# SPEECHES for SOCIALISM

JAMES P. CANNON

# SPEECHES for SOCIALISM

*Pathfinder*
New York • London • Montreal • Sydney

Copyright © 1969 by Pathfinder Press
All rights reserved

ISBN 978-0-87348-198-4
Library of Congress Catalog Card Number 72-92843
Manufactured in the United States of America

First edition, 1971
Sixth printing, 2023

COVER PHOTO: James P. Cannon at Webster Hall in New York City at his first public speech after release from prison, May 1, 1945. (Pathfinder archives)

COVER DESIGN: Eva Braiman

**PATHFINDER**
www.pathfinderpress.com
Email: pathfinder@pathfinderpress.com

*To the memory of*
**Rose Karsner**
*1889–1968*
*Great companion and collaborator
over the long road*

❖

# Contents

*Introduction by Peggy Brundy and Dianne Feeley*     9

**The first decade of American Communism**
   1. Speech at the first Workers Party convention (1921)     25
   2. Our appeal against expulsion
      to the Communist Party members (1928)     33

**The Russian Revolution**
   3. The fifth year of the Russian Revolution (1923)     47
   4. The twenty-fifth anniversary
      of the Russian Revolution (1942)     71

**American unionism at a turning point**
   5. The AFL and the start of the CIO (1935)     87

**Sixty years of American radicalism**
   6. Sixty years of American radicalism (1959)     95

**Stalinism**
   7. The end of the Comintern and the prospects
      of labor internationalism (1943)     119
   8. The downfall of Browder (1945)     139
   9. The trial of the Stalinist leaders (1949)     151
  10. The end of the Stalin cult (1956)     163
  11. Khrushchev's report to the Twentieth Congress
      (1956)     181

**Trotsky and Trotskyism**
  12. Leon Trotsky:
      To the memory of the Old Man (1940)     203
  13. How we began and where we are going (1953)     219

**The struggle against imperialist war**
  14. How to put an end to imperialist war (1942)     235

**The youth and revolution**
- 15. Youth and foreign policy (1951) — 241
- 16. What it means to be a young revolutionist today (1964) — 257

**The Smith Act case**
- 17. Before the Minneapolis trial (1941) — 271
- 18. Speech on the way to prison (1943) — 279

**Personal remarks on special occasions**
- 19. Sixtieth birthday speech (1950) — 289
- 20. Revolutionary journalism (1958) — 301
- 21. The lives of two revolutionaries (1962) — 315
    - Remarks by Rose Karsner — 315
    - Remarks by James P. Cannon — 321

**Comrades in the struggle**
- 22. Bill Brown: A proletarian fighter (1938) — 333
- 23. Address at the funeral of Inger Swabeck (1948) — 341
- 24. Goldie Geldman (1952) — 347
- 25. Joseph Vanzler (1956) — 355
- 26. A wake for Usick (1956) — 359
- 27. A tribute to Miles Dunne (1958) — 363
- 28. Carl Skoglund: One of the old guard — 369
    - The man who had no papers (1954) — 369
    - Speech at memorial meeting (1961) — 373

**Policy and perspectives of socialism**
- 29. Socialist electoral policy (1958) — 383
- 30. Socialism and democracy (1957) — 397
- 31. The trend of the twentieth century (1949) — 417
- 32. The coming American revolution (1946) — 437
- 33. What socialist America will look like (1953) — 459

*Notes* — 485

# Introduction

This is a special kind of collection. These are speeches given by an American revolutionary orator, agitator, and educator in the tradition of Eugene V. Debs. For most of this century, James P. Cannon, the National Chairman of the Socialist Workers Party, has been a prominent speaker for the revolutionary socialist movement in this country.

Schooled in the American radicalism of the Wobblies, Cannon learned the art of speaking as a soapboxer in 1911. As a traveling organizer for the IWW, he learned early how to draw a crowd on the street corner, stand up to the hecklers, and win his audience over to the defense of the rubber workers, the coal miners, the iron workers—all workers in their strikes and free-speech battles with bosses, police, and army.

This collection brings together over thirty of Cannon's speeches, given over four decades and documenting sixty years of labor and radical history. These speeches deal with many different topics, but they share a common theme: a firm conviction that there will be a better world, a socialist world, and that people must join together to bring it about. They share a common purpose: to build and strengthen the organization that can lead the struggle for socialism.

Some of these talks were historic: they helped to shape events in America's left-wing and labor movements. Others are historical: they recount the early years of the socialist movement; they describe the Soviet Union in its fifth year of revolution; they sum up the state of the left at the low tide of the fifties. Several speeches mark turning points in our epoch: at the beginning of the CIO, on the eve of World War II. One talk was given by Cannon on his way to prison with seventeen other comrades, the first victims of the witch-hunting Smith Act.

Whether Cannon is summing up the lessons of an era or teaching fellow socialists how to analyze political events, whether he is speaking on party matters or delivering a memorial talk, he always portrays an alternative to the narrow and pinched life people are forced to live in today's oppressive class society. Cannon, like Debs, is the eloquent bearer of the message of a better world to come. This revolutionary socialist saw a vision of the future in his youth, and never lost it. He says, "I came out of Rosedale, Kansas, forty years ago looking for truth and justice. I'm still looking, and I won't give one percent discount."

The stereotyped image of the socialist put forward in most of the American press is that of a humorless dogmatist scribbling or shouting an incomprehensible "Marxist" jargon. Cannon's speeches shatter that image. He is always clear and to the point, no matter how complex the issues, and he has a light touch that never fails, no matter how serious the subject matter.

Cannon is also a fine debater. As a veteran revolutionary politician, Cannon has often had to put his polemical skills to good use. "I learned from Engels," he says, "that when you go into revolutionary politics you should put on an old pair of pants. And I learned from Marx that you must not let people get you down with pinpricks. So I dressed for battle and developed a tough hide."

But Cannon's personality also shows through the tough hide. The socialist revolutionary, according to the stereotype, lives only for abstractions called "the masses" and "the cause." But these talks—especially those given at memorial services—demonstrate the opposite. Cannon expresses the socialist ideals of solidarity and comradeship in his appreciations of the unique qualities of individual comrades.

Cannon's greatest virtue as an orator is his ability to evaluate the political lessons of the day and to explain these succinctly. This is an art. And, like Debs and Malcolm X, he is a master of the art. He excels at pulling apart the specious reasoning of the propagandists of the status quo and revealing them as fakers, charlatans, and pitchmen.

His speeches are excellent examples of socialist propaganda. Each was carefully constructed and thought out in order to meet some need of the revolutionary movement. Cannon takes the most complicated ideas of Marx, Engels, Lenin, and Trotsky and explains them so that they have meaning to rebels fighting against oppression today.

Finally, taken as a whole, these speeches illustrate the continuity of the radical movement in this country and the process by which American revolutionists have learned the lessons of how to struggle against capitalism. Today's socialists do not start to analyze world events or plan strategy from scratch; they can build on the ideas of Lenin and Trotsky and the lessons derived from the revolutionary experiences of the past half-century. Cannon and his contemporaries who entered the socialist movement before the First World War and the Russian Revolution had to make their way at first with a lesser heritage. But these speeches show how he, along with others, absorbed the best of the revolutionary traditions of the IWW and the Debsian socialist movement in the United States, which prepared them to take giant steps forward after the experience of the Russian Revolution. In his speeches, Cannon passes on the distilled experience of sixty years of struggle, in which he played no small part as a living bridge to the present.

James Patrick Cannon was born in Rosedale, Kansas, in 1890, of Irish immigrant parents. His parents were Irish nationalists, in the tradition of Emmet and Parnell. His father was an active member of the Socialist Party for twenty years. *Appeal to Reason,* the popular socialist weekly, was the household's newspaper. His first public speech was a debate with another Rosedale high school student on the question, "Should Women Be Allowed to Vote?" Cannon defended the affirmative and won the debate at a time when women were ridiculed for seeking their democratic rights.

At sixteen, Cannon became outraged by the attempt to frame up three members of the IWW, Moyer, Haywood, and Pettibone, as "accomplices" in the murder of a former governor of Idaho. They were arrested in Colorado and "officially" kidnapped to Idaho for trial. *Appeal to Reason* put out a special Kidnapping Edition of four million copies, and Cannon began his radical activity by helping to distribute the paper.

Inspired by its militancy, Cannon joined the IWW in 1911, and became one of its traveling organizers. He worked in the Duluth-Superior iron range strike with Frank Little, who was later to become a Wobbly martyr. He helped to publicize the Akron rubber strike and helped edit the eastern IWW paper, *Solidarity.* During World War I, he vigorously preached continuation of the class war and opposition to the war of the imperialists.

The successful proletarian revolution in Russia in 1917 had a tremendous impact on the radical movement in the United States. To the Wobblies, it was a strike action on a grand scale; the workers had organized and taken control of every aspect of the society that affected their lives. Debs and the best revolutionary militants in the Socialist Party rallied to the defense of the Russian Revolution.

At that time, Cannon was a midwest leader of the left wing of the Socialist Party. He and Earl Browder launched a weekly paper in Kansas City, *Workers World,* supporting the Russian Revolution and the ideas that had made its victory possible. Cannon was arrested in 1919 under the wartime Lever Act for agitating in the Kansas coal fields, where the miners were on strike in defiance of a government injunction. The paper folded.

The most conscious rebels in the United States, Cannon among them, began to study just how the first workers' state had come into existence. Clearly, the decisive element in the success of the Russian Revolution was the character of the Bolshevik Party, a party vastly more effective than either the IWW or the Socialist Party in the United States.

The Socialist Party sought to be "all-inclusive," accepting into its ranks all who favored social progress. But there was no general agreement among party members on the main questions of political program and strategy, so whenever the party faced a situation demanding decisive action, it was either paralyzed or seriously divided. Thus one section of the party opposed the First World War, another endorsed it, and a third tried to reconcile these irreconcilable positions.

The IWW, seeking to be an industrial union and a revolutionary party at one and the same time, couldn't fulfill either of these functions successfully. It had no rounded program or clear strategy for a socialist revolution, beyond strikes and union organization.

Lenin's Bolshevik Party, by contrast, brought together only those rebels who could agree on a clear-cut, principled revolutionary Marxist program and organized them into a disciplined unit capable of taking swift and concerted action. Such a party is not only able to lead day-to-day struggles, but can draw upon the collective experience of its members to determine the policies enabling it to overthrow capitalism. The Bolshevik Party proved its worth on both counts.

Along with many others, Cannon concluded that the task of American revolutionists was to build that sort of party in the United States. He was a leader of one of the communist groupings that arose in response to the inspiring example of the Russian Revolution.

But the aftermath of World War I was the setting for race riots and the Palmer raids. There was a period of intensive governmental repression. Thousands of people were rounded up in police raids. Many foreign-born radicals were deported, although most had lived all their adult lives in the United States. The newborn communist movement was driven underground.

A prolonged period of underground activity would have left the new movement ingrown and isolated. Cannon was among the leaders who saw the need to break out of that trap by building a legal party at the earliest possible opportunity. But others, mechanically following their idea of Bolshevik clandestine activity under Czarism, made a principle of being underground. The question was fought out over some months. Cannon's position won out. In 1921 Cannon was the keynote speaker at the founding convention of the legal Workers Party, which later took the name Communist Party of the United States. That speech is the first in this volume.

In 1921 Cannon was elected Chairman of the National

Committee of the Workers Party. In 1922 he went to Moscow as a delegate to the Fourth Congress of the Communist International. While there, he also worked in the Red International of Labor Unions. On his return to the United States in early 1923, he went on a national tour, speaking on "The Fifth Year of the Russian Revolution," also included in this collection.

Big Bill Haywood, who had chosen exile in Moscow instead of twenty years' imprisonment in the U.S., encouraged the American Communist movement to organize a committee which could help free political prisoners. After discussions with Haywood in Moscow, Cannon helped to initiate the International Labor Defense (ILD) in 1925. The ILD publicized the cases of class-war prisoners throughout the world in its magazine, the *Labor Defender;* it raised money for the prisoners' families and for legal fees, and it planned demonstrations on their behalf. The most famous cases taken up by the ILD were those of the Centralia prisoners, Mooney and Billings, the McNamara Brothers, and Sacco and Vanzetti. Cannon served as National Secretary of the ILD from its founding convention in 1925 until his expulsion from the Communist Party three years later.

Cannon's expulsion from the Communist Party marked an important turning point, not only in his own political life, but in the entire radical movement in the United States, for it was intimately bound up with the struggle against Stalinism that was then raging in the worldwide communist movement.

From 1925 on, Cannon was increasingly disturbed by the direction being taken by the American Communist Party and the Comintern representatives' manipulations in the faction-ridden party. But he was unaware of the international political issues behind this disruptive influence, and he could not find a way out of the blind alley until the Sixth Congress of the Comintern in 1928.

In 1928, Cannon went to Moscow again, as an American delegate to the Sixth Congress. While there, he was placed on the Program Commission, where he received a copy of Trotsky's "Criticism of the Draft Program of the Communist International." Trotsky had written this document from his exile in Alma Ata. In it, Trotsky denounced the growing bureaucratic and dictatorial trends in the Soviet Union. He showed how Stalin's policy of trying to build socialism in one country represented a fundamental break with Leninism and undermined the original revolutionary character of the Communist parties throughout the world.

Recognizing in Trotsky's analysis the answers he had been groping for, Cannon resolved to go back home and fight for the program of Trotsky. In October 1928, Cannon, Martin Abern, and Max Shachtman were expelled from the Communist Party for circulating and defending the views of Trotsky's Left Opposition. Cannon's appeal against their expulsion is the second speech in this volume.

An entire section of speeches in this book is devoted to exposing and denouncing Stalinism's betrayal of the authentic principles of revolutionary socialism. Because of the prestige of the Russian Revolution and the authority of the Soviet Union, millions of revolutionary-minded militants mistakenly believed that the Communist Party under Stalin represented the continuation of this heritage. And so, no matter how unpopular and little understood such actions were at any particular time, it was an obligation for Cannon and the adherents of revolutionary socialism to expose the Communist Party for what it had really become: a roadblock to socialism.

That was the prerequisite to building a genuine revolutionary party capable of leading the fight for socialism in the United States.

The Communist Party was very large and influential in the radical movement in the 1930s, and in that position it helped divert the radicalization into support of New Deal liberalism. But today, radicalizing youth do not look to the Communist Party to provide leadership in the struggles of the oppressed. Its authority has been undermined, not only by its past record of betrayal, but also by the tireless work of Cannon and his comrades in creating an alternative revolutionary political leadership. As a result, today's movements of struggle have the best possible chance to grow independently and develop to their fullest capacity.

In the first few years after their expulsion from the Communist Party, the American Trotskyists had some very tough times. Attempting to win over other militants from the increasingly bureaucratized Communist Party, they had to fight to establish their democratic right to speak and sell their press in the face of physical assaults by the Stalinists. They were a handful at first—generals without an army, as the Communist Party mockingly described them. There were Cannon, Max Shachtman, Martin Abern, Rose Karsner (all close collaborators with Cannon from the ILD), Dr. Antoinette Konikow (the pioneer socialist and birth-control advocate), and a nucleus of revolutionists in Minneapolis.

But these "generals without an army" were armed with a revolutionary socialist program far superior to the political strategies of their more numerous rivals on the left. In his *History of American Trotskyism,* Cannon relates how he and his comrades set out to build the nucleus of a revolutionary party around this program. They had learned from Lenin and Trotsky that, in the long run, a correct program is decisive for building a revolutionary party. It enables the party nucleus to retain its bearings under the impact of great world events, to withstand internal splits and strengthen itself from them, to increase its forces through principled unifications with other groups, to act effectively in day-to-day struggles, and to grow over time into a mass revolutionary party capable of overthrowing capitalism.

In 1934 the original Trotskyist cadres succeeded in carrying out a unification with the American Workers Party, headed by A.J. Muste. This united grouping then entered the Socialist Party during 1936–1937 in order to reach a militant left wing which had developed in that organization. The much-augmented revolutionary cadres were then in a position to found the Socialist Workers Party in 1938. Cannon was elected National Secretary of the party and has been one of its main leaders ever since.

Cannon's major contribution to the American revolutionary movement has been his work in building a Leninist party in the United States. Taking Lenin's organization as a model, and drawing upon his own long experience in the American labor and radical movements, he built an effective team of revolutionary socialist politicians. He taught them how to apply Bolshevik methods to the very different circumstances of the class struggle in the United States.

In 1934, when teamsters' strikes broke out in Minneapolis, the American Trotskyists had the chance to show what they could do in the class struggle. They were in the leadership of the strikes, one of three major labor struggles in 1934. The American Trotskyist movement mobilized its whole national organization behind the strikes, and during one of the high points, Cannon went to Minneapolis. This time he was not a traveling union organizer, but a party organizer. He worked with the Dunne brothers, Carl Skoglund, Farrell Dobbs, and other comrades who were leading the strikes, and with the Trotskyist organization in Minneapolis. Their revolutionary outlook enabled them to see through the maneuvers of the bosses. Collectively, they were able to draw upon scores of strike experiences, from the days of the Wobblies on. Despite the organized opposition of the Citizens Alliance (the employers' organization), the police, the state militia, and despite a barrage of red-baiting attacks, the Trotskyists proved their worth as leaders. Even when the militia arrested the central strike leaders and put them in the stockade, the strike continued, because a secondary leadership had been prepared. In the end, it was the government and the companies that backed down. The successful Minneapolis strikes provided a model for the whole labor movement, were a key factor in building the Teamsters union, and helped to lay the groundwork for the formation of the CIO. The example and the lessons of Minneapolis are a recurrent theme in several of Cannon's speeches.

The concept of independent political action, also a recurrent theme here, has been a central feature of the revolutionary movement since Debs's time. In the midst of the labor upsurge of the 1930s, the Socialist Workers Party projected a program for challenging the political control of the two capitalist parties by forming an independent labor party. Cannon explains the principled approach to electoral action in several of these speeches.

When the Second World War broke out, every other radical grouping in the United States capitulated to it politically. But the Socialist Workers Party, in the tradition of the Wobblies and Bolsheviks during World War I, opposed the war and refused to subordinate the needs of the working class, of Blacks and other oppressed peoples to the wartime demands of the ruling class. They described the war as an interimperialist conflict rather than a struggle between essentially different systems, and they pointed out that a truly successful fight against fascism could only be carried out by a workers' government. They were not afraid to call attention to the scandal of war profiteers disguised as patriots and saviors of democracy. Because of their ideas, Cannon and twenty-seven other leaders of the Socialist Workers Party and the Minneapolis truck drivers' union were indicted as the first victims of the Smith Act. Cannon and his fellow defendants mounted a nationwide defense campaign which has served as a model in civil liberties cases ever since, based on the old IWW principle "an injury to one is an injury to all." The defense committee was open to everybody, regardless of their attitude toward the political views of the defendants, who supported the defendants' civil liberties. The committee won the support of unions with over two million members. And when the case came to trial, Cannon was able to turn the courtroom into a political forum. The transcript of his testimony, later published as *Socialism on Trial,* became a widely circulated handbook explaining the views of the Socialist Workers Party.

Despite the committee's efforts, Cannon and seventeen other Trotskyist leaders were convicted and sent to jail. This collection contains two of Cannon's speeches on the trial, one shortly before it began, the other before his imprisonment. In 1944–1945, while serving his sentence in the Sandstone, Minnesota, penitentiary, Cannon carried on an active correspondence with the interim party leadership, covering a wide range of organizational aspects of party building. From prison, he helped to prepare the party for the new wave of working-class militancy and radicalism that was then beginning as the war drew to a close. These letters have been published in the book *Letters From Prison,* an invaluable sequel to his earlier work, *The Struggle for a Proletarian Party.*

At the war's end, a great strike wave spread across the country; the workers demanded higher wages, better working conditions, decent child care, an end to the hoarding of meat and other rationed commodities. The revolutionary movement grew rapidly. The Socialist Workers Party prepared to transform itself from a nucleus of cadres into a revolutionary party of many thousands. During this period, Cannon gave his speech, "The Coming American Revolution," in which he analyzes the deep-going, historically insoluble problems of American capitalism and outlines the conditions preparing the way for an American socialist revolution.

Then the post–World War II upsurge was cut short by the cold war, reaction, and witch-hunt, historical events which undercut the developing radical potential of the mid-1940s. The long-term validity of Cannon's thesis, however, is revealed in the radicalization of today.

Although he has seen many setbacks in the revolutionary movement, Cannon has never lost his optimism. What sustained him in the dog days of reaction and isolation, when so many of his generation grew tired and cynical, was the knowledge that the masses of people, united in action, would prove capable of building a better world. He continued the work of educating younger comrades, preparing them for a new American radicalization.

The retention of its revolutionary heritage and a homogeneous cadre educated in its principles enabled the

Socialist Workers Party to emerge from the witch-hunt of the 1950s confident, strong, and ready for the radicalization of the 1960s. Today, the party that James P. Cannon has done so much to build is fast becoming the most influential and effective party on the American left.

Since the beginning, Cannon has frequently concerned himself with the task of assimilating younger revolutionaries into the movement. Many of these speeches are specifically addressed to the youth. In one talk, Cannon describes the differences between what it meant to be a young socialist before World War I and what it means today. He describes the period of his youth, which was ruled by belief in slow but steady progress, as one when being a socialist meant being committed to an ideal considered realizable only in the distant future. The era of gradual progress, Cannon points out, was brought to an end by World War I and the rapid succession of wars, economic crises, and revolutions which followed. Today the problems confronting humankind have a far greater magnitude, and socialism has a greater immediacy than ever before. Cannon explains that today the fight for a socialist society is also the struggle for human survival; the decision will be taken, he declares, within the lifetime of this revolutionary generation. Their task will be to clear away the oppressive class society and build a world in which people have control over their lives. That the youth to whom he spoke have learned how to begin the job can be seen in the growth in influence of the Young Socialist Alliance, today the largest socialist youth group. With Cannon, they believe that even the best revolutionary ideas are sterile unless they mobilize people for action and inspire them with confidence in the socialist future. "There is no eloquence," Cannon says, "equal to the eloquence of action."

For them, this book shows that James P. Cannon has known how to be eloquent in action. They will agree, too, we think, that he has been equally eloquent in expression.

*Peggy Brundy*
*Dianne Feeley*
JUNE 1971

Cannon speaking at the 1940 convention of the Socialist Workers Party.

Chapter 1

# Speech at the first Workers Party convention

The following was the keynote speech at the founding convention of the Workers Party, which met at the Star Casino in New York City, December 23–26, 1921, marking the emergence of the Communist movement from underground into a legal, public party. Cannon was subsequently elected the party's National Chairman. The Workers Party altered its name in 1925 to Workers (Communist) Party and in 1929 to Communist Party, USA.

Comrades:
After our long struggle to unite our forces, we have succeeded. We have brought them together to unite them, and we will not listen to any man who speaks any other word than unity in this convention.

We have had for two years many struggles and much strife in our ranks. This was inevitable after the great upheaval of the World War and the Russian Revolution that shook all of our organizations to their foundations and put every one of our old theories and dogmas to the acid test. Every one of us was compelled to revise some of his theories and some of his plans. It was no more than natural, I might say it was inevitable, that in the beginning we should have some confusion and some disintegration.

Many of us who are here in this convention responded and reacted very quickly to the call that came from Russia. Many who are here in this convention answered the call of the Third International the first day its banner was raised. Others moved slowly. Others at times became impatient with us because they felt that we were too impatient, but we have all moved steadily and consistently to the position where we stand today, where, I think, there is not a single man or woman in this convention who is not ready to say in categorical terms that he looks for leadership and guidance, not to the Second International that betrayed the workers and led them into the universal slaughter, not to the compromisers and evaders of the Two-and-a-half International, but I think every man and woman in this hall will say with me that we look for our guidance to the inspirer, organizer and leader of the world proletariat, the Communist International.

I say, comrades, we have come here by different roads. Some moved by one, some by another. By many methods and as a result of many struggles, we have come to a common ground where we shall unite. There are no fears on our part, and there need be no fears on the part of anyone about the character of the party we are launching today, because the people who are here to do it are not men who have sprung up overnight.

It is not an artificial gathering manufactured by our conference committee. The men and women who are here to make the Workers Party are the men and women who, for many years past, have been in the vanguard of the movements that have led to it. They have struggled and suffered and they bear the scars of battle, and that is the guarantee of the revolutionary integrity of this organization. Now, I think that there is no one here who is more optimistic about the task before us than the circumstances warrant. I think we know enough, comrades and fellow workers, of the colossal tasks ahead of us not to take them lightly, not to take them in a spirit that we are going to accomplish them by passing resolutions or by an excessive amount of phraseology in our programs. We know that we are going to accomplish them only if we try in a true Marxist spirit to analyze them and understand them, and then face and fight out the issues.

The task is before us. We have a labor movement that is completely discouraged and demoralized. We have an organized labor movement that is unable on any front to put up an effective struggle against the drive of destruction organized by the masters. We have a revolutionary movement which, until this inspirational call for a Workers Party convention, was disheartened, discouraged and demoralized. Our labor unions, upon which the workers build their first line of resistance—and I want to say right here, comrades, that you must face it as the most menacing thing on the horizon—the labor unions of America are being broken up because there is not sufficient unified understanding, because there is not sufficient leadership to save them. And I say that unless we, comrades, unless we, the revolutionary workers—we who know that only on a program of the class struggle can they mass and fight victoriously—unless we organize and prepare to unify and direct them, to lead their struggles, then, I say, the American labor unions will be destroyed and black reaction will settle upon this country. We have a responsibility upon us, and we must find the way out.

Yes, reaction is in full sway in America. Many of our finest spirits, our bravest boys, our best fighters, wear their lives away in the penitentiaries of America. The boys that threw themselves into the struggle during the war, those who did not take down their flag when the persecution became severe, the very cream of the movement, have languished in prison for over two years, and I say it is a shame and a disgrace that we have not made any effective protest against it. It is a pitiful thing that for two years the campaign for the release of our fellow workers and comrades, which should have been carried on upon the basis of the class struggle, which should have been the rallying cry to arouse the workers and inspire an irresistible campaign for amnesty, has been left almost entirely to such as the American Civil Liberties Bureau on the one hand, the Socialist Party's Amnesty Committee on the other, and the IWW lawyers on the third; and there is very little difference among them.

Now, I say, we are going to stem the tide. We are going to stop the stampede by putting up a program and plan of action with a set of fighting leaders and give out the rallying cry: Fellow workers, stand and fight! It is better to die in the struggle than to be crushed to death without resistance!

I think that everyone who was present at our great mass meeting last night had an answer to the question upon everybody's lips: Is this real unity, is this at last a real getting together?

At last night's meeting the question was answered as it is today. There came to that meeting fighting men and women from all fields, from all movements. From the IWW Committee for the Red Trade Union International came George Hardy. From the American Federation of Labor came J.W. Johnstone. From the Socialist Party, from the left wing, from those who long ago left the Socialist Party, from all parts of the country they came; they—the battlers—came, showing the marks and scars of conflict and persecution. They came together in the name of unity, and they sealed and guaranteed our pledge to present a unified movement to the workers of America.

There are only a few things I wish to touch upon further. They are a few suggestions upon the nature of our organization. In our conference call you will notice we are not very verbose. We did not put in very many revolutionary words or foreign phrases because that period is past and the time has come for action. We laid down in our convention call the definite and emphatic principles upon which we stand. We want a fighting party, and that is the difference between us and other political organizations claiming the support of the workers. The difference between us and the Socialist Party or the Farmer-Labor Party or the Gompers bureaucracy does not arise just because we declare for the final revolution and they do not, nor because we are willing to hold before the workers the final goal and all of these others are not, but because, upon the basis of the class struggle, on questions of bread and butter, on housing, on labor organization, wages and hours, they are afraid to fight, and the Workers Party says it will fight on every single one of these issues. That is the difference between a betrayers' organization, a cowardly organization, and a workers' organization.

I have talked to comrades who have fears of reformist tendencies. They are afraid we did not put enough revolutionary words in our program. Comrades, there is no danger of reformism in a party that is organized and led by class-conscious fighters. Reformism comes only from those who do not want to fight, and the guarantee that our organization will not be reformistic is not alone in our program, but in the composition of the delegates who have fought consistently and determinedly on the basis of the class struggle in the past, and that is the guarantee of our activity in the future.

With regard to the form of organization, we also speak specifically. We want a centralized party. Now what do we mean by that?

We want to build a serious movement that will be bound together by enough discipline to enable it to act as a united body. We are not going to have an excessive amount of referendums in our organization, because those go with organizations that are more concerned with talk than with activity. We want an organization able to move as one man, and effectively, in the right direction, and for that purpose we build it up on the basis of democratic centralization. We bind it together by discipline, and we call upon every man and woman to enter it in the spirit of the soldier, ready to give everything the organization asks, and willing to do everything the organization says. We want to make it, consequently, a party of action, a centralized party, a fighting party. These are our slogans, comrades. If we will follow them, we will build up an organization to which the disheartened and demoralized workers of America will rally. They will hail it as the morning star. They are looking for it. I say, comrades, they are looking for it with longing eyes. The workers do not like division. There is nothing that dispirits them more than to see their own battlefront divided, their own leaders demoralized. In the past we were not able to give them unified leadership. Let us move quickly away from past mistakes. The past is dead. Let the dead past bury its dead. We have come together to face the future. Let us judge each other upon the activities of the future and not upon the activities that lie behind us.

The final word is for unity, unity of the revolutionary workers.

Down with those who speak against it! Down with those who seek to divide the revolutionary movement! Long live the unification of revolutionary forces! Long live the Workers Party! Long live the workers' republic that the Workers Party fights for!

Chapter 2

# Our appeal against expulsion to the Communist Party members

The Political Committee of the Workers (Communist) Party expelled Cannon, a member of that committee, along with Martin Abern and Max Shachtman, member and alternate respectively of the party's Central Executive Committee, on charges of Trotskyism on October 27, 1928. But they had the right of appeal to the approaching plenary session of the Central Executive Committee. The following is the speech delivered to that plenum on December 17, 1928.

Comrades:
Many of the most important events and turning points in our party's life have been summed up in party gatherings, which stand out in party history as the expression of these events. The present meeting of the Central Executive Committee, called to confirm the control of the party by an opportunistic and bureaucratic leadership and to endorse the expulsion of its opponents, is such a gathering. It will represent in party history a downward curve.

In most of the significant party meetings of the past, certain features, certain details, stood out and gave in themselves an indication of the whole character of the gatherings. That is true also of this one. Let me mention a couple of these characteristic features of the present meeting of the Central Executive Committee.

We were impressed as we entered the hall to see Comrade Devine occupying the post as chairman—a new distinction for him—and you have all heard him tell us with a brusque authority—which is also new for him—that we will be given one hour and no more to answer the three hours of reports against us. The chairmanship of Comrade Devine will not be forgotten for it is a symbol of the meeting.

He is the district organizer in that district [Minnesota] where the expulsion of proletarian Communists for their views has attained the widest proportions. Twenty-one comrades there have already been expelled, and they are precisely the comrades whose names have stood out in the labor movement of Minnesota for years as the very banner of Communism. The prestige our party enjoys in the labor movement there is due mainly to them. And it is to their loyal, untiring and sacrificing work that we owe the five thousand votes—more than 10 percent of the total votes for our presidential candidates—which we received in the elections in Minnesota.

The election of Comrade Devine, who is responsible for the expulsion of these Communists, as chairman of the plenum, has a meaning in the light of those facts. It signifies the conferring of exceptional honors upon the district organizers who bring about the greatest disruption. It puts the seal of approval upon the policy of mass expulsions of proletarian Communists. Thus the chairmanship of Devine is a symbol of the plenum.

The second significant detail I wish to mention is the selection of Pepper as the reporter against us. This fact epitomizes the plenum and the whole issue around which it centers better than anything we could say. It demonstrates in deed that the fight against us, because it lacks all principle, must be placed from the beginning on the lowest basis and must use the vilest instruments. The selection of Pepper, the bearer in the Communist movement of all that is most corrupt and most detestable to revolutionaries, as the reporter against us, to bring here the demand for our expulsion, in itself discredits that demand.

The very fact that the sewage of slander against us and our comrades is poured out officially here through the mouth of Pepper puts an evaluation on this slander—it answers and refutes it. I will not insult a single Communist by "defending" him against the accusations of this characterless adventurer whose unspeakable record shames the Communist movement of the world. The Communist militants who constitute the forces of the Opposition, with the honorable record of the years behind them, are in no need of such a defense. For revolutionaries, the calumny of a Pepper is only a mark of distinction and a badge of honor. It is those who elected Pepper as the reporter against us who will have need of this defense before the party and before the proletariat which judges the party by its spokesmen.

In the period that has intervened since our expulsion on October 25, we have continued to regard ourselves as party members and have conducted ourselves as Communists, as we have done since the foundation of the party, and even for years before that. Every step we have taken has been guided by this conception. Those acts which went beyond the bounds of ordinary party procedure in bringing our views before the party were imposed upon us by the action of the party leadership in denying us the right and opportunity to defend our views within the party by normal means. Our views relate to principled questions, and therefore it is our duty openly to defend them in spite of all attempts to suppress them.

We are bound to do this also in the future under all circumstances. However, we said on October 25, and we repeat now, that we are unconditionally willing to confine our activity to regular party channels and to discontinue all extraordinary methods the moment our party rights are restored and we are permitted to defend our views in the party press and at party meetings. The decision and the responsibility rest wholly with the majority of the Central Executive Committee.

Events since our expulsion have only served to confirm more surely the correctness of the views of the Russian Opposition, which we support. The momentous developments in the Communist Party of the Soviet Union and throughout the Comintern have that meaning and no other. Life itself is proving the validity of their platform. Even those who fought that platform, who misrepresented it and hid it from the party and the Comintern, are today compelled, under the pressure of events and forces which overwhelm them, to give lip service to it, to pretend to adopt it. Many of the statements and proposals of the Opposition which were branded "counterrevolutionary" a year ago are today solemnly repeated, almost word for word, as the quintessence of Bolshevism.

Meanwhile their sponsors—the true leaders and defenders of the Russian Revolution—remain in exile, and there is no guarantee whatever that the presently advertised "left course" will mean anything more than a cover for further concessions to the right wing, whose policy directly undermines the dictatorship. The victorious fight of the party masses in Russia and throughout the Comintern against this disgraceful and dangerous course cannot be much longer postponed. . . .*

Our views on the problems of the American party and its leadership, outlined in our statement to the Political Committee on October 25, hold good today and have been underscored by the whole conduct of the Pepper-Lovestone faction since that time. We spoke then of "its opportunist political outlook, its petty-bourgeois origin, its corrupt factionalism, its careerism and adventurism in the class struggle" as "the greatest menace to the party." To speak now about the present party leadership with objectivity and precision, we could not use different language to characterize it. This estimate is written in unmistakable words in the election campaign, the trade-union work, the inner-party regime and in all phases of party life and activity.

Since October 25, the Pepper-Lovestone leadership has taken further steps on the course of bureaucratic disruption which confronts the party today as a deadly menace—a course which began with the expulsion of Communists, copied from the labor fakers, and which has already taken another weapon from the same arsenal: the weapon of gangsterism. Everyone sitting here knows the facts about this. You know that inspired and organized gangster attacks have been made against us on the public streets, not once but several times.

Woe to the party of the workers if its proletarian kernel does not arise and stamp out these incipient fascist tactics at the very beginning! The blows from the blackjacks of

---

* The text of this speech, as published in *The Militant*, January 1, 1929, here omits an exposition of various aspects of the platform of the Russian Opposition covered in other articles in the same issue of the paper; the deleted portion of the speech has since been lost.—*Editor.*

gangsters which have descended on the heads of Opposition Communists are blows at the very foundation of the party. This abominable gangsterism, for which the leaders of the two factions collaborating against us, the Lovestone faction and the Foster faction, are directly responsible, is hated by every honest worker. It discredits the party before the working class and threatens to deprive the party of its moral and political position in the struggle against these methods of the trade-union reactionaries.

Only the blindest bureaucrat, or the most irresponsible dilettante adventuring in the movement, can fail to see the unbounded consequences of the bureaucratic expulsion policy of the Lovestone-Pepper leadership and to react with alarm against it. It directly threatens the existence of the party. The first step was the expulsion of three members of the Central Executive Committee, in the futile hope that the issues could thereby be disposed of. But the very next day these issues arose again in a wider circle as a result of the action against us and called forth new expulsions. In the six weeks which have elapsed since that time, more than sixty proletarians have been expelled from the party for their views and glibly denounced as "renegades" and "counterrevolutionaries" by people who are scarcely worthy to criticize them in any respect.

Bureaucratic suppression has its own logic. It begins with the expulsion of individuals and ends with the disruption of the movement. Yesterday we saw the attempt to suppress the views of the Oppositionists who fight the party regime on principled grounds. Today already, inspired resolutions from the party units are making the same demand against the limited criticisms of the Foster group, with the threat of organizational measures after the packed and gerrymandered convention has "endorsed" the regime. Bureaucratism is alien to the proletarian

Communist movement. Bureaucratism cannot stand criticism. It cannot stand discussion. Bureaucratism, which is an expression of bourgeois influence, and Lenin's proletarian doctrine cannot live together.

The regime of bureaucratic strangulation, which expels its outspoken opponents and bludgeons the party into silence, has become an international phenomenon of the period. This is the only key to an understanding of its absolutely unprecedented excesses. A real struggle against it cannot be made without an understanding of its international scope. On this, as well as on the other principled questions, the fight of the proletarian Communist elements in all parties unites with the Bolshevik fight of the Russian Opposition under the leadership of Trotsky.

At the Fourteenth Congress of the Communist Party of the Soviet Union, Stalin issued a warning against the course he later adopted, and predicted its disruptive consequences. He defended there the refusal to expel Trotsky from the Political Bureau and said: "We are against the policy of lopping off, of bloodletting (it was blood they wanted). It is a dangerous thing. One day you lop off this limb. Tomorrow another, and the next day a third. And after a while, what becomes of the party?"

Stalin forgot these words so full of prophetic significance. He formed a factional combination with the right wing to suppress and expel the left, the Opposition. He gave the signal for the same line in all the parties of the Comintern. As a result, in the recent years we have seen everywhere a strengthening of the opportunist elements, an enormous development and entrenchment of bureaucratism, and wholesale expulsions of the proletarian left—the core of the workers' vanguard. All the little Stalins in all the parties are bolstering themselves up by these means.

This meeting of the Central Executive Committee has

an unusually large attendance, which has been gathered together to applaud our expulsion. The composition of the audience is also symptomatic. Of the two hundred or more in the hall, almost everyone is a functionary or employee of the party, or of an organization or institution closely related to the party. There are not half a dozen workers from the shops present. The opportunist leaders of the needle trades are here, but the rank-and-file Communists, who fight for Communist policies against them, are barred. The fiction of "proletarian representation" was never more clearly exposed than it is by these simple facts. All this is in correlation to the shifting class composition of the upper circles of the party.

The wholesale expulsion of proletarian fighters goes hand in hand with the steady recruitment of all kinds of dubious, petty-bourgeois careerist and half-baked intellectual elements. The class composition of the party, particularly in the New York district, has been seriously affected by this process in recent years and has had a direct expression in the opportunistic policies of the party and the strengthening of the opportunist elements generally.

In the upper circles of the party, in the party apparatus, this increased proportion of nonproletarians is enormously expanded. Under the Lovestone regime, these elements are appearing more and more on all sides as party representatives, officials, managers, directors, teachers, supervisors. Coming to these positions without sufficient prerequisites, they bring with them the detestable careerist attributes of insolence, arrogance and pride of office, antagonizing and alienating the worker elements and thrusting them aside.

The "education" dispensed in the party school under such auspices is becoming a distorted caricature of revolutionary training. It is led almost exclusively by schoolteachers, dentists, "professors," journalists—everything except proletarian leaders tested by the class struggle.

The party must examine this question in direct connection with the struggle against the right danger and the opportunist leaders who are its bearers. It is necessary at once to take a complete registration of the party membership with the object of precisely determining its class composition. A reorganization of the party apparatus from top to bottom, up to and including the Central Executive Committee, placing the overwhelming majority of the positions in the hands of experienced and tested party workers of proletarian origin, must be effected at once. For the next period, until a proletarian stabilization has been achieved in the party and its apparatus, the party membership must be closed entirely to nonproletarian elements. Even then, their admittance to the party must be carefully restricted and supervised.

The failure of the party to grow in the favorable objective circumstances, the defeats it has suffered where victories were possible, its poor showing in the election with the field to itself as the party of the class struggle, the collapse of its trade-union work, etc., are due primarily to the false leadership. Official bombast and factional trickery can no longer obscure or hide these condemning facts. The fight for the party is a fight against the systematic opportunist policy of the leadership and the bureaucratic regime with which it fortifies itself against control and correction from below.

This internal regime is tied up with the external opportunistic line and is an expression of it. A serious struggle for a correction of the opportunist external policy, which weakens the party and consequently the class before its enemies, is impossible without the most determined, stubborn and relentless fight for party democracy. Party democracy is the means whereby the policy of the party can be corrected and its leadership reorganized on a proletarian Communist basis.

The raising of the issue of party democracy and the education of the party membership on its meaning and significance are made all the more necessary by the confusion that prevails on the whole question of party government, of forms of working-class organization, of centralization and discipline. This confusion is fostered by the monstrous distortions of Lenin's teachings disseminated by the party leadership and is the direct result of them.

The Tenth Congress of the Communist Party of Russia, held under Lenin's leadership at the end of the civil war, said: "The form of organization and the methods of work are entirely determined by the specific character of the given historic situation and the problems which arise directly out of that situation."

The resolution of the Tenth Congress said further: "The needs of the current movement demand a new organizational form. That form is workers' democracy." We do not advocate the mechanical adoption of the forms and methods prescribed by Lenin for the Russian party, which works under vastly different conditions from ours. But if workers' democracy could be proclaimed by Lenin for the Russian party, with the responsibility of the proletarian dictatorship on its shoulders, then it is a hundred times more applicable to our party under the given historic circumstances in America.

The present leaders and teachers of the party distort and misapply all these conceptions. They substitute the idea of discipline in the formal mechanical sense for the Leninist doctrine of democratic centralism. Our party, which ought to be the champion of workers' democracy throughout the entire labor movement, is making the very words taboo. All democracy is indiscriminately labeled bourgeois democracy. This false and thoroughly reactionary idea is heard on all sides, and Comrade Weinstone, who has become the full-blown type of party martinet, has made an interjection here to the same effect. Party democracy, of course, does not exclude but presupposes centralization and discipline. It is just the bureaucratic distortions and mechanical conceptions of discipline which give rise to syndicalist prejudices in this respect.

The party must make an end of this by struggle against the leadership that fosters and expresses it. The first step is the breaking down of the disruptive expulsion policy and the reinstatement of the expelled Communists, with the right to express their views in the party by normal means. The policy of administrative gagging, suppression and terrorism must be overthrown. The worker-Communist must be able to feel at home in his own party. He must have the right and feel the freedom to open his mouth and say what he thinks without being called into the office of some petty official or other, like a recalcitrant workingman in a factory, and threatened with discipline. All talk of party democracy in the face of suppression on all sides and the wholesale expulsion of comrades for their views is a swindle.

The party needs a real and free discussion. The suppressed documents of the Russian Opposition, dealing with the vital world problems of the period, must be printed and made available for the party members. The party must have the right to discuss the questions upon which there are differences and not merely those upon which there is general agreement. The party must discuss the international questions and not merely the national and local ones. The party must have the right to discuss the questions confronting the Communist Party of the Soviet Union in order to participate intelligently in their solution. The party members must have the right to discuss *all* the questions of the Comintern, since they are part of the Comintern and should not regard it as an institution standing apart from them and making decisions without their participation.

There is one feature of the proceedings against us which gives them a tragicomic aspect. We see sitting here, ready to raise their hands to expel us, not a few comrades who exercised this privilege once before. Olgin, Trachtenberg, Kruse and others raised their hands just as high to expel us Communists, us defenders of the Russian Revolution, us followers of Lenin and Trotsky, from the Socialist Party in 1919. Then as now, they did not spare slander and vituperation in the process. We were also in those days called "renegades," "agents of the capitalists" and even "spies" and "provocateurs." It was not we, but they, who had to repent the actions and swallow the words. We survived all that—the expulsions and the slander—because we were Communists; and we will survive it now for the same reason.

We live and struggle in "the epoch of wars and revolutions," when the events of days and weeks transcend in their magnitude and importance the events of years and decades of other times. We Communists, who are the standard-bearers of the interests of the proletariat and the fighters for the future of humanity, cannot for a moment forget the immensity of our historic responsibilities, which are only magnified by the fewness of our numbers here in the reactionary citadel of world imperialism.

The sharpening international complications which push us every day nearer to the verge of imperialist war, the great and unavoidable difficulties of the Soviet Union in its capitalist encirclement, the colossal problems and tasks confronting our party in the class struggle—these facts are raising the question of party unity, of the full utilization of all the tested forces, in all its insistence. The burning issue of party unity demands a solution, not on the basis of bureaucratic machinations, but on the basis of Lenin's teachings.

We speak here for this unity. We declare ourselves ready to do all in our power to bring it about and make it secure, disregarding all the slander against us. We make one demand only: that we have the right to maintain our views and to defend them within the party by party means.

We pioneers of Communism in America, standing here at the plenum of the Central Executive Committee, fully conscious of the great solemnity of the occasion, and with a full sense of responsibility for our words, say openly to the plenum and to the entire party: the views for which we have been expelled are Leninist views. We stand by them. As revolutionists we can do nothing else, and we will continue to stand by them and work for their victory in the future. On this basis we present our appeal for the reinstatement into the party of ourselves and the other expelled comrades who share our views.

Pepper ended his report against us with the prophecy that this will be the last time we will ever address a party gathering. But this statement will be refuted by the facts of the future just as his other statements are refuted by the facts of the past. In the past, during our entire lives, we have always fought on the side of the working class when some of those who expel us, including Pepper, stood on the other side of the barricades. We will be at our posts also in the future. Let the Peppers make predictions to the contrary if they wish. It is not we revolutionists with unsullied records who will be discredited thereby. For such talk of the future only invites a recollection of their own dishonorable past, which discredits them.

The party needs the scores of loyal and tested Communists

who are being expelled today, and cannot spare them. The party will make its voice heard and assert its will. The party will call us back to our rightful places in the ranks, and will do this sooner than you dream. We say this because the platform of the Opposition represents the class interests of the proletariat on an international scale, and the Communist Party will adopt that platform. We say this because we have confidence in the proletarian ranks of the party, in their revolutionary spirit and will. Therefore our final words at this meeting are a revolutionary salutation to the party that we have helped to found and build, and from which no power on earth can tear us away.

## Chapter 3

# The fifth year of the Russian Revolution

After his return from an eight-month stay in the Soviet Union, Cannon, in his capacity as National Chairman of the Workers Party, made a tour of the United States in 1923, giving the following speech.

The story of Soviet Russia for the first four years after the revolution was a story of desperate struggle against tremendous odds. The fight of the Russian workers did not end with their victory over the bourgeoisie within Russia. The capitalist class of the entire world came to the aid of Russian capitalism.

The workers' republic was blockaded and shut off from the world. Counterrevolutionary plots and uprisings inside of Russia were financed and directed from the outside. Mercenary invading armies, backed by world capital, attacked Soviet Russia on all sides. On top of all this came the terrible famine which threatened to deal the final blow.

In those four years Soviet Russia indeed went "through

the shadows." But now, after five years of the revolution, we can tell a brighter story. In 1922 Soviet Russia began to emerge from the shadows and started on the upward track. The long and devastating civil war was at an end and the counterrevolution stamped out. The great famine was conquered. The last of the invading foreign armies—except the Japanese in the Far East—had been driven from Russian soil; and the workers' government, freed from the terrible strain and necessity of war, was enabled for the first time to turn its efforts and energies to the great constructive task of building a new Russia on the ruins of the old.

While I was yet in Russia the Red Army drove the Japanese out of Vladivostok and set up the soviets again. And before the Fourth Congress of the Communist International was ended, we had the joy of hearing Comrade Lenin say that all the territory of Russia was at last living in peace under the red flag of the Soviets.

I reached Moscow on the first day of June [1922]. Signs of recuperation from the long travail were already noticeable. The streets and sidewalks were being repaired and buildings were being painted, for the first time in five years, they told me. During the war all resources and all energies went for bitter necessity; everything else had to wait. Even the buildings in the Kremlin got their first coat of paint this year.

I was riding on a Moscow streetcar, one day soon after my arrival, with a comrade who had once been in America and who now holds a responsible position in the Soviet government. I spoke of the good appearance and condition of the car; it had just been newly painted, and looked very pretty. They know more about blending colors than we do; and they care more about it, too. He told me that the Moscow streetcar system had been greatly improved during the past year. The number of cars in operation had been greatly increased, the trackage extended, and a fairly reliable schedule maintained. The Moscow streetcar workers were very proud of their achievement; especially so because the improvement in the service had brought with it a corresponding improvement in their own living conditions.

The famous Genoa Conference was still alive at that time; the conference which Lloyd George called to settle the problems of Europe, but which didn't succeed in settling anything except the career of Lloyd George. France and Belgium, you will remember, were demanding that the property in Russia, which had been confiscated by the revolution, should be restored to the original foreign owners. Russia had not yet given her final answer, and I asked my friend in the streetcar what he thought it would be.

He said, "Most of the big industrial plants in Russia, and even a part of the railroad system, belonged to foreign capitalists before the revolution. Russia was practically a colony of European capitalism."

"Do you know," he asked me, "who used to own the streetcar system in Moscow? It belonged to the poor Belgian capitalists, and they are trying to get it back at Genoa."

I asked him what chance the poor Belgian capitalists had to get their streetcars back. He answered, "No chance at all."

He told me that as soon as that demand became known the Moscow streetcar workers—as well as the workers in the other important industries—called meetings and passed resolutions to this effect: "The foreign capitalists tried for four years to take these industries away from us by armed force, and they couldn't succeed. Now, we are certainly not going to let them *talk* us out of them at the diplomatic table."

Before I went to Russia I had read much about the

impending collapse of the Soviet government. A story of this kind used to appear on an average of about once a week in *The New York Times* and other capitalist newspapers; and no doubt you have all read them. Here, lately, the capitalist press has dropped that story and the Socialist Party and the IWW papers have taken it up. I spent seven months in Russia and I assure you that I looked diligently for the signs of this famous "collapse," but I couldn't find it. On the contrary, the more I investigated, the more I saw of the attitude of the Russian workers, the more I became convinced that the Soviet government, under the control of the Communist Party, is firmer and stronger now than at any period in its history.

I saw the power of the Russian Communist Party tested by an historic conflict with another party which challenged its control. The occasion was the trial of the leaders of the so-called Social Revolutionary Party.

These Social Revolutionaries were brought to trial before the proletarian court. When I was in Moscow I was present, with an interpreter, on the day it opened in the Labor Temple, and at many of the other sessions. It was a fair trial—nothing like it ever occurred in America. The defendants were allowed to talk as freely and as much as they pleased. There was no restriction whatever on their liberty to speak in their own defense. The trouble with them was that they had no defense. The Soviet government had the goods on them. A number of the prisoners had repented of their crimes against the revolution and they testified for the Soviet government.

The case was clear. The leaders of the SR Party, defeated in the political struggle with the Communist Party, resorted to a campaign of terror and assassination. They murdered Uritsky and Volodarsky. They dynamited the building which housed the Central Committee of the Russian

Communist Party and killed fourteen people. They had Trotsky and Zinoviev marked for assassination. It was an SR bullet that brought Lenin down and from which he still suffers today. They went even further than that. They went to the point that all the opponents of the Soviet system go to in the end. They collaborated with the White Guards and they took money from the French government to do its dirty work in Russia. All this was clearly proven in the trial; most of it out of the mouths of men who had taken active part in the campaign.

While the trial was in progress there occurred the anniversary of the assassination of Volodarsky, one of the most beloved leaders of the revolution, who had been shot down by the SRs; and the Communist Party called upon the workers to honor his memory by a demonstration for the Soviet government and against the SR Party. The Communist speakers went to the factories and requested that no worker march except of his own free will.

I stood in the Red Square and watched that demonstration. Practically the whole working-class population of Moscow marched that day, carrying banners which proclaimed their solidarity with the Soviet government and the Communist Party and demanded the death penalty for the leaders of the counterrevolutionary, White Guard SR Party.

I was standing in the reviewing stand with the members of the Executive Committee of the Communist International. It was five o'clock in the evening. The demonstration had commenced at noon and the workers of Moscow were still marching in wide streams from all directions through Red Square. One of the leaders of the Russian Communist Party turned to us and said, "Comrades, this is the funeral of the counterrevolution in Russia!"

So it was. The counterrevolution in Russia is as dead as

the King of Egypt. The only places there is any life left in it are Paris, London, and the East Side of New York.

Politically, the Soviet regime, under the leadership of the Communist Party, greatly strengthened itself in the past year. And economic progress went hand in hand with political improvement. Much of this economic progress, and its reflection in the field of politics, was due to the timely introduction of the New Economic Policy or, as they say in Russia, the NEP.

Early in 1921 it became evident that some of the drastic economic measures taken by the Soviet government, under the pressure of political and military necessity, could not be adhered to. The backward social and industrial development of Russia, together with the failure of the European proletariat to succeed in making a revolution, compelled the Soviet government to make a retreat on the economic field.

The Soviet government had been forced to adopt many of these extreme economic measures by political and military necessity. But Lenin did not hesitate to say that they had been going too fast. The economic development of Russia did not permit the direct transition to a system of pure socialist economy.

When this frank and obvious statement was made by Lenin, the yellow socialists of the Second International, as well as some so-called Marxians of this country, who have been against the Russian Revolution because it wasn't made according to their blueprint, found much satisfaction. They say: "Ha! Ha! We told you so. The Bolshevik Revolution was a mistake!" Their conclusions are that the workers of Russia should give up the political power and go back to capitalism.

But the Russian Bolsheviks are practical people. They have made the revolution once and they don't intend to go back and do it over again. They say: "No, the revolution was not a mistake, and we will not go back to capitalism. We will make a retreat on the economic field, but we will keep the political power in the hands of the proletariat, and use that as a lever to develop our industry to the point where it can serve as a base for a system of socialist economy. And if we can't find anything in the books to support this procedure, we'll write a book of our own."

There are people who say that Russia has gone back to capitalism, but that is not true. In Russia they say, "It is neither capitalism nor communism, it is *NEP!*" Trotsky described the present situation in Russia as follows:

"The workers control the government. The workers' government has control of industry and is carrying on this industry according to the methods of the capitalist market, of capitalist calculation."

I think that is the best concise definition of the NEP.

The state controls commerce and has a monopoly of foreign trade. The state owns all the land, and from the peasants who cultivate the land it collects a tax in kind of approximately 10 percent of the crop. Free trade is permitted. Peasants may sell or exchange their surplus products after the tax has been paid.

Private enterprises exist alongside of state enterprises. The workers in both state and private enterprises are paid wages in money and the medium of calculation and exchange is money. That is the NEP.

The New Economic Policy was first introduced in the spring of 1921, but it was not until 1922 that the effects of it began to be felt on a wide scale. During the period that I was in Russia, the positive and beneficial results of the NEP could be seen in all fields.

The paper money of Soviet Russia, like that of all countries ruined by the war, was greatly inflated. But in 1922 it was stabilized for a period of six months, as against three months in 1921. The peasants were able in 1922 to overcome the famine, and they voluntarily brought their tax in kind to the government elevators and warehouses. Only in the most exceptional and isolated cases was it necessary to use force to collect the tax.

Before the revolution the Russian peasant had the landlord on his back. Today the landlord system has been done away with; there is not one landlord left in the whole of Russia. All that the peasant produces, above his tax in kind of approximately 10 percent, is his own, to do with as he sees fit. The result is a very friendly attitude toward the Soviet government.

The year 1922 marked the beginning of a general revival in trade and industry. The revolution inherited from the old regime an industrial system that was poorly developed, inefficiently managed and badly demoralized by the strain of the imperialist war. The long civil war, the interventions and the blockade dealt still heavier blows to Russian industry and almost brought it to complete ruin.

To try to do anything with it seemed a hopeless task. Agents of other governments, industrial experts, went to Russia, investigated her industries and reported that they couldn't be revived without assistance from the outside. It was reports of this kind that bolstered up the hope of European and American capitalists and their political agents that the Soviet government was certain to fall. These gentlemen reckoned without the Russian working class and the Communist Party that leads and inspires it.

In the revolution and the war which followed it for more than four years, the Communist Party dared the "impossible"—and accomplished it. The same courage and determination characterize its attack on the problem of industry. Seval Zimmand told me a story of a meeting which he had an opportunity to attend in the Ural industrial district. It was a conference of engineers, factory managers and trade-union leaders presided over by Bogdanov, the Commissar of the Supreme Council of Public Economy. After discussing all features of the situation with the engineers and managers and hearing their reports, Bogdanov said, "I know that it is hard to improve the industries in the Ural. But the industries of the Ural can be improved and the industries of the Ural must be improved."

There in one word, is a definition of the Communist Party of Russia—the party of *must!* While others say "it is impossible" and "we had better wait" or "it can't be done," the Communist Party says, "it must be done!"—and the Communists go ahead and do it.

In 1922, Russian industry on the whole registered a general increase of production of more than 100 percent. This brought the standard of production up to 25 percent of the prewar condition. This condition is bad enough, but the Russian workers lived through a worse one, and they have begun to make headway.

Russian exports in 1922 were six times greater than the year before. In 1921, the exports were only 5 percent of the imports. Last year they were brought up to 25 percent. All the light industries, that is, those which produce for the market, improved remarkably last year and are now in pretty fair shape. The heavy industries, that is, the coal, iron, steel, and oil industries, whose product goes mainly to the other state industries—only about 10 percent of it being sold in the market—recover more slowly. Here the problem is a colossal one. For a long time after the revolution all these basic industries were in the hands of counterrevolutionary armies. The iron region in the Urals, the coal, iron, and steel in the Donetz Basin—the Pennsylvania of Russia—and the oil fields around Baku, were all held by hostile armies. When the Red Army recaptured these territories, the industries were in ruins.

The Soviet government bent itself to this task and in 1922 made substantial headway. Coal production was increased 25 percent over 1921, naphtha 20 percent, cast iron 42 percent, while iron and steel production in 1922 doubled that of the year before. In 1913, before the imperialist war began, the Russian railroads loaded 30,000 cars a day. In 1918, at the low tide of the revolution, when the blockade was still in effect and hostile armies surrounded Russia with a ring of steel, the number of railroad cars loaded daily dropped to 7,590. By 1921 this figure was brought up to 9,500. In 1922 the improvement was continued and 11,500 cars were loaded; this is more than one-third of the prewar volume.

Russia's great problem today is the problem of heavy industry. The leaders of the Russian Revolution recognize this and are concentrating all their energies on that task. The Soviet government is saving on everything in order to help the heavy industry. All state appropriations, even those for schools, are being reduced for this purpose. When some sentimental people complained that the reduction of school appropriations was a backward step, Lenin answered that the chance for Russia to become a really civilized and cultured nation depended on the improvement of heavy industry. That is the foundation.

The Soviet government last year made a profit of twenty million gold rubles on its trading activities. That is the equivalent of ten million dollars, and the whole of it was given by the government as a subsidy to heavy industry. Likewise a considerable portion of the tax collected from the peasants and from the Nepmen engaged in commerce goes for that purpose.

One way of attracting outside capital, which has attained

some degree of success, is through the formation of so-called mixed companies. The Soviet government goes into partnership with private capitalists in commercial enterprises by, for example, putting up part of the capital and sharing in the management and the profits. Lenin told us that by this means a large number of workers are enabled to learn from the capitalists how to carry on commerce; and the Soviet government retains the right to dissolve the companies later.

The wages of the Russian workers have kept pace with the improvement of production, increasing in just about the same proportion. Wages are not yet up to the prewar standard. The Russian shoe workers today get 33.3 percent of prewar wages. The metal workers get 42.9 percent, the textile workers 42.1 percent, and the wood workers 57.9 percent. Wages vary according to the conditions of the various industries. The foodstuff industry is pretty well on its feet, and the bakery workers get 81.9 percent of prewar wages, while the tobacco industry pays 73.1 percent. These figures do not tell the whole story. Because the workers, under the Soviet government, get many special privileges such as cheap rent, food at cost, etc.

The Russian worker, after five years of the revolution, is not as well off materially today as he was under the Czar. But his condition is now steadily improving, and the political and spiritual gains of the revolution are beyond calculation. There is no sentiment among the workers for a return to the old regime. To those who measure everything in terms of concrete, immediate material gains, and who ask the Russian workers what they have to show for their five years of revolution, they answer: "The revolution is not over yet."

Trotsky pointed out at the Fourth Congress of the Communist International that the French standard of living, ten years after the great revolution which smashed the feudal system and opened the way for the development of the capitalist mode of production, was far below that which prevailed immediately before the revolution. Revolutions destroy before they can build anew; and in this destruction the people suffer. But the destructive phase of the Russian Revolution is already past, and in five more years, at the present rate of progress, there is no doubt that the material conditions of the Russian workers, as well as their spiritual, intellectual and political conditions, will be far better than ever before.

Since private industrial and commercial enterprises exist alongside of state enterprises, the question naturally arises—and it certainly is a most important question: What is the relative strength of the two? This question is answered by the figures on the number employed by each. The state controls all means of transport, including the railroads, and in this transportation industry 1,000,000 are employed. The state trusts—these are corporations organized by the state for the commercial and financial management of the various industries under its control—employ 1,300,000. And in nontrust state enterprises there are another half-million workers. This brings the total of state employees up to 2,800,000. Private enterprises employ only 70,000.

There is little danger in this ratio. And that danger is lesser still because the state holds all the big and important industries which are the bases of power, while private capital is confined to smaller factories and to commerce. The average number of workers employed in state enterprises is 250, while private plants have an average of only 18.

Practically all the workers employed in both state and private undertakings are organized into the Russian trade unions. These trade unions are organized according to the industrial form; there is but one union for each industry. The membership of the Russian trade unions is 3,000,000. Before the revolution, the total membership of all the trade unions of Russia was only 1,385,000.

The trade unions have played a great part in the revolution. During the period of "War Communism" they were closely united to the apparatus and took upon themselves a number of government responsibilities. But under the New Economic Policy they have completely separated from the state machinery and have reorganized as independent bodies, having for their main function the defense of the interests of the workers in the factories.

Strikes were never prohibited by law under the Soviet government, but during the period of the civil war the Trade Union Congress voluntarily decided to forego that method of struggle. Under the New Economic Policy, however, the right to strike has been reaffirmed. Strikes are discouraged and do not occur very often. Boards of conciliation, courts of arbitration and mutual agreements are first resorted to, and as a rule all controversies are settled by these means.

I never saw a strike in Soviet Russia and never heard of one taking place while I was there. But Comrade Melnichansky, the head of the Moscow trade unions, told me of a few that had occurred under his jurisdiction. In those cases all the methods and forms of industrial warfare familiar to European and American labor movements automatically developed, such as strike committees, pickets, strike benefits, etc. There had been rare cases, he told me, when unscrupulous employers had tried to operate the struck plant by means of ignorant peasants recruited from the villages. The government gave no favor to this "freedom of contract" so popular with our own government. And a visit from the pickets usually sufficed to convince the strikebreakers that they had better go back where they came from. I asked Comrade Melnichansky if they had encountered any strike injunctions. He laughed and answered, "My dear comrade, you must understand that this is not America!"

I attended the Fifth All-Russian Trade Union Congress. It is analogous to the national convention of the American Federation of Labor, but it was quite a different-looking delegation than the sleek, fat, overdressed "men of labor" who meet once a year under the chairmanship of Gompers. There were more than a thousand delegates present at this congress; and I saw only one man who appeared to be overweight.

The congress was held in the Moscow Labor Temple, which in the old days was the Nobles' Club. It is a gorgeous place, with marble pillars, crystal chandeliers and gold-leaf decorations. One could imagine that the "Nobles" had many a good time there in the "good old days." But, in the words of the comic-strip artist, "Them days is over." The workers are the ruling class today, and they have taken all the best places for their own purposes.

I saw something at that congress that never yet happened in America. Zinoviev and Rykov came to the congress to make a report on behalf of the government. I thought how natural it was, in a country ruled by the workers, for the government to report to the trade unions. It is just as natural as it is in America for the government to report to the Chamber of Commerce. The same principle applies. Governments have the habit of reporting to those whom they really represent. The old proverb says, "Tell me whose bread you eat, and I'll tell you whose song you sing."

The Soviet government is a labor government and it makes no secret of the fact that it is partial to the working class. It doesn't pretend to be fair or neutral. They frankly call the government a dictatorship. "It's just like your own government in America," they told me, "only it is a dictatorship of a different class."

"Otherwise the two governments are much alike," they said. "They are both dictatorships. But there is another difference. The Russian government says it is a dictatorship and makes no camouflage about it. The government of the United States pretends to be fair and democratic, to represent both the workers and the capitalists, but whenever you have a big strike the government soon shows whom it belongs to."

Ninety-eight percent of all the delegates to this Fifth All-Russian Trade Union Congress were members of the Communist Party. Those figures constitute another answer to the question: "How does the Communist Party keep in power?" When more than a thousand trade-union delegates come together from all parts of Russia, and more than 98 percent of them are Communists, it is a pretty reliable indication, I think, that the Communist Party has its roots very deep in the basic organizations of the workers.

Referring to the fact that wages of the Russian workers had been increased 100 percent during the past year, keeping even pace with the increased production, Zinoviev laid before the congress the program of the Communist Party on the question of wages and production. He said the two must go forward together, hand in hand.

"Every country in the world," he said, "outside of Russia, has built up its industrial system at the price of an impoverished and exploited working class. The capitalist countries have built a marvelous industrial system; they have erected great structures of steel and stone and cement; they have piled up wealth that staggers calculation. And alongside of all this they have a hungry and impoverished working class which made it all. For all their toil and accomplishments the workers have reaped a harvest of poverty and misery."

"Russia," he said, "must not go that way. We are a working-class nation and we must not forget that the interest of the workers must be our first concern, always. We will strain all energies to increase production, but here at the beginning let us lay down an iron rule for our future guidance: that every improvement in industry must bring a corresponding improvement in the living standards of the workers in the industry. We want to build a big industry and we want to build it quickly. But we also want to build a bigger and better human race."

Between the trade unions and the Red Army there is a close and fraternal unity that does not prevail between the labor movement and the army of any other country in Europe. The trade unionists regard the Red soldiers as the protectors and defenders of the labor movement, and they treat them with the highest honor.

There is a reason for this attitude. When some of the industrial districts of Russia fell into the hands of the counterrevolutionary armies, the first thing the White Guards did, after dissolving the soviets, was to break up the trade unions, shooting or jailing the leaders; it was something like West Virginia. And when the Red Army reconquered those territories, the trade unions were immediately reorganized under the protection of its bayonets. This is the reason for the brotherly solidarity between the unions and the army.

It was not surprising, therefore, that the Red Army should send a representative to the Trade Union Congress. General Budenny, the head of the famous Red Cavalry, was there, and he was given a tumultuous reception. For several minutes they applauded and shouted for General Budenny. He was embarrassed and had difficulty getting started. His speech consisted of only one sentence, but it was enough. Drawing himself up to a military posture, he clicked his heels together and saluted the delegates and said, "Comrades, just tell us what you want us to do, and we'll do it!"

The Red Army is a new factor in the international situation, and a very important one. The diplomats cannot meet today to partition off the earth without asking, "What will the Red Army do?" The Red soldier is present at all the councils of the war-makers. He puts his fist on the table and says, "I am in on the war game in Europe from now on!"

The Red Army is something new under the sun, a proletarian army, made up exclusively of workers and peasants, with most of its officers drawn from the working class. It proved its mettle in the long and successful struggle against the interventionist armies. It has a morale, spirit and discipline unknown to the military history of Europe. There is not an army on the continent of Europe that, man for man, can stand up against it.

When I was in Russia, the size of the Red Army had been reduced to 800,000 men. Since I left, it has been still further reduced to 600,000. But that is not its full strength by any means. The standing army of 600,000 is only a skeleton around which five million men, already trained for service, can be quickly organized. The Red Army is a powerful military machine, but that is not all. It is a school, the greatest school on earth. The great bulk of its soldiers come from the peasantry; and 80 percent of the Russian peasants are illiterate. But in the Red Army they are all taught to read and write. Last May Day they celebrated the liquidation of illiteracy in the Red Army. Trotsky made the statement that on that day there was not a soldier in the army who was not able to read and write. The Russian

Bolsheviks have taken an instrument of destruction and utilized it for a great constructive purpose.

I visited some Red Army camps and learned something about the spirit of the soldiers at first hand. I had read something about it and wished to check up on what I had read. I asked Trotsky about it and he said, "Go to the camps and see the soldiers themselves. Then you will understand it." I asked him why the Red soldier has a different attitude toward the government from that of the other soldiers of Europe, and he answered, "The attitude of the Red soldier toward the Soviet government is determined by the attitude of the Soviet government toward the Red soldier."

That is the secret of it. That is the reason for the intense loyalty of the Red soldier, which the old-school militarists cannot understand. The Red soldier is respected and honored in time of peace as well as in war. He is not made into a hero as he marches off to battle and then chased up a back alley when he comes home. He is not given a medal when he is needed and refused a job or a handout when the war is over. In the working-class society of Russia, the Red soldier has a place of dignity and honor. In Russia, the soldiers and the workers are the real "people of importance."

I saw another phase of the educational work of the army in one of the camps. It was a moving-picture show attended by about two thousand soldiers. It was a moving picture of large-scale grain farming in Canada. Most of the soldiers in the audience were peasant lads. They had come from the villages and their idea of agriculture was founded on the primitive, individualistic methods they had always known. Most of them had never seen a farming implement larger than a one-horse plow. Here on the screen before them was flashed a picture of modern farming on a big scale, with tractors, gangplows and great threshing machines; a single working unit covering hundreds of acres at a time.

They drank in that picture very eagerly. As I watched them, I saw another picture. I saw those peasant lads going back home when their service in the army would be ended, with their newly acquired knowledge and their vision of the great world outside their little villages, telling their friends and their old folks of the great farming machinery that the city worker will manufacture for the peasants, which will be the means of developing large-scale communal farming instead of small-scale individual farming, and which will transform the individualist peasant of today into the communist peasant of tomorrow.

I found the Red soldiers pretty well informed as to what is going on in the world. They spoke of the prospects of revolution in Germany with the air of men who had read and talked much about it. That is part of their education. Trotsky keeps them fully informed about international developments, and there are special Communist detachments in all regiments who carry on a constant propaganda for internationalism.

Capitalist journalists write a great deal about the intense national patriotism of the Red Army. These stories are usually written by journalists who sit around in Moscow hotels and cook up stories about it, and, as a rule, they are very far from the truth. As a matter of fact, the main effort of Communist propaganda in the army is to overcome tendencies toward Russian national patriotism and to develop a patriotism to the international proletariat. Since the army quit singing *God Save the Czar* it has had no national official hymn. The official air played in the Red Army is *The Internationale*. Internationalism is the watchword.

This was impressed upon us very vividly by a speech we heard at the graduation exercises of the school of Red Cavalry commanders at Moscow. A number of international delegates attended those exercises and spent the entire day with the young students who were just finishing their studies. For several hours we watched them perform hair-raising feats on horseback, and late in the afternoon we had dinner with them in the mess hall. After dinner, the delegates from the various countries each spoke a few words of greeting to the graduates, and then they put up one of the graduates to respond. He was lifted up on the table from which we had just eaten our dinner, a young Communist lad who only a short time before had been taken from the factory, put through an intensive course of instruction, and on that day was being turned out as a Red commander.

"Comrades," he said, "we greet you as comrades and brothers in the same army with us. We do not want you to think of us as soldiers of Russia, but as soldiers of the international proletariat. Our army is a working-class army, and the working class of the world is our country. We will be very glad when the workers of Europe rise in revolt and call on us for assistance; and when that day comes, they will find us ready."

It is not only the Red soldiers in Russia who are internationalists. Internationalism permeates the entire working class. When the Russian workers rose in revolt five years ago and struck the blow that destroyed Russian capitalism, they were confident that the workers throughout Europe would follow their example. They have been waiting five years for the international revolution, and they still believe it is coming. Nothing has been able to shake that faith. They believe in the workers of Europe as they believe in the sun.

Ah, the faith of those Russian workers! It is so strong that it communicates itself to others. All of us who saw and felt it came away with our own faith surer and stronger. One afternoon I heard a band playing in the street outside the hotel where I was living. I looked out the window and saw a big parade marching with banners flying. I took a Russian comrade with me and we followed the parade. It wound up at the Labor Temple with a mass meeting. There were enthusiastic speeches; the band played *The Internationale,* and the crowd sang it. It was a demonstration of the bakery workers of Moscow for the bakers of Bulgaria, who were out on a general strike. And those bakery workers of Moscow, from their meager wages, raised a fund to send to their comrades in faraway Bulgaria, to cheer them on in the fight.

On the fifth anniversary of the revolution, the delegates of the Communist parties and Red Trade Unions were the guests of the proletariat of Petrograd. A great throng of workers met us at the station. We symbolized to them the international labor movement, and they gave us a warm and generous welcome. Red Army troops were drawn up before the station; the streets in all directions were packed with workers who had come to greet us; and from every building and post flew banners proclaiming the fifth anniversary of the Russian Revolution and hailing the international revolution.

That day we saw a demonstration of the workers of Petrograd. I shall never forget it. They had built a special reviewing stand for us before the Uritsky Palace, and we stood there and watched them march by in detachments according to the factories where they worked. They carried the same old banners which they had carried five years before, many of them torn by the bullets that flew during the decisive battle.

I never saw before such an outpouring of people, nor such enthusiasm. The parade commenced at eleven o'clock in the morning. Hour after hour we saw them come in wide streams across the square. The afternoon wore away and turned to dusk. It was six o'clock and we grew tired of standing and had to leave; and still the workers of Petrograd were coming by the thousands, carrying their revolutionary banners and singing *The Internationale*. All the workers of Petrograd marched that day to show their solidarity with the international proletariat and to prove to us that they still believe in the revolution they made five years before.

The next day, as though to show us that the Russian Revolution and *The Internationale* have not only spirit and solidarity on their side, but military power also, they let us see a parade of the Red Army.

It was a cheering and inspiring sight to see the Red soldiers on the march, with their rifles over their shoulders and their bayonets shining in the sun. They marched in perfect step, with heads erect, the picture of physical prowess. As they passed the reviewing stand they all shouted, "Long live the Communist International!" and we shouted back, "Long live the Red Army!"

In the reviewing stand that day were delegates of the Communist parties of other countries; and beside us sat the diplomats of foreign governments in Russia. It is the custom to invite them whenever there is a parade of the Red Army. They say that when the diplomats see the Red soldiers march, it cools their enthusiasm for another war against Soviet Russia.

Before we left Petrograd we made a pilgrimage to the Field of Mars, where in one great grave are buried the victims of the November Revolution. Five years before it was the scene of desperate battle. The air was torn by rifle fire and the cries of those Petrograd workers who had risen in revolt and staked their lives on the issue. On the seventh of November, five years before, the workers of Petrograd fought there the battle of the human race and of the future. Many of them fell, never to rise again.

We stood there, with heads uncovered, in a cold, drizzling rain. The once noisy battlefield was quiet. There was no sound but the soft music of the *Funeral Hymn of the Revolution,* and the ground, once spattered with the blood of our heroic dead, was banked high with flowers, placed there in gratitude and love by the delegates of the Communist parties and Red trade unions of all lands.

Those Petrograd workers put their lives in the scale. They had lived lives of misery and oppression, but they were possessed by a daring vision of the future when the lives of all men will be better and fairer. They were the heralds of a new day in the world, when there will be no more masters and no more slaves, and they gave their lives to hasten that day. There is an end now to their labor, their struggle and their sacrifice. They rest beneath the Field of Mars and their mouths are stopped with dust. But still from the grave they speak, and their voices are heard all over the world. They lighted an everlasting fire in the sky, which the whole world is destined to see and follow.

Those Petrograd workers struck the blow that shattered the capitalist regime in Russia and put the working class in power. But they did more than that, because the Russian Revolution did not stop in Russia. It found its way over the borders. It broke through the blockade and spread all over the earth. The Russian Revolution was the beginning of the international revolution.

Wherever there is a group of militant workers anywhere in the world, there is the Russian Revolution. The Russian Revolution is in the heart of every rebel worker the world over. The Russian Revolution is in this room.

Comrade Trotsky told us, just before we left Moscow, that the best way we can help Soviet Russia is to build a bigger trade-union movement and a stronger party of our own. Recognition by other governments will be of some temporary value; but the real recognition Soviet Russia wants is the recognition of the working class. When she gets that, she will not need the recognition of capitalist governments. Then she can refuse to recognize them! For, after all, Soviet Russia is not a "country." Soviet Russia is a part of the world labor movement. Soviet Russia is a strike—the greatest strike in all history. When the working class of Europe and America join that strike it will be the end of capitalism.

Chapter 4

# The twenty-fifth anniversary of the Russian Revolution

Delivered to a meeting at Irving Plaza, New York City, on November 8, 1942.

Comrades:

We meet on the twenty-fifth anniversary of that great day when the world-encircling chain of imperialism snapped at its weakest link, and the workers of Czarist Russia, supported by the peasants, broke through to victory and established the first workers' state. We are meeting tonight, as we and our kind have been meeting on each succeeding anniversary throughout the years since 1917, as partisans and defenders of the Russian Revolution and of the workers' state which the Russian Revolution created.

We are not alone today. The whole world is taking notice of the USSR on this anniversary. Everybody is recognizing the Soviet Union, each in his own way. Churchill, who tried his best to overthrow it in the early days, and Roosevelt, who—to judge by the indictment which his administration drew up against us—was, to say the least, not very friendly to the Russian Revolution—Churchill and Roosevelt pay hypocritical tribute today to "the great Russian people" and "the heroic Red Army." Hitler looks toward the East through dark glasses tonight, with fear and trembling, wondering whether his insane dream of empire hasn't been shattered on the Russian front.

Remembering the Russian Revolution of 1917, the workers of Europe and the colonial slaves lift up their hearts in hope once more today. Each in his own way, for reasons of his own, takes notice of this twenty-fifth anniversary. But the differences in the reasons—and they are whole worlds apart—change nothing in the decisive fact that everybody is saluting, recognizing, or cursing a state and an army that issued from a victorious revolution of the workers. This revolution is in the greatest crisis of its entire history at this hour, in its greatest peril. We know this and we say it openly. And we say also, and with truth, that in its greatest crisis and danger, we Fourth Internationalists, we disciples of Lenin and Trotsky, remain the best defenders of the Soviet Union. The fact that we are celebrating the revolution and not announcing its funeral shows that we are still fighting. We are fighting for a revolution that is still living.

War and revolution are the most authoritative of all tribunals. It is there, in war and in revolution, that all the great questions are decided in our epoch. The outbreak of the First World War in August 1914 demonstrated that capitalism, as an economic and social system, had exhausted its progressive historic mission. The Russian Revolution of November 1917 served notice that a more powerful class than the class of capitalists had come to maturity. The modern proletariat, the progressive force in modern society, the herald and representative of a new social order—this class, as demonstrated by the revolution, took the offensive in the class battle that can only end in worldwide victory.

November 7, 1917. The death sentence on the old order of capitalism and the beginning of the new order of world socialism were both proclaimed on that day. And whatever vicissitudes, whatever setbacks, betrayals or defeats may overtake the proletariat on the road to that final goal; however sharp and deep may be the zigzags in the line which charts the course of the struggle through which humanity shall pass from capitalism to socialism; whatever may befall: the starting point in the line of development will always be traced to that great day which we commemorate tonight—November 7, 1917.

I can remember the dark days of the First World War, 1914–1918. Then as now, all the hopes for humanity's progress seemed to be drowned in the blood of the war. Reaction seemed to be triumphant everywhere. The enemies of the proletariat gloated over the treachery and capitulation of the socialist parties; and to many—to the great majority, I venture to say—the theory and the hope of socialism seemed vanished like a utopian dream. And then, as now—as has already been remarked here tonight—fainthearts and deserters mocked at those who continued the stubborn struggle and held on to the revolutionary faith. The whole world labor movement was overcome with depression and despair in 1914–1917.

But the Russian Revolution of November 7 changed all that overnight. At one blow, the revolution lifted the proletariat of Europe to its feet again. It stirred the hundreds of millions of colonial slaves who had never known political aspiration before, who had never dared to hope before. The Russian Revolution awakened them to the promise of a new life.

Here in the United States, the progressive sections of

the socialist and labor movements were reinvigorated by the Russian Revolution. The morale of the movement grew stronger than ever before. For the first time, concentrated in revolutionary action, we had a demonstration of the real meaning of the doctrines of Marxism. For the first time we learned, from the example and teachings of Lenin and Trotsky and the leaders of the Russian Revolution, the real meaning of a revolutionary party. Those who remember that time, whose lives became welded to the Russian Revolution, must think of it today as the greatest inspiring and educating force that the oppressed class of the world has ever known.

Marx and Engels lifted the conception of socialism from utopia to science. The Russian Revolution developed scientific socialism from theory into action, and proved several things that before had been abstract generalizations and predictions. The Russian Revolution proved in action that certain things were true beyond all further doubt. The first of these things proved by the revolution was that it is possible for the workers to take power. It is possible for the workers to forge out of their ranks a party that is capable of leading the struggle to victory. And the workers in all countries will everlastingly remember that. Nothing can erase from history that example. Victory of the proletariat is possible—the Russian Revolution in action, in blood and fire, proved that it is so.

We all know that the authentic leaders of the revolution, Lenin, Trotsky, conceived of it not as an end in itself but as a first step, the first stage, in the world revolution that alone could complete what had been started in the Soviet Union. The conditions objectively were already mature in 1917–1919 for such a world revolution, beginning in Europe. What was lacking was the leadership, the party, without which the workers cannot succeed. The leadership of the old party, the social democrats, who had betrayed the workers under the test of war, supported the bourgeoisie in their counterrevolutionary fight against the workers in the period following the war. The young and hastily organized Communist parties, which had been formed in European countries in response to the example of the Russian Revolution, were as yet too weak and too young, too inexperienced, for their historic task.

Thus the revolution, which objectively had every possibility of succeeding on the whole continent of Europe, failed in the postwar years. The workers today have to pay for that failure, and for the consequent isolation of the Soviet Union, with another and even more terrible world war.

The capitalist world surrounded and isolated the Soviet Union. For three years, 1918 to 1920, the revolution had to fight for its life in the civil war financed and supported by the world imperialists, and against the interventionist attempts in which the great majority of the capitalist powers participated. The economy of Russia, terribly backward when the war began, a heritage from Czarism, was almost completely ruined in the war and the civil war which followed. Hunger and famine ravished the whole land, but the first workers' state survived all of that. It survived the isolation and the blockade imposed upon it by world imperialism. It survived the civil war, the intervention, the famine, the hunger, the economic disorganization and demoralization. The Soviet Union survived because, contained within that effort of the proletariat of Russia, there was a dynamic power such as had never been released before in the whole world, the power of the revolutionary proletariat.

The revolution survived, but not without terrible cost. On the basis of the hunger and the scarcity and the backwardness and the isolation arose the reactionary, privileged bureaucracy, personified by Stalin. The crimes of the Stalinist bureaucracy are known to everyone present here. They debased the theory which had guided the revolution. They destroyed the party that had made the revolution. They destroyed the soviets and the trade unions as self-acting organisms of the workers. They assassinated a whole generation of the leaders of the revolution. They beheaded the Red Army, and they capped their series of unprecedented crimes against the people by the assassination of the most authentic representative of the revolution—Comrade Trotsky.

But they haven't, in spite of all that, been able to kill the revolution. There was something there that proved itself to be stronger than all the imperialist powers of the world in the early days, something stronger than the corroding and degenerating bureaucracy. We alone know the full extent of the bureaucratic degeneration that has taken place in the Soviet Union since the death of Lenin. And we, following Trotsky, exposed it and explained it before others without any embellishments whatever. We know the full extent of the degeneration, but we also know the limits of the degeneration. We know that the basic conquests of the revolution, the nationalized industry and the planned production, remain at the base of the Soviet state. That is why the revolution stays alive in spite of all the premature announcements to the contrary.

The vitality of the revolution is demonstrated in every test: first of all in the most decisive field, the field of economy, the base of society. The Russian Revolution proved for all time, in spite of bureaucratic mismanagement, the superiority of the Soviet system of planned economy over the capitalist system of private property and anarchy in production. This superiority of Soviet economy was first demonstrated, most dramatically and convincingly, in that very period, after 1929, of the worldwide crisis of the capitalist nations. When capitalist economy was plunging down to unheard-of depths of stagnation and demoralization—in that very period, in spite of the backwardness of Russia, in spite of the isolation of Russia and its unworthy leadership—in that very period the Soviet revolution showed its power in a tremendous advance and development of industry.

That economic strength of the Soviet regime, and the strength of the revolutionary tradition, are being reflected now in the military field. The whole world has been surprised and astounded by the military prowess of the Red Army. All the military experts counted upon a defeat of the Russian armies in the space of a few weeks or months. But this Red Army has stood up for seventeen months, despite bad leadership and almost continuous retreats and defeats, without cracking. I say the whole world has been surprised, including Stalin, who had no more confidence in the Red Army than he had in the Soviet economy, than he has in the revolutionary powers of the workers generally. The Trotskyists were not taken by surprise. Trotsky predicted that imperialist attack on the Soviet Union would unleash marvels of proletarian enthusiasm and fighting capacity in the Red Army. He could do that because he, better than others, understood that the great motive power of the victorious revolution had not all been expended. The Red Army that the world hails is an army created by a proletarian revolution. This revolution lives in the memory of the Soviet people. That and the basic conquests, which they still retain and upon which they stand, constitute the basis upon which the Red Army has unfolded such unparalleled capacity for defense and resistance and heroic sacrifice.

The war put to a test the fetish of fascism. In the period

of the great reaction following the death of Lenin, the betrayal of the Chinese revolution, the defeat in Germany, and the fascist victory in Italy, followed by the fascist victory in Germany—all these events gave rise to a fetish of fascism as of some new, great, invincible power which might possibly have a progressive historic role to play. Along with that, we have seen developed in recent years the theory of the identity of fascism and Sovietism. The identity of the political methods of Stalinism and fascism led philistines and renegades to identify the Stalinist and fascist regimes altogether, to say they are the same thing, national sectors of a new social order that is developing, creating some new class of "bureaucratic collectivists," or something of that sort.

Our movement, the movement of the Fourth International, long ago refuted these superficial theories. Trotsky's analysis has been fully confirmed in the war. Trotsky, in his analysis, did not proceed from the estimation of single events or isolated symptoms. Reasoning as a Marxist, he took this theory of the identity of fascism and the Soviet Union and he first of all put the question: How did each one arise? Here the most profound difference is revealed at the very start. In Russia, the Soviet regime arose as a product of the proletarian revolution, as a victory of the workers against the Czarist police, Black Hundreds, and White Guards. Fascism in Italy, on the other hand, arose as a counterrevolution of Black Hundred gangs, financed by the big capitalists, against the workers. Italian fascism did not come to power as an imitation of the Russian Revolution, but as a counterrevolutionary answer to it.

Secondly, Trotsky put the question: How did each regime—the Russian and the fascist—develop in its first stage, and whom did it benefit? In Russia, the Soviet regime developed as a power of the workers and peasants, expropriated the capitalists and landlords and enhanced the strength of the workers and peasants. In Italy, the counterrevolution of fascism immediately and directly strengthened and benefited finance capital at the expense of the interests of the workers and the peasants and all the poor.

What was the world attitude toward Soviet Russia and fascist Italy in the beginning? That part of the world which is made up of workers and colonial slaves hailed the Russian Revolution with enthusiasm and surrounded it with their sympathy in the early years. The capitalists, the foreign money-sharks, the exploiters of all lands, ardently supported Mussolini. American money—Wall Street money—helped to prop him up in the earliest days.

Next, take the most important criterion, the economy of the country. What was the effect of the fascist counterrevolution on the one side, and the workers' revolution on the other, on the development of the productive powers of the workers, which is the decisive and basic criterion for all regimes? In fascist Italy, economy was stifled, put in an iron grip of the big monopolists, and twisted to serve their private interests at every turn. The hideously distorted and declining economy has cursed Italy ever since the fascist counterrevolution. The Soviet revolution in Russia liberated the forces of production from the straitjacket of private ownership and made possible a development of the productive powers of the workers and an expansion of industrial development on a scale never seen before in history, through the medium of nationalized industry and planned economy.

All these profound differences in the two regimes, which superficial people wanted to identify, show their significance now under the test of the war. And what does the war say about the theory that fascism and Sovietism are the same thing? Ten days ago, on October 29, Italian fascism celebrated its twentieth anniversary. But it wasn't much of a celebration. It was more like a funeral. Mussolini didn't even appear in the arena to puff out his chest and make threatening speeches. Very little was said, because all the dreams of the fascist Roman Empire of Mussolini are gone with the wind. The people of Italy are starving. The economy is bankrupt. The country seethes with revolution. The fascist masters of Italy are no longer able to control the people; they have to rely on Hitler's troops and secret police.

The soldiers of Italy will no longer fight anymore anywhere in the world. And we have this absurd explanation of cowardice. Every time a serious military struggle begins, the Italian soldiers retreat or surrender. We hear this stupid, chauvinistic explanation that this is due to the racial inferiority of the Italians, to their cowardice. But, of course, it is ridiculous to speak about the cowardice or the military incapacity of the Italian soldiers. There are no braver people than the Italians. They are the equals in every way of any other nationality in Europe or America. The true explanation of the Italian military debacle is very simple.

The Italian workers and peasants don't want to fight because they haven't got a particle of confidence in the regime and don't consider it worth fighting for. That is the explanation of the Italian military defeats everywhere. In Greece, the Italian soldiers on one front laid down their arms and marched in as prisoners, not with their heads bowed, seeking pardon from the conquerors; they marched in singing *Bandiera Rossa,* the great suppressed marching song of the Italian workers' movement. That song will resound again in mighty chorus in the streets of Italy.

The truth is that the fascist regime of Italy, after a brief twenty years, is bankrupt through and through and cannot stand defeats, while the Soviet Union, the product of a proletarian revolution, has shown a mighty strength in war in spite of the most terrible defeats caused by bad leadership. And if the German fascist, Hitler, brooding over the Eastern front and the steadily growing wave of discontent and revolt throughout the mass of the people at home, wants to know the fate of his dream of a thousand years of German fascist domination, he can look to Mussolini—there he will see the image of his own future. Fascism cannot stand the test of war, cannot stand defeat. Those who say that fascism and Sovietism are the same are completely refuted by the realities of the war.

Fascism and the Soviet system are not the same. Fascism is a desperate and short-lived final expedient of a dying social system. In a brief twenty years, Italian fascism has exhausted its economic, its military, and all its moral reserves. On the other hand, the Soviet system is the historically necessary birth of a new social order, better and more progressive than capitalism in either its democratic or its fascist form, and historically destined to supersede capitalism.

The Russian Revolution proved three things for all time. Two of them have been mentioned. First, it proved that the party and the leadership necessary for victory can be created by the proletariat, as they have been created by the Russian proletariat.

Second, the Russian Revolution proved—I am now repeating what I said before—that the system of nationalized industry and planned economy, introduced by a Soviet revolution, is superior, more progressive, more productive, than any device of capitalism, whether democratic or fascist.

And the third thing which we can say is demonstrated by the revolution, and proved now in the test of war, is that only one class is capable of solving the great social problems of our epoch. That class is the proletariat.

The Fourth International, with its program and its tactics anchored to these three propositions, has been proven correct by the whole test of events. Therefore, on the twenty-fifth anniversary of the revolution, we do not change our course. We see not only the Soviet regime's terrible weakness, which derives from bureaucratic mismanagement and control. We see also the strength and the power which derives from the revolutionary origin of the Soviet Union and its basic conquests.

I think it is quite clear that Hitler made a mortal error in attacking the Soviet Union. Fascist thinking was far too superficial for the complicated problem involved in the attempt to destroy the Soviet Union and its Red Army and its economic system. Hitler made a very common mistake. He saw only the bureaucracy, which is weak, inefficient and cowardly; and he did not see and did not understand the vitality of the still-living revolution and the mighty sources of achievement and heroism that this revolution could call forth in time of war. All the petty-bourgeois political thinkers overlook this point—the difference between the Soviet Union, which is the product of a great revolution, and the usurping bureaucracy, which is a parasitic tumor on the Soviet Union. It is quite obvious that Hitler is no genius but just another petty-bourgeois thinker.

For our part, we have always rejected these superficial conclusions of the vulgar thinkers, who judge every feature or incident out of its historic context, without regard for what went before and what must come after. To our way of thinking, to the Marxist method of analysis, the origin of the Soviet state had to be taken as the point of departure. This origin was in revolution. We studied it, aided and directed by Comrade Trotsky. We studied the Soviet Union, not as an isolated, static phenomenon but as a process. We studied it in its changes, and tried to determine in each case what was fundamental and what was secondary, what had been gained and what had been lost in that changing process. And by this method of thinking we arrived at our conclusion: the Soviet Union does not and cannot represent fascism or a social order ruled by a new exploitive class; but it is a deformed and degenerated workers' state. And from that we proceed to our fighting motto: "Never surrender a position before it is lost!" We know all the defects of the Soviet Union. We know all the crimes of the bureaucracy. But we know also all that mighty power of those conquests of the progressive revolution which remain still intact, and therefore we continue to defend the Soviet Union.

Some may say, "Defense of the Soviet Union in the present circumstances can be only moral support. Of what use is it?" We can answer—and I can tell you from my personal knowledge and recollection—that the moral support of the international proletariat was the force which saved the Soviet Union from destruction in its earliest years, and even later. The interventions against the Soviet Union could not succeed because the sympathy of the masses of the people of Europe for the Soviet Union was so great. It was impossible for the imperialists to organize mass armies or take any serious military measures because of the threats of the workers against any government that would try it.

Moral support is what we give here in America, as always since 1917, but our policy is not only for the United States. Our policy is a world policy, as that of the Marxists and Bolsheviks has always been. Our policy is the policy of the Russian section of the Fourth International, which lives and fights. And they continue at their task—to defend the country, to rebuild the Bolshevik party, to revive the soviets and the trade unions, and to overthrow the Stalinist bureaucracy. Whether, with the help of the international proletariat, they shall succeed or fail, history has yet to show.

Stalin's speech the other day, printed in all the capitalist newspapers, only shows that he is still doing all that he can to ensure the defeat of the Soviet Union in the war with Hitlerism. Stalin rejects the real allies of the Soviet Union—the workers of Europe and America and the colonial people and, above all, the workers of Germany—and he directs his appeal and his alliances to the imperialists of the United States and Great Britain. He looks for the salvation of the Soviet Union, rather of the bureaucracy, in a victory of the so-called United Nations against the Axis powers. If they defeat the Axis, if America and Great Britain crush fascist Germany in the war, would that ensure the safety of the Soviet Union? Those who may be deluded by that thought for a moment should remember 1918–1920.

No sooner had an armistice with the Central Powers been arranged, before peace was concluded, than the former allies of Russia, the champions of democracy—England, France, and America—turned all their force against the Russian Revolution. If they succeed in establishing a front in the Balkans and defeat Hitler, who can imagine, in the absence of a European revolution, that the sword of Hitler having been broken, it will not be replaced by the sword of Anglo-American imperialism pointed at the Soviet Union, as it was in 1918–1920? How can it be otherwise? The conflict between the Soviet Union and the imperialist powers is something different from and more profound than the rivalry between one imperialist power and another. Here is involved the clash, the irreconcilable conflict of two contrasting social systems. One or the other must prevail in the world; one or the other must go down. And whoever preaches trust in the Anglo-American imperialists is a traitor to the Soviet Union.

We, for our part, turn to the workers—above all, to the German workers—and to the colonial people, and we say they are the only true allies of the Soviet Union. They are the only true allies because they alone have their fundamental interest bound up with the preservation of the Soviet Union, just as the fundamental interests of the Soviet Union are indissolubly connected with the fate of the uprisings of the colonial masses and the victory of the workers in the world. And let those doubt who will. We believe in the workers. We believe in the colonial slaves awakened to new life by the Russian Revolution.

We don't doubt that in India tonight millions of the colonial insurgents are thinking, on this anniversary of the Russian Revolution. They are thinking simply but strongly, and saying to themselves: "The Russians did it; why can't we?" Once the oppressed masses of the world begin to think that way, the realization of that aspiration will be placed on the order of the day. We believe that before this bloody carnage is over, the workers, the people, will say their decisive word. And when they speak to the imperialists, they will speak Russian.

The Russian Revolution is in the greatest peril today. We do not delude ourselves about that. We do not deceive ourselves or others with any false optimism about the danger confronting the Soviet Union. We see the situation as it really is. We know that the fate of the Soviet Union hangs in the balance, that it depends now, more than ever, on the world revolution of the proletariat and the colonial masses. But we have faith in the world revolution, and because of that, we retain our hope in the ultimate regeneration of the Soviet Union. We keep undimmed our faith that the world revolution will release humanity from this terrible vise of the war and open up a new stage of progress on the way to the communist future. Because of that, here on the occasion of the twenty-fifth anniversary, as we celebrate the living revolution, we can still express the confident hope that the funeral of the Russian Revolution, which so many renegades and traitors are announcing, will not merely be postponed, but will never take place.

Chapter 5

# The AFL and the start of the CIO

Delivered to a public meeting of the Workers Party in Minneapolis, November 26, 1935.

The impulse of the masses, with the coming of the NRA, was "into the unions." Millions of workers could have been organized at that time. These workers longed for a union—the most elementary organization of the workers. Without a union, the workers felt, they had nothing. But the AFL craft unions came between the workers and the employers and betrayed the interests of the workers. This happened all over the country. In Minneapolis, Tobin, president of the Teamsters International, tried the same stunt. But he didn't succeed.

In Minneapolis, real organization survived as testimony to the real possibilities in the organization of the workers. What was the answer of the AFL leadership? Before the July strike, just when the bosses were trying to welsh out of their May agreement with 574, the Teamsters president fired a blast which was printed in the newspapers as a weapon against the union. And no sooner had the union buried its dead, no sooner had the smoke of battle cleared and the wounded been gathered together, than Tobin came along and tried to break up the union because it wouldn't allow itself to be cheated and browbeaten. Tobin connived with Green to show the workers that they might perhaps beat the bosses—but, by God, they couldn't beat the AFL and its almighty "principles." Tobin would show the union that he was better than the Citizens Alliance in busting up unions. Well, he tried. And the score is nothing to nothing for both Tobin and the Citizens Alliance.

Thus, in spite of the accumulated discontent of the workers, the AFL as such made only the most miserable showing. But the workers, for this reason, didn't say "to hell with unions!" Instead there was a tremendous pressure to change the form and methods of organization. Every worker reflects this discontent with the old methods and forms. Every discontented worker rallies around any union capable of fighting the incompetency of the old craft unions. Suppose you took 574 to Detroit or Pittsburgh—what unions you would have in rubber, in steel, in autos! You can't fool the workers with craft unionism any more. They don't want it. They want industrial unionism. When the craft unionists come in and try to tell them how to run their unions, they revolt. The automobile workers, in their convention, called on the eve of the Atlantic City convention, rejected the proposals of Green. In Akron, the rubber workers elected their own president and rejected the protege of Green. And then come the teachers—the teachers, who have never been known to be radicals—the teachers in Ohio rejected the ultimatum from Green that they reorganize the New York local. The teachers told Green to go to hell. Three times before the

Atlantic City convention Green got official rebuffs and defeats—unheard-of before! And in Minneapolis, Tobin had also failed.

All these accumulated forces pressed in on the Atlantic City convention—forces which guarantee that there will be no patching up between the contending forces in the AFL. First, then, there is the revolt from below. Secondly, there is the fear on the part of certain of the shrewder leaders. This fear is not unjustified. It is the fear that if the AFL doesn't quit monkeying around, there will grow up an independent union movement outside of the AFL, leaving the old leaders high and dry without their highly remunerative "pie cards." They have seen the handwriting on the wall, these more farsighted leaders; they have looked across the Atlantic and seen what happened in Europe. Take John L. Lewis. Lewis is no radical, yet he says that if there are no industrial unions there will be none at all. Hillman, too, in the AFL conventions made the same point. Thus we find forces pressing for more modern types of organization both within and without the official AFL.

While on the surface it may appear that the contest is only between two types of leaders—between the industrial unionists and the horse-and-buggy unionists—there is also a tendency which is even more progressive than the official sponsors of industrial unionism. This tendency aims at more than merely winning a strike. It aims at the foundation of a workers' republic. This tendency is ours; and it will come more and more to the front.

The difference between Lewis and Green is one of intelligence and not of radicalism. The old Bourbons never learn anything new. They call the unskilled workers riffraff; they try to keep the unions small and divided into crafts. These old fossils have lived their time. There are going to be many types of labor leaders before we have a workers' republic in the United States, but you can be sure that the Green-Hutcheson type will be among the first to be pushed aside.

The younger leaders know that if you don't organize the strategically situated basic industries you have practically no organization at all. How can you speak of the American trade-union movement when the basic industries are not unionized? These younger leaders are goaded on, also, by another fear—that unless they organize the basic industries first, more radical leaders will come in ahead of them. They don't want to be left on the outside. But they are not radicals, either. They want to deal with the bosses, but in an organized way. The bosses would have liked to cooperate with Meyer Lewis in Minneapolis. But Lewis had no power—he didn't control any unions—so they said to him, "We're sorry, but we can't do any business." The same principle applies to the John L. Lewis-Hillman-Dubinsky crowd. They know they can't deal with the bosses unless they have powerfully organized industrial unions behind them.

Now it is one of the nine wonders of the world that John L. Lewis & Co. have been catapulted to the leadership of the movement for industrial unionism. Their record is not so good. Nobody suppressed trade-union democracy more ruthlessly than John L. Lewis. Nobody expelled more honest radical workers from the unions. Nobody forced more "provisional reorganizations" of local unions. Nobody was more violent and unscrupulous in his methods. Yet this man has been projected to the front.

Nevertheless, his interests and ours to a limited extent coincide. Our tendency is not that of John L. Lewis. We believe in militancy, and our final aim is the foundation of the workers' republic. We don't believe in class collaboration. We don't believe that the workers can get anything without militancy. But we do stand for industrial unionism because it is a necessary step—because it is a step forward. It is a curious fact that the interests of the most revolutionary and the extremely conservative tendencies coincide to a certain extent. Industrial unionism is objectively progressive. Therefore revolutionists must support it regardless of who is at the head of the movement for its realization. But we must not lose our heads and think that industrial unionism is all. We must forge ahead. We must retain our independent position. We must take advantage of every division between the reactionaries and the conservatives.

The situation is this. The Lewis clique can't leave the workers unorganized. In Detroit, the first strike of the season was conducted by an independent union consisting of three unions outside the AFL that came together and amalgamated. This was a warning to the AFL. Minneapolis is also a warning. Here was a deliberate attempt to break up a union and drive it out of the AFL for ninety-nine years. And this attempt failed. The idea may get into the minds of the workers: "To hell with an AFL charter. Maybe it wasn't the AFL charter that got us our wage increase. Maybe it was our own organized strength!"

That is the meaning behind the resignation of John L. Lewis. Lewis doesn't agree with Green—who issued a warning on the "serious consequences" of forming organizations within the AFL and of entering into relations with non-AFL unions (except the Civic Federation, or any other boss union). Lewis is just going ahead the same as before.

What does this mean for us? Now is the time for progressive and militant elements to push forward. Now is not the time to be cautious. Now is the time to press our demands and to get consideration for them. Now is the time to press further and further into the AFL.

Now you may want to know why Lewis rather than the radicals is leading the fight for industrial unionism. The answer is that in the five years of the crisis, the most radical group, the Communists (Stalinists), left the AFL. They went out of the AFL and pulled many others out with themselves. That's why when all this upsurge from the ranks is taking place, there have been no militants ready to spring into a place of leadership.

That is why, too, we must, wherever possible, fight for a policy of unity. But not unity at any price. We won't purchase unity at the cost of breaking up our organizations and of giving up our fundamental rights. We must, wherever possible, go into the AFL and fertilize it, while there is still time, with genuine militancy. We must inspire the unions not only to fight for a loaf of bread but to conquer the world, or else the world will be taken away from them, as happened in Germany.

In the days of reaction, the Gompers and Green policy of weeding out radicals worked like a charm. But now the workers are discontented. There is no hope of inciting them against radicals. If you go to a worker and say to him, "A radical is the leader of your union," he will answer, "I'm damned glad to hear that." The sentiment of the masses has changed. I predict with absolute confidence, for example, that Meyer Lewis will be a complete flop. The victory of 574 is due not only to its own strength but to the favorable national situation. But it will be so decisive that it will put steel and courage into the movement everywhere else. The reactionaries' hands are too full—they have too many irons in the fire. There are too many issues at stake here and elsewhere.

We must take advantage of this favorable objective

situation. We must push the industrial union struggle forward. But at the same time we must inspire the workers with the revolutionary idea that they must establish themselves as the masters of the whole world.

## Chapter 6

# Sixty years of American radicalism

Delivered to a meeting at the West Coast Vacation School and Camp, Labor Day, 1959.

The biographical information which the chairman provided in his introduction doesn't necessarily qualify anyone to give a coherent account of what happened in the past fifty years or so in the movement of socialist and labor radicalism. The woods are full of people who have been through at least a large part of this experience, but their accounts of it may vary widely. The stormy events of American radicalism during this century may be compared to a long series of explosive and catastrophic experiences after which every survivor tells a different story.

It is not only necessary to have been a participant and an observer to explain the ups and downs of American radicalism in this century. It is equally necessary to have understood what was happening in the world over that period, and to relate it all to a consistent historical theory.

You'll be better able to judge at the end of my speech than at the beginning whether I, in part at least, meet those qualifications.

This is a very big and complicated subject to be compressed within an hour or so. But we need a general view of the preceding events of the present century as a means of giving us some perspective on the years that remain in it.

Let's begin with the present reality, with what might be called the great American contradiction. Here we live in the most advanced country in the world from the point of view of its technological and industrial development and its productivity. Because it is the most advanced country in these respects, it is the country where the material conditions and foundations for the socialist transformation of society are prepared to a degree not yet existing anywhere else in the world.

Marx explained that capitalism not only greatly advances the forces of production and is therefore a more progressive stage of society than the feudal past, but, in developing the forces of production and proletarianizing the great mass of the population, capitalist society also prepares its own gravedigger in the person of the industrial proletariat. That also has been provided in the United States to a greater extent than anywhere else in the world. The gravediggers of capitalism are more numerous here and, in some respects, better organized than elsewhere on a trade-union level. It is potentially the most powerful working class in the entire world.

The contradiction to all these prerequisites for the socialist transformation of society is the other side of the picture, which we all have to recognize. We have here the most conservative political climate of any country in the world, at least among the great powers, and the weakest movement of labor radicalism and socialist consciousness.

Despite all the rich experiences of the working people in the rest of the world which should have come to our aid—and eventually, inevitably will—despite all the favorable developments for socialism on a world scale, the situation of American radicalism today, from the point of view of socialist consciousness, socialist organization and socialist morale, is worse than it was thirty years ago. It's even worse than it was sixty years ago, at the turn of the century, when the first modern movement of socialist and labor radicalism in this country began to get a popular hearing.

There are objective causes for this tremendous depression of the radical movement at the present time. They are well known and don't need to be elaborated here. The unprecedented boom, prosperity based on war expenditures and preparations for war, and so forth, have had a tremendously conservatizing influence. In any case, radicalism would very likely be on the defensive in this country under such conditions. But our concern today is not with these *objective* causes of the present conjuncture in the development of the historical movement toward socialism. I propose to deal mainly with the *subjective* causes of the present weaknesses of American radicalism: above all, the failure of leadership which has made conditions ten and a hundred times worse than they needed to be, and which makes our problem of preparing the great socialist revival more difficult.

The present situation which I have briefly sketched can change very rapidly into its opposite. That's what happened in the thirties, following the first postwar boom of American capitalism together with the concomitant decline in radicalism of the twenties. Very few of you may remember that we went through a period in the 1920s, after the rise of radicalism in the first twenty years of this century, when the unprecedented boom of American capitalism on the one side and the inadequacies of the revolutionary leadership on the other produced a collapse, and nearly a dispersal, of the previous radical movement. But within the next decade that entire situation was turned upside down in a few years' time.

The subjective reasons for the current depression of United States radicalism cannot be understood without a critical analysis of the inner history of the American socialist and labor radical movement in the sixty years since the turn of the century. We can learn something from this review of the past that will be useful both for the present and for the future. Of course, in a single lecture we can only hit the high spots and must omit many interesting and significant details. But such a condensed review may make the main aspects of the historical development stand out more clearly.

In our century we have seen two widespread and popular movements of socialist and labor radicalism. If we examine what they were, how they came into existence, what they did and failed to do, and what happened to them—we can draw some useful conclusions about the prospects of a new revival of American radicalism and about the nature of our problems and our tasks in preparing the way for it.

At the turn of the century, there was a great upswing of radicalism in this country prompted by the objective conditions of the time—the accelerated development of industrial and monopoly capitalism, the dispossession of small businessmen and farmers, the unbridled exploitation of the workers who were without organization, and so forth. This rebirth of American radicalism got its big impetus in 1901 with the formation of the Socialist Party of America as a fusion of different socialist currents that up to that time had been isolated groups without any wide, popular influence. The distinctive factor that made possible the development of this new socialist movement at that time was the turn of a number of influential individuals and groups away from the policy of class collaboration in politics to the policy of independent socialist action.

Many of you have heard of the great role played by Debs and the *Appeal to Reason,* the socialist agitational paper which had a half-million and more circulation. What is perhaps not so well known to comrades of the younger generation is that Debs, the *Appeal to Reason,* and a very large percentage of the people who were influential in giving the Socialist Party its start in the first years of this century, had previously been Populists. They had supported the Populist movement, and then in 1896, when the Populist Party was swallowed by the Democratic Party, they went along with it. Debs, the *Appeal to Reason,* Victor Berger, and others who promoted the formation of the Socialist Party in 1901, had supported Bryan and the Democratic Party in 1896. But by the turn of the century, they had broken out of that blind alley and had come to the conclusion that it was necessary to have an independent socialist position. That's what made the big difference.

The most significant change in the attitude of these influential people, and of tens of thousands of others who supported them, which made possible the emergence and growth of the Socialist Party in the first years of this century, was their break with capitalist politics altogether and their espousal of socialism. They emphasized and acted on the fundamental principle that a socialist movement must have its own party and its own candidates and cannot combine with or support any capitalist party, whether Republican, Democratic, Progressive or Populist. This new revelation inspired the emergence for the first time of a popular socialist movement in this country.

The Socialist Labor Party and other socialist sects which had existed prior to that time had never gained a popular hearing. But the Socialist Party brought into its ranks a great number of people who had had their fill of experimentation in one form of capitalist party politics or another. They gave a great impetus to the new Socialist Party. So much so that by 1912 the Socialist Party of the United States had 100,000 members and got almost a million votes in the presidential election. That was before women's suffrage, and was about 6 percent of the total vote cast. This would be equal to between three-and-a-half and four million votes at the present time. That gives you an idea of the popular appeal of the Socialist Party in that period.

The IWW, which was a very militant organization on the industrial field, was a part of this first popular *movement* of American radicalism. It is important to recall that the IWW was founded by socialists. At the founding convention in 1905 all the leading figures were from a socialist background; they came from the Socialist Party, the Socialist Labor Party, some anarchists and other kinds of radicals. This sentiment predominated in the IWW throughout its first twenty years of existence. It called itself not merely an industrial union, but a *revolutionary* industrial union.

In these early years of our century, socialist and labor radicalism attained something of a mass character in this country. The movement had its weak sides. In the course of its electoral activities, as we look back on it now, we can see that it placed too much emphasis on municipal politics and reform. The reformist tendency within the Socialist Party was quite strong, although I believe a fair assessment of the history would show the majority were revolutionary.

But the composition of the party was also unfavorable

in some respects. Comrade White told us last night that the Populist movement in the South was deflected into a reactionary channel. But there was another part of this Populist movement which was drawn into the Socialist Party. The Socialist Party in many parts of the country consisted of a very large percentage of former Populists. The composition of its membership in the western part of the country was very heavily weighted on the side of the petty bourgeoisie in the cities and in the countryside. At one time the largest single state membership of the Socialist Party, and, if I'm not mistaken, the largest socialist vote proportionally, was in the state of Oklahoma. In the other western agrarian states also, the hard-pressed tenant and mortgaged farmers and desperate petty bourgeoisie streamed into the Socialist Party from the Populist movement and swelled its ranks. So the class composition of the party was not as proletarian as an ideal socialist movement should be.

Another terrible defect of the socialist and radical movement of that time came from the weakness of the organized labor movement. The great mass-production industries in this country were completely without trade-union organization. Trade unions were limited almost entirely to the skilled crafts, and were very weak in many places even in that field. Outside of the mines and the railroads, it was very hard to find a single union in the big industries. As I listened the other night to the report about the present steel strike, a general strike shutting down all the mills of the country, with the union so strong it doesn't need to send more than token pickets—I recalled a very different steel strike in 1913 that I participated in as an IWW organizer. There we ran up against company thugs dressed up in police uniforms who sometimes outnumbered the pickets. And that was a single local strike on the ore docks in Duluth and Superior.

This was a common experience of the IWW and socialist attempts to organize in the steel industry or anyplace else. The most you could do was conduct a guerrilla attack at a single locality. The idea of a general strike, which was our ideal and our program, was far from realization. Yet that's taken as a matter of course today.

This weakness of the trade-union movement naturally was a weakness also of the socialist movement of the time. Without a strongly organized working class in the basic industries, it is quite futile to expect a socialist and revolutionary transformation of society. The IWW, which had played a prominent part in the general radicalization of the period, turned to syndicalism, and that was a big defect of the movement too. The unfavorable class composition of the Socialist Party, the weakness of the trade-union movement, the mistakes of syndicalism and reformism—all these defects prepared the way for the decline and eventual collapse of the first big experiment in socialist labor radicalism after twenty years of upswing.

The real trouble began with the First World War, and then with the Russian Revolution. The movement as a whole proved unable to assimilate the lessons of these world-shaking experiences. They produced a deep division in the socialist movement, a split in 1919, the formation of the Communist Party as a separate organization, and the great weakening of what was left of the Socialist Party.

This split in the forces of American socialist and labor radicalism, beginning with 1919, was followed by the tremendous postwar boom of the twenties.

Of course this wasn't anything like the current boom. But considering the conditions that had previously been known in the country, it was pretty lush. From the end of the war in 1918 up until the stock-market crash in

1929, there was a continuous upswing of production, interrupted only by a recession in 1921, which was overcome within a year. And, for the first time in this country, there was year after year of almost full employment, fairly good wages, lots of overtime, and all the rest. Some workers even began to own automobiles. That was a sign of what we called their "bourgeoisification." Everything is relative—and relative to the previous period, the automobiles of the twenties were a sign of workers' prosperity.

The big boom of the twenties was interpreted by all kinds of learned people as the final solution of the contradictions of capitalism. Then as now, that was a common theme of the economists and intellectuals: Karl Marx was out of date. His theory of the cycle of boom and bust had been overcome by the genius of American capitalism. We were going to have ever-rising permanent prosperity from now on. A great many people, including workers, believed that; and radicalism lost its previous attraction.

The result was that by the end of the twenties the original movement had become dispersed. At least 90 percent of the people who had been active socialists and labor radicals in the two decades before had fallen aside. There was nothing left except a weak and rotting right-wing Socialist Party and the Communist Party, with a greatly reduced membership.

That was, you may say, the end of the Debsian movement. It had lasted twenty years. What remained after that was merely a hangover, a survival of remnants—never the dynamic center of radicalism as it had been before. But despite that eventual failure of the movement, I think the overall judgment of the Debsian period must be favorable, because out of this movement came the cadres and some of the main ideas for the second big upsurge of American labor radicalism in the thirties.

There never could have been a Communist Party in this country in the twenties if there had not been a socialist movement in the twenty preceding years. This first big experiment in socialist and labor radicalism failed in its ultimate mission. But it left behind—and this is what we should remember in our historical appraisal, because it is so pertinent for today—it left behind a residue, in the form of cadres, ideas and attitudes which continued and advanced the socialist tradition. What was left from that older movement eventually became the leaven in the movement of the thirties.

After the split of 1919, the new Communist Party took over and rapidly displaced all other contenders for supremacy in the field of radicalism, as the Socialist Party had done in the preceding two decades. What was the Communist Party like in the twenties? I was there and I remember, and in the light of later thought and study, I think I understand it and can report it truthfully.

The CP in its early years had certain basic characteristics. Its cadres, formed in the previous radical movement, consisted of younger comrades who were conditioned to irreconcilable struggle against capitalism. It was inspired by the Russian Revolution and was the carrier of its ideas as well as it understood them. Its message was revolutionary, not at all moderate, not in the least compromising, or liberalistic, or conciliationist. The idea of class collaboration was simply anathema. Its guiding doctrine was the *class struggle.*

One of the main slogans of the Communist Party in that period was: "Organize the unorganized!" That was a bold program that only revolutionists could take seriously. If you think it is tough in the steel union or any other union today, look back to those days. Steel, rubber, auto and every other big industry had no unions at all, or else they had company unions controlled by the companies and led by company stooges. The Communist Party conducted a struggle against company unions for bona fide unions of the workers under the slogan: "Class struggle versus class collaboration!" That was a revolutionary slogan for the time, and it did a lot to prepare the great upsurge of union organization in the next decade.

In the main, the composition of the Communist Party in the twenties was young. The age level of the Communist Party today, or what's left of it or its peripheral circles, doesn't resemble what the Communist Party was in the twenties. That was a young movement, as dynamic revolutionary movements always are.

The "old men" of the party at its inception among the leaders were Ruthenberg, Bedacht, Wagenknecht, Katterfeld, later Foster—they were all turning forty years old. A second layer of leaders, represented by Earl Browder, Bill Dunne, Arne Swabeck, myself, and others, were turning thirty. And a third layer of the top leaders, represented in the Central Committee and the Political Committee by Lovestone, Weinstone, and Wolfe, were in their early twenties—fresh out of college.

That was the composition of the leadership. The ranks, I believe, were even younger. The old men of the Socialist Party—of the period before the split—did not come with the Communist Party. It took the youth to understand the war and the Russian Revolution and to make the new movement fit for new times.

This Communist Party held the line of class struggle and revolutionary doctrine in that long, ten-year period of boom, prosperity and conservatism before the crash of 1929. It was in that period—fighting for revolutionary ideas against a conservative environment as we are trying to do today, refusing to compromise the principle of class independence—that the Communist Party gathered and prepared its cadres for the great upsurge of the thirties.

Not more than 10 percent were left from the old prewar movement. Although the Communist Party itself continued to recruit individuals from day to day and month to month, it also continued to lose people, and its overall membership declined. The left-wing leaders in the Socialist Party had claimed, with some justification, that they had 60,000 votes supporting them in the Referendum of 1919—shortly before the split. But then followed the Palmer raids, the witch-hunt, the deportations, the illegality of the party, and the long boom. It was tough going.

By the time the party came to the stock-market crash in 1929, which ended the myth of permanent capitalist prosperity, the Communist Party had under 10,000 members. Ninety percent of these were foreign-born. But it was a young movement—and primarily proletarian.

That was what the CP had to start with at the end of the twenties. It was up against the fact that the trade-union movement was even weaker than it had been at the beginning of the twenties. A peculiar phenomenon was recorded: for the first time in modern history, a protracted period of prosperity, with its increase of production and increase in the size of the proletariat didn't increase the size of the unions. On the contrary, it depleted and replaced them in many instances by company unions. The country was so conservative, the bosses were in such firm control, the union leadership was so weak, and its craft form of organization was so inadequate, that the trade unions embraced not more than three million at the time of the stock-market crash in 1929. As far as CP influence in the unions was concerned, it was pretty well purged, except in the garment trades and among the miners.

Although the CP wasn't in first-class shape in those

earlier days, it was young, confident and revolutionary—even ultraradical at times. The Socialist Party and the IWW had withered on the vine. In the Communist Party itself, the corruption of Stalinism had already started but as yet had not deeply affected the consciousness of the rank and file. Despite its reduced membership, the Communist Party entered the thirties—the period of the great radical revival—as the dominating center of American radicalism. It had no serious contenders. It had to its left only the dissident group of the Trotskyists, who were numerically small and isolated. The right-wing group of Lovestoneites was equally weak; the attenuated and decrepit Socialist Party offered no real competition; the IWW had fallen victim to its syndicalist dogmatism and become a sect. That was the shape of American radicalism when the thirties began.

Then the situation changed, almost overnight. The terrible financial and social crisis really shook up this country—and the workers. The radicalism produced by this shake-up was far stronger than the radicalism of the previous two decades. It had a much firmer social composition. This time the industrial workers in the main centers were the spearhead of the radicalism and gave the new movement a class composition of invincible power. It had the advantage of a more advanced ideology. The inspiration and ideas of the Russian Revolution permeated the Communist movement of that time and gave it a tremendous advantage over all other tendencies.

And then, in the changed situation in the thirties, the impossible was accomplished. The impossible task of organizing the automobile industry, the rubber industry, the electrical manufacturing industry, the steel industry, the maritime industry—and of actually bringing the monopolistic powers of American capitalism to the point where they had to recognize the unions—all that was accomplished in the great days of the CIO uprising in the thirties.

Along with that there was a growing sentiment for a labor party, which, under proper leadership, could have brought this whole movement of labor radicalism toward a glorious new epoch of independent class political action in this country. But that didn't happen. And the main reason it didn't happen was that the Communist Party, which was the main leader of this new movement of labor radicalism, failed in its mission, even more shamefully, even more disgracefully than the Socialist Party of the previous two decades. And more catastrophically, because it was not defeated in battle; it was corrupted from within. The Communist Party has left less behind it from the great radical movement of the thirties than the Socialist Party left at the beginning of the twenties.

You know the CP expanded its organization and influence in all directions in the thirties. Why did it collapse so miserably in the fifties? In fact, it had collapsed before then, but we have only seen in recent years how catastrophic it was. Although many, like John Gates, ex-editor of the *Daily Worker,* (I use him only as a symbol, because his name is legion) went through the experiences of the thirties, they didn't understand what happened and they can't make a true report about what they saw. They attribute the successes of the CP to the party's cleverness in putting on the mask of "progressivism," supporting Roosevelt and the New Deal in the late thirties and in the war period. And, conversely, they think the collapse of the CP was caused by sectarianism, which is the way they describe the policy of class struggle and revolution.

But that's a complete misunderstanding of what really happened. The main cadres of the Communist Party, which played such a big role in the second big wave of American radicalism in this century, were forged, as I said before, in the twenties. Then they were renewed and greatly expanded in the early thirties by the policy of the class struggle. (In fact, during the first half of the thirties the Communist Party was devoted to what we called ultraleftism, ultraradicalism, not at all "progressivism." It did not maneuver with capitalist politics.)

In 1932, the Communist Party nominated a Negro, James Ford, for Vice-President, with Foster. And the slogan of their 1932 campaign was: "Class against class." There was no mealymouthed "progressivism" about that. With this slogan and the spirit emanating from it, the main cadres of the young unemployed workers of that time, the student youth without prospects, and, for the first time in the history of American radicalism, significant numbers of Negroes—thousands of them, and displaced intellectuals in droves, were recruited to the party. In this period of the depression they were not repelled by the party's radical and revolutionary aspect, but were attracted precisely because of it; not in spite of its appearance as the representative of the Russian Revolution and the Soviet Union, but, in large measure, because of it.

That was the big appeal of the Communist Party in the first years of the thirties. The discontented turned to the most radical and aggressive movement they could find, and thought they had found it in the Communist Party. In that, I think, is a lesson for the future. In times of social crisis, when the workers, the Negro people, the troubled students and the intellectuals of many kinds see no prospect in capitalism, they want to hear the word of a radical social transformation and a new beginning. That's what the Communist Party represented in the eyes of these people; and that's why it grew.

In the early years of the thirties, the program and tradition of independent class politics completely dominated the Communist Party and its tremendous periphery. So strong was this principle and this tradition that it couldn't be changed abruptly. The rank and file of the movement, educated in the principle of the class struggle—which has its highest and sharpest expression in independent socialist political action—had to be corrupted gradually, a step at a time. Snuggling up to Roosevelt and the Democratic Party couldn't be presented directly to the Communist Party membership and its supporters in the middle of the thirties. It had to be presented as a maneuver to fool the class enemy.

Of course, it was really a Stalinist maneuver to fool the communist workers; they were the real victims. This new turn was inspired and directed by the Stalinized bureaucracy of the Soviet Union, and designed to use the promising movement of American radicalism as a pawn in its diplomatic game. The leaders in Moscow were concerned with the short-term interests of their foreign policy, and not at all with the American workers and the American revolution. Roosevelt had recognized the Soviet Union, and the Stalinists, in turn, decided to recognize Roosevelt. They looked upon the great movement of American radicalism as something to be expended cheaply. They diverted it, through the leadership of the Communist Party, into the Roosevelt camp. They steered it away from the movement for an independent labor party, which was called for by the conditions of the time and the sentiments of hundreds of thousands of workers. The big switch in policy, from class struggle to class collaboration, was made in the shortsighted temporary interest of Stalinist diplomacy.

That's the great divide between the rise and the decline, and the eventual complete collapse of the radical movement of the thirties and of the Communist Party that led it. The big turnaround began with disguise and double-talk.

Just think what was done and how it was done in 1936! There was a presidential election. The Communist Party leadership didn't yet dare to endorse the candidates of a capitalist party. They had a grand convention and nominated their own candidates, Browder and Ford, as independent candidates of the Communist Party. This was a concession to the traditional purpose of a socialist or communist party. Then came the double-talk. They said: We're nominating our own candidates, but—"Socialism is not the issue!"

This crooked formula was the great contribution of Browder, as the agent of Stalin, to the betrayal of American radicalism. "Socialism is not the issue"? Well, people might logically ask, if socialism is not the issue, what in the hell are you nominating a socialist candidate for? The Stalinist leaders didn't answer that question directly. They worked their way around it deviously.

They didn't call for people to vote for the Communist Party candidates. And they did not come right out for Roosevelt. They conducted the campaign on the slogan—What do you think? Well, by now you know; it happens in every election. "Beat Landon at all costs!" That was the slogan of the Communist Party in 1936, in the middle of the social crisis, when the possibility of a ringing campaign to further radicalize the workers was on the agenda. "Beat Landon at all costs!" meant, of course, "Elect Roosevelt at all costs!" That's what such a slogan always means in reverse.

It was supposed to be a very slick maneuver to fool everybody. "No, we're not voting for Roosevelt, we're putting up our own candidates." But all the trade unionists who were under the influence of the CP got the word: "Vote for Roosevelt." It was presented to the communist workers as a maneuver to fool the class enemy. But those who started out that way, thinking to outwit the class enemy by supporting him, eventually became victims of their own deception. They began to play the capitalist party game in earnest.

The most incredible thing, for one who has been raised in the old socialist tradition, is to run into people by the score, and, if you look around for them, by the hundreds and thousands, who have been educated in the Communist Party of recent years, who think they should play the Democratic Party game for keeps. They believe it. The mask has become the face. The dupers have become the duped.

Of course, the Stalinists didn't capture the Democratic Party. I can tell you that, in case you have any doubts about it. But class-collaborationist politics did capture the Communist Party. The Stalinists went to work, running errands and ringing doorbells, in order to beat some capitalist political faker at all costs in order to elect some other capitalist political shyster at all costs. Over a period of time, the program of the class struggle and independent class politics was lost sight of altogether by the bulk of these people. The Communist Party members and sympathizers forgot the ABC of socialism that Debs understood sixty years ago. They continued to support the Democratic Party long after the Democrats had no further need of them and gave them the boot.

Of course, there were other causes for the catastrophic decline and disgraceful collapse of the Communist Party and its peripheral movement. But that's the basic cause, because it goes right to the fundamental class issue of independent politics. That's the basic cause of the defeat, demoralization and dispersal of the great movement of labor radicalism generated by the crisis of the thirties.

In the thirties and since, the Communist Party, as the leading center of the new radicalism, directly reversed the trend of their predecessors of the turn of the century. That unspeakable betrayal stands out strikingly as you see it in historical perspective. Debs and Wayland, who had supported the Populist Party and the Democratic Party, turned around and led the movement forward from Populism and the Democratic Party and all kinds of class-collaborationist politics. The Stalinists reversed this whole trend and led communist and socialist workers back from independent class politics, back to class collaboration, to support of capitalist politicians.

The leading forces of the Debsian period had the benefit of far less experience and far less study. Yet they did far better than their successors of the thirties. That's a striking historical fact that ought to induce younger people to study the history of the movement. In this study of history they will see how colossal has been the loss of the tremendous potentialities of the radical movement of the thirties under the Stalinist leadership.

If we're going to make a new start and prepare for the next wave of radicalism in this country, there's only one way to begin. We have to go back to fundamentals, at least to the one big fundamental of class politics. If some people, who still call themselves socialists or communists, can't go back to Marx and Lenin in one bound, they ought at least, for a start, to try to go back to Debs and the *Appeal to Reason,* to the break with the Democratic Party in 1900.

The great movement of socialist and labor radicalism that was generated by the crisis of the thirties has completely spent itself. That's what we have to understand if we are going to get a realistic picture of the actual situation. Due to the combination of circumstances, the objective difficulties, plus the corruption of leadership, this movement is worn out. All that remains of it, outside the cadres of those who remain faithful to the fundamental ideas of socialism, is a big lost generation of radicals.

They're very numerous in this country. But when I see these people—or hear about them, which is more frequent—who have fallen out of the Communist Party by the tens of thousands, who still want to consider themselves socialists and even communists, who want to gather every now and then to have a discussion—providing you don't bring up any fundamental questions or propose any action—they strike me as people suffering from political amnesia. They can't remember where they came from— from that revolutionary movement of the early thirties. They have a nostalgia for big masses and big deals, but they've forgotten that that mass movement was produced by policies of the class struggle, not by class adaptation.

The radicalism generated by the social crisis in the thirties is not a total loss by any means. Like its predecessor of the Debsian time, the new movement of the thirties left something behind it to build on. First of all, and this is a tremendous thing, out of that great upheaval of the thirties came the CIO movement and the organization of the big industrial unions in the mass-production industries. They have softened up, shackled by government controls and saddled with a conservative, capitalist-minded bureaucracy. But the unions, as organizations, have survived. We see them in action every once in a while, as in the present steel strike. And they remain a great potential power.

It needs just a little shift in the situation to bring it forth. We got a slight intimation of this a year ago when the bosses went a little bit too far and attempted to pass "right-to-work" laws. They could have passed them in the twenties without any strongly organized opposition. When they tried it in 1958, they were suddenly made aware of the fact that a seventeen-million-strong trade-union movement, created by the upsurge of the thirties and inspired by radicals, didn't want to be broken up by "right-to-work" laws. That was a sort of political uprising, a portent of things to come, that upset all the calculations of the capitalist politicians.

Right now they're probing again, provoking the steel workers, and provoking the unions generally with the Landrum-Griffin antilabor law. Let them go a little bit too far, let a political aggressiveness of the capitalists coincide with some social disturbance and workers' discontent, and you'll see what a colossal power this seventeen-million-strong trade-union movement really has. And what a hearing you'll get from the workers then if you speak the true and honest word of class struggle against class collaboration! There's an immense reservoir for genuine radicalism in this great trade-union movement. That's something left behind from the uprising of the thirties.

No less important, perhaps even more important in the long run, are the surviving cadres of class-conscious revolutionists who preserve and represent the ideas, who are the continuators of the doctrine and the tradition of socialism. They are important because without the ideas, without the cadres, even though small, you can't hope to build a consistent revolutionary movement. And the conjunction of cadres of class-conscious revolutionists, who have assimilated the experiences of the past, with a new upsurge of labor militancy will release a great power.

It is another advantage of great import for the future, that this surviving nucleus of the continuators is organized and active, and is recruiting, even though slowly, but quite consistently and noticeably, a new cadre of young revolutionists. That is the touchstone. That is ground for confidence. The living movement always appeals to the young, and the mark of a living movement is its ability to attract the young. Wherever you see a party anywhere that has no young people, you can say for sure that its prospects are dim. The experienced troops of every army, even the best, always need renewal and replenishment.

Here is the central point I have been building up to. The radical movement of the thirties, with all its grandeur, glory and power, has spent itself. Individuals and small groups of the old, fallen-away radicals may be reactivated under new conditions; but the main forces of the new movement of American socialist radicalism have to come from a new generation. There is no room for doubt or misunderstanding on this score. The evidence of the recent years is conclusive. Our task is to hold the line and help the process along, provide some of the ideas, and make room for the new contingents of young militants.

That was Lenin's idea a long time ago. Only, he was more radical about it than we are today. *The New Republic* a few weeks ago carried a review of a history of the Russian Komsomol—the Russian Young Communist League. Here's a quotation from it:

"At the outset of a history of the Soviet Young Communist League or Komsomol, the author, Professor Fisher, cites a remark of Lenin's, made long before the Revolution to someone who complained that the Russian Social Democrats were mostly mere youths. Lenin said, 'It's perfectly natural that youth should predominate in a revolutionary party, since this is the party of the future, and the future belongs to the young. . . . We will always remain the party of the youth, of the most advanced class, i.e., the working class.'"

We have the same general idea and we take the attraction of the upcoming young rebels to our banner as a sign of things to come.

As Marxists, we count on the objective developments to prepare the ground for a great new movement. Trotsky, like all Marxists, based his revolutionary optimism on the contradictions of capitalism generating a revolutionary movement. So do we. In 1931, in the second year of the crisis, Trotsky wrote about America as follows:

"In the past, America has known more than one stormy outbreak of revolutionary or semirevolutionary mass movements. Each time they died out quickly, because America each time entered a new period of economic upswing and also because the movements themselves were characterized by crude empiricism and theoretical helplessness. Those two conditions belong to the past. A new economic upswing (and one cannot consider it excluded in advance) will have to be based not on the internal 'equilibrium,' but on the present chaos of world economy. American capitalism is entering an epoch of monstrous imperialism, of uninterrupted growth in armaments, of intervention in the affairs of the entire world, of military conflicts and convulsions."

Remember, this was written in 1931, when the official policy of the United States was isolationism. Then Trotsky continued: "On the other hand, in Communism the masses of the American proletariat have—or rather, could have, provided with a correct policy—no longer the old melange of empiricism, mysticism, and quackery, but a scientific doctrine equal to any event. These radical changes permit us to predict with certainty that the inevitable and relatively rapid revolutionary transformation of the American proletariat will not be the easily extinguishable bonfire of old, but the beginning of a veritable revolutionary conflagration. In America, Communism can confidently face a great future."

The first part of Trotsky's prediction about the militaristic eruption of American capitalism has been confirmed to the letter. The second part was only partly carried out;

the revolutionary prospects of the upsurge of the thirties were not realized. But even there, Trotsky had qualified his prediction. He said, the American workers could possess a scientific guide in the form of communism provided its representatives had "a correct policy." The American Communist Party failed to provide that correct policy. Trotsky saw on the one hand the transformation of American capitalism into a world-embracing imperialist power; on the other hand, he also saw a revolutionary proletariat as a possible outcome of the thirties. And it really was possible. For the reasons we have cited, that possible outcome was lost the first time. We owe that failure, above all, to Stalinism.

But the prospect remains fully valid for the next upsurge. The movement of revolutionary socialism has a great future in this country. And if we face it with confidence, and put our trust in a new generation, the future will become the present all the sooner.

Chapter 7

# The end of the Comintern and the prospects of labor internationalism

Delivered to a meeting at Irving Plaza, New York City, May 30, 1943.

Comrade Chairman; Comrades:
The formal dissolution of the Communist International is undoubtedly an event of great historical significance, even though everybody understands that it is simply the formal certification of a fact that was long since accomplished. Some of the bourgeois commentators and politicians may exaggerate a bit when they speak of the dissolution of the Communist International as the greatest political event since the beginning of the war. But, in any case, there is no question of its transcendent importance. This is recognized on every side, and the event has called forth discussion from every quarter.

There are two ways to view the question. One is from the standpoint of the United States and Allied capitalist powers in their war against the Axis powers and their struggle to maintain the capitalist system of oppression of the workers in the home countries and enslavement of the great masses of the colonial world. The other standpoint from which the dissolution of the Comintern can be discussed is from the standpoint of the liberation struggle of the workers, which has had a conscious expression now for ninety-five years, since the publication of the *Communist Manifesto* in 1848.

The discussion has all been one-sided so far. All the discussion outside our ranks begins from the premise of its effect upon the fortunes of American imperialism, with particular reference to the war. It is remarkable how so many people, in so many supposedly different camps, take this as their starting point in analyzing the burial of the Comintern. It was to be expected that the bourgeois press would take this point of view because all their interests lie in that direction. But we notice also that such labor leaders as have pronounced themselves show the same bias. They inquire, with straight faces, whether Stalin's action is sincerely meant as a gesture of help and cooperation with our war leaders in Washington and London, or whether it is a mere maneuver. No other aspects of the question seem to concern them.

The same thing is true of the social democratic press. You might think that people who used to have an International of their own would have something to say about the unburied corpse of the Second International, but they pass over that as a matter of no interest. Perhaps they are right in this respect. They sagely discuss the recent events in Moscow and put seriously to themselves—these "socialists"—the question: Will this help America in the war or not?

Even the Stalinists, who up to a few days ago were the adherents and representatives—even if not formally, owing to the Voorhis Law—of the Communist International, solemnly discuss the action like imitation Congressmen. They defend the burial of the Comintern without reference to its effect on the struggle of the workers for better conditions and eventual liberation—the original aim of the Comintern—but solely from the point of view of the interests of the American ruling class. Browder writes a letter to *The New York Times* and attempts to reassure this extremely perspicacious organ of America's Sixty Families that the action taken in Moscow is in good faith and in their interests, and that it is not quite sporting of them to raise a questioning eyebrow about the fact.

So far nobody has discussed the question from the point of view which brought the Communist International into existence, that is, from the point of view of organizing and furthering the worldwide struggle of the proletariat for emancipation from capitalism. But it is this point of view that I want to bring to the discussion here this evening.

Of course, the announcement of the formal dissolution of the Comintern is simply the news account of a burial that is ten years overdue. It serves a certain purpose in that it puts an end to a fiction and clears the air of illusions and misunderstandings, to say nothing of very bad odors.

This belated burial of the corpse of the Comintern is a climax, we might say, to a long sequence of events which has extended over two decades. These events, in their highlights, can be noted: the death of Lenin; the promulgation for the first time, in 1924, of the theory of socialism in one country; the bureaucratization of the Comintern and all of its parties; the expulsion of the Bolshevik-Leninist Opposition, first in the Russian party and then in the other parties of the Comintern; the capitulation of the Communist Party of Germany, with its 600,000 members and its six million voters, without a struggle and without a fight, to Hitler fascism in 1933; the organized, systematic betrayal of the proletariat of the world in the interest of the diplomatic policy of the Kremlin; the murder of the Old Bolsheviks; the assassination of Trotsky; the betrayal of the proletariat in the Second World War, first to Hitler and then to Roosevelt and Churchill.

Since the beginning of the war the Comintern, the unburied Comintern, was silent as the grave. Now it is formally buried, and that, at least, is a good thing. It is somewhat late, but the old proverb says, "better late that never." By the formal burial of the Comintern, Stalin, for once on the international arena, has unconsciously performed a progressive act.

The bourgeois press and public generally, the political leaders and spokesmen, are very well pleased with the recent pronouncement, even if they understand that it is only a formality. They have good reason to be pleased. The dissolution of the Comintern, and the cynical repudiation of internationalism and the international proletarian organization, is an ideological victory of vast importance for capitalism and reactionary nationalism. They have been quite true to their interests in hailing this action and pushing aside the quibblers who wonder if, after all, it isn't another maneuver.

They have good reason to applaud the action of Stalin, taken through his puppets in the so-called Executive Committee of the nonexistent Comintern, because the renunciation of internationalism is a renunciation of the basic premises of scientific socialism. It is a renunciation of the cardinal doctrine which has guided and inspired the struggle of the workers for generations, since Marx's day. The modern movement of international socialism began with the *Communist Manifesto* in 1848, ninety-five years ago, with its battle cry: Workers of the World Unite!

The *Communist Manifesto* proclaimed the doctrine that the emancipation of the workers could be achieved only by their common actions on an international scale. Against the cardinal principle and battle cry of Marx and Engels, and of all revolutionary socialists since that time—Workers of the World Unite!—Stalin has announced a motto of his own: Disband your international organization; give up all thought of international collaboration; support your own imperialists; and confine your activities to the national framework of the country in which you are enslaved.

Internationalism was not a dogma invented by Marx and Engels, but a recognition of the reality of the modern world. It proceeds from the fact that the economy of modern society is a world unit requiring international cooperation and division of labor for the further development of the productive forces. The class struggle arising from the class division between workers and exploiters within the countries requires class unity of the workers on an international scale. From the beginning, the program of scientific socialism has called for the international collaboration of the workers and oppressed peoples in the different countries, with all their different levels of development, in order that each might contribute their strength as well as their weakness to a unified world program and world cooperative action. The *Communist Manifesto* called for common efforts of the workers in all countries for the common goal of workers' emancipation.

After the downfall of feudalism, the national states played a progressive role as the arena for the development and expansion of the forces of production in the heyday of capitalism. But these very national states, whose sanctity is proclaimed by Stalin in 1943, became obsolete long ago. They have become barriers to the full operation of the productive forces and the source of inevitable wars.

The whole pressure of historic necessity is for the breaking down of the artificial national barriers, not for their preservation.

Just as the petty states and principalities and arbitrarily divided sections of the old countries under feudalism had to give way to the consolidated, centralized national states in order to create a broader arena for the development of the productive forces, so, in the same way, the artificially divided national states have to give way to the federation of states. In the future course of development this must lead eventually to a world federation operating world economy as a whole without class and nationalistic divisions. From this it follows irrevocably that such an order can be created only by the international collaboration and the joint struggle of the workers in the various countries against their own bourgeoisie at home and against capitalism as a world system. So preached and so practiced the great founders of socialism, Marx and Engels; so preached and practiced their great continuators, Lenin and Trotsky.

Among the immortal achievements of Marx as a revolutionist, side by side with his monumental work on capital, will always stand his creative labor in the building of the first international organization of the workers, the International Workingmen's Association. From the time that the ideas of internationalism were propounded in the *Communist Manifesto* to their first realization in 1864 in the First International, up until the present time, the conflict within the labor movement between revolutionists and reformists has revolved around this fundamental question. At the heart of every dispute, socialist internationalism on the one side has been contrasted to nationalistic concepts on the other.

We can see in the whole period down to the present day the deadly parallel between revolutionary internationalism, pointing the way to the socialist future, and opportunistic adaptation to the decaying order of capitalism. Marx and Engels were the champions of this idea of internationalism and of corresponding action. The nationally limited, narrow-minded trade-union reformists of Britain and other places renounced the idea of internationalism. With the idea of gaining small favors for the day at the expense of the interests of the class as a whole and of the future, conservative trade unionism, even in Marx's day, took a nationalistic form and had a nationalistic outlook. In the First World War of 1914–1918, the great resounding struggle which took place between the revolutionary wing, headed by Lenin and Trotsky, on the one side, and Kautsky & Co. on the other, had as its great criterion, its touchstone, the question of international organization.

Lenin, the Russian, living as an emigre in Switzerland, with no more than a dozen or two followers that he could name and place, rose up against the whole so-called Second International and the social democratic parties in the war. He rose up against the bourgeois world and announced the necessity for the Third International in 1914. Similarly, in the period of the decline and eventual decay and death, up to the formal burial of the Communist International, the great dividing line between the real inheritors of Marx and Lenin on the one side, and Stalin and his cohorts on the other, has been this principle we are discussing here tonight—the principle of internationalism.

Since it was first proclaimed nearly a century ago, in the historic ebb and flow the idea of internationalism and the organization of the international workers has suffered three great defeats. The organizations have been destroyed, but always the idea rose again after each defeat, corresponding to historical necessity, and found the necessary organizational form on higher ground.

The First International, that is, the International of Marx and Engels, was founded formally in 1864. Seven years later came the tragic defeat of the Paris Commune. Along with that great defeat and the great impetus it gave to reaction on the continent of Europe, there was the unprecedented rise and expansion of capitalist industry. The productive forces began to expand and develop on a capitalist basis at an unprecedented rate. This temporarily weakened the revolutionary movement. It was the expansion of capitalism still reaching toward its apex of development which decreed the end of the First International by its formal dissolution in 1876. But the First International didn't die like the Second or like the Comintern. It was dissolved with its honor unsullied. It remained an inspiration and an ideal which still continued to work in the vanguard circles of the workers and in time bore good fruit.

The Second International followed. It was formally launched in Paris in 1889, thirteen years after the formal end of the First International, and died as a revolutionary organization on the fourth of August, 1914. The fourth of August was the day when the social democratic deputies in the Reichstag voted for the war credits of German imperialism. But between the manner and form of the end of the Second International and that of the First, there is a great contrast that we should not forget. The First International succumbed to external conditions, to the defeats, the spread of reaction and the expanding development of the capitalist productive system. It went down gloriously. The Second International, on the contrary, ended as a result of the betrayal of the leadership in a period when capitalism had already long passed its peak and had entered into its decline and bankruptcy. The Second International capitulated at a time when the necessity and urgency of international revolutionary organization were a thousand times more apparent than in the case of the First International.

The Third International was born of war and revolution and struggle against nationalism in March 1919, twenty-four years ago. This International, too, died ignominiously from a false theory, from capitulation and betrayal, and is buried in 1943, without honors, without regrets.

As far as the revolutionary vanguard of the proletariat is concerned, the formal event was anticipated and nobody was taken by surprise. We have been struggling against the national degeneration of the Comintern for a long time. This struggle, as a matter of fact, began in 1923. That is twenty years ago. It is startling in these days, in contemplation of this final ceremony of burying the nonexistent Comintern, to read the polemics of Trotsky written twenty years ago in Russia. At the very first signs of national degeneration, Trotsky, like a physician, put his finger on the pulse of the organization and detected the fever of nationalism and pointed out what it was and what it would lead to. He began a struggle twenty years ago in the name of internationalism against the theory of socialism in one country, against the conception that the workers could find any other way to salvation except through international organization and joint struggle against capitalism on a world scale.

This fight began in the factional and ideological disputes of 1923. The fight took international form in 1930 in the organization of the International Communist League, shortly after Trotsky was exiled from Russia and began, from his refuge in Turkey, to communicate with cothinkers on a world scale. The unceasing struggle of Trotsky and his disciples was climaxed by the World Congress of the Fourth International in 1938.

Trotsky, the unfailing champion of internationalism

in the uncompromising struggle against every form and trace of nationalist degeneration, was finally assassinated by an agent of Stalin. But his imperishable ideas are incorporated in the new international organization of the communist workers, the Fourth International.

Stalin's action, formally dissolving the Comintern, was taken in the midst of the Second World War, an appropriate time. The international organization which was presumably formed to enable the workers to take advantage of the difficulties of national capitalist states to promote the international revolution, is dissolved with a cynical explanation that it doesn't fit the conditions of the war. Kautsky, in 1915, explaining the collapse of the Second International when the war started, said that the International is an instrument of peace, not of war. Kautsky was the originator of this monstrous theory. Stalin simply repeats it, nearly thirty years later when it is thirty times more false.

Lenin said in 1914: *"Because of the war,* we must build the Third International in order to coordinate the activities of the workers in struggling against the war and in all that will follow from it." Stalin says to the workers of the world in 1943: *"Because of the war,* dissolve international organization and confine yourselves to the framework of your own bourgeois fatherland." In this contrast between the words of Lenin, who thought the war was a means of underscoring and emphasizing the necessity for an international organization of workers, and the words of Stalin, who says the war is a sufficient reason to disband international organization—in this contrast you have the measure of the two men and of what they represent in history.

Already in 1914 the First World War had demonstrated beyond all question that the bourgeois national states, as an arena for the development of the productive forces of mankind, were already outlived and had to give way to a broader basis. National capitalism had already entered into its bankruptcy in that time, more than twenty years ago. The most tragic expression of the bankruptcy of capitalism was the fact that it could find no other way out of the conflicts between outlived national states than in the explosion of the terrible war that cost ten million lives and crippled and maimed twenty million more.

And it was precisely the demonstration by the terrible fact of the war, it was precisely the war that caused Lenin and Trotsky, and such as they, to realize that even the Second International as it had existed before the war—as a rather loose federation of national parties—could not be rebuilt. As Trotsky expressed it, the war had sounded the death knell of national programs for workers' parties. They drew the lesson from the experience of the last world war, 1914–1918, not only that the workers must reconstitute their organization on an international scale, but also that they must base this reorganization on an international program and not on the sum of national programs.

Thus, the war of 1914, which signalized the bankruptcy of the national capitalist states, was, in the eyes of Lenin and Trotsky, the greatest motivation for an extension of the idea of internationalism in program as well as in form of organization. Now, a quarter of a century later, when the bankruptcy of capitalism has developed into its death agony, when an explosion takes place in the form of a Second World War, in even more tragic loss in human life and material culture—now, after this, Stalin and his traitor gang have the cynical effrontery to tell the workers that there is no need of international cooperation and international organization.

There isn't a shadow of logic or reason, if you proceed from the point of view of socialism and the cause of the proletariat, in any of the explanations given by the Stalinists for the renunciation of internationalism. The explanation given by the bourgeois press and bourgeois political leaders is more correct and honest because it frankly proceeds from the point of view that is of interest to them, that is, to the capitalist world order, and they can see in it a very good thing. But that it is no good for the workers is quite obvious.

Even the bourgeoisie recognize internationalism in their own way. The bankruptcy of national limitedness has become so clear to the bourgeoisie that all their most perspicacious leaders have been compelled to renounce the idea of national isolation altogether. Isolationism as a political tendency stands discredited in bourgeois politics. And in this situation, in this terrible war that is caused by the artificial prolongation of the life of national states as separate economic units, Stalin and his puppets tell the workers: "Confine your efforts to the national limits in which you find yourselves. Support one set of bandits against another set of bandits." That, workers of the world, heirs of Marx and Engels, heirs of Lenin and Trotsky and the Russian Revolution, that is your destiny in 1943, pronounced by Stalin and his gang.

This treacherous advice not only defies Marxist doctrine and tradition but it violates the most fundamental features of the prevailing world situation. It betrays the workers in the metropolitan centers and even omits any mention of the many-millioned masses in the colonies and the semicolonies who were awakened by the Russian Revolution and the Communist International to the struggle for life and freedom.

I think that the frankest and most heartfelt expressions of opinion by the chosen leaders of the democratic world bourgeoisie—Mr. Churchill and Mr. Roosevelt—really were off the record. They didn't have the heart to put down in public print what they really think of Stalin and his order dissolving the Comintern. They could only make fun of the explanation that the time has come in 1943 to go back to the national boroughs and forget the world arena at the very moment when they, the leaders of the bourgeoisie, are looking over the whole world and talking only in global terms. Stalin's explanation, intended to deceive trusting workers, can cause only the most cynical amusement to Churchill and Roosevelt, tinged with contempt plus a little appreciation for a very valuable favor. They at least have no illusions about national limitations either of economy or of politics, and certainly not of war.

If you take down from the bookshelf that imposing library of polemics, manifestos, appeals, and analyses written by Lenin from the fourth of August, 1914, on, you see running through the whole collection, like a red thread, the idea of internationalism. His manifesto, the manifesto of the Bolshevik Central Committee against the war, raised the demand already in 1914 for the creation of the new Third International. His attitude led him and the Bolsheviks to the Zimmerwald Conference in 1915, to Kienthal in 1916, and then to the revolution in 1917 in Russia.

Now, in all the plans of the social democrats, to say nothing of the imperialists, in 1914—in all their plans to do away with international organization, to harness the workers to the war machines of their respective capitalist masters in the different countries, the one thing that was not counted upon occurred in Russia, a little surprise— merely a revolution. The revolution that first overthrew the Czar in February and then overthrew the bourgeoisie in October was one of those unheralded events of the past world war which upset all calculations.

We do not see any mention of that in the order of

dissolution, as we may call it. There is no talk about revolution. There is no talk about socialism. There is no talk about anything except winning the war against Hitler. Lenin's steps, from 1914 on, led through these events I have mentioned to the Russian Revolution, the conquest of power by the proletariat of Russia, supported by the peasantry and led by the Bolshevik Party of Lenin. That didn't end Lenin's fight against the theory of Kautsky, that internationalism is an instrument of peace, not of war. In view of the collapse and bankruptcy of capitalism, as well as in anticipation of another war, Lenin and his party sponsored in 1919 the formation of the Comintern.

So, you see, throughout the whole course of Lenin's work, his manifesto after the betrayal of the German social democracy, his participation in the conferences at Zimmerwald and Kienthal, in the revolution of 1917, and the formation of the Comintern in 1919—every act of Lenin from first to last took place under the banner of internationalism. The premises of the Third International were that the dissolution and collapse of the capitalist world order made necessary the organization of the proletariat for the seizure of power in the capitalist states, the federation of the socialist states into a world federation, and the inauguration of the world socialist order.

Lenin saw the Russian Revolution as only the beginning of this worldwide process. Lenin and Trotsky and the Bolshevik Party as a whole understood that Russia could not stand isolated in a capitalist world; it could not remain as a national utopia. They saw it as a fortress of the world proletariat. Their policy was to unite the Soviet Union, representing the fortress of the world proletariat, with its allies in the world. And who were the allies of the Soviets as Lenin and Trotsky saw them? Not Churchill. And not even Roosevelt. Their allies were the world proletariat in the developed capitalist countries, and the colonial peoples. Under this leadership the workers of the war-torn countries lifted their heads again. They were reinspired with socialist ideas. They reorganized their ranks. They formed new revolutionary parties. They made heroic attempts at revolution in Europe. The colonial masses were awakened for the first time to political life, to revolt against age-old slavery, and were inspired to throw off the imperialist yoke altogether.

Such was the course of development under Lenin's leadership of the Comintern. Under Stalin's leadership, which was tainted from the start with narrow-minded nationalism, the world movement was betrayed; the Soviet Union was isolated; the services of the Comintern and its parties were sold like potatoes on the market to the various camps of imperialists for dubious pacts, for dribbles of material aid, at a very cheap price. Lenin and Stalin—the creator of the Third International and its gravedigger—these two represented ideas and actions which are in polar opposition to each other. They can in no way be reconciled. I notice that while they had the effrontery to refer to Marx in the order dissolving the Comintern, they left unmentioned its founder. That at least was a wise omission, because Lenin's name would have been out of place there, as Marx's was also.

In the course of twenty years, from 1924, when the fatal theory of socialism in one country was first promulgated, to the sorry, dishonorable end of the Comintern in 1943, in that whole tragic degeneration, we can see above everything else the decisive role of theory in political action. Stalin didn't begin with the dissolution of the Comintern. He began with the theory of socialism in one country. From this false theory everything else has followed—the betrayal of the world proletariat, the isolation of the USSR behind her national barriers, the purges, the Moscow trials, the mass murders, the assassinations, and finally the dissolution of the Comintern.

There is a profound lesson in this terrible sequence of events for all the generation of the young proletariat awakening to political interest and political life. Trotsky explained it in 1928 in his book, which was here referred to by the chairman. In the "Criticism of the Draft Program of the Comintern" he explained to the communist workers of Russia and the world that precisely this theory of socialism in one country, with its inevitable nationalistic implications, would inevitably lead to the degeneration and downfall of the Comintern. When this was written fifteen years ago, the great majority of Communists considered this a great exaggeration and even an insult to Stalin and his coworkers in the Russian party. But Trotsky, who did not impute design but only ignorance to these people at that time, explained that good intentions cannot help you in politics, if you proceed from a false theory. It is like a mariner setting a false course that can only lead the ship to an unintended destination.

The struggle against the theory of socialism in one country was conducted in the name of internationalism. And in the name of internationalism Trotsky and his disciples struggled against its disastrous consequences, as they began to reveal themselves in life. As the tragic course of events unfolded, Trotsky, step by step, analyzed; he explained; he threw the Marxist light on all the great events as they happened, before they happened; and afterwards he drew the necessary conclusions. He was not deterred by persecution; he was not dismayed by the fewness of those who surrounded him, nor by the renegacy of others, nor by the sneers of philistines.

Trotsky did not consider in the first place numbers,

popularity, success of the moment, any more than did Marx and Engels, and Lenin. He considered historical necessity. He considered the task of formulating for the proletariat the program showing the shortest road to the realization of its historical goal. His work and struggle bore fruit in the creation of an international nucleus of revolutionary fighters, and eventually in the formal organization of the Fourth International, in the World Congress in 1938.

At the time it was formed, the great politicians of the mass parties of the social democracy used to sneer at Trotsky's little handful and his insignificant Fourth International. The heroes of the London Bureau, the centrists who, if they could not organize mass parties could at least talk about them, used to argue against Trotsky that he didn't have many followers. And the Stalinists, backed by the limitless material resources of the Soviet Union, with money, a tremendous apparatus, a subsidized bureaucracy, and the GPU murder machine at their disposal—with all this tremendous weight at their side, they derided, hounded, and persecuted Trotsky and the Fourth International.

But in the brief period since the Founding Congress of the Fourth International, in a brief five years, every other international organization of the workers has been hurled down to ruin as Trotsky predicted they would be, without one stone left standing on another. This was the fate of the Second International of the social democracy, of the London Bureau of the centrists, and now it is the fate of the Stalinists, admitted and acknowledged by themselves. They have all been destroyed by the war, as Trotsky said they would be. But the Fourth International remains. And with it lives the principle of internationalism, which alone can show the tortured masses of the world the way out of war and slavery to the socialist future of humanity.

In this past period since 1864, each international

organization of the workers, in passing from the historical scene, left something accomplished, left something behind upon which its successor could build for the future.

The First International left an imperishable ideal, an unsullied record, as an inspiration for the workers from that day to this, a glorious memory.

The Second International died ignominiously through betrayal in 1914. Nevertheless, in the period from 1889 to that fatal day in August twenty-five years later, it built great mass organizations of the workers, and handed on experience in organization of incalculable value, upon which the Third International was able to build. Also, the initial cadres of the Third International didn't fall from the sky. They came right out of the heart of the Second International. Thus, in spite of everything, the Second International left a great heritage.

The Third International, which has ended now in shame and disgrace, has nevertheless left behind the richest treasures for the future. Its founders, Lenin and Trotsky, belong to us; nobody can dissolve the tie that binds the new generation of revolutionary workers to Lenin and Trotsky, to their teachings, their example, their beautiful memory. The record of the long internal struggle from 1923 to this date, the struggle of Trotsky and his cothinkers and disciples, belongs to the proletariat of the world. The record of that struggle is the basic literature upon which the whole new generation which is destined to lead the world will be educated and trained. The first four congresses of the Comintern, held under Lenin's leadership in 1919, 1920, 1921, 1922—four congresses in four years—produced documents which are the basic program of the movement that we uphold today.

And, in addition to that, out of the Third International, before it died and long before it was buried, came the initiating cadres of the Fourth International. Thus, looking at the thing always from the standpoint of the international proletariat and disregarding no elements in the whole survey, whether they are positive or negative, we have a right to say that the balance sheet of the Communist International, in spite of everything, shows a great historical credit balance.

Stalin can bury the dead organization but he cannot bury the great progressive work the Comintern accomplished in its first years. He cannot bury the Fourth International, which has risen, phoenix-like, from the ashes of the Third. We know very well and we don't try to conceal the fact that the numbers of the Fourth International are small. But its ideas are correct, its program represents historical necessity, and, therefore, its victory is assured. Its program consciously formulates the instinctive demands of the workers and the colonial peoples for emancipation from capitalism, fascism, and war.

Even today, striking workers who never even heard of the Fourth International, are denounced as "Trotskyists" whenever they stand up for their rights, just as the workers and soldiers in Russia in 1917 under Kerensky were denounced on every side as "Bolsheviks" and heard then, for the first time in the denunciations, the word "Bolshevik." Trotsky relates in his *History of the Russian Revolution* how they began to say to themselves, "If what they are accusing us of is Bolshevism, then we had better be Bolsheviks."

So it will be again wherever workers stand up for their rights, express their instinctive will to struggle for a better future, and are denounced as Trotskyists. In good time they will learn the name of the Fourth International, its meaning, its program, and ally themselves with it.

No one can dissolve the Fourth International. It is the real Comintern and it will keep the banner unfurled in the faces of all traitors and renegades. And we assert confidently that it will be strengthened and grow and triumph until its organized ranks merge with the whole mass of humanity. The song that no Stalin can render obsolete ends its chorus with the words: "The International shall be the human race." And this chorus has a profound political meaning. It is not merely a poetical expression.

The peoples of the world in the various countries, through coordinated international effort, will pass, in their great historic march from capitalism to socialism, through the transitional period of the dictatorship of the proletariat. As they progress toward the completely classless socialist society, all the various workers' organizations which have been instruments and mechanisms of the class struggle, that is, the parties, the unions, the cooperatives, the soviets, will gradually lose their original functions. As the classes are abolished and class struggles consequently ended, all these instruments of class struggle will tend to coalesce into one united body. And that one united body will be the organized world society of the free and equal. The International shall really be the human race.

We disciples of Marx, Lenin, and Trotsky, we partisans of the Fourth International, retain undimmed that vision of the future. To see that vision even now, to see it clearly through the fire and the smoke of the war, is simply to be in accord with historical development, to foresee the inevitable march of events and to prepare for them. To fight for this vision of the socialist future, to hasten its realization, is the highest privilege and the greatest happiness for a civilized man or woman in the world today.

# Chapter 8

# The downfall of Browder

Delivered to a meeting at Webster Hall, New York City, August 3, 1945.

What has transpired in the ranks of American Stalinism in recent weeks is something more than a "change of line," as they say. It is a confession of failure of a policy carried out in the United States by Browder, but inspired and directed from Moscow: the policy of selling out the American workers in the interests of the Soviet bureaucracy, of harnessing them to the imperialist war machine, and of attempting to represent that policy as service to the workers and to the cause of socialism.

The Stalinist party, which during the current war has been the most enthusiastic advocate of the cause of the imperialists, the worst enemy of the workers, the most criminal strikebreaker, did not arrive at this depth of degradation and treachery at one step. When the bureaucracy in the Soviet Union consolidated itself on the basis of the reaction which set in after the failure of the German revolution in 1923, it began to renounce the theory and practice of international revolution in favor of a new theory of socialism in one country.

Trotsky and his collaborators, the best of the leaders of the Russian Revolution, warned the workers of Russia and the world that this theoretical revision of Marxism, this turn from internationalism to a narrow-minded national policy, would result in the downfall of the Communist International and the social-patriotic degeneration of all the parties. That prediction seemed remote and farfetched in those days, but how truly it was fulfilled. Year by year, step by step—once the Comintern, and the American Communist Party with it, got off the theoretical rails of Marxism, they departed further and further from the original program of the Communist International. This theoretical deviation led to a complete betrayal of the interests of the workers of the world in the second imperialist war.

These traitors counted upon the hysteria of patriotism, the repressions of the government, and the befuddlement of the workers to give them the opportunity to dispose, once and for all, of that hated group of Trotskyists who remained true to the ideas of Marx and Lenin, true to the ideas of communism. And for a time it appeared that they might have success. The leaders of the American Trotskyist movement were finally imprisoned. But the enthusiasm of the workers for the war and for patriotic strikebreaking did not measure up to the expectations of these finks at all. Quite the contrary. The American workers accepted the war very sullenly. They had not forgotten World War I and they already had in their minds the specter of World War III. And they did not believe the workers should surrender all their rights during the war.

They maintained the right to strike in case after case,

and to the great surprise of the Stalinist strikebreakers and superpatriots, great numbers of workers manifested sympathy and admiration for the genuine communists in this country, the Trotskyists of the Socialist Workers Party. Union after union gave us moral and financial support. There was so much sympathy for us the government did not deem it expedient to keep us in jail too long. And the net result of the war experience has been that the Socialist Workers Party, instead of being crushed and driven out of existence, gained by leaps and bounds, precisely in the mass workers' unions in the country where the Stalinists formerly had been so powerful. The Stalinist traitors finally had to realize that they had overplayed their hand a little bit. Browder is the scapegoat for this mistake.

They made a great success in Washington. They even did pretty well in Wall Street. Even J. Pierpont Morgan, if he didn't accept Browder's offer to shake hands, accepted Browder's offer to grovel before him, and said, "Good boy, that is all right." But the Communist Party began to lose thousands and tens of thousands of militant workers, and tens of thousands of Negroes whom they had deserted and betrayed in the war. And they began to realize that if they wanted to stay in business as a bargaining agent for Stalin, they had better repair their fences and get an organization together that would have some real influence among the workers. That is the real reason for the so-called change of line in the Stalinist party, in the course of which a little man named Browder, who was standing on the stair, wasn't there anymore.

The order for cutting off Browder's head came straight from Moscow via Paris. You know the Comintern was dissolved; so instead of sending cables direct from Moscow, now they send letters to Paris and print them in a magazine and transport them by boat to the United States. But the authenticity of the direction, the origin of it in Moscow, was known to all the dearly beloved collaborators of Browder in the National Committee of the Communist Political Association.

And strangely enough, every single one of the national and district leaders of the Communist Political Association, every editor and organizer, every functionary and every flunky, who in May 1944 had voted unanimously for Browder as the leader of the party, as the representative of Marxism—every single one, without exception, voted in July 1945 against Browder as the representative of what they call "revision of Marxism." But that really isn't what it was at all. Browder is a victim of Stalinist reconversion. He was caught in the cutback to peacetime production.

Another victim of the cutback is a very prominent scoundrel of an especially unattractive type, named Robert Minor. Robert Minor was leaning too close to Browder, was his alternate and deputy when Browder was in Atlanta. Minor was one of those functionaries in the Stalinist hierarchy who combined the repulsive traits of sycophancy toward those above him and brutality toward those below him, each in the highest degree imaginable. Minor was one of the most despicable of all the functionaries of the Communist movement who entered into the service of Stalin.

Browder once told a story about Minor in one of the old faction fights. I always remembered it because it was the only witticism I ever heard this pompous jackass perpetrate. He said Minor used to be an anarchist, which is true, if I may say so without meaning to offend any anarchists who may be present. But, said Browder, as an anarchist he had the idea, which is part of the antipolitical teachings of anarchism, that politics is a very dirty business; and then Minor became converted to communism without changing his idea of the nature of politics and engaged in it in a very dirty way. It was fitting that Minor and Browder should be the two chief partners in that game of crime and betrayal which passed as political leadership in the Communist Party. And it is rather poetic justice that they should go out together.

I was reading the other day, in preparation for these remarks, a book which previously had not come to my attention. It is a very well printed official record of the convention of the Communist Political Association of May 1944. Looking through this volume, I could see that in May 1944 one leader after another was called on to speak at the convention. Browder spoke in favor of his policy; then Minor, then Dennis, then Williamson. Then all the rest of the trained seals of the Communist apparatus got up, one after another, and expressed complete approval of everything Browder had said. I turned from that book to the file of *Daily Workers* containing the recent discussion and convention reports. The very same people who spoke so devotedly in echo of Browder in 1944 said the exact opposite in 1945. All, without exception, denounced Browder as a revisionist of Marxism, as a peddler of bourgeois ideas, etc. And Browder, who had unanimous support in May of 1944, had not a single vote in July of 1945.

Now, what kind of a movement is it and what kind of leaders are they who can be unanimously elected one year and unanimously rejected the following year without any change on their part whatsoever? That is the type of leader who is not elected, but is appointed from above. Such people are all the same type; they are fit to run a bureaucratic machine but never to lead a real struggle. I can't imagine anything more personally degrading than to be in a formal position of "leadership" by the sufferance of another; to have all the external trappings of office and yet to know that there is nothing real or solid about it; to know that the whole thing is a fake and a buildup; that one does not represent a real movement; that one's position is not based on the confidence of comrades gained in struggle, but on the appointment of someone higher in power. That is the fate of Browder, as it has been the fate of all others who succeeded the genuine leaders of the early communist movement.

Stalin needed people of this type, not only in central positions, but all the way down the line. In the course of years of struggle, all the independent, honest and revolutionary types of worker-leaders, who could not fit into the machine of Stalin, who could not obey the instructions to betray the workers, were expelled from the party, slandered, hounded, and their places taken by manufactured leaders. These leaders have no personal authority, no independence. When Stalin wishes to depose one of them as a scapegoat, it is not necessary to do more than send a letter, a note, and the job is completed.

In sacrificing Browder they have tried very hard to make it appear that this time there is really a change of line; that Foster, who has been dug up out of the reserve list and placed in Browder's seat, really represents something different from Browder; and that they are not going to betray the workers anymore. They say openly now that the whole policy of Browder was a policy of betrayal, but "We are going to change that now. We are going to be honest for a change. Foster is the representative of real Marxism."

What did Browder do? Browder's policy was to send the workers into the war; to tell them they should follow the leadership of the Wall Street gang; that they had a vital stake in the war adventures of the imperialists; that they should not strike, they should not protest; that they should hunt down and even lynch the incorruptible communists who called upon the workers to defend their rights even in the war. Under Browder, the Stalinists tried to break every strike of the workers, no matter how great were the wrongs.

What did Foster do? Foster supported that whole basic policy throughout the war, and even today his first pronouncement upon entering the place of Browder calls for the same program, supporting the imperialist war in the Orient. On what grounds? As a war for the liberation of the colonial peoples! Never could a more scoundrelly lie be told than that. Can you imagine a more monstrous lie than that—to say that the imperialist war machine is going into the Orient, burning and destroying the people of the Orient, for the purpose of their liberation?

Yet that is the first plank in Foster's program. Foster pledges no strikes while the war is going on. Just last week there was a strike of the workers at the Wright Aeronautical plant in New Jersey. The Stalinists in this plant, under the leadership of Foster, acted in the strike as finks and strike-breakers, just as they acted under Browder in the Detroit strikes, in the coal strikes and in all others. In principle the policy of Browder and Foster is the same thing. They both lie and they both betray.

But Browder wants to pledge also for the future, beyond the present war in the Orient. On the other hand, Foster says—and herein comes his "radicalism"—"That is going too far. That," says our uncorrupted Marxist, "that is revision and I won't stand for it." What a travesty, what a farce, what a deception of the hundred-times-deceived workers in the Stalinist party! The whole thing is a skin game; an attempt to continue the same policy with a change of faces and the promise that in the future, perhaps, if Stalin gets into a conflict with Truman, they may get a little more radical as a form of pressure on Truman.

This sham battle between Foster and Browder appears to me like an argument on the price of virtue between two cut-rate prostitutes. Foster says, "After the war we should make a small service charge." That is about the worth of the disagreements between them.

The fundamental reason for all this stage play, for this chopping off the empty head of Browder, for sacrificing the little man who wasn't there, is to call a certain halt to the idea that the American Communist Party, which is an agency of the Soviet bureaucracy, should become too completely merged with the governmental apparatus in this country.

Stalin has need of the Communist Party in this country, as in other countries, for only one purpose—as a bargaining agency in the diplomatic conflicts with the various imperialist powers. But in order to fill this mission the Communist Party must keep a certain influence over the workers. If it becomes a stench in the nostrils of every independent militant, as the CP did under Browder, then it has no bargaining power left. In order to keep it from becoming completely discredited, they had to go through this comedy of repudiating Browder, to denounce him as a "revisionist." They had to dig up Foster from the reserve list and put him forward as a labor leader who is in favor of strikes sometime in the future and so on, in order to overcome the demoralization and discouragement in their own ranks and to find a new basis for deceiving the awakening militant workers.

The necessity for this stratagem was emphasized in the reports of the district organizers. One report after another explained: "Under the policy we have been following we have been losing influence in the trade unions, and the Trotskyists have been gaining with their policies. As we have been fighting against strikes and following the government too uncritically, the Trotskyists who kept agitating on the same program as before have been making gains. We have got to correct our policy a little in order to head off the Trotskyists."

That is the real basis for their change in leaders and their so-called change of line. By adopting a new facade and a little more radical phraseology they hope to gain a new credit with the militant workers of America. They are coming too late. The crimes of Stalinism have gone too far and are too widely known. Corruption has entered too deeply into the bones and marrow of that party for anyone to have any realistic hope of reforming it. They cannot and do not mean a return to the policy of the proletarian revolution. The degeneration of the cadres of that party, of its officials—national, district and local—is not only political, it is moral too. They have not been able in seventeen years—since they expelled us from the party—to train any new cadre of leaders. So corrupt, so sterile is the life of the Stalinist party that the whole party has to be dominated and controlled by the same old gang of case-hardened hacks. Old functionaries and pensioners that we haven't heard of for years reappear, crawling out of forgotten corners of the party like cockroaches out of old woodwork. This is the "new leadership" which is supposed to regenerate the party.

Stalinism, with all its power and all its money, can train only functionaries, never independent leaders; whereas the Socialist Workers Party, which began as a small persecuted group, in seventeen years has developed on a national scale a whole new staff of younger leaders who have been trained exclusively in our movement. They have come forward and developed their capacities in the free democratic atmosphere of an honest revolutionary party. When our eighteen leaders were put in prison for a whole year, the party did not lack for qualified younger people to take their places.

Our whole party life has been a constant process of selecting, educating and training new people, younger and more revolutionary than any the Communist Party can dream of. These Stalinist functionaries, who have been selling principles for more than seventeen years—how can anyone have the slightest hope that they will turn revolutionary, suddenly become honest and virtuous again? That is impossible. A political error can be corrected, but moral degeneration has to run its course. These people are traitors to the marrow of their bones.

They betrayed the United States workers in the war. They betrayed the workers of Europe. They betrayed the Negroes of this country in the most shameful and cynical manner. Then, on top of that, at the very moment when they are promising to be good and honest and revolutionary again, we read of this cynical and despicable alliance of the Communist Party in New York City with Tammany Hall. They put up Davis, this cynical traitor to the Negro people, as a candidate of Tammany Hall.

They say to the people of Harlem: "We and Tammany Hall will fight for your freedom and liberties." Could there be a greater cynicism, a more shameful betrayal than that? No, you cannot hope for any regeneration of this thoroughly corrupt party.

It is not a question of "revisionism" at all. It is a question of complete degeneration, complete abandonment of vital principles of the proletarian revolution which are represented by Marxism.

We are the real communists, the Trotskyists. And in that we are the polar opposites of the Communist Party of Stalin and Browder and Foster and all the rest of them. Some people make a great misidentification; some people are inclined to consider Stalinism and communism as the same thing. That is false to the core. In one case, it might be passed off as ignorance of the general public who have not studied the question closely. In the other case, it is conscious misrepresentation and miseducation. They point to the American Communist Party and Browder and Foster and say, "that is communism," in order to discredit the very idea of communism in the eyes of the workers. That is not true. We denounce the Stalinists, not because they are communists but because they have betrayed the cause of communism.

The Socialist Workers Party goes straight back to Lenin and Trotsky. We uphold the old program. We carry on the great tradition of the Russian Revolution and the Comintern. All those members of the Communist Party who may have been shaken out of a coma by the present discussion, who are looking for the real party of communism, must come to our party and they will find it there. Our party stood up under persecution in the war and grew stronger in the struggle. We build our party on the organizational principles and methods of Lenin. The spirit of our party is the spirit of socialism. Socialism is the only salvation of humanity. The Stalinists are the greatest obstacles in the fight of the workers toward socialism.

The Socialist Workers Party is confident of the future in Europe, in the colonial countries, and in America too. The workers of starving and tortured Europe and the great colonial peoples—they see America today as the most predatory of all the imperialist powers, casting a dark and menacing shadow over the whole of humanity. That is the America these people see throughout the world today.

But we shall make it our task—and we invite you to join us in it—to show the people of the world another America, a different and better America—the America of the people, the America of the workers, the America of the proletarian revolution, which will lead the way to peace and cooperation of all peoples and all nations in the Socialist United States of the World.

Cannon addressing a meeting of the International Labor Defense, October 1926. Meeting is chaired by Elizabeth Gurley Flynn.

# Chapter 9

# The trial of the Stalinist leaders

Delivered to a protest meeting at Beethoven Hall, New York City, February 4, 1949.

There is a widespread popular impression that the Communist Party leaders in the dock in the federal courtroom on Foley Square are criminals and ought to be brought to trial. I personally agree with that popular sentiment. The Stalinist leaders are indeed criminals, and they should be tried for their crimes. But we don't agree with this trial. This is a case of the right criminals charged with the wrong crime. And they are being tried in the wrong court.

Like Comrade Dobbs, I could testify as an expert witness on these questions. I hereby publicly offer the lawyers for the Stalinists on trial my services in their defense against false accusations. I have qualifications as such an expert, as follows:

I was an active member of the Communist Party from its foundation in 1919 until 1928, that is, nine years. I am a student of Marxist and Leninist theory, which the Stalinists are falsely accused of teaching. I have been a working opponent of Stalinism for twenty years.

And, finally, I am familiar with the free-speech section of the United States Constitution which provides that "Congress shall pass no law . . . abridging the freedom of speech, or of the press." I learned that in school, and then had an opportunity to read it over again and ponder over it for thirteen months in a federal university at Sandstone penitentiary.

So, armed with these qualifications, I would challenge the indictment of the leaders of the Stalinist party on three grounds:

1. The crime charged against them—that they "conspired to advocate" the overthrow of the United States government by force and violence—is not a crime in this country under the Constitution.

2. The Stalinists are not even guilty of this crime that is not a crime. They do not advocate the overthrow of the United States government by force and violence, or otherwise.

3. The federal court of American capitalism has no right to try them, because the crimes of Stalinism have not been directed against the system this court represents. The Stalinist leaders should be placed on trial before a court of the international working class for high crimes and misdemeanors against the working class of the world, and of this country, too, over a long period of years; high crimes and misdemeanors ranging from perversions of Marxism to class collaboration and support of the imperialist government of the United States in the Second World War, and including every kind of offense against the ethics of the workers' movement from falsification and forgery to frame-up and murder.

The Stalinists are guilty of these crimes. The Stalinists are the greatest criminals in history. But the present trial in the federal court of the Southern District of New York in Foley Square is a frame-up against them. They are not guilty of the charge brought against them, that they advocated the overthrow of the capitalist government of the United States.

The whole course of Stalinism, since its inception, has served to support world capitalism and not to overthrow it. Stalinism began twenty-five years ago with the promulgation of its basic theory of "socialism in one country," meaning Russia. That signified: "No socialism in any other country." It signified the renunciation of all perspectives of international revolution: an offer of the Soviet bureaucracy to compromise with world capitalism at the expense of the international workers' movement. That is the theory from which Stalinism originated.

The practice followed from the theory: the expulsions, the frame-ups and mass murders of tens of thousands of Bolsheviks who made the revolution and stood in reality for international revolution against all capitalist institutions; the conduct of the Stalinists in Spain, where they propped up and supported the bourgeois government at the cost of mass murders of Spanish revolutionists; the "people's front" policy of collaboration with capitalist parties and participation in capitalist governments; the Soviet-Nazi pact whereby the Stalinists joined hands with Hitler in launching the Second World War; the Anglo-Soviet-American Pact, under which the American Stalinists sold out the working class of the United States and lined up to support the war.

Yes, the record clearly shows that the Stalinists are criminals. But the capitalist court is disqualified—by this record of known facts and by the clear provision of the United States Constitution and even by considerations of gratitude for services received from the Stalinists, especially during the war—to try them.

On the other hand, despite the fact that we indict the Stalinists as criminals on the record, we and all other workers' organizations, who have reason for neither love nor gratitude toward the Stalinists, have a vital interest in protesting against their prosecution in this particular case. This is the purpose of our meeting tonight.

This is not a criminal trial of alleged actions in violation of definite constitutional laws. This is a political trial. The freedom to "advocate" any doctrine, including revolution, is basic to free speech and democracy. This trial strikes at the very roots of these democratic rights of all workers' organizations.

It should be borne in mind that the indictment against the Stalinists does not charge them with a single action against the United States government. The sole basis of the trial is that they conspired to "advocate" the overthrow of the United States government. That is to say, they conspired to speak and to write.

The very provision of the Constitution, which I have referred to, was designed specifically to prevent Congress from passing laws which would proscribe the "advocacy" of any doctrine. But this indictment under the Smith Act—the same law under which we were prosecuted and convicted in Minneapolis—is an indictment against speaking and writing. Now, once you establish the precedent that it is possible to proscribe one kind of talk or "advocacy," you lay the ground for the suppression of any other. You legitimatize the suppression of free speech and the free press.

Unfortunately, our trial and conviction under the Smith Act in Minneapolis and our subsequent imprisonment, and the refusal of the Supreme Court to review the case, has already set one precedent. This was a heavy blow at free speech and democracy in this country, and the Stalinists on trial are suffering from this precedent.

It is true, as Comrade Dobbs pointed out, and as I think all of you know, that the Stalinists did all they could, in every dirty way they knew, to help the prosecution put us in prison. They did everything they could to keep us in prison for our full term. It is true that these scoundrels even tried to sabotage and break up our defense committee, to prevent it from raising funds from sympathetic organizations to pay the lawyers. If the Stalinists had had their way, we would not have been able to employ a legal defense to make a legal record. Their shameful conduct paved the way for their own prosecution under the same law.

That is all true, as has been related so graphically here tonight by Comrade Dobbs. But that cannot determine the policy of a revolutionary organization, or of any workers' organization for that matter. Sheer self-interest, for us and for every honest workers' organization, weighs more than sentiments of revenge in this case.

If the precedent established in our case is reinforced by another conviction in this case of the Stalinists, and sanctioned by public opinion until it becomes accepted as custom, the traditional freedoms which the workers' movement needs for enlightened advancement will yield to new encroachments all along the line. The ominous trend toward thought control under a police state will be greatly accelerated.

That is the larger issue, transcending all other considerations, in the trial of the Stalinists now going on. That is why we are so deeply concerned about it and appeal to all workers' organizations, especially to those who supported us in our trial, to protest against the political trial of the Stalinists. I think we have made it sufficiently clear that our point of view in this case is not motivated by

Christian forgiveness or softheadedness, and even less by political conciliation with perfidious Stalinism. Our stand is based solely on our concept of the most vital interest of the working class and its future struggles.

It used to be taken for granted in the labor movement that, despite all differences and disputes between different parties, factions and groups, all would unite and cooperate when any section of the labor movement was under attack in the courts of the class enemy. We have come a long way from the old tradition of solidarity against persecution and frame-up. It was a good tradition and we should try in some measure to restore it.

Some of the brightest pages of American labor history were written in united struggles for justice and free speech. The labor movement of today, which did not fall from the skies, is the product and fruit of many struggles in the past, and owes a great deal to these united-front struggles for free speech and justice and freedom of organization.

My first interest in the socialist and labor movement was aroused by the great protest movement in behalf of Moyer and Haywood in 1906. They were arrested and brought to trial on trumped-up charges of murder, but their real offense was their labor activities, their militancy and incorruptibility. They were not left alone to defend themselves as best they could. They were leaders of the Western Federation of Miners, which was then affiliated to the IWW. Nevertheless, all sections of the labor movement recognized the threat to themselves and their whole future in the attempt to legitimatize the framing-up of the labor leaders.

A tremendous machinery of protest and defense was built up, from one end of the country to the other, in the form of "Moyer-Haywood Conferences." All kinds of organizations, representing every section of the labor movement and all points of view, sent delegates to these united-front conferences. AFL and independent unions, the IWW, the Socialist Party, the Socialist Labor Party, the anarchist groups and groups of liberals, and people of good will—all marched together under the "Moyer-Haywood Conferences" to make a mighty movement in defense of the accused. The ground shook with their tread.

The conspirators who had sought to take the lives of Moyer and Haywood were pushed back. The frame-up was defeated by the threat of the united workers' movement. The great Bill Haywood, of beloved memory, was right when he spoke to the first great mass meeting of 200,000 in Chicago that greeted him on his release from jail, and said: "We owe our lives to your solidarity."

The same solidarity was shown in defense of Ettor and Giovannitti, leaders of the Lawrence strike of 1912; and in the defense of Mooney and Billings. It was true to a considerable extent in the case of the IWW leaders during the First World War, and in the cases of Debs and of Sacco and Vanzetti. All class-conscious workers felt it to be an elementary duty, as a matter of course, to join together against the attacks of the class enemy.

The Communist Party itself was once the exponent of this proud tradition of solidarity. The International Labor Defense, which was formed in 1925 under the direct inspiration of the Communist Party, was specifically dedicated to the principle of nonpartisan labor defense, to the defense of any member of the working-class movement, regardless of his views, who suffered persecution by the capitalist courts because of his activities or his opinions.

I can speak with authority about that because I participated in the planning of the ILD and was the National Secretary from its inception until we were thrown out of the Communist Party in 1928. The International Labor

Defense was really "born in Moscow"; that I must admit, although it was strictly an American institution in its methods and practices. The ILD was born in Moscow in discussion with Bill Haywood. The old fighter, who was exiled from America with a twenty-year sentence hanging over him, was deeply concerned about the persecution of workers in America. He wanted to have something done for the almost forgotten men lying in jail all over the country.

There were over a hundred men—labor organizers, strike leaders and radicals—in prisons at that time in the United States: IWWs, anarchists, Mooney and Billings, Sacco and Vanzetti, McNamara and Schmidt, the Centralia prisoners, etc. In discussions, there in Moscow in 1925, we worked out the plan and conception of the International Labor Defense as a nonpartisan body that would defend any member of the working-class movement, regardless of his opinion or affiliation, if he came under persecution by capitalist law.

I never will forget those meetings with Bill Haywood. When we completed the plans, which were later to become reality in the formation of the ILD, and when I promised him that I would come back to America and see to it that the plans did not remain on paper, that we would really go to work in earnest and come to the aid of the men forgotten in prison, the old lion's eyes—his one eye, rather—flashed with the old fire. He said, "I wish I could go back to give a hand in that job." He couldn't come back because he was an outlaw in the United States, not for any crime he had committed but for all the good things he had done for the American working class. Up to the end of his life he continued to be an active participant in the work of the ILD by correspondence.

The plans for the International Labor Defense as a nonpartisan defense organization, made there in Bill

Haywood's room in Moscow, were carried out in practice during its first years. There were 106 class-war prisoners in the United States—scores of IWWs, members railroaded in California, Kansas, Utah and other states under the criminal-syndicalist laws. We located a couple of obscure anarchists in Rhode Island; a group of AFL coal miners in West Virginia; two labor organizers in Thomaston, Maine—besides the more prominent and better-known prisoners mentioned before. They added up to 106 people in prison in this land of the free at that time for activities in the labor movement. They were not criminals at all, but strike leaders, organizers, agitators, dissenters—our own kind of people. Not one of these 106 prisoners was a member of the Communist Party! But the ILD defended and helped them all.

The ILD adopted as its policy to remember them all and raise money for them. We created a fund so that five dollars was sent every month to each of the 106 class-war prisoners. Every Christmastime we raised a special fund for their families. The Centralia IWW group, almost forgotten for years, were remembered; publicity was given their case and efforts made to help them. The same with all the old half-forgotten cases. The ILD was the organizing center of the great worldwide movement of protest for the two anarchists, Sacco and Vanzetti. All this work of solidarity had the backing and support of the Communist Party, but that was before it became completely Stalinized and expelled the honest revolutionists.

The principle of the International Labor Defense, which made it so popular and so dear to the militants, was nonpartisan defense without political discrimination. The principle was solidarity. When you consider all this and compare it with the later practices of the Stalinists; when you recall what has happened in the last twenty-odd years, you must say that the Stalinists have done more than any others to dishonor this tradition of solidarity. They have done more than any others to disrupt unity for defense against the class enemy.

That terrible corruption of disunity in the face of the class enemy has penetrated other sections of the labor movement too. The social democrats do a great deal of pious moralizing about the Stalinists, but their conduct isn't much better, if any. For the greater part, they make no protest against the persecution of the Stalinists. The labor officials, both of the CIO and AFL, stand aside, and many even support the prosecution.

They think there is no need to worry about the Smith Act, that it is only for Stalinists. That is what the Stalinists thought when we were on trial seven years ago—that this evil and unconstitutional law is only for Trotskyists. I heard in San Francisco that a Stalinist party speaker, harassed by an interrogator as to the relation between their trial and ours, said, "This whole trial is a mistake and a misunderstanding. The Smith Act was meant for the Trotskyists." But the Smith Act chickens came home to roost for the Stalinists, and the same thing can happen to others, too.

If the Stalinists are convicted, establishing another precedent to buttress the precedent of our case, the same law can be invoked against other political organizations, against college professors, and even preachers who happen to have opinions contrary to those of the ruling powers and the courage to express them. It is a great error, a terrible error, to neglect this trial and refuse to protest, an error for which we will all have to pay—they and we, and all of us, all who aspire by whatever means, or by whatever program or doctrine, toward a better and freer world through the unity and solidarity of the workers. We will all have to pay if the federal prosecutor wins this case and makes it stick with the support of public opinion. That is why we would like to see every effort made, even now while the trial is going on, to reverse the present trend, to overcome the passivity and indifference.

It is, of course, utopian to hope or expect that a great united movement, cooperating loyally as in the old days, can be formed with the Stalinists. The Stalinists cannot cooperate loyally with anyone. We offered them a united front. They refused it. Even now, when the witch-hunt and loyalty purges are directed against them, they refuse to say one word in defense of James Kutcher, the legless veteran, who was removed from his Veterans Administration job in New Jersey because of his political opinions as a member of the Socialist Workers Party.

Because of the attitude of the Stalinists, as well as for other considerations, it would be utopian to hope for an all-inclusive united front. But the trade unions and anti-Stalinist political organizations should join together, for their own reasons and in their own interest, to protest this prosecution. We would join and give our support to such an effort. But in any case, whether it can be done cooperatively or separately, all should raise their voices in protest against the political trial going on in Foley Square. Not for the sake of the Stalinist gang, but for the sake of free speech, for those democratic rights which the labor movement has dearly won and badly needs for its informed and conscious struggle to reach higher ground.

Chapter 10

# The end of the Stalin cult

Delivered at the Friday Night Forum, Los Angeles, March 9, 1956.

Three years ago Stalin, the bloodthirsty tyrant, the betrayer of revolutions and the murderer of revolutionists, "the most sinister criminal in the history of mankind," unfortunately died in bed. Two weeks ago his personally selected and handpicked heirs, the beneficiaries of his monstrous tyranny and the accomplices in all his crimes, used the occasion of the Twentieth Congress of the Soviet Communist Party to denounce the cult of Stalin and to declare that his dictatorial rule for twenty years was wrong.

The congress pronouncement is true, as far as it goes. And it is the first official truth that has come out of Moscow for more than thirty years. Truth is a slow starter. Mark Twain said a lie can travel halfway around the world while the truth is putting its shoes on. But the truth has more endurance than the lie, and eventually catches up with it. The truth is on the march again—even in Moscow.

According to press reports, after they had repudiated and buried the cult of Stalin by official decree, they wound up the congress by singing *The Internationale*. But I think their tongues must have twisted over the chorus, which says that those who have been naught shall be all. The chief business of their congress was to say that Stalin, who had once been "all," was henceforth to be nothing. The prophecy of *The Internationale* was shifted into reverse gear at the Moscow congress, and the cult of Stalin happened to be in the way and got run over. The Stalin cult is dead, never to rise again.

One of the Moscow correspondents of the Associated Press reports that he asked a congress delegate what would now be done about all those plaster monuments of Stalin standing around in Moscow and all over Russia, and the delegate answered: "The monuments can stand." But he's mistaken about that. They will stand for a while until somebody gets the idea for a badly needed road program in the Soviet Union, and looks at all this plaster standing around for no good reason, and says it ought to be put through the rock crusher and ground up into material for concrete. That's where the monuments of Stalin will eventually end.

There is even a rumor that Lenin addressed a message to the congress through a spiritual medium. You know, in a mistaken impulse right after the death of Stalin, his successors buried him in the Red Square right beside Lenin. According to the rumor, Lenin sent a request to the congress to have him moved out of there because, he said: "I don't want to be found dead in the same mausoleum with Stalin."

Shakespeare must have been looking ahead to this day when he wrote:

"But yesterday the word of Caesar might
Have stood against the world; now lies he there,
And none so poor to do him reverence."

Not even the poor American Stalinists do reverence to Stalin anymore, and they're about as poor as you can get. I noticed in the *Daily Worker* a piece about the seventy-fifth birthday of William Z. Foster, the chief and chairman of the American Stalinists. Some time ago, Foster published an autobiography that he entitled, without knowing what was coming, *From Bryan to Stalin*. In the *Daily Worker* article relating Foster's accomplishments this volume is not listed among the products of his pen.

The article states that Foster "was in the forefront of the struggle" against Jay Lovestone, and also in the forefront of the struggle against Earl Browder, and then it stops. It doesn't say that Foster was in the forefront of the struggle against Trotskyism, hand in hand with Browder and Lovestone. It doesn't say that he was the promoter of the cult of Stalinism. On the contrary, it says—this is really rich, and it must have been an afterthought that they put in after the proofs were already drawn, and they got the reports from the Moscow congress—"Comrade Foster has fought at all times for collective leadership in the party." No mention of Stalin and Foster's services to Stalin.

The Stalin cult is a dead duck; there is no question about that. Even the third anniversary of Stalin's death on March 5 was ignored by the Soviet press. The Moscow correspondent of *The New York Times* reports under that date: "The Soviet press, radio and most of the people made no comment today on the third anniversary of the death of Stalin.... Only foreigners seemed to be aware of today's anniversary. An effort to bring up Stalin's name in conversation with an English-speaking Soviet citizen brought only a nod of the head."

The press of the American Stalinists also forgot to mention the third anniversary of Stalin's demise. And the blanket of silence covered China, too. A March 5 dispatch from Hong Kong in *The New York Times* says: "The Chinese Communists maintained a discreet silence on Stalin today. Neither the Hsinhua news agency nor the Peiping radio marked the anniversary."

I mention these news items neither in sorrow nor in anger. Whatever the reason for this action of the Soviet congress, the repudiation of Stalin by his heirs is big news and good news—the biggest news and the best news since the death of Stalin himself three years ago. We can recognize this without exaggerating the significance of the congress action or deceiving ourselves and others about its purpose.

It does not mean the end of Stalinism in the Soviet Union and on the international field. Far from it. The assembled bureaucrats at the congress, who are the product of the abominable system and the representatives of its privileged beneficiaries, hope to preserve Stalinism by unloading Stalin and repudiating the hateful cult associated with his name. But the repudiation of the cult may very well mark the beginning of the end of the system just the same.

It is remarkable how differently the successors of Stalin treat his name from the way Stalin found it necessary to treat the name of Lenin. Stalin, the impostor, treated the name of Lenin with a great outward show of reverence. He claimed to be the best disciple of Lenin. The whole development of Stalinism, which was a counterrevolutionary reaction against the heritage of Lenin, was passed off as a continuation of Leninism. The international revolution, the heart of Lenin's program, was betrayed by Stalin in the name of Lenin.

All this deceitful pretense of reverence for Lenin was necessary because Lenin lived in the memory of the Russian masses as the personification of the great revolution, and the masses loved his name for that. But how different it is with the name of Stalin. The bureaucrats assembled at the Twentieth Congress, who are the true heirs of Stalin and owe their positions to his favor, are already ashamed and afraid to acknowledge him. They found it necessary and expedient, only three years after the tyrant died, to repudiate his name at a formal congress.

There was a profound reason for their action, and that reason is the key to the riddle. I think it is clear now, as Trotsky always said, that the cult of Stalin was the cult of the privileged bureaucrats. It was never the faith of the masses of the Soviet workers. Despite all the years that Stalin ruled after the death of Lenin; despite all the falsification of history, all the crooked, lying propaganda; despite all the suppression of free opinion, all the terror, all the frame-ups and murders; despite all the attempts to bury the murdered opponents of Stalin under tons of official slander, and the official deification of Stalin—despite all that, the cult of Stalin never took hold among the Soviet workers. They never believed it.

That is now implicitly recognized by the proclamations of the Twentieth Congress. The simple fact that the congress felt impelled to repudiate Stalin, bears testimony to a powerful revulsion of the Soviet masses against everything connected with his name. That revulsion of the masses against the name and the memory of Stalin was the mass pressure behind the congress. And now, with the stamp of "legality" placed on the true sentiments of the masses, this pressure will grow stronger and will bring far greater repercussions than this first formal action.

We see proof every day that the Supreme Court decision outlawing segregation in the public schools in the United States stimulated the struggle of the Negro people for equal rights all along the line. So, in the same way, we can expect that the Moscow congress action will encourage the workers in the Soviet Union and the satellite countries to demand the real thing as well as the promise.

There cannot be the slightest doubt that the long-oppressed Soviet workers have received the congress reports as tidings of great joy, and have lifted up their hearts in hope. There is jubilation in the factories and dancing in the streets of the forced-labor camps. The political prisoners of Stalinism, who number millions in the Soviet Union, look forward now to the end of their long agony. There can be no doubt that the Soviet masses will seize upon these congress pronouncements as a banner in their struggle to end the long nightmare of police-state tyranny which bears the name of Stalinism.

History does not know another repudiation of a cult coming so soon after the death of the individual who personified it, without a revolution accompanying the death of the tyrant. It is true that the cult of Mussolini died with him on the same day, on the same meathook from which the fascist monster was hanged upside down on the public square by the revolutionary partisans of Italy. Stalin escaped the fate of Mussolini, which was his due. Stalin didn't die in the right way, and that caused a slight delay in the burial of his cult along with its author. But this discrepancy has finally been made up; the cult of Stalin has followed him in death after only a brief three-year interlude.

The repudiation of the Mussolini cult was thoroughgoing and unconditional, and included everything connected with his name after he came to power. That was possible because Mussolini himself was executed by his enemies, the revolutionary masses of Italy, and revolutions do not stop at half measures. The repudiation of the Stalin cult by the friends and heirs of Stalin was more limited. They were willing, so far, to say only that Stalin's regime had been wrong for twenty years before his death, without naming the most atrocious crimes of Stalinism in that long time.

Those twenty years, which they have now proscribed and repudiated, include the 1936–1937 period. The years during which they say his rule was wrong are the years in which the Old Bolsheviks—the noblest, the most heroic generation in all history—were framed up and murdered by Stalin. They have not yet said so specifically, but by inference they have repudiated all the frame-ups and all the murders. They have even begun to rehabilitate some of the victims of the purges, specifically by name.

I read one dispatch which said that Bela Kun, the Hungarian leader who perished in one of the purges, has now been officially recognized as falsely accused; and a eulogistic article was published in *Pravda* as if nothing had happened. Another victim of the purges, the Ukrainian, Kossior, is now discovered to have been falsely accused and framed up in the great purge. The leadership of the Polish Communist Party, which was expelled in 1938, is now declared to have been framed up—eighteen years after the event.

Declarations were made at the congress that Stalin's *History of the Communist Party of the Soviet Union* is false and has to be rewritten. That follows from the present decision to repudiate the last twenty years of Stalinism. But that still leaves ten years unaccounted for—the crucial first ten years when the regime of Stalin was consolidated in the course of a political counterrevolution against the heritage of Lenin, which was defended by Trotsky.

They swear off the cult of Stalin without specifying and repudiating the specific crimes that were committed in the name of that cult; without repudiating the whole theory and practice of Stalinism on a national and international scale since the death of Lenin. They haven't yet said anything about the long, monstrous record of Stalinism in the international labor movement.

That record includes the betrayal of the Chinese revolution in 1926; and the betrayal of the German workers in 1933, which made possible the victory of Hitler and all its terrible consequences for the German working class and for the people of Europe. They haven't said anything yet about the betrayal of the Spanish revolution in 1936, and the murder of the Spanish revolutionists by the Stalinist gunmen sent there for that purpose. They haven't mentioned yet the Stalin-Hitler pact, which precipitated the Second World War.

They haven't mentioned the policy of social patriotism adopted by all the Stalinist parties allied with the Soviet Union during the Second World War. Under this policy the shameful Stalinists in this country joined the camp of the imperialist masters and became the chief advocates of the no-strike pledge and the most zealous strikebreakers. In the service of Stalin they applauded our prosecution in Minneapolis in 1941—the first prosecution under the Smith Act—and appealed to the unions to refuse contributions to our legal defense.

The Moscow congress didn't say anything about the betrayal of the revolution in Europe immediately after the war. The French partisans and the Italian partisans had power in their hands, but they were disarmed by the policy of Stalinism. The communist workers were demoralized by the Stalinist policy of collaboration with the bourgeoisie. Representatives of the Communist parties in Italy and France went into bourgeois cabinets and helped to stabilize the regime and stifle the revolution.

They haven't yet repudiated another typical manifestation of Stalinism here in the United States. That is the present policy of the Communist Party, advising the workers to be good Democrats and join the Democratic Party along with the bankers and the industrialists and the Dixiecrats, and vote for the Democratic Party in order to serve the diplomatic interests of the Kremlin gang.

They have repudiated the cult of Stalin, but they haven't yet repudiated Stalinism and the crimes of Stalinism. That is something like a professional criminal pleading guilty to spitting on the sidewalk in the hope of avoiding trial on the charge of murder.

The Moscow bureaucrats have made a start—that cannot be denied, or ignored. They have confessed something, but they haven't confessed enough yet. They said $A$, but they choked over $B$. But in the political alphabet, $B$ follows after $A$, and we can be confident that it will be said in due time. If the heirs of Stalin cannot yet say $B$, because to do so they would have to repudiate themselves, the Soviet workers, whose burning hatred of every memory of the Stalinist regime is the driving force behind these first partial disavowals, will say it for them—and against them.

The repudiation of the Stalin cult at the Moscow congress is an echo in the top bureaucratic circles of the ominous rumble of the coming political revolution in the Soviet Union. Nothing less than a complete political revolution will do there. It is not merely the cult of Stalin as a person, but Stalinism as a political system, that must be repudiated and overthrown. That can be done only by a revolution of the Soviet workers.

The goal of this revolution is the unconditional repudiation of the Stalinist theory of "socialism in one country," which was the motivation of all the crimes and betrayals, and the reaffirmation of the Lenin-Trotsky program of proletarian internationalism; the overthrow of the Stalinist police state in the Soviet Union and the restoration of

Soviet democracy; the abolition of the privileged caste; a complete review of the frame-up trials and purges and a vindication of their victims. These are the demands and the program of the political revolution in the Soviet Union.

The Moscow congress was not the revolution, and it does not signify the restoration of Soviet democracy, as fools and traitors may suggest, but it was an incident on the road to it. A faltering, hesitant reflection in the Soviet tops of a mighty revolutionary impulse from below; a promise of reform in the police-state regime, a verbal gesture of appeasement in the hope of heading off the storm—that is what the pronouncements of the Moscow congress are really intended to signify. That and nothing more is what is intended.

But the results of the gesture and the promise of reform may be entirely different than the Stalinist bureaucrats at the congress intended. It has happened that way more than once in history. An outlived autocracy, whose continued existence is made impossible by new objective conditions, can hasten its own downfall by inadequate concessions as well as by ineffective terror. Reforms granted in the hope of staving off a mass revolt can, by their revelation of fear and weakness, act as a spur to the revolt. This can also be the result of the new turn of events in the Soviet Union.

The congress repudiation of the Stalin cult was prompted by internal Russian conditions, not by external ones. The whole world is laughing at the claim of Dulles that he caused the Moscow turn by shooting off his big mouth. The claim that the Washington imperialists compelled the repudiation of the Stalin cult; or that they care a hoot about it; or that, as a matter of fact, in the present world situation they are in any position to compel serious concessions of any kind from the Soviet bloc and the colonial people, is really enough to make the world laugh. Nobody in the world believes that—except Dulles; and he doesn't believe it either—he only says it.

No, that part of the congress—the repudiation of the Stalin cult—was determined by internal considerations. It was meant as a concession to the Soviet masses—and, in part perhaps, as a concession to the democratic-minded workers in the capitalist world, and to the colonial masses, who have been repelled by the police-state terror of the Stalinist regime. It is meant above all as a gesture of conciliation with the deepest sentiments of the Soviet workers and the workers in the satellite countries—offered in the hope of heading off the gathering storm by the promise of reform.

The congress action is not the first indication of this storm. As I see it, we have already had four signs of the real trend of thought in the Soviet masses since the death of Stalin—two of them from the top and two from below.

The first indication, from the top, intended to forestall the masses, was the promise of reforms in the regime as soon as the successors of Stalin took over. Before they had the tyrant buried they were promising a relaxation of the Stalinist terror. Hardly a week had gone by when they announced that the big case against the Jewish doctors had been exposed as a frame-up and would not be carried through.

The first promises of reforms in the regime had a double effect. They not only encouraged the Soviet masses and the workers of the satellite countries to demand more. They also nourished some delusions in a minority in our own ranks about the "self-reform" of the Soviet bureaucracy.

The Soviet workers labored under no such illusions about the voluntary self-reform of the Stalinist bureaucracy. The second and third powerful indications of their real sentiments came from below. The East German workers rose in revolt in June 1953. That was followed—in July 1953, and as a result of it—by the mass strike in the Vorkuta forced-labor camp. There can be no doubt that these momentous actions, lightning flashes of the coming revolutionary storm, were sparked by the death of Stalin and the first promises of reforms by his successors. The revolt of the East German workers and the strike of the prisoners in the Vorkuta forced-labor camp, were deadly serious revolutionary actions—glorious harbingers of great events to come.

The fourth indication and recognition of the anti-Stalinist sentiment of the masses in the Soviet Union, comes now in a new set of promises from the top by the Twentieth Congress. They are far more sweeping than the original promises of three years ago, and their effects can be all the greater. We ought to see these decisions in their true light, as another incident in the interaction of movements from below and gestures from the top; as a possible, and indeed probable, factor in the acceleration of the whole process, which is moving toward the goal of a complete political revolution in the Soviet Union.

The political revolution against Stalinism in the Soviet Union will give no support to the imperialists' dreams of a capitalist restoration. On the contrary, it is an essential part of the international revolution against capitalism, and will coincide with it. The destruction of Stalinism brings with it the destruction of capitalism.

Stalinism is the most monstrous perversion of the workers' movement ever known in history. It has been and remains the chief support of world capitalism and the chief obstruction to the revolution in the labor movement of the world. But Stalinism's days are numbered now. The basic conditions for its emergence and triumph have radically changed, and are still changing in the same direction. The

Russian workers—and this is the big new fact—the Russian workers today are no longer the weak and scattered mass of a few million, surrounded by a peasant sea, who succumbed to the Stalinist terror thirty years ago.

At that time, their ranks had been decimated in the revolution and the long civil war and the war of intervention that followed it, and the survivors were worn out from their superhuman exertions. At that time, the international revolution, to which they had looked for aid and reinforcement, had been defeated and pushed back all along the line. World capitalism had attained a new stabilization after the first postwar upheavals, and the young Soviet Union was isolated and encircled by the capitalist powers. The monstrous phenomenon of Stalinism grew up out of these unfavorable conditions, and represented a national-reformist adaptation to them.

Stalinism, which impressed the philistines and the superficial observers as all-powerful because it ruled by terror, in reality arose in the twenties out of the weakened position and the capitalist encirclement of the Soviet Union, and the defeats of the workers and colonial peoples on the international arena. Stalinism contributed more than anything else to the defeats of the international revolution, and it flourished on these defeats. Stalinism was the reactionary ideology of the ebb tide of the revolution.

All the old conditions that favored Stalinism in that time are changed now. The laws of permanent revolution, elucidated by Trotsky, proved to be stronger than the Stalinist terror and treachery. Despite Stalinism, isolated, backward, peasant Russia, thanks to the revolution that gave it birth, has become the second industrial power in the world. Despite Stalinism and its theory of socialism in one country, the capitalist encirclement has been broken by the extension of the Soviet system to

Eastern Europe and China.

The colonial revolution is on the rise everywhere. The labor movement of Western Europe is strongly organized and militant, and since the end of the Second World War has been restrained from revolution only by Stalinism. Only the cursed influence of Stalinism stands today between the European workers and their victory over their own capitalism. But the great masses of the revolutionary workers, who have been deceived and befuddled by Stalinism, are also changing and are also demanding a different policy.

I pick up this issue of the Sunday *New York Times*. Here's a dispatch on the front page about the revolutionary developments in the ranks of the Stalinist party of Italy. It is headed "Dissident Red Bloc in Italy Protests 'Soft' Party Line"—and the first two paragraphs read as follows:

"*Rome*, March 3—Six hundred avowed but rebellious Communists, wearing cloth caps and red scarves as a kind of uniform, marched through the streets of Rome this morning shouting protests against their party's leadership. They accused it of being inept and lacking in the courage to lead the Italian proletariat in a revolution against capitalism.

"The 600 marchers, who boasted that they represented 1,000,000 Communists, were delegates from all parts of Italy to a meeting of self-styled Democratic Communists. This is a movement that aims to lead communism back to its Marxist and Leninist line."

Good news from Italy, right after the good news from Russia!

And the American workers, who were an atomized mass when Stalinism first came to power, without even trade-union organization, except in a small stratum of skilled workers—these same American workers have arisen out of nothingness in the meantime. Out of a semirevolution of their own in the thirties, they have built a great trade-union movement of seventeen million, and are on the eve of the next advance to political and class consciousness.

While all these favorable changes take place in the camp of the working class and of the colonial people, the decaying system of world capitalism is plunged deeper into a crisis from which it cannot escape, and grows weaker by the day.

This radical change of the whole world situation is the objective basis, first, for the formal repudiation of the Stalin cult in words, and next, for the revolutionary overthrow of Stalinism in deeds. And there is the power to make good that program.

The Soviet proletariat today is a new, young class of more than forty-eight million. Its ranks have been multiplied ten times in the thirty years since the first rise of Stalinism. It has become a skilled and trained working class, grown strong and self-confident in great achievements in the Second World War and in the postwar reconstruction. These forty-eight million Soviet workers are a mighty power. Taking all their resources together, they may be an even greater power than the American working class in the big events next on the agenda, for they are inspired by the memory and the tradition of three revolutions in the past fifty years.

The tradition of revolutionary victories in the past multiplies the powers and potentialities of the class. Once they begin to move again, after the long suppression and the long terror, they will shake the world again—as they did in 1917. The appearance of the mighty Soviet proletariat as an independent force on the international arena, which is now clearly foreshadowed, can qualitatively change class relationships on a world scale in favor of the workers and the colonial peoples.

Once again, as in 1917, the Russian workers can inspire a revival of the revolutionary movement in America. And the politicalization of the American workers, which would be the first result, in turn would add all that is needed for the victory of socialism on an international scale. That, plus the other forces already maturing, would signify the end of capitalism and the beginning of the socialist reorganization of the world.

The perspectives before us are breathtaking. And they are not the perspectives of a dim and distant future, but of the epoch in which we live and struggle now. We should take heart, for we have great allies. The Russian workers, breaking out of the prison of Stalinism and taking the road of international revolutionary action once again; great China and the revolutionary movement of the whole colonial world; and the mighty working class of the United States and Europe—here in these three forces is the invincible "Triple Alliance" which can change the world and rule the world, and make it safe for freedom, peace and socialism.

The end of the Stalin cult, which is a part of the revolutionary development in the world, signifies the beginning of the vindication of Trotsky. His theory of revolutionary development is finding confirmation in world events in one country after another—and now, once again, in Russia. All that he foresaw and explained to us, his disciples, is being demonstrated in life as true. And we, who have fought long years under his banner, salute his glorious name again today. We are surer than ever that we have been right. We have more reason than ever to fight without compromise for the full program of Trotskyism. And we have more reason than ever for confidence in victory.

Our victory will be more than the victory of a faction

or a party—for the factional and party struggle is and has been the expression of the international struggle of classes. The vindication and victory of Trotskyism will coincide with, and fully express, the victory of the international working class in the struggle against the capitalist exploiters and the Stalinist traitors, for the socialist reorganization of the world.

**Chapter 11**

# Khrushchev's report to the Twentieth Congress

Delivered to a meeting at Channing Hall, Los Angeles, June 15, 1956.

Comrade Chairman; Comrades:

As the chairman has indicated, and as many of you know, a speech about the Soviet Union is not a new experience for me. In fact, I have been talking about it ever since 1917, and always from the same point of view.

I wish to begin my remarks tonight by restating the opinion I have held about the Soviet Union ever since it first arose out of the revolution thirty-nine years ago, and by presenting my credentials to talk once again about the great new things that have been happening there—to an audience which, I take it, is friendly, as I am, to the Soviet Union, and believes, as I do, that the interests and the destiny of the international working class are indissolubly bound up with the interests and destiny of the Soviet Union.

We Trotskyists regard the Russian Revolution of 1917 as the great dividing line in human history. Ascending world capitalism came to a halt there, met with its first defeat, and entered into its decline. The Russian Revolution signalized the real beginning of humanity's march to the higher and better order of socialism. All social progress in modern times dates from November 7, 1917.

We Trotskyists are internationalists. We have always regarded the Russian Revolution not as an end in itself, but as the starting point of the worldwide socialist revolution. For that reason, from that socialist internationalist standpoint, we have been partisans and defenders of the Soviet Union and the Russian Revolution which brought it into existence, ever since 1917.

Everything that has happened in the thirty-nine-year evolution of the Soviet Union has always had a burning interest for us from that internationalist socialist point of view. Everything we have said and done, either in praise or in criticism, in all the intervening time, has been governed by the single criterion: what is good for the revolution, for the defense of the Soviet Union, for the extension of the revolution throughout the world?

That was our criterion in defending the revolution in its first difficult years when the combined imperialist nations tried to strangle it in the cradle.

That was our criterion in 1928 when we first came out in support of the Left Opposition in the Russian party, in the internal struggle against the bureaucratic degeneration of the revolution under Stalin. The Left Opposition fought under the great slogans of soviet democracy, industrialization, and revolutionary internationalism. It stood for the defense of the Soviet Union by the policy of international class struggle.

We were governed by the same criterion, what is good

for the Soviet Union and for its extension throughout the world, in the thirties when we denounced the Moscow trials as frame-ups and protested against the physical extermination of the Old Bolsheviks who were the victims of those trials.

We bring the same criterion, the same basic point of view about the Soviet Union, to the present consideration of the new revelations now coming out of Moscow about the monstrous crimes of Stalin and Stalinism. We discuss them as partisans and defenders of the Soviet Union. I state that by way of introduction, to establish the theme of all I have to say tonight.

The news coming from the Twentieth Congress of the Communist Party of the Soviet Union represents progress in all respects.

In the first place, the economic reports show the tremendous development of the productive forces of the Soviet Union, including its military potential. Thanks to the revolution and the new social system of nationalized property and planned economy created and made possible by the revolution, the Soviet Union is no longer a backward country. In industrial development it stands second only to the United States, and its rate of productive development is greater than that of the United States.

In the second place, the Twentieth Congress occurred at a moment when the extension of the revolution, the abolition of capitalist property forms in Eastern Europe and in China, and the rising tide of the colonial revolution coincided with innumerable weaknesses and dislocations in the world capitalist front. This combination of circumstances has greatly improved the position of the Soviet Union in relation to the imperialist powers. Thanks to this extension of the revolution, the Soviet Union is no longer isolated and surrounded in a capitalist world.

In international relations today the Soviet Union obviously leads not from weakness but from strength. It is the strength of the Soviet Union that compelled the imperialist powers headed by the United States to pause before the reckless gamble of a military attack, which has been the central feature of their world program for a long time.

And finally, the events of the Twentieth Congress represent progress because a part of the truth of what has been going on inside the Soviet Union for a long time—to undermine it and endanger it—a part of the truth about that was revealed at the Twentieth Congress for the first time. Truth is always the ally of progress.

In the new revelations, and others that are yet to come, we see the distorted reflection in the top circles of the Soviet bureaucracy of a deep-going movement of the Soviet masses. We are witnessing a new stage in the development of the Russian Revolution, a progressive stage. The Soviet masses are beginning to stir. That's why the tops are shaking.

The wholesale denunciation and repudiation of Stalin, three years after he is safely dead, sensational and far-reaching as it is, marks only the beginning. The whole story of the monstrous crimes of Stalin and Stalinism has not yet been told. Far from it. But the heirs and accomplices of Stalin, by their preliminary revelations, have set in motion a process that they will never be able to control.

It will not stop until the full truth is known, and until every vestige of Stalinism in the Soviet Union has been swept away by the Soviet masses, and until this foul disease is eradicated from the international labor movement. The truth is on the march again and nothing can stop it. The truth is always progressive. The truth is revolutionary.

The subject of our discussion tonight is provided by the speech of Khrushchev at a closed session of the Twentieth Congress, February 24 and 25. The text of this speech was leaked to the diplomatic representatives of various foreign powers, and was freely referred to in the world press more than two months ago.

On June 4, the text of the speech of 26,000 words was issued to the press by the U.S. State Department. It was published in full in *The New York Times* the next day, and has brought no denial or repudiation from the Kremlin. The current issue of *The Militant,* which went to press a week ago and is now in your hands, carries the full text of Khrushchev's speech in a four-page supplement. And now the New York *Daily Worker,* in its weekend edition, has also printed the entire text, as released by the U.S. State Department, without in any way challenging its authenticity. So when we discuss the speech as it was printed in the various publications that I have named, we can safely assume we are discussing the speech, or at least part of the speech, as it was actually given.

The *Daily Worker* says it is publishing the speech as a contribution to the effort "to explore ways of uniting socialist-minded Americans and advancing socialist ideas." And then it adds: "We hope, too, that Communists, readers of our paper and other socialist-minded Americans will contribute their thinking on the problems confronting the Marxist movement in the discussion of this subject."

I agree with this sentiment expressed in the *Daily Worker.* I am assuming that the invitation to "other socialist-minded Americans" to join in the discussion also includes me, and

I hope I am not mistaken about that. My remarks tonight can be taken as a response to the invitation of the *Daily Worker*—although, to be perfectly frank with you, I freely admit that the preparations for this meeting had already been made before the weekend edition of the *Daily Worker* went to press, and I would very probably be making my speech anyway, even if the invitation to join the discussion had not been so kindly extended.

The *Daily Worker* sets a good theme for the discussion when it says in its editorial:

"The State Department is dead wrong when it suggests that the evils of the Stalin era are inherent in socialism. The fact is that the development of those evils created a peril for socialism. The repression, the injustice, the frame-ups, the torture, are a gross perversion of socialist principles."

That's what the weekend *Worker* said. I fully agree with that statement. That has always been our opinion and we see less reason than ever to change it now.

What is new and important in the Khrushchev report is that some of the crimes of Stalin against the Soviet Union, against the international working class, against socialism, are now admitted and confirmed by Stalin's most intimate collaborators, his handpicked disciples, who were accomplices in those very crimes. Khrushchev's report is the testimony of an expert. Khrushchev is the man who knows. He was there!

The long history of Stalinism and the struggle against it encompasses all the problems of the international labor movement for the past thirty-three years. Many articles, pamphlets and books—classics of Marxism—have been written in the course of this long struggle. It is the most important question in the world because it directly affects the struggle for socialism at every point. Many lectures would be required to cover this vast field. Here tonight I wish to single out and quote Khrushchev's testimony about Stalin's method of dealing with honest, revolutionary critics and opponents; how Stalin wiped out the whole generation of the companions of Lenin. That is the question that goes to the heart of all the other questions. It is the most terrible story in all history, for the companions of Lenin, whom Stalin murdered, were truly the advance guard of humanity. They were the noblest and the best history has yet seen. We weep for the slaughtered saints of the great revolution.

Three months ago, when the first reports of the Twentieth Congress came out, William Z. Foster, the national chairman of the Communist Party, tried to sweep the whole business under the rug. In a *Daily Worker* article, this old hack of Stalin's who has been applauding all Stalin's crimes for thirty years, came to Stalin's defense once again. That was three months ago. We haven't heard from him lately. But three months ago he told the young Communist Party members, who were alarmed about the reports, to take it easy and wait till we get the official word from Moscow. Stalin did a lot of good, he said; don't "tear him to political shreds." There might have been a few small mistakes, but nothing to get excited about. Then he asked, with an air of innocence—as if he didn't know—"Were injustices committed in the purges?"

Well, we now have the official word Foster said he was waiting for. I am now going to quote, chapter and verse, from Khrushchev's answer to Foster's question: "Were injustices committed in the purges?"

Remember, as I quote, that this is not Trotsky talking. It is Khrushchev, repeating what Trotsky said twenty years ago, before he was assassinated by an agent of Stalin.

I am reading now direct quotations from Khrushchev's speech:

> Stalin acted not through persuasion, explanation, and patient cooperation with people, but by imposing his concepts and demanding absolute submission to his opinion.
>
> Whoever opposed this concept or tried to prove his viewpoint, and the correctness of his position, was doomed to removal from the leading collective and to subsequent moral and physical annihilation.

So says Khrushchev. Again:

> Stalin originated the concept "enemy of the people." This term automatically rendered it unnecessary that the ideological errors of a man or men, engaged in a controversy, be proved; this term made possible the usage of the most cruel repression, violating all norms of revolutionary legality, against anyone who in any way disagreed with Stalin. . . .
>
> This concept "enemy of the people" actually eliminated the possibility of any kind of ideological fight, or the making of one's views known on this or that issue, even those of a practical character. In the main, and in actuality, the only proof of guilt used, against all norms of current legal science, was the "confession" of the accused himself; and, as subsequent probing proved, "confessions" were acquired through physical pressures against the accused.
>
> The formula "enemy of the people" was specifically introduced for the purpose of annihilating such individuals.
>
> It is a fact that many persons who were later annihilated as enemies of the party and people, had worked with Lenin during his life.

Khrushchev speaks of the purges, frame-up trials and false confessions again, as follows:

> Government and economic activists who were branded in 1937–1938 as "enemies" were actually never enemies, spies, wreckers, etc., but were always honest Communists.
>
> They were only so stigmatized, and often, no longer able to bear barbaric tortures, they charged themselves (at the order of the investigative judges—falsifiers) with all kinds of grave and unlikely crimes. . . .

And how were the false confessions obtained? Here again I quote directly from Khrushchev's report:

> Now when the cases of some of these so-called "spies" and "saboteurs" were examined, it was found that all their cases were fabricated. Confessions of guilt of many, arrested and charged with enemy activity, were gained with the help of cruel and inhuman tortures.

Khrushchev doesn't rest with general statements. He gives a number of specific examples which you can read for yourself in the printed text of his speech.

"But they confessed, didn't they?" We heard that over and over again when we were fighting against the Moscow trials in 1936 and 1937. Day after day the *Daily Worker* boasted triumphantly: "They confessed, didn't they? That proves they're guilty." And here's what their confessions were worth, according to Khrushchev:

> How is it possible that a person confesses to crimes which he has not committed? Only in one way—because of application of physical methods of pressuring him,

tortures, bringing him to a state of unconsciousness, deprivation of his judgment, taking away of his human dignity. In this manner were "confessions" acquired.

What I have just quoted from Khrushchev's speech is only a small part of Khrushchev's testimony, which you can read for yourself, and his whole testimony tells only a small part of the whole truth.

These terrifying revelations which have come out of the Twentieth Congress of the Communist Party of the Soviet Union raises questions which every honest communist is asking, and they're asking them today at every meeting of the Communist Party where they have a chance.

One, how was such a monstrous regime of frame-up and murder possible in the Soviet Union, created by a workers' revolution which was led by the most honest, the most truly democratic party in all history?

Two, who, if anybody, opposed this degeneration and spoke out against it, and what happened to them?

And three, the $64,000 question, which all those who have been duped by the official Communist Party press are asking: Why weren't we told this before?

Khrushchev's answer to this last question, "Why weren't we told before?" is not so much an answer as an excuse: it was dangerous to speak, he said; they were afraid for their lives. But since when do revolutionists tell the truth only when it is safe? What has become of the principle that a revolutionist must tell the truth to the people under all circumstances, as the Bolsheviks did under the Czar? It is always dangerous to oppose a tyranny and tell the truth about it. It was dangerous for the Bolsheviks in Czarist times, but that didn't stop them. They told the truth just the same, at the cost of imprisonment and death for many of them—and they organized an underground movement that eventually led the greatest revolution in all history.

There were people in the Soviet Union who recognized the danger of Stalin and Stalinism from the very beginning. They told the truth about it too, and they led the fight against it from the beginning, in 1923, thirty-three years ago. The organizers of the fight against Stalinism were the very same people who organized and led the October Revolution in 1917. The first one to denounce Stalin in writing and to demand his removal, was Lenin. And the second was Trotsky. The same two men who led the great revolution, led the fight against its bureaucratic degeneration under Stalin.

On his sickbed, December 25, 1922, Lenin wrote his testament to the party. In this testament of Lenin, he said: "Comrade Stalin, having become general secretary, has concentrated an enormous power in his hands; and I am not sure that he always knows how to use that power with sufficient caution." That was the first warning of Lenin, dated December 25, 1922.

While Lenin lay helpless in his last illness, Stalin was moving to consolidate his power, and Lenin became alarmed. Then on January 4, 1923, a couple of weeks later, he added a postscript to his testament. And here is what he wrote:

"Postscript: Stalin is too rude, and this fault, entirely supportable in relations among us Communists, becomes insupportable in the office of general secretary. Therefore, I propose to the comrades to find a way to remove Stalin from that position and appoint to it another man who in all respects differs from Stalin only in superiority—namely, more patient, more loyal, more polite and more attentive to comrades, less capricious, etc."

So wrote Lenin in his testament to the party.

Lenin, struggling with death, appealed to Trotsky at that time and offered to make a bloc with him to fight the growing bureaucratism in the party and in the state machine. Trotsky agreed. In the last months of Lenin's life they made a bloc to fight the bureaucratic degeneration. Lenin died in January 1924, without ever having been able to return to his duties throughout the preceding year. Trotsky carried on the fight.

That's the true explanation of how the struggle against Stalinism was started in the Soviet Union. It is all coming out now. It is all documented from the beginning, from the very beginning up to the latest events, and cannot be suppressed any longer.

It is not true, comrades, it is not true, as Khrushchev represents, that nobody dared to speak out against Stalin. Lenin and Trotsky spoke out. The Old Bolsheviks spoke out. It was dangerous, but they conducted the struggle just the same, as was their revolutionary duty, and they paid for it with their lives. Trotsky was assassinated in 1940 because he had told the truth about Stalin, and for no other reason. And tens of thousands of the Old Bolsheviks were slaughtered in the Soviet Union because they spoke out against Stalinism, and for no other reason.

The revolutionary struggle against Stalinism has been the greatest political and ideological struggle in all history, and it has left the richest documentary record. The truth is in that literary record—in books and pamphlets and innumerable articles and mimeographed bulletins. It is a great treasury of Marxist thought, and all who want to know the truth must study it conscientiously.

If Khrushchev & Co. were opposed to the Stalinist regime, and could not speak out openly against it because of the terror, why didn't they organize an underground movement and leave a printed record of their opposition which could be referred to now? They never made such a record and they have nothing to refer to, because they were not revolutionists, they were not opponents of the regime which they now condemn. The truth is that they were the handpicked accomplices of Stalin, and they owe their careers and their privileges to him and his regime. They want to blame everything now on Stalin as an individual. There is nothing Marxist in such an explanation of any social regime.

The fact is that the Stalin regime, like every other, had a social basis. Stalin was the representative of the Soviet bureaucracy. Many people, including Khrushchev & Co., enjoyed rich benefits and privileges under the rule of Stalin. They grew prosperous and sleek and fat under Stalin. They drove automobiles and lived in summer cottages and enjoyed all the fruits of the labor of the heroic Russian working class. They were the ones who supported Stalin, and they were well satisfied with his regime. And they supported it in all its crimes.

The privileged beneficiaries of the Stalin regime numbered millions in the Soviet Union. It was not one man alone; there were millions tied to that regime and prospering under it. They were a small minority of the Soviet population, but still they numbered millions. This privileged minority formed the social basis of the Stalin regime.

Khrushchev's explanation explains nothing about what really happened. The bureaucrats' method today is the same as their method yesterday, turned upside down. Yesterday, Stalin was pictured as the infallible, benevolent leader who could do no wrong, who was responsible for all progress and all victories in the Soviet Union in peace and in war. Today, the same Stalin is presented as a paranoiac criminal who was personally responsible for all mistakes, who brought the Soviet Union to the brink of ruin—all by himself.

The great man theory is replaced by the devil theory.

The devil is dead, but the privileged bureaucrats still live. They remain in power in the Soviet Union, and don't you forget that. And their sole concern is to stay in power and hang on to their privileges at the expense of the working masses in the Soviet Union, who are our concern.

Why do these bureaucrats speak out now, three years after the death of Stalin, and begin to tell a part of the truth about that terrible regime? Is it because they have suddenly turned honest and are no longer afraid? Some people are asking you to believe that, but they are liars and deceivers. There have been some concessions and some reforms—no question about that—but there has been no basic change in the bureaucratic regime of special privileges for a minority and hard times for the majority, established under Stalin. The bureaucracy still has all the privileges. The workers have no rights and no freedom, and anybody who says they do, lies. There is no such thing as a free worker in the Soviet Union under Khrushchev any more than there was under Stalin. That is yet to come. The workers have to get that freedom for themselves.

I think many of you who are present in this hall know the name of I.F. Stone, the distinguished journalist who used to write for the *New York Compass* and the *New York Post*. I.F. Stone has a great reputation for integrity as a journalist, justly earned. He went over to Russia after the Twentieth Congress to take a look for himself. And because he has always been known as an honest liberal and a friend of the Soviet Union, many people were expecting and hoping that he would send back a favorable and perhaps a whitewash report that everything is lovely now.

He looked around and summed up his impressions in one sentence. For the benefit of people who want to deceive themselves that everything has been changed in the Soviet Union, I.F. Stone simply said: "This is not a good regime, and it is not run by honest men."

No, Khrushchev & Co. are the same bureaucrats, the same cynical careerists they were when they served Stalin and climbed into high office over a mound of corpses, the corpses of better men than they are. They have not turned honest and they are still afraid. But they are afraid now, not of the dead Stalin, but of the living wrath of the Soviet masses, who have been so long oppressed and who have begun to rise against their oppression.

The irresistible pressure of the Soviet workers was the power behind the Twentieth Congress. That, comrades, is the key to an understanding of what is taking place. The bureaucrats assembled at that congress had had warning signals of a coming storm, and they began to respond to these signals. The uprising of the East German workers in June 1953, that was followed a month later by a general strike of the Vorkuta slave-labor camp—those tremendous actions under the guns of police-state terror, when workers took their lives in their hands to strike, gave notice of a coming revolutionary storm, just as the general-strike movement of the Russian workers in 1905 gave notice of the first revolution against the Czar.

Khrushchev & Co. want to exculpate themselves. They want to throw off the blame and escape the consequences of the people's hatred and the people's wrath. I do not say this to minimize the importance of what was said and done at the Twentieth Congress, or to pass it off as if nothing had happened. No. Great things indeed are happening in the Soviet Union these days. And their importance becomes magnified if we see them in their true light, as a reflection, a distorted reflection in the top circles of the privileged bureaucracy of a profound movement from below, a movement of the oppressed Soviet workers, a revolutionary movement for the overthrow of the privileged bureaucracy and the restoration of Soviet democracy.

That's what the Soviet workers mean when they say: "Back to Lenin." That was the slogan of the Left Opposition in the twenties and thirties. That was the slogan of the Vorkuta strike in 1953, and that's the slogan of the Soviet workers today. No wonder the bureaucrats assembled at the Twentieth Congress gave three cheers for the slogan "Back to Lenin." "Back to Lenin" is nothing less than what the Soviet workers really demand, but they demand the substance and not merely the form.

We put all our faith in this revolutionary movement of the Soviet workers and no faith whatever in the good intentions of the bureaucratic heirs of Stalin. I think the best way to muddle up the discussion of the new events, and the worst crime against the truth in the discussion opening up now, is to say that the Soviet bureaucrats have already reformed themselves or are in the process of doing so, that they have "mellowed" and that all they need is to be left alone to bring about a gradual elimination of all the hated features of Stalinism and the restoration of a democratic workers' regime.

If they are trusted and left alone everything will remain basically the same. These bureaucrats are the privileged upper crust. They will never give up their privileges voluntarily. They have to be overthrown like every other privileged group in history had to be overthrown. Trotsky said on this subject twenty years ago, in his great book, *The Revolution Betrayed*, "No devil ever yet voluntarily cut off his own claws."

We can be confident that the Russian masses will not let them alone to reform themselves, and that the changes now taking place in the Soviet Union represent not the end, but the beginning of a revolutionary transformation which will sweep out the last remnants of Stalinism. The political revolution against the privileged bureaucrats has nothing in common with the imperialists' hopes for a capitalist counterrevolution. That's not on the order of the day in the Soviet Union. The political revolution will not bring the return of capitalism. On the contrary, in the final analysis, the political revolution is the one sure way to prevent the return of capitalism in the Soviet Union.

That's the way Trotsky explained it twenty years ago in the book I have mentioned. His theoretical exposition has burning actuality for all of us who want to follow this question in its further development in these days.

Now, if we give Khrushchev no credit for his claim that he and his associates did not tell the truth before because they were afraid for their lives, what shall we say about the leaders of the American Communist Party, who hid the truth about the Stalin regime from their own party members and from the readers of their press, and defended all its monstrous crimes at the top of their voices all these many years? What were they afraid of? The most they stood to lose was their positions, and their false importance as little Stalins.

To be sure, if they had told the truth they would have been slandered, they would have been expelled. They would have been denounced as fascist spies and counterrevolutionists. But it's possible to survive all that if you have some integrity and some courage. We have proved that—for twenty-eight years.

The skins of the American Stalinist leaders, whatever they may be worth, were never in very great danger. The only thing they were afraid of was the truth, because the truth would have demolished all their claims to leadership. What I.F. Stone said about the Khrushchev regime can be said of the so-called Communist Party leadership in this country: this is not a good regime, and it is not run by honest men. That's a growing conviction in the rank and file of the CP, growing so strong that you even see it printed in the *Daily Worker* letters column. They get so many letters stating this opinion that they have to print some of them.

I want to make it very clear that I am talking now about the official leaders of the Communist Party, and not about the honest communist workers whom they duped and deceived and betrayed. The American Stalinist leaders are now apparently proceeding on the theory that confession is not only good for the soul, but also that it wipes out all responsibility for the crimes confessed. You merely have to say that you made a "mistake" and then everything is cleared up. They now admit that they were wrong all the time, and pat themselves on the back for their "self-criticism"—as if that rights all the wrong. "We were wrong," they say. "We defended all the crimes and all the lies of Stalin and Stalinism. We cheered for all the frame-ups and all the murders of honest revolutionists. We denounced all who protested against the frame-ups and murders as counterrevolutionists and fascist spies. Our careers were built on lies. We are sorry. Now let's all get together and trust each other." That's the sum and substance of the propaganda of the leaders of the Communist Party since the Twentieth Congress in Moscow.

At more than one meeting of the Communist Party in recent days, CP members and sympathizers who have been duped and deceived so long, have asked the question: "How can we now trust anything you say?" My opinion is that you can, but you shouldn't. When these careerist leaders of the Communist Party try to make a virtue of their claim that "they are now correcting their mistakes," merely by admitting some of them, they ought to be asked the simple question which was asked of a Stalinist speaker at a trade-union conference in England. The trade unionist asked the Stalinist speaker, who had been explaining that they had made mistakes but were now correcting them: "How do you correct such a mistake as the frame-up and murder of innocent people?" The account I read didn't give the answer of the Stalinist speaker. I don't know what he said, but I imagine it would be very hard to answer.

You can be sure that in every discussion looking toward the regroupment and reconstruction of an honest movement of revolutionary socialists in this country we will be on hand to ask just such questions as that. And many more questions, equally inconvenient for people who want to wipe a sponge over all the crimes of the past and pretend that the slate is now clean, that there is no more blood on it.

The new program the American Stalinists are offering, as far as I can make out—I have been reading it in the *Daily Worker* and to a certain extent in the *People's World*— is nothing but Stalinism without Stalin, and Browderism without Browder. That's no good. And they make it worse when they drag in the name of Lenin. You can't say "Back to Lenin" and "Forward to the Democratic Party." Or rather, you can say both, but you can't do both, at the same time. These two slogans run in opposite directions.

We, for our part, can't join the Democratic Party because we are revolutionary socialists, not bourgeois democrats. This Democratic Party is a capitalist party. I knew that much when I was sixteen years old. I heard it explained by Eugene V. Debs fifty years ago. The Democratic Party is a capitalist party representing the interests of the bankers, the monopolists and the Dixiecrats. Isn't that true? Well, let the bankers and the monopolists and the Dixiecrats have it. That's what we say. Let them have it, and let the workers organize a class party of their own. That was Lenin's idea. Anyone who wants to go back to Lenin can't escape the fact that

Lenin insisted, first of all and above all, on a class party of the workers. He didn't ask them to join Miliukov's party of "Constitutional Democrats" in Russia, which was just as good as the Democratic Party of banker Harriman, Stevenson and Eastland in the United States. He said, "Organize a workers party to overthrow this Miliukov gang!" And even before Lenin, Karl Marx over a hundred years ago said the workers must have a class party of their own.

We are heartily in favor of a full and free discussion among all people and all tendencies friendly to the Soviet Union and professing devotion to the socialist idea. We hope and believe that out of such a discussion—a full and free and unregulated discussion—can come a new understanding among honest, socialist-minded workers, a new solidarity, so long disrupted by Stalinism, and a regroupment in an honest party of American socialism.

We Trotskyists are ready and willing to contribute our part to bring about this new understanding and this new solidarity in a common struggle for a common cause. We don't demand that anybody take our word for it. We don't demand that anybody accept what we say out of hand. We are ready to listen as well as to speak, to learn as well as to teach. But, after all the years of wholesale lying, misrepresentation and bureaucratic violence brought into the movement by Stalinism, let us have now, for the first time in thirty years, a really free and honest discussion! Let us have old-fashioned open forums and fair debates where all points of view are fairly heard. Let us put all questions on the table and hear all points of view. Let the articles, pamphlets and books of all sides be studied conscientiously. Let us agree to search together for the truth that will make us free—the truth, the whole truth, and nothing but the truth.

And finally, let us search for the truth with free and

independent minds, as befits revolutionists, each one thinking for himself, and nobody taking anybody's word for it. That was the advice of Lenin, long ago. That was the way he trained his Bolsheviks to think independently, to know all sides of the subject, to make up their minds on the basis of independent inquiry. That was the advice of Lenin put in specific words which we printed in the first issue of *The Militant* when we began our struggle against Stalinism twenty-eight years ago, in November 1928. Lenin's advice still holds good today, and it reads as follows, as we printed it on the masthead of the first issue of our *Militant:*

*"It is necessary that every member of the party should study calmly, and with the greatest objectivity, first the substance of the differences of opinion, and then the development of the struggles within the party. Neither the one nor the other can be done unless the documents of both sides are published. He who takes somebody's word for it is a hopeless idiot, who can be disposed of with a simple gesture of the hand."*

So said Lenin. Take nobody's word for it! Think for yourself! Study all points of view calmly and with the greatest objectivity! So said Lenin.

Let that advice of Lenin be the motto for the new discussion in the ranks of radical workers in this country. And by that method of Lenin let us strive for a new understanding, and a new solidarity, and a new regroupment of all honest, socialist-minded workers in a common struggle for a socialist America.

Trotsky Memorial Meeting, New York, August 28, 1940. Behind Cannon on platform is Dr. Antoinette Konikow.

# Chapter 12

# Leon Trotsky: To the memory of the Old Man

Delivered to the Leon Trotsky Memorial Meeting at the Hotel Diplomat, New York City, August 28, 1940.

Comrade Trotsky's entire conscious life, from the time he entered the workers' movement in the provincial Russian town of Nikolaiev at the age of eighteen up till the moment of his death in Mexico City forty-two years later, was completely dedicated to work and struggle for one central idea. He stood for the emancipation of the workers and all the oppressed people of the world, and the transformation of society from capitalism to socialism by means of a social revolution. In his conception, this liberating social revolution requires for success the leadership of a revolutionary political party of the workers' vanguard.

In his entire conscious life Comrade Trotsky never once diverged from that idea. He never doubted it, and never ceased to struggle for its realization. On his deathbed, in his last message to us, his disciples—his last testament—he proclaimed his confidence in his life-idea: "Tell our friends I am sure of the victory of the Fourth International—Go Forward!"

The whole world knows about his work and his testament. The cables of the press of the world have carried his last testament and made it known to the world's millions. And in the minds and hearts of all those throughout the world who grieve with us tonight one thought—one question—is uppermost: Will the movement which he created and inspired survive his death? Will his disciples be able to hold their ranks together, will they be able to carry out his testament and realize the emancipation of the oppressed through the victory of the Fourth International?

Without the slightest hesitation we give an affirmative answer to this question. Those enemies who predict a collapse of Trotsky's movement without Trotsky, and those weak-willed friends who fear it, only show that they do not understand Trotsky, what he was, what he signified and what he left behind. Never has a bereaved family been left such a rich heritage as that which Comrade Trotsky, like a provident father, has left to the family of the Fourth International as trustees for all progressive humanity. A great heritage of ideas he has left to us; ideas which shall chart the struggle toward the great free future of all mankind. The mighty ideas of Trotsky are our program and our banner. They are a clear guide to action in all the complexities of our epoch, and a constant reassurance that we are right and that our victory is inevitable.

Trotsky himself believed that ideas are the greatest power in the world. Their authors may be killed, but ideas, once promulgated, live their own life. If they are correct ideas, they make their way through all obstacles. This was the central, dominating concept of Comrade Trotsky's philosophy. He explained it to us many, many times. He once wrote: "It is not the party that makes the program [the idea]; it is the program that makes the party." In a personal letter to me, he once wrote: "We work with the most correct and powerful ideas in the world, with inadequate numerical forces and material means. But correct ideas, in the long run, always conquer and make available for themselves the necessary material means and forces."

Trotsky, a disciple of Marx, believed with Marx that "an idea, when it permeates the mass, becomes a material force." Believing that, Comrade Trotsky never doubted that his work would live after him. Believing that, he could proclaim on his deathbed his confidence in the future victory of the Fourth International which embodies his ideas. Those who doubt it, do not know Trotsky.

Trotsky himself believed that his greatest significance, his greatest value, consisted not in his physical life, not in his epic deeds, which overshadow those of all heroic figures in history in their sweep and their grandeur—but in what he would leave behind him after the assassins had done their work. He knew that his doom was sealed, and he worked against time in order to leave everything possible to us, and through us to mankind. Throughout the eleven years of his last exile he chained himself to his desk like a galley slave and labored, as none of us knows how to labor, with such energy, such persistence and self-discipline, as only men of genius can labor. He worked against time to pour out through his pen the whole rich content of his mighty brain and preserve it in permanent written form for us, and for those who will come after us.

The whole Trotsky, like the whole Marx, is preserved in his books, his articles and his letters. His voluminous correspondence, which contains some of his brightest thoughts and his most intimate personal feelings and sentiments, must now be collected and published. When that is done, when his letters are published alongside his books, his pamphlets and his articles, we, and all those who join us in the liberation struggle of humanity, will still have our Old Man to help us.

He knew that the super-Borgia in the Kremlin, Cain-Stalin, who has destroyed the whole generation of the October Revolution, had marked him for assassination and would succeed sooner or later. That is why he worked so urgently. That is why he hastened to write out everything that was in his mind and get it down on paper in permanent form where nobody could destroy it.

Just the other night, I talked at the dinner table with one of the Old Man's faithful secretaries—a young comrade who had served him a long time and knew his personal life, as he lived it in his last years of exile, most intimately. I urged him to write his reminiscences without delay. I said: "We must all write everything we know about Trotsky. Everyone must record his recollections and his impressions. We must not forget that we moved in the orbit of the greatest figure of our time. Millions of people, generations yet to come, will be hungry for every scrap of information, every word, every impression that throws light on him, his ideas, his aims and his personal life."

He answered: "I can write only about his personal qualities as I observed them; his methods of work, his humaneness, his generosity. But I can't write anything new about his ideas. They are already written. Everything he had to say, everything he had in his brain, is down on paper. He seemed to be determined to scoop down to the bottom of his mind, and take out everything and give it to the world in his writings. Very often, I remember, casual conversation on some subject would come up at the dinner table; an informal discussion would take place, and the Old Man would express some opinions new and fresh.

Almost invariably the contributions of the dinner-table conversation would find expression a little later in a book, an article or a letter."

They killed Trotsky not by one blow; not when this murderer, the agent of Stalin, drove the pickax through the back of his skull. That was only the final blow. They killed him by inches. They killed him many times. They killed him seven times when they killed his seven secretaries. They killed him four times when they killed his four children. They killed him when his old coworkers of the Russian Revolution were killed.

Yet he stood up to his tasks in spite of all that. Growing old and sick, he staggered through all these moral, emotional and physical blows to complete his testament to humanity while he still had time. He gathered it all together—every thought, every idea, every lesson from his past experience—to lay up a literary treasure for us, a treasure that the moths and the rust cannot eat.

There was a profound difference between Trotsky and other great men of action and transitory political leaders who influenced great masses in their lifetime. The power of such people, almost all of them, was something personal, something incommunicable to others. Their influence did not survive their deaths. Just recall for a moment the great men of our generation or the generation just passed: Clemenceau, Hindenburg, Wilson, Theodore Roosevelt, Bryan. They had great masses following them and leaning upon them. But now they are dead; and all their influence died with them. Nothing remains but monuments and funeral eulogies. Nothing was distinctive about them but their personalities. They were opportunists, leaders for a day. They left no ideas to guide and inspire men when their bodies became dust, and their personalities became a memory.

Not so with Trotsky. Not so with him. He was different. He was also a great man of action, to be sure. His deeds are incorporated in the greatest revolution in the history of mankind. But, unlike the opportunists and leaders of a day, his deeds were inspired by great ideas, and these ideas still live. He not only made a revolution; he wrote its history and explained the basic laws which govern all revolutions. In his History of the Russian Revolution, which he considered his masterpiece, he gave us a guide for the making of new revolutions, or rather, for extending throughout the world the revolution that began in October 1917.

Trotsky, the great man of ideas, was himself the disciple of a still greater one—Marx. Trotsky did not originate or claim to originate the most fundamental ideas which he expounded. He built on the foundations laid by the great masons of the nineteenth century—Marx and Engels. In addition, he went through the great school of Lenin and learned from him. Trotsky's genius consisted in his complete assimilation of the ideas bequeathed by Marx, Engels and Lenin. He mastered their method. He developed their ideas in modern conditions, and applied them in masterful fashion in the contemporary struggle of the proletariat.

If you would understand Trotsky, you must know that he was a disciple of Marx, an orthodox Marxist. He fought under the banner of Marxism for forty-two years! During the last year of his life he laid everything else aside to fight a great political and theoretical battle in defense of Marxism in the ranks of the Fourth International! His very last article, which was left on his desk in unpolished form, the last article with which he occupied himself, was a defense of Marxism against contemporary revisionists and skeptics. The power of Trotsky, first of all and above all, was the power of Marxism.

Do you want a concrete illustration of the power of Marxist ideas? Just consider this: when Marx died in 1883, Trotsky was but four years old. Lenin was only fourteen. Neither could have known Marx, or anything about him. Yet both became great historical figures because of Marx, because Marx had circulated ideas in the world before they were born. Those ideas were living their own life. They shaped the lives of Lenin and Trotsky. Marx's ideas were with them and guided their every step when they made the greatest revolution in history.

So will the ideas of Trotsky, which are a development of the ideas of Marx, influence us, his disciples, who survive him today. They will shape the lives of far greater disciples who are yet to come, who do not yet know Trotsky's name. Some who are destined to be the greatest Trotskyists are playing in the schoolyards today. They will be nourished on Trotsky's ideas, as he and Lenin were nourished on the ideas of Marx and Engels.

Indeed, our movement in the United States took shape and grew up on his ideas without his physical presence, without even any communication in the first period. Trotsky was exiled and isolated in Alma Ata when we began our struggle for Trotskyism in this country in 1928. We had no contact with him, and for a long time did not know whether he was dead or alive. We didn't even have a collection of his writings. All we had was one single current document—his "Criticism of the Draft Program of the Comintern." That was enough. By the light of that single document we saw our way, began our struggle with supreme confidence, went through the split without faltering, built the framework of a national organization and established our weekly Trotskyist press. Our movement was built firmly from the very beginning and has remained firm because it was built on Trotsky's ideas. It was nearly a year before we were able to establish direct communication with the Old Man.

So with the sections of the Fourth International throughout the world. Only a very few individual comrades have ever met Trotsky face to face. Yet everywhere they knew him. In China, and across the broad oceans to Chile, Argentina, Brazil. In Australia, in practically every country of Europe. In the United States, Canada, Indochina, South Africa. They never saw him, but the ideas of Trotsky welded them all together in one uniform and firm world movement. So it will continue after his physical death. There is no room for doubt.

Trotsky's place in history is already established. He will stand forever on a historical eminence beside the other three great giants of the proletariat: Marx, Engels and Lenin. It is possible, indeed it is quite probable, that in the historic memory of mankind, his name will evoke the warmest affection, the most heartfelt gratitude of all. Because he fought so long, against such a world of enemies, so honestly, so heroically, and with such selfless devotion!

Future generations of free humanity will look back with insatiable interest on this mad epoch of reaction and bloody violence and social change—this epoch of the death agony of one social system and the birth pangs of another. When they see through the historian's lens how the oppressed masses of the people everywhere were groping, blinded and confused, they will mention with unbounded love the name of the genius who gave us light, the great heart that gave us courage.

Of all the great men of our time, of all the public figures to whom the masses turned for guidance in these troubled terrible times, Trotsky alone explained things to us, he alone gave us light in the darkness. His brain alone unraveled the mysteries and complexities of our epoch. The great brain of Trotsky was what was feared by all his enemies. They couldn't cope with it. They couldn't answer it. In the incredibly horrible method by which they destroyed him there was hidden a deep symbol. They struck at his brain! But the richest products of that brain are still alive. They had already escaped and can never be recaptured and destroyed.

We do not minimize the blow that has been dealt to us, to our movement and to the world. It is the worst calamity. We have lost something of immeasurable value that can never be regained. We have lost the inspiration of his physical presence, his wise counsel. All that is lost forever. The Russian people have suffered the most terrible blow of all. But by the very fact that the Stalinist camarilla had to kill Trotsky after eleven years, that they had to reach out from Moscow, exert all their energies and plans to destroy the life of Trotsky—that is the greatest testimony that Trotsky still lived in the hearts of the Russian people. They didn't believe the lies. They waited and hoped for his return. His words are still there. His memory is alive in their hearts.

Just a few days before the death of Comrade Trotsky the editors of the Russian Bulletin received a letter from Riga. It had been mailed before the incorporation of Latvia into the Soviet Union. It stated in simple words that Trotsky's "Open Letter to the Workers of the USSR" had reached them, and had lifted up their hearts with courage and shown them the way. The letter stated that the message of Trotsky had been memorized, word by word, and would be passed along by word of mouth no matter what might happen. We verily believe that the words of Trotsky will live longer in the Soviet Union than the bloody regime of Stalin. In the coming great day of liberation the message of Trotsky will be the banner of the Russian people.

The whole world knows who killed Comrade Trotsky. The world knows that on his deathbed he accused Stalin and his GPU of the murder. The assassin's statement, prepared in advance of the crime, is the final proof, if more proof is needed, that the murder was a GPU job. It is a mere reiteration of the lies of the Moscow trials; a stupid police-minded attempt, at this late day, to rehabilitate the frame-ups which have been discredited in the eyes of the whole world. The motives for the assassination arose from the world reaction, the fear of revolution, and the traitors' sentiments of hatred and revenge. The English historian Macaulay remarked that apostates in all ages have manifested an exceptional malignity toward those whom they have betrayed. Stalin and his traitor gang were consumed by a mad hatred of the man who reminded them of their yesterday. Trotsky, the symbol of the great revolution, reminded them constantly of the cause they had deserted and betrayed, and they hated him for that. They hated him for all the great and good human qualities which he personified and to which they were completely alien. They were determined, at all cost, to do away with him.

Now I come to a part that is very painful, a thought which, I am sure, is in the minds of all of us. The moment we read of the success of the attack I am sure everyone among us asked: couldn't we have saved him a while longer? If we had tried harder, if we had done more for him—couldn't we have saved him? Dear comrades, let us not reproach ourselves. Comrade Trotsky was doomed and sentenced to death years ago. The betrayers of the revolution knew that the revolution lived in him, the tradition, the hope. All the resources of a powerful state, set in motion by the hatred and revenge of Stalin, were directed to the assassination of a single man without resources and with only a handful of close followers. All of his coworkers were killed; seven of his faithful secretaries; his four children. Yet, in spite of the fact that they marked him for death after his exile from Russia, we saved him for eleven years! Those were the most fruitful years of his whole life. Those were the years when he sat down in full maturity to devote himself to the task of summing up and casting in permanent literary form the results of his experiences and his thoughts.

Their dull police minds cannot know that Trotsky left the best of himself behind. Even in death he frustrated them. Because the thing they wanted most of all to kill—the memory and the hope of revolution—that Trotsky left behind him.

If you reproach yourself or us because this murder machine finally reached Trotsky and struck him down, you must remember that it is very hard to protect anyone from assassins. The assassin who stalks his victim night and day very often breaks through the greatest protections. Even Russian Czars and other rulers, surrounded by all the police powers of great states, could not always escape assassination by small bands of determined terrorists equipped with the most meager resources. This was the case more than once in Russia in the prerevolutionary days. And here, in the case of Trotsky, you had all that in reverse. All the resources were on the side of the assassins. A great state apparatus, converted into a murder machine, against one man and a few devoted disciples. So if they finally broke through, we have only to ask ourselves, did we do all we could to prevent it or postpone it? Yes, we did our best. In all conscience, we must say we did our best.

In the last weeks after the assault of May 24, we once again put on the agenda of our leading committee the question of the protection of Comrade Trotsky. Every comrade agreed that this is our most important task, most important for the masses of the whole world and for the future generations, that above all we do everything in our power to protect the life of our genius, our comrade, who helped and guided us so well. A delegation of party leaders made a visit to Mexico. It turned out to be our last visit. There, on that occasion, in consultation with him, we agreed upon a new campaign to strengthen the guard. We collected money in this country to fortify the house at the cost of thousands of dollars; all our members and sympathizers responded with great sacrifices and generosity.

And still the murder-machine broke through. But those who helped even in the smallest degree, either financially or with their physical efforts, like our brave young comrades of the guard, will never be sorry for what they did to protect and help the Old Man.

At the hour Comrade Trotsky was finally struck down, I was returning by train from a special journey to Minneapolis. I had gone there for the purpose of arranging for new and especially qualified comrades to go down and strengthen the guard in Coyoacan. On the way home I sat in the railroad train with a feeling of satisfaction that the task of the trip had been accomplished, reinforcements of the guard had been provided for.

Then, as the train passed through Pennsylvania, about four o'clock in the morning, they brought the early papers with the news that the assassin had broken through the defenses and driven a pickax into the brain of Comrade Trotsky. That was the beginning of a terrible day, the saddest day of our lives, when we waited, hour by hour, while the Old Man fought his last fight and struggled vainly with death. But even then, in that hour of terrible grief, when we received the fatal message over the long-distance telephone: "The Old Man is dead"—even then, we didn't permit ourselves to stop for weeping. We plunged immediately into the work to defend his memory and carry out his testament. And we worked harder than ever before, because for the first time we realized with full consciousness that we have to do it all now. We can't lean on the Old Man anymore. What is done now, we must do. That is the spirit in which we have got to work from now on.

The capitalist masters of the world instinctively understood the meaning of the name of Trotsky. The friend of the oppressed, the maker of revolutions, was the incarnation of all that they hated and feared! Even in death they revile him. Their newspapers splash their filth over his name. He was the world's exile in the time of reaction. No door was open to him anywhere except that of the Republic of Mexico. The fact that Trotsky was barred from all capitalist countries is in itself the clearest refutation of all the slanders of the Stalinists, of all their foul accusations that he betrayed the revolution, that he had turned against the workers. They never convinced the capitalist world of that. Not for a moment.

The capitalists—all kinds—fear and hate even his dead body! The doors of our great democracy are open to many political refugees, of course. All sorts of reactionaries; democratic scoundrels who betrayed and deserted their people; monarchists and even fascists—they have all been welcomed in New York harbor. But not even the dead body of the friend of the oppressed could find asylum here! We shall not forget that! We shall nourish that grievance close to our hearts and in good time we shall take our revenge.

The great and powerful democracy of Roosevelt and Hull wouldn't let us bring his body here for the funeral. But he is here just the same. All of us feel that he is here in this hall tonight—not only in his great ideas, but also, especially tonight, in our memory of him as a man. We have a right to be proud that the best man of our time belonged to us, the greatest brain and strongest and most loyal heart. The class society we live in exalts the rascals, cheats, self-seekers, liars and oppressors of the people. You can hardly name an intellectual representative of the decaying class society, of high or low degree, who is not a miserable hypocrite and contemptible coward, concerned first of all with his own inconsequential personal affairs and saving his own worthless skin. What a wretched tribe they are. There is no honesty, no inspiration, nothing in the whole of them. They have not a single man that can strike a spark in the heart of youth. Our Old Man was made of better stuff. Our Old Man was made of entirely different stuff. He towered above these pygmies in his moral grandeur.

Comrade Trotsky not only struggled for a new social order based on human solidarity as a future goal; he lived every day of his life according to its higher and nobler standards. They wouldn't let him be a citizen of any country. But, in truth, he was much more than that. He was already, in his mind and in his conduct, a citizen of the communist future of humanity. That memory of him as a man, as a comrade, is more precious than gold and rubies. We can hardly understand a man of that type living among us. We are all caught in the steel net of the class society with its inequalities, its contradictions, its conventionalities, its false values, its lies. The class society poisons and corrupts everything. We are all dwarfed and twisted and blinded by it. We can hardly visualize what human relations will be, we can hardly comprehend what the personality of man will be, in a free society.

Comrade Trotsky gave us an anticipatory picture. In him, in his personality as a man, as a human being, we caught a glimpse of the communist man that is to be.

This memory of him as a man, as a comrade, is our greatest assurance that the spirit of man, striving for human solidarity, is unconquerable. In our terrible epoch many things will pass away. Capitalism and all its heroes will pass away. Stalin and Hitler and Roosevelt and Churchill, and all the lies and injustices and hypocrisy they signify, will pass away in blood and fire. But the spirit of the communist man which Comrade Trotsky represented will not pass away.

Destiny has made us, men of common clay, the most immediate disciples of Comrade Trotsky. We now become his heirs, and we are charged with the mission to carry out his testament. He had confidence in us. He assured us with his last words that we are right and that we will prevail. We need only have confidence in ourselves and in the ideas, the tradition and the memory which he left us as our heritage.

We owe everything to him. We owe to him our political existence, our understanding, our faith in the future. We are not alone. There are others like us in all parts of the world. Always remember that. We are not alone. Trotsky has educated cadres of disciples in more than thirty countries. They are convinced to the marrow of their bones of their right to victory. They will not falter. Neither shall we falter. "I am sure of the victory of the Fourth International!" So said Comrade Trotsky in the last moment of his life. So are we sure.

Trotsky never doubted and we shall never doubt that, armed with his weapons, with his ideas, we shall lead the oppressed masses of the world out of the bloody welter of the war into a new socialist society. That is our testimony here tonight at the grave of Comrade Trotsky.

And here at his grave we testify also that we shall never forget his parting injunction—that we shield and cherish his warrior-wife, the faithful companion of all his struggles and wanderings. "Take care of her," he said, "she has been with me many years." Yes, we shall take care of her. Before everything else, we shall take care of Natalia.

We come now to the last word of farewell to our greatest comrade and teacher, who has now become our most glorious martyr. We do not deny the grief that constricts all our hearts. But ours is not the grief of prostration, the grief that saps the will. It is tempered by rage and hatred and determination. We shall transmute it into fighting energy to carry on the Old Man's fight. Let us say farewell to him in a manner worthy of his disciples, like good soldiers of Trotsky's army. Not crouching in weakness and despair, but standing upright with dry eyes and clenched fists. With the song of struggle and victory on our lips. With the song of confidence in Trotsky's Fourth International, the International Party that shall be the human race!

Chapter 13

# How we began and where we are going

*Delivered at a rally at the Cornish Arms Hotel, New York City, celebrating the twenty-fifth anniversary of the Socialist Workers Party, October 30, 1953.*

The first speech I made for the program of Trotsky was at a meeting just about this size twenty-five years ago this week. It was a joint meeting of the Central Executive Committee, Control Commission, the functionaries and goon squads of the Communist Party. They rose up too, but not in so friendly a manner as you did tonight, when I hurled into their faces, for the first time, the announcement that the banner of struggle against Stalinist revisionism and degeneration was going to be raised in this country and fought for.

I recall that meeting and that speech tonight with pride, because that's where our party began. It began in struggle, for principle, as outlined in the teachings of the great Marxists all the way from Marx and Engels to Lenin and

Trotsky. I'm going to make the same kind of speech tonight.

But first I want to tell you it's a great joy and satisfaction to be here with you tonight, to join in the celebration of our twenty-fifth anniversary. And it's especially satisfying that the celebration of our glorious anniversary is held in connection with an election-campaign meeting, that it is linked to an action in the class struggle, of which election campaigns are a part.

That is symbolic of the character of our party—not a critical propaganda circle of wiseacres, but a part of the working class, participating in the fights of the workers and trying to rouse them to action in their own interests, even when they as yet fear to speak, and some of them even fear to listen.

The party throughout the country is proud of Local New York for this great campaign, by far the best, the most militant, the most genuinely Trotskyist campaign we have ever conducted. For that the whole party gives its thanks to our candidates, David Weiss and Cathy Gratta and Joyce Cowley, and to all the rest of you who helped to make the campaign possible, helped to contribute one more great action, to stamp on the minds of hundreds of thousands of workers the fact that there is one party, even in the midst of all the reaction and the witch-hunt and the indifference, that is not afraid to tell the truth, and tells it straight.

I don't think I need to tell you that I'm strongly in favor of these candidates. I am. I gravely regret, however, that I can't vote for you, Cathy, and Joyce, and David, because they took my vote away from me. That's one of the things I'm sore about. During the Second World War, I suppose most of you know, they put me and seventeen other comrades in prison, because we were opposed to the war and we said so—out loud.

But they weren't satisfied just to put us in prison. They slandered us, accused us of disloyalty to our country. And I resented that. Because I love this country and I'm loyal to it. All I want to do is to get it back into the hands of the people who made it, and take it away from the Sixty Families and the other grafters and hangers-on who've stolen this country from the people who made it. I consider our whole work of organizing this party, which is going to organize the masses in struggle for a revolution, as nothing more nor less than an operation for recovery of stolen property. There's nothing disloyal about that. The accusation is a slander.

All this talk of disloyalty is a slander added to the indignity of depriving us of our liberty, which was an injustice. And then on top of that, because we had become convicts, they took our vote away from us. That's when I really got mad. They said that since we belonged to the Socialist Workers Party, we had to go to prison. And then because we had been in prison, we couldn't vote for the party we belonged to. They got us on a runaround there, and I'll never be reconciled until we get our vote back, and get our country back, and either tear down those damned prisons or put some other class of people in them.

I want to talk a little bit tonight about the party. The Socialist Workers Party represents a program, first of all and above all. This program, as Engels once expressed it, is the conscious expression of the unconscious historic process which is operating relentlessly and inexorably to transform society from capitalism to socialism. But when we say that we and our program are the conscious expression of this unconscious historical process, it does not mean that we are simply observers, analysts and commentators. Just because we are the conscious expression of the historic process we also have the duty to participate in the process and help it along. That's the difference between a party of action in struggle and a mere circle of academicians, analysts and observers. Quite different.

It has also been said by Engels that we, the Marxists, the revolutionists, represent the future of the labor movement in its present. That is another excellent and accurate way to present it. But we don't merely represent the future in the present. As active revolutionists, we strive, by every means, every day, by every form of activity, including such great activities as you carried on in this election campaign—we strive to transform the present into the future at a little earlier date.

The program we stand on goes back a long way. It is by no means our invention, by no means new. It goes back in an unbroken line of continuity to the *Communist Manifesto* of Marx and Engels of 105 years ago. Our party goes back to that program along an unbroken line of continuity and, by that same token, is connected in its actions with all the actions and efforts of all the working class of all countries of the world for 105 years; and all their experiences, all their victories and defeats, are assimilated and generalized into the program of the party today, and are a part of our strength and our confidence.

More specifically, in this country the Socialist Workers Party goes back to all the great struggles and movements of the past, of the American working class, and represents their tradition too. So we speak here not only for ourselves. We speak for all those who went before us, and whose banner we carry, and whose cause we represent.

We are the direct descendants and the sole heirs of the Haymarket martyrs of 1886, the pioneer fighters for the eight-hour day, to whom every union man who enjoys a shorter workday and union conditions today, whether he knows about it or not, whether he ever heard their names or not, owes a debt of gratitude that someday will be recognized. We go back to the old Socialist Party of the time of Debs, which roused a whole generation to an elementary understanding of the class struggle, and to the movement which they created, which made it possible for us to build on, and to be here today. We are the direct descendants and heirs of the old IWW, the heroic IWW of Bill Haywood and Vincent St. John and Frank Little.

And we are also the heirs and the sole continuators of the early Communist Party in this country, which was founded in 1919. It grew up out of the left wing of the Socialist Party which had fought the struggle against the first imperialist war, and out of a section of the IWW which had suffered persecution of all kinds in its strikes and battles during the war and the prewar period.

That whole movement of left-wing radicalism of the American workers, which was unified and given a sharpened program by the great Russian Revolution of 1917, was all brought together and concentrated in the Communist Party as it was launched in 1919. That's where we come from. We come from the party that took shape in the fight against the first imperialist war, out of the cadres of American radical workers who first responded to the great Russian Revolution led by Lenin and Trotsky.

The Socialist Workers Party is the heir of all that. It represents all of that. And we can say proudly that in its twenty-five years it has represented it honorably and creditably. In addition to all that has gone before us, on which we built and which is part of our strength and our confidence, we have made our own contribution in twenty-five years of battle.

We date the origin of our party to twenty-five years ago because it was at that point when it seemed, for a time, that the chain of continuity of the revolutionary movement and of revolutionary thought and revolutionary program was almost broken. Under the impact of world events, the reaction that set in after the first revolutionary postwar wave, the old program of revolution, the old program of Lenin, was revised and discarded by the usurping clique of Stalin, which had gained power in the Soviet Union.

The Communist Party in this country had been softened up by the long prosperity, the long period of hopes deferred. Its leadership had turned conservative and Stalinized—and it seemed, for a moment, that the continuous line of revolutionary activity according to the program of Marxism was suddenly about to break. But not everybody gave way. Not everybody capitulated.

Those who resisted the degeneration in this country found inspiration and guidance from the writings of Trotsky in faraway Russia. Trotsky was conducting the great heroic fight against the degeneration, against the revision and discarding of the program. And we who heard his voice, who had the opportunity, after many years of suppression, to get hold of his writings, revolted against the Stalinist degeneration of the Comintern and of the Communist Party in this country. We raised the banner of Trotsky on October 27, 1928.

That's why we trace the origin of our party, the origin of the SWP as a distinct party, of our own making and our own building, to that day, twenty-five years ago this week, when a small group in the Communist Party raised the banner of Trotsky and his program. They expelled us for that, and we struck out on a new road, to build a new party, to replace the one that had been corrupted and degenerated, to build a new party on the old program.

The issues that were raised that day, at that meeting, have been put to the test of twenty-five years—and surely, those have been the biggest and the most eventful years in all history. I think no one can deny tonight that the test has shown who was right and who was wrong. You have it vividly illustrated at this very meeting in the speech of David Weiss, recounting the campaign of the Socialist Workers Party against the whole capitalist war setup, and his scornful denunciation of the campaign program of the miserable Communist Party, wiping the spittle of Wagner off their faces and still saying "Vote for Wagner."

In that alone is strikingly illustrated the verdict on the dispute that was raised in the meeting twenty-five years ago—who would be revolutionary and who would capitulate. And by showing who was right, and who was wrong, the events of the last twenty-five years have shown to whom the future belongs. The future belongs to those who link themselves with the progressive course of the historic process and help it along. The future belongs to those who stand firmly by the program.

That wasn't so clear to many people in October 1928. Now, if some comrades, feeling the weight of the long war boom and the conservatizing effect of it on the working class, and on the labor movement, and the accumulated effects of the reaction and the witch-hunt—if they find that it is not so easy to stand firm for revolutionary principles and to be active and aggressive for them—if you think it's difficult now, I can tell you there have been harder times.

There have been harder times to be a revolutionary socialist, and October 1928 was one such time. The situation then was somewhat different from now. Certainly the prospects for socialism didn't look very promising to anybody. And many got discouraged and lost all perspective of the future. The reason was they saw things from too close a view—what was before their eyes—and did not see them in process, with a historical perspective and a Marxist analysis.

Why, in 1928, don't you know, there were people who thought that the boom was going to last forever! The world situation seemed to have turned definitively to the stabilization of capitalism. The great hope that had been raised by the Russian Revolution of 1917, which carried with it a great revolutionary wave across Europe for five years, had finally subsided. The Russian Revolution survived, but it was isolated in a capitalist world. The German revolution, which had been counted upon as the great reinforcement, which would seal the doom of capitalism all over Europe, which had every possibility of success, had been finally defeated in 1923 for lack of a revolutionary party capable of leading it to victory as Lenin's party did in Russia.

And on the basis of that terrible defeat, capitalism got restabilized in Europe. Reaction set in. In one country after another, the labor movement, the communist movement was pushed backward. And in America, the great boom of the twenties was roaring along at such an unprecedented rate that almost everybody began to believe—it's hard for you to realize it now, perhaps, or to recall it, after the experiences later—but almost everybody believed, including the capitalists themselves!—they thought that out of their own thick heads they had found the solution of the contradictions of capitalism. And the economists in the colleges were writing, writing, writing: "Marx has been refuted! American capitalist genius has solved the problem!"

And social democrats from Germany sent delegations over here to study the workings of American capitalism, so that they could go back home and tell their own capitalists: why don't you do like that and solve the problem, and then we won't need a revolution or anything like that! And every labor faker in the country was sure that what was going on then would go on forever. And virtually all the leaders of the Communist Party eventually got reconciled to the idea that the Marxist prognosis of the contradictions of capitalism leading to crisis and revolution were no longer operating in this country, that the "old books" didn't have the answer anymore.

The Stalinist gang in the Soviet Union, nationally limited and narrow in their outlook, concerned only with their own privileges, abandoned all hope of the international revolution. They began to think only in national terms and evolved a new "theory," revising Marx and Lenin and their theory of the international revolution developing in stages from one country to another until it engulfed the world and transformed the world. They evolved the monstrous conception of "socialism in one country," by which they really meant—revisionists never tell the truth, they never say what they really mean, they always speak in double-talk—"No revolution outside of Russia!"

One revolution is enough, they thought; let us try to save what we have here, come to terms with the capitalists on the status quo in the rest of the world, and transform the Communist parties from revolutionary organizations, aiming to lead the masses in revolution, into miserable pressure groups in the service of Soviet diplomacy. That was the program foisted, step by step, upon the Communist Party of the Soviet Union by the Stalinists in the period of reaction in the twenties. This monstrous revisionism and betrayal—revisionism has always been the prelude to betrayal—culminated in 1927 with the expulsion from the Communist Party of Trotsky and the other great leaders of the revolution.

Here in the United States the long boom of the twenties, with no intervening crisis, softened up the Communist Party in this country and got it ready for the corruption of Stalinism. The leaders of the Communist Party became convinced that there could be no revolution in this country in the foreseeable future; that the United States, in any case, was an "exception" to the Marxist law.

Now I must say the theory of the leaders of the Communist Party, as it was evolved in that long, difficult period of the boom and the prosperity, was agreed to by nearly everybody else in the country. That was almost a unanimous opinion.

But we didn't agree. A few of us didn't agree. A few of us had read "the books." And from the books we derived a theory and a conviction that what was before our eyes was only temporary and superficial. We held on to the old theory that the contradictions of capitalism would explode and upset it and create the conditions for revolution.

In the very first issue of *The Militant*, comrades, in the very first issue of our *Militant*, published a few days after we were expelled from the Communist Party, we printed an assertion that the boom, which had everybody fascinated, already showed signs of cracking and was heading for a bust and a crisis; that this crisis would shake U.S. capitalism to its foundations, and that out of that crisis and the misery and oppression and horrors that would follow would come a new working class and a new labor movement and the conditions for building a revolutionary party.

And we said about the Soviet Union and the Stalinist program, in our first number of *The Militant* twenty-five years ago: the Stalinist program of socialism in one country is a revisionist betrayal of Marxism. The Trotsky program of international revolution is realistic and right and we will support it at all costs, no matter how small our numbers may be, because we believe the program will carry us to victory in the end.

And we said that the issue would not be decided by the vote at the meeting where we made our declaration and were expelled from the Communist Party. We said we would support the program of international revolution as advanced by Trotsky, and on that rock we would build a new party in this country. That's what we started out to do twenty-five years ago.

I'll admit now what I wouldn't admit then—that it was not easy at the start. The Stalinists gave us a rough time. We were only a handful of people. They expelled us. They broke up our meetings. When we tried to hold a meeting they brought in a mob and broke up meeting after meeting, and beat up all the Trotskyists. Beat us up on the streets. Burglarized our houses. In the same *Daily Worker* that is today boosting Wagner the Democrat for mayor, they slandered us every day as "agents of American imperialism" and "counterrevolutionists."

That sounds funny doesn't it? That the supporters of Wagner, the finks who broke strikes during the Second World War, the finger-men of the FBI during the war, the advocates of the incentive-pay speedup of the workers during the war—that these people called us "agents of American imperialism" and "counterrevolutionists" twenty-five years ago! I say it sounds funny now, but it wasn't so funny then.

We were isolated and alone. They had the audience; they had the daily press; they had the apparatus; they had the money—and nobody was listening to us. It makes me laugh ironically when I hear people say these days, "What's the use of running an election campaign, nobody is listening to you." I wonder what such fainthearted people would have said in 1928, when we tried to explain the problems arising out of the great theoretical fight in the Russian Communist Party and nobody would listen because nobody was interested.

Did I say nobody listened? That's not quite correct. A few listened. And a few more. And out of our constant pounding and pounding and talking and talking, whether the people would listen or not, we assembled the original cadres of this party. People listen now a hundred and a thousand times more. We didn't have the forces for an election campaign then. We couldn't dream of getting on the radio. We couldn't dream of having a meeting of this size, to say nothing of having a television audience in those days.

But we had something else. We had conviction in our program, and that's a mighty strong prop of support. In the fight for socialism you have to expect and encounter difficulties. You have to expect hard times on some occasions. But you can stand them on certain conditions—if you have a clear historical perspective, if you are not overwhelmed by the events of the moment, but see in the events of the moment that a different thing will develop tomorrow. If you have a class historical perspective and a clear head, you can be a revolutionist under any conditions. Of course, it helps too if you have a good "belly," as the boys say, to be able to take punishment. That helps. As a matter of fact, if you haven't got a good "belly" it's very difficult to be a consistent revolutionist in good times and bad.

We had all that in the early days. That's a fact. And we still have it. And in addition, we had on our side in that unequal fight in the beginning, we had the greatest political thinker of modern times. That was Comrade Trotsky. That made the difference.

When we started our fight, he was in exile in Alma Ata, in Asian Russia, thousands of miles away. We had no contact with him, but we had some of his writings in our hands, his criticism of the program. That was our only connection with him at the start. Later on, after he was deported to Turkey, we got direct contact with Trotsky and had him and his advice and his thinking all the time.

And we still have Trotsky, despite the fact that the Stalinists finally assassinated him. The greatest political thinker, the greatest revolutionist, the most heroic man of modern times—they finally assassinated him in 1940. But we still have Trotsky's writings and example as our guide.

And we are convinced by all the evidence that the whole course of world development in the last twenty-five years has confirmed Trotsky's analysis. The stabilization of capitalism in 1928, which the Stalinists took for permanent, which was supposed to last indefinitely, lasted only one more year. Just one year and two days after I made my speech in that Stalinist Central Committee meeting, and told them that this boom would not last and would run into a crisis which could change the whole thing and open up the perspectives of the revolutionary party—just one year and two days after we were expelled and organized the original nucleus of the SWP, the great boom blew up.

On October 29, 1929, the stock-market crash sent its reverberations throughout the world, and capitalism began to writhe in the death agony of crisis and war and revolution, from which it can never be extricated. We were confident of that when we started out twenty-five years ago. Today, on our twenty-fifth anniversary, we are more confident than ever for firmer reasons and with stronger proofs from all the events of the past twenty-five years.

We are frequently spoken of as "optimists." Throughout the labor movement we Trotskyists have become known far and wide in these twenty-five years because we have been active on many fronts. They all see the Trotskyists always with the same attitude and the same spirit, and our "optimism" has been frequently noted and spoken about by friends as well as by enemies. "The Trotskyists," they say, "are very optimistic people." Now, there's a certain justification for this opinion of us, but it shouldn't be taken one-sidedly. We are not cheerful idiots by any means. We are not optimistic about everything. Our optimism is a discriminating, selective, reasonably based optimism.

About some things we are pessimistic. For example, we are pessimistic and have not a trace of confidence in the future of capitalism. In that, I think, we have a common bond with the highest brains of American capitalism who are very doubtful in their own minds too. They don't know what's going to be, and say so frankly in their financial organs. In 1928 they were all happy and confident, but now they're all full of doubts and gloom, and they wish somebody would tell them that things are not as bad as they look. We can't tell them that because we're honest, we always tell the truth, and the truth is that things are worse than they look for capitalism. That's all we can tell them. We have not a trace of confidence in the future of capitalism in this country or in any other country.

On the other hand, we are optimistic, and for good sound reasons, about the prospects of revolution in all countries, including this one.

We are pessimistic, profoundly pessimistic, about anybody's chances to revise the basic program upon which our party and our world movement has been founded and built. Our party was born in struggle against Stalinist revisionism, don't forget that. Our party began in a doctrinal struggle against a revision of the Marxist program. The party was steeled and strengthened in a great doctrinal battle against Burnhamite revisionism in 1939–1940, in the last year of Trotsky's life, when he directly participated and led the party in our fight against the revisionists. In the course of these and other doctrinal battles we became real Trotskyists, and proud to bear the name.

Trotsky's teachings have been assimilated into our flesh

and blood and bone. His teachings have sustained us for twenty-five years, and enabled us to stand up against all pressure, and to endure all hardships, and still persevere and continue and fight and hope and believe in the future. And if someone asks: "What are the chances now to change us after all this, to 'revise' us, so to speak, at this late date?" we would have to answer pessimistically: "No chance whatever." The Trotskyists are fixed the way they are and there's no chance to tamper with their orthodox doctrines or the program of their party. That they will not allow, and it's an utterly pessimistic enterprise for anybody to even contemplate.

On the other hand, we are optimistic and we have unlimited confidence in the program upon which we have built our party—the program derived from the basic doctrine of Marx, Lenin and Trotsky. As we start off on the second twenty-five years of our struggle for a socialist America there are only two things we need, and these two things we've got. First, we have the conviction, based on theoretical analysis and living evidence of development in the last twenty-five years, that capitalism cannot survive and that international socialist revolution is already knocking at the door. That's our profound conviction of the state of the world as it looks from here tonight. And the second asset we have is the conviction that the program formulated by Trotsky in his lifetime—in the latter eleven years in direct collaboration with us—is the only program to organize the revolution and to lead it to definitive victory and the transition to socialism.

We celebrate our glorious twenty-fifth anniversary tonight at the halfway mark of our journey and our task, with our work only half done. Twenty-five years ago last Wednesday, we started from scratch, with only a handful of people and a program, to build the new party of the

American Revolution. We've succeeded with that half of the task. On the basis of the Trotskyist program, we have built a party whose cadres can never be broken.

In the next twenty-five years the cadres of this party, armed with the same program, will grow and expand and become the leaders and organizers of the socialist revolution in the United States. That's the way it's going to be.

Chapter 14

# How to put an end to imperialist war

Radio speech delivered over station WPAT, Newark, New Jersey, October 31, 1942.

For the second time within the brief span of twenty-five years, imperialist war is reaching into every home. Sons, husbands, brothers, sweethearts are being torn out of every family circle in order to build up the largest military machine the world has ever seen. Women and children are forced to take the place of men in the factories and on the farms. Sugar, gasoline and tires are already rationed. Meatless days are here. There is an ever-increasing shortage of the basic necessities of life. Prices are skyrocketing. Wages have been frozen. One tax after another has been heaped upon us until they have become a staggering burden. At the same time big business, which is raking in profits from the war industries exceeding those of even the 1929 boom year, has launched an unprecedented assault against the labor movement and against such basic rights of the people as freedom of speech, freedom of the press and freedom of assembly.

Yet the Second World War has scarcely begun.

Not until the casualties are listed, and the maimed, the mutilated, the shell-shocked and the blind come back home to finish their lives in wheelchairs and hospitals—not until millions upon millions of young men discharged from the armed forces start hunting for jobs—will we feel the full impact of this war.

Not until big business has bankrupted the nation, ruined the economy, plunged the people into mourning and despair and commenced organizing and financing gangs of American fascists to put an American Hitler in power—not until then will we realize the full horror of the imperialist war that has been thrust upon us.

What is involved is nothing less than the fate of mankind. If the capitalist class continues to rule, civilization will go down. The entire world will enter the eclipse of a new dark age.

But intelligent workers with the real interests of our country at heart are beginning to ask, isn't there a way out? Isn't there some way to escape the abyss? Yes, there is a way. But it is not the way of capitalism and its wars, its lies and false promises.

Remember the various promises and assurances which big business and its representatives in Washington made to the people in the First World War. We will then be better able to judge the promises they have made in this war.

They assured the people that there would be no more wars if the Allies won. They promised that an Allied victory would make the world safe for democracy. They assured the people that it was a war to end wars. They declared that the Kaiser and his followers were solely responsible for the war, and that it was only necessary to do away with the Kaiser to usher in peace and prosperity. That was what they promised.

But what were the realities?

Instead of a world made safe for democracy, we got a world converted into a foul prison and made safe only for fascism. Depressions swept through nation after nation. Unemployment became a worldwide plague. Instead of a war to end wars it turned out to be a war to breed wars. Mussolini came to power in Italy; Hitler in Germany; Franco in Spain.

Great Britain continued to oppress one-fourth of the world's population. Wall Street maintained its grip on the Philippines and Puerto Rico and moved deeper into Latin America. Wall Street sent troops against the Russian Revolution of October 1917, quarrelled with the other imperialist powers over China, and drove the Bonus Army out of Washington at bayonet-point. All this has now been climaxed with a Second World War.

All the promises of big business and its representatives about the First World War turned out to be treacherous lies. That is the cold fact. The promises of the present administration give us no reason whatsoever for expecting that they will turn out one iota better than those of Wilson.

Like the First World War, the Second World War is a product of capitalism. It is a struggle for markets, for colonies, for spheres of investment, for control of raw materials and control of trade routes. The conflicts now raging are for oil fields, rubber plantations, mines, food-producing areas, and strategic military bases. The imperialist armies follow the trade routes and entrench themselves where the rich sources of raw materials exist.

Imperialist war is a struggle for these concrete material things in a period when the world has already been divided up. It is not a struggle for fine ideals such as democracy and freedom of oppressed peoples, but a brutal, ruthless, bloody struggle to redivide the world in the interests of different warring gangs of capitalists.

For more than a hundred years, Great Britain extended her seizures of backward and undeveloped world areas and policed the seven seas to maintain her ill-gotten empire. German, Italian and Japanese capitalism grew strong enough to challenge her world position and to attempt to carve up this old empire.

But big business in the United States decided to establish its own empire over the world. Big business decided to make itself heir to the dying British lion and to meet the challenge of the Axis for control of the world. Where the British policed the seven seas, Wall Street has a program of policing the five continents in addition. Wall Street's dream is to establish a super-British empire.

The imperialists of both sides promise a lasting peace if they win the war. But there can be no lasting peace unless this war ends the causes of imperialist war, that is, ends the system of capitalist private property and the economic rivalries among the capitalist nations. Since neither side seriously proposes or can propose to end these rivalries, neither side will be able to assure genuine peace to the world.

The postwar programs of the Axis and the United Nations look like identical twins. Neither intends, if victorious, to disband its armies after the armistice; on the contrary, they aim to maintain the mightiest military machines in history. Both propose to "police the world" for a hundred years or longer. Both propose an armed "peace" resting solely on the bayonets of a conqueror. Such a "peace" would undoubtedly prove the most short-lived in history. Such a peace would inevitably breed a third and more terrible war, just as the peace following the First World War bred the Second World War. Imperialist war would break out again as soon as the defeated capitalist nations felt strong enough to try to redivide the world—or as soon as the rivalries among the victorious nations drove them to quarrel among themselves over the spoils. Such are the perspectives of capitalism.

The future of mankind would be dark indeed if there were no hope of ending the capitalist system. Capitalism is no longer capable of advancing society. It is useless and outlived. Prolongation of its death agony is solely at the expense of the vast majority of the population. It can offer nothing now but decay, stagnation, unemployment, hunger, and the terrible catastrophe of imperialist war.

A new social system is required. A new government must be placed in power.

Karl Marx almost a hundred years ago foresaw the development of capitalism and the blind alley it would reach. His predictions have been borne out with almost machinelike precision. Karl Marx and his disciples not only saw what was going to happen, they worked out a program to save humanity and to open up a road to the future. That road is socialism.

Socialism would end imperialist war forever because it would remove forever its basic cause, the ownership of the means of production by a small minority. Socialism would place the natural resources, the mines, the factories, the transportation and banking system in the hands of the people where they belong. Socialism would introduce a planned economy. Instead of the present chaos, where each business, each industry, each nation is run according to blind chance or the greedy interests of a small clique, a master plan would coordinate the entire economic system of the world. Instead of recurring and ever more violent struggles between the capitalist classes of the leading nations for profits and the sources of profits, there would be genuine cooperation between all the nations, a pooling and exchange of resources and technique that would result in a higher living standard for all the peoples of the world.

Under such a system we could rapidly forge ahead into a new era where peace, prosperity and good will would reign.

The socialist program against imperialist war is the most important issue in the present election. The people of New Jersey have the opportunity to cast their vote on November 3 for a candidate who advocates and fights for the future socialist society. That candidate is George Breitman, Socialist Workers Party nominee for the United States Senate.

A vote for George Breitman is a vote for the abolition of the present capitalist system and its by-products—imperialist war, fascism and depression—and for the establishment of a Workers' and Farmers' Government functioning in the interests of the great majority of the people, and leading the way to the socialist society of peace and security and freedom for all.

## Chapter 15

# Youth and foreign policy

Delivered to a meeting of students at New York University, April 25, 1951.

The subject of our discussion today, the foreign policy of the United States, is now recognized on every side as the burning question of the day. It monopolizes the attention of the statesmen, the generals and the diplomats. It is a sign of the times that the specialists in the art of propaganda, true and false—mostly false, concentrate on this subject nowadays, each from his own point of view and special interest. Through this poisonous fog of slanted propaganda the truth has a hard time making its way.

The people of America, as distinguished from their rulers and misleaders, in their great majority have been traditionally peace-loving, nationally exclusive and self-sufficient, even isolationist in their sentiments. But they have long since been convinced by the course of events that foreign policy is their greatest concern today and the source of their greatest fears. For they know in their bones, no matter what the statesmen and the propagandists say, that U.S. foreign policy is driving not toward peace but toward war.

And I believe that of all the elements and age brackets in the population of the country, those who are most acutely sensitive to this relationship of foreign policy and war are the youth, that is, those who will have to do the fighting and the dying in the ultimate execution of our foreign policy as it is directed today. For the young people, foreign policy is no academic disquisition, but a question of life and death.

Therefore, I am glad of the opportunity you have given me to speak to an audience of young university people on this subject today. First of all, I wish to express my appreciation of the spirit of fair play and free speech which has been manifested on so many sides, especially in the student body, and I assume also in the administrative staff, which has made my discussion with you possible.

I believe in free speech. I have fought for it a long time, for others as well as for myself. Free speech is a necessary instrumentality for the dissemination of full information and the clarification of ideas which can lead to correct decisions. In the early days of the pioneer socialist movement in this country and of the IWW, with which I was affiliated, we put up many battles, not without hazards and penalties for some of us, for the right of free speech. I first came into collision, and eventually to an irrevocable break, with the Communist Party over this question—over the attempt to suppress the rights of a minority faction, to which I belonged, to present their views and defend them in fair debate. For forty years I have been mixed up one way or another in the fight for free speech, either as a defendant under prosecution, defending my own rights, or as an active participant in organizations and committees defending the rights of others. I know all about free speech.

I speak here today on the subject of foreign policy from the viewpoint of Marxist socialism, the socialism of the class struggle. I have lived to see the United States take part in two world wars. As a socialist I opposed them both, and I am opposed now to the American intervention in Korea and the program of spreading it into a third world war. As a socialist I know that capitalist wars are waged not for high moral principles, as the lying propagandists say, but for profits and plunder, for territories, for markets and fields of investment. I cannot conceive of a more disgraceful act of self-repudiation for a socialist than to support a capitalist war.

The great debate, so-called, which is proceeding with feverish intensity today in the halls of Congress and in the press, on radio and television, in forums, on platforms and in pulpits, does not in my opinion touch the real problem of war and peace. The differences of Truman and MacArthur, the two protagonists in the debate as it is presently unfolding, are only tactical and strategic, not fundamental. They differ on where to begin and when to begin to drop the atom bomb and start the third world war. But both policies, the policy of Truman and the policy of MacArthur, are imperialistic. They both aim at war and hope to solve the economic problems of the United States by means of war.

Hoover is rather on the sidelines, a third party in the discussion whose influence is declining. The Hoover policy is imperialistic also, but in too limited a way to serve the economic requirements of American capitalism. His conception of a Western Hemisphere fortress is too small for the present-day world. *The New York Times,* in my opinion, correctly disposed of the Hoover thesis from the point of view of big finance, with the editorial observation that his program would signify "economic strangulation" for the United States—as a capitalist nation, that is.

In the last analysis, the same thing holds true for the programs of Truman and MacArthur and ultimately condemns them both to bankruptcy. The dilemma of United States capitalism arises from the fact that it has come to the apex of its riches and its power, as the heir of bankrupt Europe, in a world that has no room for expanding capitalism as was the case half a century ago. It is not only the Western Hemisphere that is too small. Europe and Asia are also too small. In fact, the whole world is too small to meet the demands and needs of American capitalism with its ever-accumulating surpluses of capital and manufactured goods, which cannot be absorbed at home on a capitalist basis.

The Soviet Union, one-sixth of the world's surface, is closed off to the capitalist world as a market and field of profitable investment. Eastern Europe in the recent period has been closed off. And now China, the great object of the war in the Pacific, the prize for which the war against Japan was waged, has not only been wrested from the control of Japanese imperialism; in the process of war and revolution China has torn itself out of the orbit of capitalist exploitation. And the colonial revolutions have just begun. The world open to capitalist exploitation is narrowing down, while the demands of American imperialism for markets and fields of investment grow ever more rapacious and insatiable. That is the dilemma of a bankrupt social system which "foreign policy" cannot conjure out of existence.

The bankruptcy of capitalism is registered in terms of human poverty and misery, of which it is the primary cause. As we here today discuss the question of American foreign policy and the dilemma of American imperialism, just let one simple fact have the floor. There are two billion people in the world which capitalism has ruled so long, and more than one-half of these people never get enough to eat all their lives. This is an established fact, undisputed by anybody. It is a matter of common knowledge.

These hungry people don't want propaganda. It is the biggest illusion and delusion to imagine that hungry people who number more than a billion are just waiting for somebody to give them the lowdown in learned professorial essays. They know what they want. They want bread and land and national independence. Capitalism cannot supply them, and has not supplied them. That is the nub of the problem of the world today. Neither Truman nor MacArthur can bomb it out of existence, although that is what their "foreign policy" stupidly aims to accomplish.

The terrible contradictions of American capitalism forbid and exclude a humane and peaceful foreign policy. The narrowing fields for capitalist exploitation on the one hand, and the constantly growing surpluses of capital and goods produced in the United States—this is the economic circumstance determining the imperialist foreign policy of the United States. It is not a matter of bad will or ignorance on the part of one statesman or another, although God knows there is plenty of that. It is an ineluctable contradiction of an economic nature. That is what determines the imperialist foreign policy of the United States and drives it to militarization and to war.

These facts are well known to the decisive ruling circles of this country, these circles who represent the great accumulations of capital, for whom *The New York Times* and *The New York Herald Tribune* speak most authoritatively. They know these facts and that is why they will not listen to any talk of isolationism; or of limitation to the Western

Hemisphere; or of making peace with China and Russia. Not at all. Such proposals do not fit into their policy in any way whatever, except as propaganda to deceive the people. To be sure, they all blandly deny any imperialist aims. They all talk for peace. But talk is cheap. That is the first lesson in politics I would recommend to you young men and women, if by any chance you are studying political science in some class or other. Talk is cheap, but facts speak louder. All this talk of peace and denial of imperialist aims is just routine propaganda, belied by deeds everywhere.

The "theoretical justification" for this phony "nonimperialist" and "peace" propaganda of the masters of America has been undertaken by some people, including your professor of philosophy, Sidney Hook, who call themselves "democratic socialists." They correspond in my opinion—you will forgive me if I unintentionally offend your religious sensibilities—they correspond to the missionaries who were sent out to soften up the native peoples in the colonies for subjugation and exploitation by the great powers in the past.

I have here a few quotations as samples of this theoretical missionary work, this shoddy attempt to prove on a theoretical basis the nonimperialist and peace-loving character of the most rapacious imperialist power that ever existed in the world. Here is a quotation from a published document entitled "To Our Friends in Europe and Asia": "The development of American capitalism has not led to imperialism; it does not fulfill Lenin's theory of imperialism as the inevitable last stage of capitalism."

Another quotation from the same document—a denial "that American capitalism depends on imperialist expansion for its very life."

And a third quotation: "The U.S. had a great internal

free trade market and such enormous natural resources that today she is an exporter of raw materials as well as of manufactured goods. The economic facts of life in America were and are very different from the facts in Europe which led Lenin to formulate his theory of imperialism."

The signers of this document—among them Lewis Corey, James T. Farrell, Sidney Hook, Upton Sinclair and Norman Thomas—attempt to convince the people of Europe and Asia that the economic laws determining the imperialist character of the old Europe, about which Lenin wrote, do not apply to its successor to the domination of the world, the beneficent United States of America.

The best I can say for this "theoretical" exercise is that it must have been written on the assumption that nobody will read it who ever read Lenin. While it is true that there were certain differences between the line of development of American capitalism into imperialism and a similar development in Europe, the differences all accentuate the imperialist drive of the United States. It is true that American capitalism had, and still has, a great internal market. It had a whole continent to exploit in contradistinction to the hemmed-in countries of Europe. The development and exploitation of this vast territory provided an expanding internal market for a long time. It also opened up a widening field for the continuous investment and reinvestment not only of the profits of American capitalism itself, but also of billions and billions of dollars imported from Europe in the development of this country. That was the case up to the time of the First World War.

Then the situation and the relationship of Europe and America began to change fundamentally. America, which was a debtor nation at the beginning of the First World War, has become the richest capitalist nation in the world and the creditor of the whole world. Meanwhile, the internal market, great as it was and still is, proved in the crisis of the thirties that it could no longer absorb the products of American industry on a capitalist basis. A slight decline in exports was sufficient to plunge American economy into the most devastating crisis the world ever saw, a crisis which lasted ten years and even then was only temporarily and artificially overcome by war expenditures.

Our theoretical justifiers say that America exports raw materials in contradistinction to some of the older European countries analyzed by Lenin, and therefore cannot be imperialist by Lenin's law. That argument wouldn't even convince Governor Thomas E. Dewey. Did you read Dewey's speech in answer to Hoover? Dewey's speech lists, one after another, the strategic raw materials which America needs from foreign sources for its industries and for its armament, including uranium. He points out the various spots around the world where they are located and cannot be obtained and incorporated into the American industrial process unless the sources are controlled by the United States or its allies.

America exports wheat and cotton, but a great number of strategic raw materials, absolutely necessary for its industry and its war machine, have to be imported at any cost, even at the cost of war. And so great is the power of America over this supply of raw materials, it caused an explosion in the British cabinet just the other day. One of the main reasons for the resignation of Bevan from the cabinet of the Labour government was that America is cornering the raw-material supplies of the world, stimulating inflation in Europe and endangering the British economy.

Lenin said the epoch of capitalist imperialism, as distinguished from the epoch of free competition, is characterized mainly by the export of capital. The development of home industry reaches the point where it can no longer absorb the accumulations of profits piled up by the capitalist investors. In addition to the export of manufactured goods, they have to find foreign fields where this surplus capital can be invested at a high rate of profit under conditions of political security for the investment.

How does that apply to America? Why, I think it applies a hundred times more than it ever did to England, France and Germany, which were the great imperialist powers before the First World War. All you have to do is look at the figures of the accumulation of capital and the rate and volume of its exportation by America since the beginning of the First World War. These figures do not lie, and cannot be lied away. To bring forward the "nonimperialist" argument at the present time, when the bulk of the surplus capital of the entire world is held here in the United States; to say that this country, which has the virtual monopoly of world capital, is not confronted by the imperialistic problem of investing outside its own borders—that is to make a mockery of facts as well as theory.

Our theoretical missionaries mention the gifts dispensed by the American Santa Claus, the loans and the donations for military purposes to foreign governments, including Chiang Kai-shek, Syngman Rhee, Franco and all the other representatives of "freedom and democracy." What is all this largesse designed for? It is represented in the document I have quoted here as a sign of the beneficence and peace-loving character of the American capitalist government.

Cutting out the buncombe and getting down to brass tacks, permit me to give you another interpretation. These loans and donations are primarily designed to prop up the shaky capitalist structures and create the political conditions for profitable investments. Not even the free-spending United States capitalists want to pour out billions of dollars in investments for the development of backward foreign countries without guarantees that their investments will be secured and pay off. What is necessary for the security of their investments? "Stable political conditions." And these stable political conditions, as they are understood in Washington and Wall Street, require puppet governments that can suppress revolutions and colonial uprisings and guarantee, at all costs, that the profits of investors will be secured regardless of the interests of the exploited people.

There is a second reason why they dole out money so freely. The Marshall Plan, etc., came at a convenient time, when America was threatened with an economic crisis which was due to the overproduction of goods that the domestic market could not absorb. The huge expenditures, creating an artificial market, alleviated and postponed the crisis. Benevolence here was happily married to expediency.

We Marxists interpret the foreign policy of the United States government from economic facts. The capitalists who own the government need foreign markets for their surplus goods. They need secure political conditions for profitable investment in foreign lands. Their demands are insatiable and cannot be restrained. Loans and investments in Russia, Eastern Europe, and now China, are considered unsafe. The policy is not to "contain" the Soviet Union in Russia and Eastern Europe. No, that is only a temporizing tactic. The ultimate aim and imperious necessity is to overthrow the governments in these countries; to open them up as markets and fields of investment under secure political conditions. This is the real goal of American foreign policy, which spells in the final analysis the drive to dominate the entire world. They select their allies to serve that end; "benevolence" and "democracy" have nothing to do with it.

Just ask yourselves a question, friends. How does it

happen that the United States government, implementing its foreign policy, which the priests of spurious theory tell us is so peaceful and so beneficent and concerned so purely with the welfare of the human race—which includes, we presume, the billion people who never get enough to eat—how does it happen that everywhere American foreign policy, backed up by American military force, supports the capitalists, the landlords, the usurers, the kings and the fascist gangs against the people?

In China they support Chiang Kai-shek whose regime was so corrupt and reactionary that the people rose up en masse to drive him out. America takes sides against the people everywhere: in Spain with its fascist butcher, Franco; in Greece with its monarcho-fascist regime; in Korea with its Syngman Rhee; in Indochina where the people are struggling for independence against French imperialism and have to fight against the overwhelming might of American financial help and military supplies; in Malaya and the Philippines; in Portugal, Turkey and South America. All over the world, wherever the hungry people are rising in a struggle for land and bread and national independence, they confront the United States of America with its money and its bombs.

The people everywhere know this fact because it brings down upon them death and destruction all the time. And because they know this fact, they are not apt to be taken in by the theory of Professor Hook, elucidated in an article in *The New York Times Magazine,* that the real need of America is a "propaganda offensive." When people know the facts, it is pretty hard to deceive them with words, especially when they feel the facts on their bodies and bones, in blows and bloody attacks.

The more practical artificers of American foreign policy, as distinguished from their professorial advisers, know that it is a waste of money to try to convince a billion people throughout the world by propaganda that America is their friend. The hardheaded statesmen gave an ironic answer to Sidney Hook and his propaganda theory the other day in Congress when they voted to cut the appropriations for the "Voice of America" by 90 percent. It was a big surprise to many people. But these realistic politicians in Washington have more faith in their guns and their bombs to make the people of the world love them, than in propaganda which is belied by all the facts.

Now a question we should ask ourselves is this: Can our life purpose be committed to the fate of this American imperialist power? Disregarding all moral considerations and all concern for the human race except ourselves and our families—our little circle—can we say, well, America is bound to dominate the world anyway, and we might as well go along and serve it and save ourselves? I would say that even from that narrow and morally impermissible standpoint the question does not have an easy and facile answer.

Is the United States of America, as it is now constituted on a capitalist basis, all-powerful? Can she lick the world with guns and atom bombs and impose her will by force everywhere, as some ignorant braggarts and narrow-minded militarists like to say? Can she enslave and exploit the whole world and make good conditions for us, the favored few, within her borders? In my opinion, an objective examination of the real facts of the world situation can only raise the gravest doubts of the capacity of American capitalism to carry out even a small part of the global designs implied in its foreign policy.

Capitalism is an outworn social system. The First World War was the sign of its bankruptcy as a world order. Prior to that, for half a century, capitalism had grown and expanded.

It had maintained an uneasy peace in the world, except for numerous local wars and colonial expeditions by which the great powers divided up the world. But things have changed since then. Just consider for a moment how much they have changed in thirty-seven years since the first shots were fired in 1914. Two world wars, devouring the lives of tens of millions of people, and wounding nobody knows how many more, and destroying so much of the material culture of the world. Two destructive world wars and a terrible worldwide depression with its unmeasured toll of misery and death. And now the mad armaments race toward another world war, the end of which no one can see or prophesy.

These are the achievements of capitalism in the last third of a century. This system, I say, is bankrupt. This system is in the twilight period of its decline and its decay. The peoples of the world are rising up against it, and especially against its chief representative, the United States of America. The rest of the capitalist world would fall of its own weight without American money and American arms. There isn't a country in Europe where a capitalist government could stand up for many months without American power and support. That applies to all of them, from Greece to Franco's Spain, to Italy, to France and all others, except possibly England, and England too would soon follow the others.

The peoples of the Orient, who have thrown off the shackles of the old colonialism, show no disposition to wear new ones. They are not asking to be taken into America's sphere of influence and exploitation. On the contrary, they are fighting against it with all of their strength and passion.

The victims of Stalinism in Russia and Eastern Europe badly need a political revolution; but they don't want any "liberation" by the arms and bombs of the United States with the consequent restoration of the capitalists and landlords, and the splitting up of their countries into colonies for American exploitation.

The workers of Europe, and particularly the workers of Germany, have made it perfectly clear in this last year that they don't intend to fight the battles of United States imperialism in another war. An expression of that attitude has come like a lightning flash from Britain this week. The resignation of Bevan from the cabinet throws the Labour government into a crisis and raises the question of the Atlantic Pact, and all the other war plans of the United States. This is a direct expression of the unwillingness of the people of Britain to be tied, as Bevan said, to the chariot of America. A dispatch from Paris in *The New York Times* this morning says that the sentiments of Bevan are echoed in socialist and labor circles all over Europe.

And finally, the workers of the United States haven't said their last word yet by a long shot. The foreign policy of American capitalism is united with its domestic policy. The war program carries with it the program of militarizing and regimenting the country, already under way; of stamping out liberties, which is in the design; and of driving down the living standards of the workers, which is in progress with the wage freeze on the one side and skyrocketing inflation on the other. All this, in my opinion, will meet resistance in the United States. The crisis in the Labor Mobilization Board may already be a sign of the coming storm.

So I wouldn't advise young people to bet their heads on the victory of American imperialism.

There is an alternative. In my opinion this alternative is to recognize the social reality of our time, to see capitalism as a world system in its death agony, completely reactionary and beyond salvation by any means. The alternative to support of this doomed social system is to ally oneself with the future, with the socialist and labor movement, and with the great colonial revolutions in process and still growing. The alternative is to work for a union of the world's workers and the colonial peoples, to put an end to imperialism and open the way for the socialist society of the free and equal. That is the way to secure peace and progress and a good life for all.

Friends, I recommend this alternative program to you. It is better. For it offers you something worth fighting for, with the prospect of victory at the end, a victory for all humanity in which you and your generation will share.

## Chapter 16

# What it means to be a young revolutionist today

Delivered to a meeting at the West Coast Vacation School, September 4 and 5, 1964.

I want to begin by explaining this delay of fifteen minutes—I was here strictly on the dot of 2:30—according to the Bolshevik custom of being on time. Any delay was due to extraneous circumstances, which I will not mention in order to spare the feelings of the delinquents who have got to face the Control Commission and explain why we were not ready on time—according to the Bolshevik custom. Lenin and Trotsky were great sticklers for being on time.

I had a chance to observe that personally, in my visits to Trotsky with delegations, several times in Mexico City. He used to have sessions something like this with a delegation from New York and Minneapolis, and all the guards and other comrades doing technical work were invited. When the hour came to begin the seminar, Trotsky would get up and ostentatiously lock the door if anybody was absent, so that when they came they would have to knock and be reprimanded for being late.

Bolshevism, in a way, is a synonym for efficiency and timeliness—they were on time for the revolution in 1917. Lenin once said, "A man who doesn't know how to show up on time is like a fellow who comes late for a wedding and finds a funeral in progress and goes around wishing everybody present many happy returns of the day."

You have wrought a miracle today. I made my first soapbox speech on the corner of Sixth and Main Street in Kansas City fifty-three years ago. I had a little stage fright and nervousness before I started, but after the first few minutes I got over it. From that time till this, according to my calculations, I've made about 15,000 speeches. And I have never had a trace of stage fright in any one of them until today.

Rose can testify that I've been quite nervous because this is a new experience for me. This is the first seminar that I ever presided over. My only time at college was like that of the thief who said, "Sure, I've been to college, I ran across the campus two jumps ahead of the sheriff."

Now, the purpose of the seminar, as we have discussed it and outlined it, is not a call to action, although we are a party of action; it's not an appeal for efficiency, although we pride ourselves on our efficiency—that's one of the ingredients of our party; it's rather an attempt to stimulate thought about new things in America and the world. Because, without thought brought up to date all the time, efficiency in action often turns into what has been called all motion and no direction. The party is not only an efficiency machine and an action machine, but, first of all and above all, it's a thinking machine. That's what distinguishes us from many others.

I thought a good way to begin on the general subject

of what it means to be a young socialist today, and the perspectives before him or her, would be to discuss it in connection with what it meant to be a young socialist when Rose and I were your age, more than fifty years ago.

That was still the Victorian age, although the queen was dead. But the general atmosphere and attitude of the people, especially in the Anglo-Saxon world, was Victorian. That was an atmosphere of confidence and optimism in steadily increasing progress, step by step, to unlimited goals without any interruptions. The theory of evolution, both social and organic, was conceived of as a steady, slow progress and improvement, not recognizing that in organic evolution as propounded by Darwin, and social evolution as propounded by Marx and Engels, there are violent explosions at various stages in the gradual evolution, which are known as revolutions. These revolutions transform the situation fundamentally, and then go on evolving further until there's another revolution or, in some cases, a counterrevolution.

Now before the First World War, to be a socialist meant above all to be committed to an idea and an ideal which you served without being able to demonstrate concretely that you were engaged in a practical task. One of the most effective arguments that used to be made against us fifty-odd years ago was, "It's a good idea, but we'll never live to see it." Or, "It can't be done, the workers won't move—look at them, how apathetic they are. Nowhere in the world have the workers ever won any real victories—the most they ever won was a few cents more an hour." And we couldn't refute that from practical experience. We couldn't refute, with practical evidence, the theory that things were just going to continue as they were, only getting a little better from day to day and year to year. So why get excited— even if you're a socialist? You go to a meeting once a week, as a religious person goes to Sunday school, and the rest of the week you devote to practical affairs and preparing for the future. Raise a family and look forward to grandchildren and great-grandchildren who eventually, some day or other, will live in a socialist society.

There was peace in the world. The great powers had not been in conflict in a military way since 1870, and it looked as if this peace was stable and permanent. Then, into this idyllic picture of slow, steady progress came the thunderbolts of the First World War, 1914—exactly fifty years ago this week. And then Rosa Luxemburg reminded people that when we said socialism was inevitable, we always coupled it with the assertion that "socialism or barbarism" was the perspective of the human race, and that world war was barbarism. The old slogan "Workers of the World Unite" had been transformed in practice into socialists and union workers in different countries murdering each other in the service of the masters. The First World War took a toll of between ten and twenty million dead and innumerable wounded and starved and deprived in various ways.

And after the First World War we had the terrible depression. Then we had the Second World War, which cost between twenty and forty million human lives and innumerable casualties wounded in various ways. Then we had the horror of six million people—men, women and children—in Germany, in Poland and other Nazi-occupied places, being murdered in gas chambers. We had the unspeakable horror of Stalinist slave-labor camps. And we had the unmentionable crime of whole cities full of people, in Hiroshima and Nagasaki, destroyed in a single moment by the first atomic bombs.

When the Second World War ended in 1945, Europe and Japan and a large part of Eastern Europe and Russia were in ruins, and America was triumphant, with a minimum of casualties, the monopoly of the atomic bomb, and an abundant prosperity built on supplying goods to the countries who had sacrificed so many millions in the war. It was then that a great genius named Henry Luce, the proprietor of *Time, Life,* and *Fortune,* came out with a jubilant editorial, waving it over the ashes of the victims of the gas chambers and battlefields and slave-labor camps, proclaiming the American Century. America was to rule the world as Rome had in her time. But what does it look like today?

I have a grandson. I told him that the American Century had been proclaimed in 1945, and asked what that proved. And he, having a sense of humor and being a good straight man, replied, "I don't know. What does it prove?" And I said, "It proves that some centuries are shorter than others."

But now 1945 seems eons and eons away. What happened since 1945 is what we, as Marxists, students of social reality which does not remain constant but changes, have to do our thinking about. Marx, in his introduction to the first volume of *Capital,* said that what he had undertaken to prove by his exhaustive examination was that human society is not a solid crystal, but an organism subject to change, and constantly changing. And our task, in the present hour and in the days that lie ahead, is to assess what has changed since 1945 and to adjust our thinking, and consequently our perspective, accordingly.

Since 1945, prostrate Europe has risen again, with the help of America, which could thereby dispose of its surplus capital and at the same time build a military barrier against the Soviet Union, which incidentally and most inconsiderately had in the meantime developed an atomic bomb of its own, thus destroying the American monopoly.

That's point one. America no longer has the monopoly

of atomic weapons or of rockets, and it's very doubtful, if we are to judge by the demonstrations that have taken place in space, whether we have rockets as accurate and deadly as the Soviet Union's.

Europe has grown from a colony, a dependent colony of the United States, into a great industrial power, more or less united in the European Economic Community, and a bitter competitor of the United States in the world market. Japan has risen from the ashes to become a competitor in the world market.

The Soviet Union and the Eastern European countries associated with it have also enormously increased their productive capacity. And then, out of a clear sky as far as the blind were concerned, came the Chinese Revolution, in which six or seven hundred million people not only chased the American satrap Chiang Kai-shek off the mainland and brought about a complete social revolution in China, but also closed China to the world capitalist market, as Russia and Eastern Europe had already been closed.

And then China triggered the further colonial revolution in Korea and Vietnam. We don't know just how things are in South Vietnam right now, but yesterday they didn't look so good. Yesterday, I read that mobs were in the streets and that the latest savior had been replaced by a triumvirate. And we're going in there to defend free people—we're having trouble locating where they are. The South Vietnamese think that they must be somewhere else—they're certainly not in Saigon, because they're storming the headquarters of the custodians of that freedom.

The Chinese Revolution triggered the colonial revolution through all of Asia and Africa; and finally, against our best wishes, it leaped across the wide ocean to Cuba, and is fermenting all over Latin America.

In the meantime, American productivity is growing at an astonishing rate, but the market in the world is narrowing. We can't sell goods to Russia, Eastern Europe, or China except on a *quid pro quo* basis. We can't sell goods to Europe except on an exchange basis. The narrowing market, along with increasing production, leads to a point at which overproduction, as foreseen by Marx more than a hundred years ago, will attack all the capitalist countries with a depression—not such as we knew from 1929 until the beginning of the Second World War, but of how great consequences nobody knows. And while all the economists are scratching their heads, they're not asking when a recession is going to come, but as I read them, they mean a depression and crisis. To complicate things further, something new has been developed which greatly increases the productivity of the system while decreasing the manpower required. Automation or, as some of the scientists want to call it, cybernation—that is, automatic machinery coupled to computers which do the thinking and directing—displaces men faster than new jobs are created by an increased demand for goods.

We know a few rough facts. For example, in the coal mines two-thirds of the people who made their living traditionally by coal, as their fathers and grandfathers did before them, two-thirds of the coal miners have been removed from the mines to make room for machines to dig coal. The same thing is happening in the packinghouses, which touches me emotionally because my first job was in a packinghouse. They've just simply been torn down and the industry has moved out to the centers where the cattle are fattened and where they are now processed in automated plants. Probably half of the packinghouse workers—skilled, semiskilled and unskilled—are roaming the streets without jobs, without a chance of finding any.

Already we have increasing unemployment—they say five million; but the true figure is probably ten million, as all the honest experts tell you. Because the other five million consists of people who have quit looking for jobs. Five million are those they have registered. I've read in a dozen places—I'm not an expert on the question, but I've been reading rather voluminously lately and discussing with comrades the increasing abundance of literature of the effects of automation and cybernation—one figure that seems to be generally agreed upon is that every week 40,000 jobs are eliminated in industry right now; that's two million a year.

And now we're reaping the full benefit of the baby boom that followed the Second World War. Two million surplus babies have become teen-agers, looking for work that they can't find. The rate of unemployment among vigorous teen-agers—dropouts from high school or graduates, it makes no difference—is especially high; and among Negro adolescents it runs to 30 and 40 percent.

On the surface, the Negro people have apparently been making advances through their newfound militancy—and, by the way, that's new, less than ten years old—that is, their self-assertion outside the framework of the ultrarespectable, reformistic National Association for the Advancement of Colored People. They have broken out of that in various forms and made a few gains and got a few laws passed.

But the conditions of the Negro people have actually worsened from year to year while they were fighting hardest and seemingly making the most important gains in the legal field. And you hear about the riots in Harlem, in Brooklyn, in Rochester, Chicago, and yesterday in Philadelphia. These are riots for the most part triggered by young Negroes who have no jobs, who can't find jobs and who, out of frustration and desperation and the brutality inflicted upon them by police, take to the streets in violent action. Nothing has been gained—at least nothing has been gained yet except a promise of a conference with the leaders. The leaders of all the various organizations that have sprung up within the last ten years have no power over these outbursts, but they try to solve the problem by negotiation. They no sooner get a meeting to negotiate with the masters of what they call the power structure—which they ought to call American capitalism, in order to call things by their right name—than a riot breaks out in Philadelphia. Nobody knows where the next one will start.

The significant thing is that we are only at the beginning of the automation revolution. We just got started. And it's self-propelling and developing to the point where a group of thinkers, none of whom calls himself a socialist, financed by—this is the magnificent irony of the whole thing—the Center for the Study of Democratic Institutions, in turn financed by the Ford Foundation, has come out with a document on the Triple Revolution. In it they list the strides already made by cybernation and extrapolate from that, as thinkers should, to estimate the trend into the future. And they come to the conclusion that there's no possibility even of merely assimilating the present ten million unemployed, not to speak of the fifteen million elderly people who are poor and living on the ragged edge of nothing, and that there will be so many millions more that if the powers-that-be want to keep their system going, they're going to have to abandon the whole idea of wages for work performed, because there will not be sufficient work. And they will have to introduce a system whose premise is that everybody who's born into this world is entitled to compensation sufficient for a comfortable living, whether he works or not.

This is the document that has been laid on the table for the consideration of the Marxists who, I'm sorry to say, didn't think of it first. But I would be sorrier still to say that some Marxists, because the original thinking came from other sources, were not flexible and subtle and intelligent enough to seize upon the evidence provided for them and make their own extrapolations as to what the perspective is.

The perspective, as I see it, is that we can't go on as usual because the cybernation or automation revolution is not merely taking place in the United States, it's already well underway in Europe and Japan and the Soviet Union. And America will, in my opinion, in the very near future run up against the fact that the world market is so flooded with goods that U.S. production will have to be slowed down. Because, for some peculiar reason, they don't produce goods for the fun of it. They don't produce goods for utility or for beauty or just for the hell of it. They produce goods for profit. And in order to get profit, they've got to sell them. Where in the hell are they going to sell them when the market is clogged not only by our overproduction, but by that of Europe and Japan and the Soviet Union?

Now, I don't see any possible solution for this except a tremendous showdown. And we must now modify the early formula of the socialists who said: socialism or barbarism. Because there has been another revolution taking place alongside the automation revolution, and that's the revolution in weaponry, as the Ad Hoc Committee calls it. That's the development of atomic and hydrogen bombs and the means to deliver them anyplace on earth. You hear the proud boast of the representatives of the military and the government that we already have enough nuclear bombs and the means to deliver them anyplace on earth—we already have enough to kill every man, woman and child four or five times over. That's what they call overkill. And then there's the sobering second statement—the Soviet Union has got a lot of these bombs too.

When they talk about a confrontation with the Soviet Union, they say—I heard McNamara and I heard Kennedy—as if they were discussing a game of chess, "We have the means to destroy the Soviet Union and China, but they have the means to kill 100 million Americans at the same time within the first hour in the first strike." And I think that when they say 100 million, they mean 200 million.

There exists not only the possibility, but the *danger,* as long as American imperialism has command of this capacity to destroy the human race, whether by direct firepower, fire storms, or by subsequent fallout of strontium 90; while they have all that, there is no security whatever in this world.

Here, I would like to make a slight correction of a remark made by the speaker last night, when he spoke of the colonial revolution as the center of the international revolution. It seems to me he should have said "at the present moment." Because the colonial revolution can't disarm the American imperialists. Neither can the Soviet Union. They can only deter them. The only one who can disarm the American imperialists of their arsenal of death-dealing hydrogen and atomic bombs is the American working class. And if they don't do it, you're in yearly, monthly, weekly, daily, hourly danger—not only you—the whole world is in danger of an accident, or of an insane person in a submarine deciding it's time to put an end to all this foolishness and defoliate some jungles with a couple of nuclear weapons, which will bring retaliation because there will be no way of knowing who fired them, where they come from. The world can be consumed in an atomic holocaust.

Now, how long can this situation last? Our international

resolution, "The Dynamics of World Revolution," which is one of the very best documents of our international movement, fully worthy, in my opinion, of its place in succession to the great documents produced by Trotsky, analyzes the whole world problem essentially correctly, I think, and comes to the conclusion, which is obvious to any thinking person, that there cannot be any final showdown until it takes place in the United States—until the American imperialists are disarmed. And they cannot be disarmed from without—only from within. And the writers of the resolution say that by the end of the century, the American working class will complete its historic mission.

Now, I would like to end my preliminary summation by saying that my difference with them is *time*. I agree with that document and I admire it enormously, but I think they are too optimistic on the time span they allow. I think it would be more realistic to say ten years. We've got ten years in this country to decide whether this terrible risk is going to be continued or whether the American working class is going to disarm the American imperialists and scrap the nuclear weapons and clear the road for a socialist world. And—to come back to our point of departure—that gives a sense of urgency to the work of a young socialist today, as contrasted with Rose's and my time fifty-odd years ago. It gives a sense of urgency to the work of those who join the socialist movement consciously and understandingly, with a knowledge of the basic premises of Marxism brought up to date and applied to these new problems, for these new problems are not fabricated by me but are known—or should be known—to all, for they are appearing in print more and more every day. Since I began to discuss this question a year ago with comrades in Los Angeles, never a week goes by that we don't get new information about some new advance of the tremendous potential destructiveness of nuclear weapons, on the one side, and the increased productivity of the automated machinery at the expense of human labor power, on the other.

So we have come to the conclusion that time is shorter. When you join a socialist movement now, you're joining the battle which in your own lifetime—not that of your children, not that of your grandchildren, but in your own lifetime—and even before you reach an advanced age, is going to be settled.

You have got to be the vanguard of the people who are going to settle it. So being a socialist becomes the central purpose of your life and your activity. And everything you do counts, however little it may signify at the moment, whether it's writing a leaflet or distributing a leaflet or making a speech or attending a meeting or taking part in a demonstration.

Or, no less important, and perhaps more important, gathering occasionally in seminars or lectures to discuss and, above all, to think—to think. And in thinking, a true Marxist does not discard any element of reality.

The essence of Marxist politics is not only to begin with reality as it is, but also as it has evolved from the past and as it is evolving toward the future, and always to look to see what's new and to ask what it signifies for us. So, the essence of my presentation is: let's have a consideration, a sort of think session among ourselves. What's new? How is it related to the past? What are we going to do about it today? And what does it signify for our lives as young revolutionists just beginning to go into action?

Chapter 17

# Before the Minneapolis trial

Delivered at the Morrison Hotel in Chicago to a mass meeting greeting the defendants in the Minneapolis Labor Case, October 10, 1941.

Comrade Chairman and Comrades:
There is one thing that never fails about a meeting or a gathering of Trotskyists—it always makes you feel good to be there. You feel inspired in the company of people who have some faith in the future, who believe in a program and are willing to fight for it and to pay for it in any way that is necessary. I was supposed to be sick tonight. I caught cold last night and didn't feel so well. But when I came to the meeting and heard some of the speeches and, above all, saw the warm reaction from the comrades in the audience, I began to feel better and decided to lay my cold on the shelf until the conference is over.

We believe in the future, and nowhere outside of the revolutionary movement in these tragic days can you find people with any faith in the future or any hope that this world, which has rolled along for so many centuries, is going to keep on rolling and that historic progress is not finished but only beginning.

When I, along with my colleagues, go on trial in the federal courtroom in Minneapolis on the twentieth of this month, it will be thirty years, almost to the day, since I formally joined the revolutionary labor movement in Kansas City in 1911. I joined the IWW thirty years ago this October because, as a young man, a young worker, I had become convinced that socialism was a good idea. And thirty years afterward I am more convinced than ever that socialism is the only hope of the world. After having seen what capitalism has been able to do with this world in the past thirty years—how in that space of time it could produce two world wars devouring the lives of tens of millions of people, and its crises and its unemployment, and its despair and its hypocrisy—one can feel fortunate indeed if he has harnessed his life's activity to a philosophy pointing the way to a better and more sanely organized social system, which is socialism.

For all of us thirty years ago, socialism was only a formula, a prophecy of our great teachers. But in the intervening time we have seen the workers in one great part of the earth—over one-sixth of its surface—actually rise up victoriously in revolution and take charge of the social system of a great expanse of territory, and demonstrate in practice, in spite of all difficulties, that the workers can organize production on a better, more planful, more productive and fruitful basis than private capitalism can anywhere. And even if after these years, even if at the end of twenty-four years, this magnificent achievement of the Russian workers is finally struck down by the hands of Hitler and Stalin, that will be only a brief episode, because the example of the Russian Revolution is imperishable and will inspire the workers of other countries, as well as Russia, to carry through that experiment and make it successful and final in its victory.

We take great satisfaction, as we stand here tonight, in the knowledge that we have followed the star of the Russian Revolution, that we have been loyal defenders of it to the very last moment, that we fought the Stalinist betrayers, that we supported the Soviet Union against all of its capitalist enemies, and that we parted company with those fainthearts, cowards, those deserters and renegades who wanted to desert the Russian Revolution in the hour of its most desperate need.

The Russian Revolution, whatever the outcome of the terrible encounter today—if the Soviet Union really comes to catastrophe under the traitorous leadership of Stalin and his gang, we will remain partisans of the Russian Revolution, and in due time we will transport it into this country and we will make a revolution which neither Hitler nor Stalin nor Roosevelt nor Biddle nor anybody else will have the nerve to try to overthrow, when we do it in the USA.

And when we go on trial, they will not drag us in like repentant slaves to repudiate what we have said and what we have done. We will go into that courtroom not as defendants at all, but as accusers of the prosecutors and the system they represent.

I was greatly interested in talking tonight to our chief counsel, Comrade Albert Goldman, who got mixed up in the law business so much that he is also a defendant in the case. So now he will have to do a little pitching. I was greatly interested in his plan for the defense. I don't know how much law he has been reading, but I suppose he and his colleagues have done enough. But the plan for the defense that is the real defense is a division of subjects that the different defendants are to speak about in court. Morrow is going to give an exposition of Marxist propaganda from the point of view of the editor of a revolutionary journal. Comrade Dunne is going to give an exposition of Trotskyist trade unionism in Minneapolis, what it has done for the workers, and why it is good. The topic assigned to Dobbs is revolutionary trade unionism in general in the epoch of wars and revolutions. I have been assigned an explanation of the revolutionary party, how we are building it and why it is going to conquer in the United States. Why, Goldman got this thing so well fixed up it almost makes you glad of the opportunity this scissorbill prosecution has given us.

This is not my first indictment. This is the third time that I have been called upon to answer a formal indictment in the course of the years I have mentioned. I almost had the honor of a sojourn in the state penitentiary of Illinois. I was indicted in 1913—twenty-eight years ago, in the spring of 1913—in Peoria, Illinois, in the course of a strike in the Avery Manufacturing Plant there. I forget exactly all that I was accused of, but I recall that among other things I was "conspiring against the people and integrity of the State of Illinois."

I was indicted again in 1919 by the federal government in the jurisdiction of Kansas City on the charge of conspiring to obstruct the production of wartime materials, namely, bituminous coal. This was the result of some activity in the coal strike in the Kansas coal fields at that time.

Well, I was lucky enough, one way or another, in these two previous indictments, to escape conviction. Things occurred and eventually they were washed out, and I didn't serve any penitentiary sentence. And this time—and it seems to me I detect just a slight note in our chairlady's remarks, as if she were saying a final farewell to us—well,

I am not ready to call it quits until they really have got us there, because something may happen in our favor. But if they really put us in the penitentiary this time, I will at least get a certain satisfaction from the fact that it took them thirty years to catch up with me.

And I have had a lot of satisfaction in those thirty years. I consider it the greatest satisfaction a man can possibly have in this period of history. That's the satisfaction of working and fighting for the cause that I believe in and of living the kind of a life that I wanted to live—the life of a rebel against capitalism. That satisfaction is enough so that even if I have to pay a little now, I am still away ahead of the game.

I got a beautiful letter the other day from Comrade Natalia Trotsky. Among other things, she expressed her great satisfaction that *The Militant,* in a recent issue, had printed a chapter from Comrade Trotsky's book, *Literature and Revolution,* that chapter where, with great masterful strokes of his pen, he draws a picture of the communist society of the future and the stature communist man will attain. She said that chapter had always attracted her, and that she loved this aspect of the movement and believed that we should more and more inspire the workers with that great, that grandiose vision of the communist future of mankind. She said Trotsky wrote the book after consultation with Lenin. He wrote it in the heat of military struggle, and the ideas in it and its method were almost a collaboration between Trotsky and Lenin.

And she said one thing more: that when she talked with Trotsky about the chapter containing the grandiose vision of the classless society based on solidarity, justice, friendship and brotherhood, which will no longer be ashamed to mention those words because they will be cleansed of hypocrisy, he told her that he personally preferred the present with its struggle for the future. And I, too, think that I do not need to see the communist society myself. I can be completely satisfied with the struggle to attain it. I think that is the spirit of all the communists who belong to this party and who sympathize with this party and who help it in various ways. We are bound together by the greatest bond that could ever be conceived of in this period of wars and revolutions—the bond of the common goal of our struggle, solidarity among ourselves, confidence in each other, and faith in the final victory. I recommend to every young man and every young woman that philosophy, that outlook, that faith and that struggle.

Fifteen of the eighteen convicted in the Minneapolis Labor Case surrender to U.S. Marshals, December 1944. Facing up to largest marshal is V. R. Dunne; behind him, Cannon, Oscar Coover, Sr., Carl Skoglund, Albert Goldman, Farrell Dobbs, Felix Morrow, Grace Carlson, Carlos Hudson, Max Geldman, Harry DeBoer, Emil Hansen, Clarence Hamel (face hidden), Ed Palmquist, and Jake Cooper. Three others (Karl Kuehn, Alfred Russell, and Oscar Schoenfeld) served their sentences in Danbury, Connecticut.

The Executive Board of Local 544 of the International Brotherhood of Teamsters in Minneapolis in 1938. Left to right: Farrell Dobbs, Grant Dunne, Carl Skoglund, V. R. Dunne, Miles Dunne, Jack Smith, Bill Brown, Nick Wagner.

# Chapter 18

## Speech on the way to prison

Delivered at a banquet at Irving Plaza, New York City, December 26, 1943.

This last opportunity to speak to you for a period, comrades, is also the first opportunity I have had to thank you all for the gifts that were presented to me and Rose on the occasion of the fifteenth anniversary of our movement. We were both given gold watches by the comrades of Local New York. While I will not be able to take the watch with me to Sandstone penitentiary, I will nevertheless be able to take something even more valuable than the watch or any other material gift. That is the memory of your kindness and your friendship.

It is always the most important thing in a new situation to understand what it is, to know exactly what has happened and why. Trotsky taught us that, among so many other things. He frequently repeated his favorite motto, from Spinoza: "Neither to weep nor to laugh, but to understand."

The new situation is very clear to us, and I think our understanding is accurate. As the United States began to gear all its machinery for entry into the new imperialist war, it became necessary again to fool the people. Here, as throughout the world, a tremendous, worldwide mechanism of deception, falsification and misrepresentation was turned loose on the people. It was once said that in every war the first casualty is the truth, and surely the truth was the first casualty of this war. The world is flooded, inundated by lies. We are living, you might say, in the epoch of the lie. Natalia Trotsky, in a letter she wrote to us not long ago, said that the lie has entered like a geologic layer into the spiritual life of the people of the world; but even geologic layers are not indestructible. The coming social revolution will blow the stratum of lies to bits, as a volcano blows up a geologic stratum.

In this time, when the people of the world, and the people of America among them, needed one thing more than anything else—to know the truth—they were fed on lies. All those in public life, all the political parties; all the preachers, priests and rabbis; all the intellectuals who had promised to instruct and educate and inform the youth—they all betrayed the people of America; they sold them out and went over to the camp of the liars and deceivers. Our party alone did not betray, did not sell out. We Trotskyists told the truth. That is the reason, and the only reason, we are on our way to prison. We obeyed the first commandment in the decalogue of Trotskyism, which reads: "Thou shalt not lie."

We are not criminals, as you know, and as all of the others know. We are not going to prison for any fault or injury committed against unoffending people. We didn't kill, we didn't steal, and we didn't lie. On the contrary, we have been just and truthful. All the criminals are on the other side. And all the liars are on the other side, beginning with the judge and prosecutor in Minneapolis and ending with the highest court in the land. That is where the criminals are. I say that those nine black-gowned justices of the Supreme Court in Washington are just as criminal as any of them. They are on a level with Roosevelt and Biddle, who started the prosecution, and the lesser figures who carried it through. The august court did not pass judgment upon us. They played the ignominious role of Pontius Pilate, who washed his hands.

The Supreme Court of the United States, many of whom were once members of the American Civil Liberties Union—democrats, if you please, and liberals who frowned upon the morality of the Bolsheviks and the Marxists—showed us what their morality consists of. They were not concerned if honest people had been condemned. They were not concerned if the treasured Bill of Rights had been trampled into the mire. They didn't see the act. They turned away. They washed their hands.

I say they are all liars and conspirators. They are all on the side of the rich and the privileged, and their actions, from beginning to end, have been entirely consistent with this position. Everything, from the time when Roosevelt gave Biddle instructions to start the prosecutions against us, up to the trial, up to the verdict and the condemnation, up to the sentencing in the federal court of Judge Joyce, up to the Pontius Pilate action of the Supreme Court of the United States—everything is consistent, everything is in order in the camp of the liars, the friends of the rich and privileged.

But how do matters stand with us? Are we consistent too? Yes, indeed. Everything is in order on our side. We neither laugh nor weep; we understand. We have understood from the beginning what might be the consequences of our undertaking. All people pay for their ideas what they think the ideas are worth. If some men are not prepared to pay with the sacrifice of one day's liberty or the missing of one meal or a little inconvenience for the sake of their ideas, they are only saying thereby that they set no serious value upon them. But we think our ideas are the most important thing in this world, that they represent the whole future of mankind. That is why, if we have to pay even a high price for the sake of those ideas, we pay it without whimpering. We are Trotskyists, you remember, and that means we are political people of a different breed.

The Trotskyist party is not like the other parties. It is a different kind of a party, different not in degree, but in kind, in quality. Other parties and other politicians set limits to what they will do. But the Trotskyists set no limit on what they will do for their ideas and, in the last analysis, they set no limits on the price they are prepared to pay for them. The others play for pennies, but the Trotskyist stakes his head. Therein is the difference. Therein is the chasm that separates the vanguard of the coming proletarian revolution from all politicians and parties who merely dabble with the idea.

I am not one of those who take lightly the iniquity that has been perpetrated against us. It is a severe and cruel punishment. We who love freedom and live for the idea of freedom are condemned to lose it for ourselves. We will not be free to come and go as we please. Our days and nights, through the long months leading up to the end of our sentence, will be regulated, and all our movements will be circumscribed by others. That will not be easy for rebels to bear. We will be forced into inactivity. What can be more cruel to a revolutionary activist than to be deprived of the opportunity to take part in the movement which means life to him—the very breath of life?

And then, also, it is no light matter that we have to be separated from our families, and they from us. True, we don't cry, and, as Rose said so magnificently in her speech here tonight, our women don't mope. But, nevertheless, we are human too. If we are struck a blow, we hurt; and if we are stabbed, we bleed. Separation from those whose lives are bound to us in an intimate personal way is no less cruel a punishment for us than it would be for others. Perhaps it is even more cruel because our personal intimate associations are bound up with a complete community of ideas and activity in every element of life. Such associations are perhaps a little closer, even a little dearer, if you will, than those of people who don't value ideas very much and who, consequently, don't attract to themselves personal associations such as ours.

But even if it hurts a little more, we can stand it better than the others because we are doing it on behalf of a cause that is more important than our personal lives. It is the cause that lifts us up and gives us strength. Socialism is greater than a mother and dearer than a wife. Knowing that, and knowing that our separation is forced upon us because of our devotion to the higher cause, is what makes it possible to bear and to withstand.

We haven't been taken by surprise. We have not been suddenly pulled up short and required to make a decision whether we are prepared to pay this price. Our decision was made in advance. We knew to begin with that to tell the truth, to take up the cause of the poor and the persecuted against the rich and the mighty, to tell the truth in the face of all the liars in the world—we knew that course entailed risks. I knew that more than thirty years ago when I entered the socialist movement as a youth.

Socialism lifted me out of the drab surroundings and meager life of the poor town of Rosedale, Kansas, and showed me the vision of a new world. I thought it was good. I thought it worth fighting for. I was ready, more than thirty years ago, to fight for it at all hazards.

Nothing has ever changed my sense of proportion and of values in that respect. Neither persecution, nor poverty, nor hardship, nor the long days of internal struggles and factional quarrels that sear the souls of men in the political movement—none of that was able to change me or break me, because I never forgot what I started out to fight for. I kept undimmed my vision of the socialist future of mankind. Having that attitude, as all of the eighteen do, we can put so-called sacrifices in their proper setting and attribute to them their right place with a due sense of proportion.

Ben Hanford, one of the best loved of all the early socialist agitators in this country, once objected to a comrade's statement that he had made great sacrifices for the movement. He said he had received from the socialist movement something far greater and far better than he had ever been able to contribute to it. He had only been able to give time, effort and material means, but the socialist movement had given him a cause that was bigger than self. Therefore, he had a warrant for living in a world of poverty, hardship, discrimination and injustice. "So please don't speak of my sacrifices," said Ben Hanford. "Socialism made a man of me, and I can never repay the movement for that."

We have not been idle in our time of comparative freedom. We have labored and we have created something that we can leave behind, very sure that it will not fall apart. A movement that is built upon ideas is a power that is hard to destroy. Indeed, it cannot be destroyed.

You remember the tragic time three years ago last August, when Trotsky fell victim to the assassin. Many people speculated that now, with the great genius-leader dead, the movement he had created would be scattered to the four winds and soon disappear. We knew it was not so, because the ideas Trotsky left behind were a mighty cement to keep the ranks together. The party didn't fall into disintegration. Far from it, the party continued to live and to grow. That will be the case now, too.

We go to prison confident that we are leaving behind us capable men and women who are qualified to take our places in the leadership of the party. They have not been selected in a hurry. When the decision of the Supreme Court was announced, we did not need an emergency meeting and a hurried search for comrades to take our places in the leading positions. That had already been decided by the fifteenth anniversary plenum of our party. But even the plenum decision was only a formality. In reality, the substitute leadership had been decided by the fifteen years of work and struggle in which certain individual comrades had been sifted out. They had shown their caliber. They had come forward, and by common consent they were designated to step into the places vacated by the eighteen.

Our party is built on correct ideas and therefore is indestructible. But, in addition to that, I believe there is in this party of ours an intangible power which reinforces the power of its ideas. That is the spirit of the party—its comradeship, its solidarity. You know the word *comrade* has been so long abused and so badly defiled by self-seekers and pretenders that honest people sometimes shrink from using the word any more. But in the movement that has been created under the inspiration of Trotsky, with his example always before us, the word *comrade* has acquired a new, fresh meaning that animates the members of our movement not only in their political work in the class struggle, but also in all their daily lives and associations with each other. It is not anymore, not with us, a formal and conventional word, but a bond of unity and solidarity. Our comrades are devoted to each other and trust each other. That is an intangible source of power that will yield great results in the days to come.

The grandest figure in the whole history of America was John Brown. In John Brown of Osawatomie, the word and the deed were always in harmony with each other, never in contradiction, never in conflict. When the old warrior went to Harpers Ferry to "interfere," as he said, against the abomination of chattel slavery, he took a small group of young men with him, among them some of his own sons. They went to Harpers Ferry where they perished because, like Luther, they could do no other. They felt required to do it. When Watson Brown, the son of the old man, lay dying in the firehouse, bleeding from his wounds, with his head resting on an old pair of overalls, the great governor of the slave state of Virginia came in to see him. He said to Watson Brown, "Young man, what brought you here?" Watson Brown answered him in two words: "Duty, Sir!"

I believe that is the case with us. I believe that we have been under the same compulsion as John Brown's young men were. We were obliged to tell the truth. We saw the abomination of the imperialist war and we were under compulsion to tell the people the truth about it. We saw the vision of a socialist society and were under compulsion to fight for it at all costs and despite all hazards. We have done our duty. And that, to me, on the eve of departure for Sandstone, is the important thing. That is why we go to the next stage of the struggle with a sure self-confidence and self-assurance.

We are historically minded. We know that in the great scale of history our personal fate is a trifle, our lives are a trifle. But the socialist goal of our struggle—that is no trifle.

To serve that goal, as we have served it, that is enough. Let the consequences be what they may. Whether we participate in the final victory of the struggle of mankind for its socialist future, or whether it has to be built on a foundation of our bones, it will still be good for us that we took part in it, and we will have our justification and our reward.

No liars and conspirators, no Supreme Court and no prison, can take that satisfaction away from us. We were obliged to do what we did. As a consequence of our truth-telling and our struggle, we are now obliged to go to prison. We go there, however, not as criminals, but because duty takes us there.

# Chapter 19

# Sixtieth birthday speech

Delivered at birthday celebration in Los Angeles, March 4, 1950.

As you know, my sixtieth birthday, which also rounds out my forty years of activity in the movement, was already celebrated at a dinner in New York. That was three weeks ago, but I haven't grown a day older since then. Time has stood still for me during these three weeks because I was waiting for this second celebration in Los Angeles. I maintained that my sixtieth birthday was not official until it was celebrated here. As you know, I am partial to Los Angeles. Perhaps that is because the Los Angeles comrades have always been partial to me, and have always given me the benefit of their most generous judgment. I like that friendly indulgence; and as a matter of fact, I need it.

In these forty years of struggle, people have been talking about me ever since I started, and most of what was said—at least what I heard—was harsh and critical. Those who might have had other opinions were not so articulate.

Rose Karsner, James P. Cannon, and Harry Ring at New York banquet on Cannon's seventieth birthday, 1960.

I never complained about the brickbats tossed in my direction, and perhaps some people thought I was indifferent to the opinions of others. But that wasn't the reason. I had simply learned to recognize hostile criticism as an occupational hazard of the political struggle. If you can't take it, you are licked before you start. I learned from Engels that when you go into revolutionary politics you should put on an old pair of pants. And I learned from Marx that you must not let people get you down with pinpricks. So I dressed for battle and developed a tough hide.

But still, I must tell you—although you won't believe me—that when I used to hear people denouncing me and criticizing me, I was hurt and bewildered, for I am by nature friendly and peace-loving. I felt something like Eddie Waitkus, the star first baseman of the Philadelphia Phillies, who was in the news the other day. He had an unfortunate experience with a deranged woman who was a total stranger to him. She lost her head and, for no reason at all, broke into his hotel room and shot him. They took Eddie to the hospital for an operation, and when he came out of the anesthesia, they told him what had happened. His only comment was a question: "Why did she want to go and shoot a nice guy like me?" That is what I have thought all these years about my critics and opponents. They have been shooting the wrong guy all the time.

On the occasion of the celebration in New York, I received letters and telegrams from friends and comrades throughout the country. In several of them there was a recurrent note somewhat as follows: "Celebrating your forty years in the movement, we expect you to give forty more." That sounds like a large order, but if, as it is said, longevity is determined by heredity, things might possibly work out that way. I come from a long-lived ancestry. All four of my grandparents lived into their eighties. Two of my aunts lived to be nearly ninety. My father lived to be eighty-nine. It may be that I still have a long way to go. But I am not making any long-range commitments tonight.

Now I must frankly tell you that I have appreciated in the highest degree the joint celebration—this prolonged birthday—in New York and in Los Angeles. I wouldn't go for the idea that I should stand in the corner and pretend not to know what was being prepared. I was the biggest promoter of the affair in New York.

I was assigned to be chairman of a public meeting where Vincent Dunne was the speaker, about a week before the birthday celebration. The New York organizer was in a dither as to how to announce my birthday celebration, with me as the chairman of the meeting. He thought it would be too delicate a matter for me to announce myself. When I called him up the afternoon of the meeting and asked him for last instructions about announcements, he said: "You don't have to say anything about the dinner; that will be taken care of by someone else."

I said, "Well, if I am chairman of the meeting, I might as well announce it."

He said, "Would you?"

I said, "Damn right, I will. I've been waiting sixty years for this birthday!"

And I used the occasion of Vincent Dunne's lecture to invite everybody down to the birthday party; and to make it very clear that I was as much in favor of it as anybody, I made only one proviso. I said: "I want it to be a real party of friends and comrades, and I don't want any enemies of our movement coming around telling me what a good fellow I am. I don't want any Farleys or Baruchs or anybody else who has been opposed to the things I've fought for, coming around to give me some hypocritical personal compliments. I would feel dishonored if those whom I've fought against all my life came around to pay tribute to me on my sixtieth birthday."

I have enjoyed it here tonight, as I did in New York, because there have been no formal compliments, no hypocritical praise—just, maybe, a little exaggeration. I understand that, and I don't take it to be flattery. Flattery means falsehood, deceit. I take all the kind words you have said, rather, as what we Irish call the blarney. The blarney is not falsehood; it is the truth exaggerated and embellished to make it sound better. We always feel that under the husk of exaggeration there is a grain of truth and sincerity in the compliments, and we love the blarney.

After forty years of experience, of ups and downs and battles and denunciations, criticism and hardships and rewards—it is nice to sit down at the end of forty years and hear the friendly words of comrades. Somebody once said: "The sweetest music man ever heard is the applause of his fellows." And if one can be sure, as I am tonight, that the applause is sincerely meant and freely given, it is doubly sweet.

I also like the fact that this drawn-out celebration,

beginning in New York and ending here tonight, has not been isolated and separated from our life and our work. In New York it was simply one of the features of the plenum of our National Committee. We had already been meeting a whole day. We held the celebration in the evening, and then we went back the next morning into another session of the plenum to deal with the problems of today and tomorrow, and not merely to confine ourselves to reminiscences.

I don't want to do that here tonight; but still I think I might be justified in making a brief review or, more correctly, a summary of these sixty years. Rose and I are the same age, with only a few weeks' difference, and we have both been in the movement all our lives. This gathering marks her sixty years of life and forty years of socialist activity too. In all the years we have been together, we never paid much attention to birthdays. The years went by. We were busy and had no time. I don't even remember celebrating birthdays in our house as a rule. Not from year to year at any rate. But when we reached the age of sixty, it occurred to both of us, as it has probably occurred to others who have reached that age, to take a little time out to think what has happened, and to make a sort of appraisal of the sixty years.

Speaking for myself, and making a bow to the acquisitive society we live in, I will begin with point one: What have you accumulated? Well, even there it's not so bad. I have a new suit of clothes which was given to me by a friend as a birthday present. I have my weekly allowance from Rose in my pocket. That's more than I had to start with, and it's as much as I ever had. So I feel that, in the matter of accumulation, if I haven't gained much ground, I haven't lost any. That's a satisfactory inventory.

The second point I ask myself: What have you

accomplished? There, I can tell you that I have perhaps made a more objective judgment than you have. I am one man who took seriously the injunction of the Greek philosophers: Man, know thyself. And if I don't know myself, I've come as close to it as a man can. Because I know myself, I don't claim great accomplishments. I am well aware of all the negligences and all the faults. I can't, in good conscience, stand up and say that I did the best I knew; I only did the best I could. That's quite a difference. I only did the best I could, falling short of the best I knew, because I am human and therefore fallible and frail, prone to error and even to folly, like all others. In summing up the answer to that question—what have you accomplished?—I can only say honestly: I did the best I could.

Then I come to the third point of my self-examination: Has your life been consistent with your youth? For me that has always been the most decisive criterion, for one's youth is the gauge to measure by. Youth is the age of wisdom, when our ideals seem to be, as they really are in fact, more important than anything else in the world. Youth is the age of virtue, or more correctly, the age of courage, which is the first virtue. Every man's younger self is his better self.

The struggle for socialism, with all its hazards and penalties, has always been comparatively easy for me, throughout the entire forty years, because my youth was always with me. My youth was like another person who never forsook me, not even in the darkest hours. It was then that he was always most vividly present as a friend, easygoing and indulgent as a friend should be, with a benign indifference to my faults and my follies which disturbed other people so much. The faults and follies never disturbed my younger self, and I liked that because I like to have a little leeway in my personal life.

I never promised anybody to be perfect. I only promised

to be myself and to be true to myself—that is, to my better self, to my youth. That in itself was a pretty big undertaking, easier to promise than to perform. And this seemed to be the view of my younger self, who followed me everywhere I went. He insisted on that, but on nothing more. He consistently checked me up on that. He was a friend, as I said, but also a censor and a judge—sometimes looking over my shoulder, sometimes looking me straight in the eye, but always confronting me with the one imperious command: Remember, I am your youth, don't betray me!

As long as I didn't do that—and I never did—I felt sure, with never a doubt, that I was on the right road, even though it put me in the minority, and more often than not in the minority of the minority. That wasn't my fault. I have been in the minority not because I don't like crowds, not because I am sectarian by nature, but because I couldn't agree with the majority. I couldn't agree with things as they are. I was in favor of things as they ought to be and will be.

That is what put me in the minority and out of step with the others. I found the explanation of that in the writings of Thoreau, and the justification for it too. Thoreau wrote: "If a man does not keep pace with his companions, perhaps it is because he hears a different drummer. Let him step to the music which he hears, however measured or faraway."

Have forty years of activity, of struggle, of life, resulted in defeat or victory? That is a fair question to put on such an occasion as this. And I say the answer depends on how you measure defeat and victory. Our goal is the socialist society, and it is clear that that goal has not yet been attained. But in my youth, when I became a socialist, I associated the ideal of socialism with my own way of life. I decided to be a socialist and to live as a socialist, insofar as physical restrictions would permit, even within the capitalist society. And having that philosophy, I have felt that every little thing I contributed from day to day to the struggle for the socialist goal of the future was a vindication of my own life that day, and that every day was a victory. If one has that conception of socialism, and lives by it, he does not need to wait for the final victory of socialism. He has his own share of socialism as he goes along.

The prophet Joel, prophesying great things for his people, said: "Your young men shall see visions." In my own youth I saw the vision of a new world, and I have never lost it. I came out of Rosedale, Kansas, forty years ago looking for truth and justice. I'm still looking, and I won't give one percent discount.

I have always agreed with Emerson, who said, "He who has seen the vision of a better future is already a citizen of that future." I take that literally. That was always true in my case. And that was all the reward I needed for anything done or given to the movement. I never found it possible, nor did I ever even think of renouncing my citizenship in the socialist future of humanity. And here with you tonight, in the midst of friends and comrades, I feel like a qualified citizen of the good society of the free and equal, of that future which Jack London so beautifully described as "the golden future when there will be no servants, naught but the service of love."

It is very rarely, and only in the most exceptional occasions, that we revolutionists dare to permit ourselves to express such sentiments, or even to utter such words. In the society in which we have been fated to live, a society divided into classes, deception and hypocrisy rule supreme. The noblest and most fraternal sentiments, which inspire the better selves of the great majority of the people in their relations with each other, are perverted for opposite uses and exploited for the selfish aims of a few.

The most beautiful and holy words that people have articulated to express their deepest feelings and their highest aspirations have been so prostituted by misuse that they have lost their original values, like coins worn smooth from too much handling. All this perversion of sentiment and prostitution of language makes us cautious and reserved in expressing ourselves, lest we too sound like the hypocrites and the vulgarians, who are so glib and free with the use of words that mean nothing to them.

But on this occasion, here among comrades, I will disregard that fear and tell you what I really think and feel, what I have always thought and felt since I became a socialist forty years ago. I believe in people and in their unlimited capacity for improvement and progress through cooperation and solidarity. I believe in freedom, equality and the brotherhood of man. That is what we really mean when we say socialism. I believe in the power of fraternity and the love of comrades in the struggle for socialism. Walt Whitman said: "I will build great cities with the love of comrades." I would go farther and say: we will build a great new world.

It is not illogical or inconsistent for us, soldiers of the revolution, to pause in the midst of our labors and our battles, as we do tonight; to rest and relax, to take it easy and have a good time. We are soldiers, that is true, and therefore we must be Spartans. We must be able to endure hardship and privation, but we should never inflict it upon ourselves. Soldiers and Spartans, yes, but not ascetics. For socialism, the philosophy of the good life and the life more abundant, is alien to all asceticism. Socialism, if you stop to think about it, is the doctrine of the good time coming and "the great gettin' up morning!"

That is how I have thought about it; and it was my good luck that this conception fitted so neatly with my own personal temperament. I just made a small amendment: If socialism means a good time for everybody in the future, why not have a good time in the struggle for socialism? I was always in favor of that. It wasn't always possible. There were some tough times. Forty years of fighting for socialism was not all beer and skittles, as the British would say. But by and large, taking the good with the bad, I had a good time for forty years and I really have no right to ask for sympathy. I had a good time, and perhaps that is one reason why I lasted longer than some of the others.

And finally, just by having patience, the greatest achievement of all became mine. Just by having patience and waiting around, I reached my sixtieth birthday, which formally ends tonight, and tomorrow morning I will be entering the first day of my sixty-first year. The question then naturally poses itself: What next? Rose and I have to answer that question, as we have answered every important question for twenty-six years, together.

When we were forty we took stock of the situation at that time. That was when we had been expelled from the Communist Party for defending the program of Trotsky, and had to start all over again. We were forty—that's older than twenty—a little tired. We realized that revolution is rather a young people's occupation, like athletics. But we had to recognize that the movement depended upon us more than ever then, and that we had to make an exception of ourselves. So we said: well, we'll give ten more years to the party; after that perhaps they won't need us so much.

Those ten years went by, busy, active years. We didn't chance to count them. Then we were fifty. That was the time of the biggest fight for the existence of the party, in 1940, the fight with the petty-bourgeois opposition. Right in the middle of that fight we celebrated our fiftieth birthday, and we had to admit that we were still needed. There was nothing for us to do but agree to give ten more years.

Those ten years went by, busy, active years. We didn't have much time to think about getting old. We were always on the go, both of us, and before we knew what had happened, we reached sixty. So here we are, and where do we go from here?

Everybody, I suppose, gives to the movement what he can. It takes all kinds of contributions from all kinds of people to keep the movement going. All we ever had to give was our time, our years. So we sat down, on the eve of our sixtieth birthday, to consider one more donation. We thought: the party is growing, and growing up, and the demands upon us are not as heavy as they used to be. The young recruits of former times have become veterans. A great cadre of leaders has developed. They can do many things that we had to do in the past. We are by no means as much needed as we were ten and twenty years ago. But still, we thought we might be useful if we're there to help a little. So we decided: all right, we'll give the party another ten years. And then we'll see.

Chapter 20

# Revolutionary journalism

*Delivered at a banquet at Forum Hall, Los Angeles, celebrating the thirtieth anniversary of* The Militant, *November 15, 1958.*

As has been announced and referred to by other speakers, we celebrate tonight the joint anniversary of the Russian Revolution and the founding of *The Militant*. It was not designed that way, but it turned out that both these events occurred in the month of November. Thirty years ago, our struggle for the ideas of the Russian Opposition had come to a head, resulting in our expulsion from the Communist Party on October 25, 1928. That imposed upon us the necessity of starting our own paper and the first issue was dated in November.

The timing was accidental; nevertheless, I think the coincidence was significant and deeply symbolic. *The Militant* and the Russian Revolution have been tied together all the time. *The Militant,* from its first issue up to the latest one to come off the press, has been the champion of the Russian Revolution and the advocate of its extension throughout the world. That has been the central meaning of every expression of revolutionary socialism in every part of the world since November 1917.

So *The Militant* began as the champion of the Russian Revolution. It began with a big idea—the biggest and best idea in the world—the idea of the Russian Revolution and its extension to all other countries, including the United States. That idea is still the chart, not only for *The Militant,* not only for us, for the Socialist Workers Party, but for the future of all humanity on this planet.

*The Militant* has carried out a great mission. It has never temporized with the concept of transforming society through a social overturn as exemplified in the Russian Revolution. The very first issue of *The Militant* declared its position foursquare with a headline that covered the entire front page: *FOR THE RUSSIAN OPPOSITION!* And the Russian Oppositionists we supported were primarily those Bolsheviks who were fighting to defend the revolution against bureaucratic and conservative degeneration.

Comrade Novack has been kind enough or mischievous enough to divert me a little bit from my main theme by stating that I worked on other papers before *The Militant.* I never agreed to make that detour. It came about this way. He came out to see me in the desert, where I was taking a rest, and I asked him: "What am I supposed to say at the banquet? '*The Militant* and the Russian Revolution' is a subject that one can talk about for hours and days and weeks. What segment of the subject can I take?"

I already knew what I was going to say, but I was just asking. You know, to make conversation. So he said, "Why don't you tell about all the other papers you worked on?"

I didn't say yes or no. I just listened. Then he came back, I am told, and announced that I was going to speak about the things he had suggested I should speak about. And he mentioned it again tonight. So here I am.

Now I have worked on radical revolutionary papers for forty-five years. The first one was *Solidarity*, the Eastern organ of the IWW which was published in New Castle, Pennsylvania, in the early days. After the 1912 convention of the IWW, I showed up in New Castle to visit with the staff and see what was going on. I didn't hitchhike there. I went by train. I got off in the freight yards with a pal of mine, and we walked down to the *Solidarity* office and said hello to the boys who worked there. They decided I should stay and work on the paper for a while.

I often recall that paper of the IWW as an example of how much the pioneers of our movement did with so little. *Solidarity* was printed in a tiny shop by one editor who spent three days a week at the type case. We had a press but no linotype, and so it was set by hand. The other two members of the staff were a fellow named Bill Wolgast and myself. We did the press work and the mailing and the clerical work. The three of us got out a paper once a week. That was common in the early radical movement.

In 1919, I helped in starting a local paper in Kansas City, Missouri. During the war—the First World War, that was—the movement was under great persecution. When we began to gather the scattered forces together in a semi-underground manner, especially after the Russian Revolution, the only thing we could think of to serve notice that we were still for socialism was to start a paper. With the resources of a single local organization in Kansas City, we actually started a weekly paper and kept the thing going for six months.

The first editor of the *Workers World* was Earl Browder. After the paper had been going for a couple of months, he and his brothers were sent to Leavenworth penitentiary because of a previous conviction for opposing the war, and I became the editor and business manager.

At that time the coal miners launched a general strike. President Woodrow Wilson demanded it be called off and got a judge to issue an injunction against it. John L. Lewis, who was then the newly crowned president of the United Mine Workers, announced that "we can't fight against the government" and called off the strike everywhere—except in the Kansas coalfields.

One reason why the strike was not called off there was because we were down in the coalfields with thousands of copies of *Workers World* advocating continuation of the struggle.

I was arrested and indicted on the accusation of conspiring to interfere with the production of a wartime necessity—namely, bituminous coal. This was more than a year after the war was over, but the wartime Lever Act had not yet been repealed. I was thrown into jail and the paper then had no staff.

*Workers World* was forced to discontinue, but it had served a certain purpose while it lasted. It gave us a little experience that was of use later. The fact that I had edited this paper was known to the national leadership of the newly formed Communist Party, and in 1920, when I had been elected to the Central Committee, I was appointed to go to Cleveland, Ohio, to become editor of the *Daily Worker*—that is, the paper that later became the *Daily Worker*. This was the *Cleveland Toiler*.

The *Cleveland Toiler* was controlled by the State Executive Committee of the Socialist Party in Ohio, a left-wing group which had joined the Communist Labor Party. After I had edited the *Toiler* for about six months in Cleveland, we moved the paper to New York because it was the only legal paper we had in the country. The official organ, *The*

*Communist,* and everything else had been proscribed.

We changed the name of the *Cleveland Toiler* to the *New York Weekly Worker.* The *New York Weekly Worker,* which was still operating on the same mailing permit eventually became the *Daily Worker,* published in Chicago, so that by a sort of remote association you can say that I am one of the former editors of the *Daily Worker*—for whatever that may be worth.

I was in Minneapolis during the 1934 strike—the strike that made Minneapolis a union town. So far as I know, this was the only long, drawn-out strike in which the union published a daily paper throughout. We Trotskyists did that in Minneapolis. The daily paper was called *The Organizer* and I served as its policy editor.

During the time we were in the Socialist Party—1936–1937—Rose and I came out to California. We hadn't been here more than about two months when we moved up to San Francisco, where a big maritime strike was brewing and there was sentiment to increase socialist activity. The State Executive Committee of the California Socialist Party agreed to publish a weekly paper in San Francisco, and I was appointed editor of that paper. Its name was *Labor Action.* That is not the same *Labor Action* some of you may have run across later.

This weekly lasted until early in the spring of 1937 when the Socialist Party leadership decided that we hadn't become social democrats after all. They didn't want Trotskyists in their organization and they prepared to expel us. That ended the *Labor Action* of San Francisco.

Shortly thereafter it was reborn in the form of the *Socialist Appeal* in New York. A little later, the *Socialist Appeal* changed its name back to *The Militant.*

So that's about the sum and substance of my participation in labor journals as an editor. The one thing that

I am proudest of is the fact that I was founding editor of *The Militant* and have always been an off-and-on contributor to its columns; and it is about *The Militant*, for which I have the most affection, that I want to speak.

The name was deliberately designed to express its distinctive character. It is not so commonly used nowadays as it was in the earlier movement. "Militant" was the word for the active, fighting member of the various radical organizations—IWW militants, Socialist Party militants, anarchist militants. Nowadays they have a much weaker word, I think, for that. They say "activists." Those that are always working for the organization. But in the old days we called these people the militants, which is activism plus.

We decided that by calling our paper *The Militant*, this would indicate our intention of appealing directly to the vanguard, to the cadre people, to the militants—a paper of and for the vanguard.

We did not pretend, when we started *The Militant*, that we were producing a great mass paper, simplifying everything to the lowest common denominator. On the contrary, our paper was devoted to the education and reeducation of the vanguard militants of the Communist movement. It was primarily a cadre paper, the educator and guide of the cadres. The people who hold the party together and keep it going in all kinds of weather. The people who never quit, who never float down the stream like dead fish, but swim against the current no matter how rough it may be. That is the meaning of "militant," and that was the meaning of the paper we started to represent such people.

We had learned a good deal by then, although we have learned a great deal more since, and were applying something from Lenin's program for *Iskra*. Many of you have read in his great pamphlet, *What Is To Be Done?*, what he considered to be the role of a national paper. As Lenin conceived it, the role of a revolutionary paper is to function not merely as an agitator dealing with protest issues, not merely as a propagandist concerned with educating people and dealing with questions of theory and politics, but as the best organizer of the party.

That was the way we conceived our *Militant* and for that reason *The Militant* never was and never could be a personal organ. It broke entirely with the earlier socialist tradition in this country, in which the most widely circulated press, the most influential press, was a privately owned and privately conducted enterprise.

You have heard many good things about the *Appeal to Reason,* the paper published in Girard, Kansas, which had at one time as high as a half-million circulation, and which undoubtedly did a great deal to popularize the general idea of socialism and the struggle against capitalism and against capitalist wars. But when the war broke out in 1917, the proprietors of the *Appeal to Reason,* this privately owned paper, decided that they did not want to get into conflict with the government. They came out in support of the war. And all the readers and supporters who had believed in the paper and trusted it, who had built its tremendous circulation, were just left helpless, completely incapable of exerting any influence on the policy of the paper. *The Militant* was never in that tradition.

From its first issue *The Militant* was an internationalist paper. It has always been concerned with the great problems of the world, and has done all it could to help the world movement of revolutionary socialism. It was through *The Militant*—and in this we take special pride—that the message of the Russian Opposition was carried to all corners of the world and even penetrated the Soviet Union itself.

In Europe, Latin America and Africa, Ceylon, India,

China, and many other parts of the world, the message of *The Militant* sparked and inspired the organization of the first cadres of the International Left Opposition, so that when Trotsky, six months later, was deported to Turkey, he found a forum all ready for him in *The Militant,* and groups and organizations springing up throughout the world very largely as the result of the preliminary message of *The Militant.*

Among the countries I neglected to mention was England. The English Trotskyist movement had its origin in copies of *The Militant* that a few members of the Communist Party got hold of in 1928–1929. *The Militant* inspired the organization of new cadres everywhere and was recognized in the early days by Trotsky and by others as the foremost journal of the cause of the International Left Opposition.

On the national field, *The Militant* has represented and protected the continuity of the uncorrupted revolutionary movement of the past. *The Militant* has always strictly defended and incorporated into its own teachings much of the early Communist Party tradition in this country—and at that time it was a real CP—and of the older movement of Debs and Haywood which helped to prepare the way. In the unions you all know that *The Militant* has always stood for militant action, for class-struggle policies, for trade-union democracy, for the rank and file against the privileged bureaucrats, for the rights of the Negro people, every day and on every occasion without any compromise.

On the political field, *The Militant* has always stood for independent political action and applies that doctrine in practice at every opportunity. If we can get anyone to cooperate with us, the party, small as it is, has tried to put up socialist candidates just to keep the idea of socialism alive and to show that even a small group that takes its socialism seriously can do things considered impossible by large bodies who are less serious.

*The Militant* fought for all these basic lines—which are ABC for anyone worthy of the name socialist—all these policies which are not new, very old in fact, but still good and far better than the new counterfeits. We have been swimming against the stream all the time.

As the chairman, Novack, mentioned, in the old days anyone calling himself a socialist wouldn't even dare to suggest that you campaign for or support a candidate of a capitalist political party; but in the last twenty-odd years we have seen a different course pursued by the majority. The net result of this trifling with principle, of this class collaboration in politics, was a demoralized radical movement, the destruction of socialist tradition and even the habit of independent socialist political action.

That took time to bring about and it had to be done stealthily and a step at a time. It began in 1936. Prior to then it was ABC for the Socialists or the Communists to nominate their own candidates and to use electoral campaigns and the expanded audience they provide to popularize the ideas of socialism and communism. But in 1936 the right-wing Socialists in New York and the Communist Party of Browder decided that these old-fashioned ideas were out of date; that it would be much smarter and much slicker to join the majority.

That was the year when Browder campaigned for President on the ticket of the Communist Party. He wouldn't have dared then to advocate not running their own ticket; so they compromised with the rank and file, who wanted the CP to have its own campaign, and they nominated Browder and Ford for President and Vice-President.

What do you think was their chief campaign slogan? "Defeat Landon at all costs!"

So, they campaigned all over the country to beat Landon at all costs with the result that 90 percent of the people under their influence voted for Roosevelt.

In New York, the radical workers, especially the great mass of needle-trade workers, had the habit year after year, of always voting for the Socialist ticket. To get around this inconvenient habit and tradition, the needle-trades union bureaucrats, in an undercover deal with Socialist and Communist Party leaders, as was later revealed, worked out a clever scheme. They couldn't ask the socialist-minded New York workers to jump over and vote straight Democrat. But they could ask them to vote for something new—a labor party. So they said, let's form another party; call it the American Labor Party; and put just one little catch in it: that the ALP endorses the Democratic ticket.

Through this little stratagem they mobilized about half a million votes that normally would have been Socialist or Communist. That was the beginning of the break in the habit and the tradition of voting for socialism or communism. The Communist union bureaucrats and the Socialist union bureaucrats got together to put this over. In the showdown they really worked very closely together. You know, as Kipling said about the colonel's lady and Judy O'Grady, they're really sisters under the skin. Later on, there was a split in the ALP, and a section of the New York garment-trades bureaucrats formed the Liberal Party, which continued the same game.

The net result of this kind of betrayal of principle was that in the elections in New York this year, that great mass of people, most of them pretty old by now, who had been raised in the socialist and communist tradition, found themselves faced with the alternative of voting either for Harriman or for Rockefeller. And that's what they did.

I don't know what conclusions they are going to draw

from it now, because this kind of shenanigans is based on the theory that you've got to be with the masses. You've got to be with the majority. They don't know that this is just a variation of the old unprincipled, ward-heeler politics that says if you can't beat 'em, join 'em.

They mobilized to vote for Harriman but it turned out that Rockefeller got elected. Rockefeller couldn't have gotten elected unless he won working-class votes. New York is an industrial state and the workers can decide any election they see fit to. So if a large percentage of workers and the Negro people voted for Rockefeller, it looks to me like they might have to revise their prescription and say we made a sectarian error. We voted for Harriman, who's in the minority, and we should have been with Rockefeller, who's in the majority. If we keep on going that way, you know, eventually we may arrive at socialism.

I think the Independent Socialist ticket in New York this year made a good showing, considering the miseducation that had gone before. I think that the ticket made a possible beginning in reviving the tradition of socialist political action.

*The Militant* did its share, perhaps a little more than its share, in this united effort, and we can be proud of our paper for that. To promote the idea of independent political action, that simple issue in itself, is the greatest possible service to the cause of reviving socialism in this country.

All I have said about *The Militant* so far is in its praise. But that is not the complete story. There have been criticisms of the paper, and I will mention three of them that have been made over the years.

One criticism was that it was against imperialist war, not only the Second World War but also the Korean War, and that it was a mistake to isolate itself this way from the great majority.

The second criticism is that it has been sectarian in general.

The third, and this is the loudest criticism I have heard lately—although in fact I have been hearing it for years, for thirty years—is that *The Militant* told the truth about Stalinism before the time was right, before Khrushchev gave permission.

The first criticism, that we were against the war, is correct. We admit it. We are guilty. *The Militant* had great difficulties with the Post Office Department and came within an inch of having its mailing rights taken away; a number of its issues were suppressed. The editors of *The Militant* were sent to prison for opposing the war. We can't get around that. We might as well admit it. But we should add that we will do the same thing again, if need be. We are not going to support imperialist war on any pretext whatever. You can't fight capitalism in peace, support it in war, and hope to take up the struggle in peace again. No, you have to fight imperialism and capitalism all the time. That is a matter of principle.

The second criticism, that we are sectarian, that *The Militant* has been a sectarian paper, is I think, a misunderstanding. We are not sectarian at all. Any time we have a chance to participate with others in class-struggle action, we are always ready to join. The most recent example of that is the Independent Socialist ticket in New York. We didn't hesitate to agree with socialists of different points of view and to make organizational concessions about the candidates and a number of other things, on the single provision that they run on a socialist platform.

I don't think that is sectarian.

Now as to the third criticism, that we criticized Stalinism before the time was ripe. That is wrong; they are mistaken. The time is always ripe to tell the truth. It is not always popular, as we have learned. *The Militant* had to pay for the privilege and we have to help it pay for this privilege in the future.

Now I believe that anything that comes from *The Militant* staff is entitled to a respectful hearing from all of us because our staff, all down through the years, has never been a privileged bureaucracy. Their only privilege has been to do more and to take less for themselves than others, and that is true of the present staff responsible for *The Militant* today.

I think they are worthy of the great tradition that they are carrying on and that we owe them our solidarity. What are we here for? I don't mean here in this room. What are we *here* for? In this poignant book on sale now, the *Diary in Exile, 1935,* there is a part where Trotsky writes down his most intimate thoughts—about growing old and his bad health and having to continue the work because of the need to prepare the succession.

We and all like-minded people all over the world are that succession, which Trotsky prepared when he was too old and tired to do any more, but which he still persisted in doing as long as he could because that was the duty imposed upon him by destiny. He said that for the first time in his life he felt indispensable, because there was no one else to prepare the succession and he had to do it.

And we in turn, whom Trotsky prepared, are confronted with the same duty right now. We have to keep going as long as we can under any circumstances, preparing our own succession so that the continuity of our movement will not be broken, so that it shall grow with new life and new blood.

In this we can't do without *The Militant*. That is the long and short of it. *The Militant* is our means and our weapon . . .

We, whose lives were made over by *The Militant*, we, who call on *The Militant* to change the lives of others, have no choice but to make a special effort once again. What else can we do when the call comes for our solidarity and support?

Old Frederick Engels, in the hard and bitter time of the movement of his day, wrote to an old comrade, an old guard of the Communist League, referring to the difficulties and troubles they were in and to the good comrades who had fallen by the wayside. And the old comrade asked, "What shall we do?" And Engels answered, "What can we do? We stand in the breach. That's what we are here for."

# Chapter 21

## The lives of two revolutionaries

Remarks by Rose Karsner at a banquet in Los Angeles celebrating the publication of *The First Ten Years of American Communism*, December 15, 1962.

Thank you comrades and friends. I'm afraid you are anticipating. I thank you for your heartfelt applause and I hope that what I say here will merit an equal applause. Now, I am not going to speak about my struggles. I am not going to speak about our struggles in particular, but I am going to have a few words to say.

The other day, on our trip in from the country for this occasion, Jim said to Oscar, "Do you know, Oscar? I am soon going to retire officially from active duty in the party. This is my last speech."

I interjected. I said, "See, Oscar? You are getting the last speech out of him."

And to myself I thought, "The last speech? Of a long career of speechmaking? And at a banquet, yet." Sounds

Early photo of Rose Karsner and James P. Cannon.

something like the Last Supper. Except, we all know, Jim is no Christ, who turns the other cheek when he or his class are wronged.

But Oscar replied, somewhat skeptically I think, "Where have I heard that before?"

And he was right. He and others have heard that before. Not once, but at least three times—on the occasions of our fortieth, fiftieth, and sixtieth birthdays. You see, when we passed our fortieth year, the average age in the Trotskyist group was twenty-seven. All things being relative, the younger people in the group naturally looked upon us as the old folks, at forty. And we were a little tired. We thought then that we had only another ten years of fruitful work to give to the party. For hadn't Lenin said: when a revolutionist reaches the age of fifty, he should be shot.

In fact, Max Shachtman—and I hope you all know who he is—began to think thirty-two years ago that Jim was already out of date. And he lost no opportunity to remind all and sundry about Lenin's half-serious pronouncement. He even said it on the floor of a branch meeting that I attended. But by implication, he reduced the age limit from fifty to forty. That meant not only Jim, but Arne, myself, and all the Minneapolis trade-union leaders, who were in their forties then, were to be shot. Nevertheless, we survived.

The Minneapolis group, with the help of the party, led successful strikes that became nationally famous. And many of the leading comrades Max was shooting at then were politically healthy enough to survive a prison term, when they were past fifty already. I'm sorry to say I can't say the same for Max Shachtman.

Well, so it went. Each ten years we would promise another ten, up to our sixtieth. Then we promised only five. Now, we thought we would have to crowd in all we had to give to the party in the remaining five years. The truth is, however, that we did not feel as old as our numerical age would indicate, and the party cadres had not grown sufficiently to be able to afford our withdrawal at that time. So here we are approaching our seventy-third birthday—mine in December, Jim's in February, Arne's in September—and we're pitching once more. So that is why I said Oscar was right. He had heard that before.

This time, however, it is different. This time Jim can confidently say, "This is the last speech I make," yet have a clear conscience about his retirement, because he knows that the party has enough competent and talented younger comrades who can take over and lead the party successfully. From here on we shall be close observers of the party's work, giving advice—only when it is asked. But don't take this promise too literally.

This dinner not only honors the pioneers of the founding of the Communist Party of the USA, and later of the Trotskyist movement. We are also celebrating. We celebrate the publication of the first book written by a leader of the Socialist Workers Party and published in the U.S. by a commercial publisher. This in itself assures a broader reading public for our ideas.

Furthermore, in my opinion, the very fact that a commercial publisher would invest hard cash in promoting a book by an outspoken Trotskyist leader is, I believe, a straw in the wind. A small straw; a small wind, perhaps. But nevertheless, a sign of a changing attitude in a section of the reading public. Otherwise, why would a sharp businessman consider a true story of communism and Trotskyism of sufficient interest to warrant an investment in its publication?

Jim does not fully agree with me on this analysis. He thinks Lyle Stuart—that's the publisher of the book—just took a wild chance. I challenge that opinion. Businessmen don't operate that way. They take wild chances, but only when they have some reason to believe there is a market for the product.

Already we received a sample of the kind of promotion the book is going to get. A review of the book, carrying that glorified photo of Jim which is used on the jacket of the book, appeared on December 2 in the Sunday edition of the *Anniston Star*. Anniston is a city in Alabama, of all places. On December 8, the New York edition of *The New York Times* carried a display advertisement of the book.

And I am sure we are going to get more of these. The book was just released November 28.

Our own paper, *The Militant,* on December 3, carried a review written by Fred Halstead. Fred, as many of you know, is, in the vernacular of the business world, the boy who went to New York and made good. I think *The First Ten Years of American Communism* is the story about the roots from which our party stems. At the same time it is a history of that era.

But Jim writes this history not in the conformist style—that is, as a chronicle of consecutive dates and events—rather, he writes it as the story of the people who used these dates and events to further their conviction of a socialist world to come. And he does this with admirable objectivity. Even though it comes from me, believe me, it is really objectively written. And he gives credit where credit is due. Even to those who later fell into the mire of the Stalin era.

Fred Halstead comments on this phase of the book. He states it so well that I would like to read some excerpts from his review, for the benefit of those who have not read it yet. I quote: "For active participants in working-class politics, the book is a manual of Leninist organizational principles, applied to American problems and explained through American experience. It is a story, too. A tale, above all, of individual human beings. What made them tick, and what made them change. It contains a number of characterizations of the early U.S. radical figures. Some of these are short sketches. And some run through large sections of the work, building like the people in a novel."

Then Fred continues, a little further on in his review: "But there is a lot of hindsight in this book, too, in the form of analysis. The old problems are dissected with current problems in mind and with tools sharpened by 56 years in the socialist movement. Not the least of these tools, are the ideas learned from the leaders of the Russian Revolution."

After a few comments by Jim about Draper's thesis regarding the degeneration of the Communist Party of the U.S., Fred continued: "As Cannon says, 'The famous bandit Willy Sutton was once asked by a reporter why he specialized exclusively in robbing banks. Willy, a thinking man's thief, answered right off the bat: "Because that's where the money is." In the entire historical period, since the collapse of the international socialist movement, in the first world war up to the present, revolutionary national parties in every country have had to look to the Russian Revolution and its authentic leaders. That's where the ideas are.'"

With this quotation Fred ends his review. But I would like to continue right here another few minutes to express a conviction. Tonight you have honored a few of us for our steadfast allegiance to ideas and principles, in face of all obstacles and difficulties. Also, we are celebrating a historical event: the publication of a party book by a commercial publishing house for the first time in the history of the Socialist Workers Party. In the future this will become the accepted procedure. Of that I am completely convinced.

You will meet in halls seating thousands, instead of hundreds. Recruits will come to the party by the tens and more, instead of by the ones as they do now. You may even hold a meeting someday honoring the memory of tonight. Because this is a historic milestone on the way to becoming a mass party of action and theory. If you do so, when we can no longer be with you, remember this— and I believe Arne and Jim will concur in it.

From the moment we threw our lot in with the socialist movement, more than fifty years ago, we have never wavered in our conviction that a socialist world will come into being. Whether we live to see it or not. That's immaterial. We never faltered in our devotion to this conviction, or in our allegiance to the party we believed was working toward that end. In times of personal difficulty, and we all had them, we sometimes took out time to straighten these matters. But never with the idea of dropping out.

Never did we feel that we were sacrificing for the party. On the contrary, we were always conscious of the fact that to have to give up the party, that would be a sacrifice. Because through activity of the party, we got fulfillment of life and satisfaction and the confidence that we were working not merely for our own little selves, but for the entire human race. We feel the same way tonight. We recommend that way to you all.

## REMARKS BY JAMES P. CANNON
## AT THE SAME BANQUET

After all these wonderful speeches, they didn't leave much for me to say. Before I made my first speech, over fifty years ago, I had a bad case of stage fright. But once I got up on the soapbox for the IWW on Market Square in Kansas City, my stage fright left me and never returned until I was notified by Oscar that I had to speak tonight, and I have been going through a period of stage fright ever since the notification. I may get over it.

Our chairman told you, most of you know, that I've had a lot of trouble with my eyes in the last four or five years. The last speech I remember making to you I was blind in one eye and half-blind in the other, so that I couldn't even read my notes. But I'm happy to report to you now that, thanks to medical science and a friendly doctor, I have recovered the sight of both eyes, and I now see out of both of them very well—but not exactly in the same way. I've got one eye to see you with and the other to see through you with—so watch out!

I was reading the newspapers lately about this Mariner (is it called?) on the trip to Venus—180 million miles. As I recall, I think it was Oscar or Rose who was saying, 180 million—that seems like an awful lot of miles. I said, it isn't so much to me, I've made that many speeches in my lifetime—I think just exactly 180 million. And Rose has made just about the same number of speeches—a few of them in public like tonight's, and the rest of them with me for the audience. I listened. That's how I got so smart.

I don't know much more that I can say, except maybe to tell a few anecdotes. First about how this book that you've been talking so much about here—making such a big fuss about—how it came to be written.

I had nothing to do with it. I didn't plan it, didn't design it. It all started with a letter from Theodore Draper, a scholar who was working on the history and wanted to know if I would answer a few questions. And it happened at that time that the Los Angeles party had provided me with one of the most competent, qualified and devoted secretaries a man could ever ask for, who was willing to do all the work as long as I just dictated a few things into the machine, or for her to take down in shorthand. So between Draper's questions, one after another, and Jeanne Morgan's work and Rose's prodding—one thing led to another and before we knew what had happened some years had gone by. And then Julia Houdek came to fill in. Reba Hansen put in a year or two with me, and between us all before we knew what had happened we had a book and there it is.

Now, that book is not complete, not perfect by any means. It's unique in one respect. I think it's the first history ever written in this country or any other—a history without footnotes, without a bibliography, without references to what somebody else said some other time. Written entirely from my memory, which is pretty good, as Draper testified. But a lot of things I remembered are not in there. But I've got a built-in alibi for any criticism. Oh, I'm slick at that. Why didn't you mention this person, why didn't you tell about that? And my answer every time is: Draper didn't ask me. So I'm in the clear.

But what's there is all true. It's funny what tricks your memory plays on you. As we get older, we have noticed that our memory of recent events isn't as sharp as it used to be, but, in compensation for that, our memory of older events stands out fresh. And as Draper began questioning me about what happened forty years ago, I went into a sort of a semicoma and shut everything else out of my mind, and I remembered things as though they happened yesterday. As I wrote to him, this is what happened. And he told me in a personal interview I had with him later—and he also testified to it in his preface to the book—that I remembered correctly. He tested it against others who had given him a different account and every time my memory was right because I was really living the old days over again. I think he paid me a very high compliment when he said, "Jim Cannon remembers because he has not wanted to kill the memory within himself." I still believe that fight was worthwhile, and, as he said, I wanted to remember and I did.

I've been goaded a great deal in the last few years by the comrades in the party center and others: "Why don't you write your autobiography?" And every chance they get they bring it up again, "What do you need? Is there anything we can do for you? Do you want some technical help, or anything? Just sit down and write what happened to you in these fifty-six years since you first distributed the *Appeal to Reason* on the streets of Rosedale carrying the story of the frame-up against Moyer and Haywood."

And I've said several times, the trouble is I can't write unless I write honestly. And if I told the truth about the scrapes I got into and the characters I have known . . . if I only told half the truth, people would say, "Cannon is the biggest liar since Baron Munchhausen!" Incredible what happened.

If I ever do write my autobiography—and this is a threat, not a promise—I wouldn't write it in the ordinary way, as I don't write history, dates and events and so on; but I would write it in a personal way about things that I recall that were interesting; mainly about people and my relations with them.

One chapter, I've thought, would be entitled "Did You Eat Yet?" The reason for that unusual title for the chapter would be my experiences as a professional soapboxer for the IWW. When I was on the road—and I was only one of many young men who traveled from one city to another wherever the organization needed a hand, to take my stand on the soapbox—we used to speak every night in the week—Minneapolis, Kansas City, Omaha, Chicago, Cleveland, Akron, etc. We were already then professional revolutionists in the modern sense, in the Bolshevik sense—although we never heard that term. We preached the gospel and we lived by the gospel.

They had a rule at the street meetings where crowds of migratory workers would gather—you'd make your speech and they would sell literature. And if we took a collection—as we did at every meeting—it was not an ordinary collection for some cause or other. The pitch was: "There's a lot of fellows here out of work who can't afford to buy the *Industrial Worker* and *Solidarity,* so if you'll give a quarter, we'll give away five copies to some fellow workers here that want to read it and haven't got any money in their pockets." And we'd take up a collection from a quarter up to a dollar. And whatever the total collection was, in return for that, for every nickel, a copy of the paper would be distributed free to the unemployed workers listening. And the soapboxer would get 40 percent commission on the sale of the literature. And that's what we were supposed to live on. It wasn't much, but it would keep you alive. What more do you want?

In addition to that in every IWW hall I went into, there were always a couple of what we called "live ones," fellow workers who had been out on a job for a couple of months and had come into town with a stake. They were very fond of the soapboxers and very appreciative of them. We were the articulate ones who got up and expounded their ideas in a way that they were not technically qualified to do. They used to have a saying. They'd come in and they'd hunt up the soapboxer, and I remember many a one of them coming up to me and saying, "Hello Jim, did you eat yet?" So I'd say, "No." "Come on." And out we'd go to a saloon where they served lunch. We'd eat lunch, drink a couple of beers, and maybe he'd slip me a dollar or something "in case you run short." In that way the IWW maintained a staff of professional soapboxers, of which I'm proud to say I was one.

How does a professional revolutionist keep it up—year after year—when you know to start with, and you know still better at the finish, there's no money in it? It's not a paying business. The best you can hope for is to keep alive. But sometimes even that becomes a problem. And then something happens that gives you a new burst of inspiration and devotion.

I would call another chapter of my autobiography "A

Suit of Clothes." Once, back in Kansas City, in 1919, the immediate postwar period, we were publishing a weekly paper all by ourselves. I was the editor and the business manager, following Earl Browder, who had been the first editor and was serving a prison sentence. Then I got indicted under a federal law for monkeying around in the Kansas coalfields, agitating among the miners to keep up a strike that had been prohibited by a federal injunction. And a year after the war was over I was indicted under the wartime Lever Act, as they called it, which makes it a crime to interfere with the production of a wartime necessity, namely bituminous coal.

So I was thrown into the clink and I lay there for sixty days before they could bail me out. I was held in $15,000 bail. And that meant you had to get property security double the value of the bail—that meant $30,000 worth of property had to be put up to get me out on bail.

And do you know what the comrades in Kansas City did? Mainly the Jewish comrades. I was sick and fed up with the Irish by then. I had been raised as an Irish patriot. But when I looked around and saw all the goddamned Irishmen were either cops or politicians or grafters and contractors and prosecuting attorneys, I said to hell with it. I disaffiliated. And then I ran into the radical socialistic Jews. And among themselves they went around from one to another; one of them put up his house, another put up his little business, another put up a little money and between them they raised $30,000 worth of security and got me out on bail. Now, how could I quit on people like that?

After I got out on bail the paper had been suppressed, things weren't going too well. I was sitting rather glumly in the office one day wondering what's going to be next and three Jewish comrades came in just suddenly, unexpectedly. They said, "Jim, come on." They came in almost like they were putting me under arrest. "Come on." I said, "What's up?" "Just come on, we'll show you."

I don't know whether they noticed that I was looking a little seedy or something. I never paid much attention to clothes. They took me and marched me down to a Jewish merchant's clothing store on Twelfth Street in Kansas City. And they told the proprietor, "This is Comrade Cannon. Fix him up a suit of clothes." "Oh, Comrade Cannon?" "Yes, he works for the movement." "Oh, yes." That was a funny thing about them. They thought somebody who worked for the movement was almost like a saint, a priest or something—entitled to special consideration. The Irish community had thought I was a damn ne'er-do-well. But there it was a great honor—editor of the paper and a speaker for socialism—OK. Fixed me up a suit of clothes that fitted me to a tee. Then began the bargaining about the price.

What's the price? The merchant said, "Thirty dollars." "Thirty dollars, that's the price, huh? OK, now just cut off all the profit and give us wholesale price. What's that?" He hesitated a little and they reminded him, this is for Comrade Cannon. "OK, cut it down to twenty." They said, "Is that the rock-bottom wholesale price?" He said, "Yeah, rock-bottom." "Alright, now you knock off five dollars more for your own contribution." And they gave him fifteen dollars. "OK." So I walked out of the store with a brand new suit of clothes and an uplifted spirit that kept me going a long time.

And things like that have been happening to me all my life. I think it says somewhere in the Bible about the early apostles, not the modern bishops who live in plush luxury, but the early apostles who went around barefooted, being instructed to go out and preach the gospel and live by the gospel. Things like that happened to me all the time.

God, I remember when I came to Los Angeles. Rose and I—I'll go back a little further than that—we came out here in 1936 at the time we joined the Socialist Party. The comrades in New York collected just about enough money to get us here, and here we were. And the comrades here just took us over without any questions at all, provided a place for us to stay with Edith's mother and a little money for us to spend. Then our darling Lillian here, Lillian Curtis, brought her mother in—she was connected with the clothing business someplace, and the first thing I knew I was measured for a suit of clothes—I was all fixed up. And that kind of thing happened all the time.

It was hard for a lot of people to believe that one can work for a cause regardless of the profit in it. And the most skeptical of all were people that I was associated with very closely at different times in my life, namely the criminals—in jail and prison. In my sixty days in the county jail in Kansas City—that was away back yonder forty-three years ago—prisoners awaiting trial were kept on separate floors or tiers, as they called them, according to the seriousness of their crimes. Sneak thieves on the first floor, burglars on the second, bank robbers, murderers and communists on the top floor. That's the way it was.

So, I was among them, and I was accepted right away as a big shot because I was under $15,000 bail. "My God," they used to say, "all we did was rob a bank; you're trying to overthrow the whole damn government." And they said it with admiration. One of them said to me one day, he said, "Hey, Jim"—we were on a first-name basis in no time—"Jim, you must be gettin' a pretty big cut out of this, aren't you?" I said, "No, all I get is $30 a week when I'm working for the party." "Now, don't kid me!" And finally I convinced him, no, I wasn't getting anything out of it. He said, "Well, there's some big guy up in Chicago or New York who's gettin' the money. You can't kid me. Somebody's gettin' the money and you ought to cut yourself in on it." And so it went.

I could start with this kind of business—little anecdotes I remember—such as the trouble I ran into in Chicago in the twenties. That's in the early years. We had the national headquarters in Chicago for three years during the twenties. That's when I was fighting the toughest bastards you ever ran up against in your life—the early leaders of the Communist Party. It was very tough. And I didn't have enough trouble with them—I had to get married to Rose.

I don't know how it happened, but it seemed like every place I'd go, a party affair, a meeting or a social, always—accidentally—she'd bump into me and say, "Fancy meeting you here." So, first thing you know, in order to quit bumping into each other, we said, "Well, let's go and live together." And we went to live in a furnished room with a daybed, if you know what that is, a daybed that folds up into a cot—and kitchen privileges—and we lived that way for three years and we never thought we were sacrificing at all. We thought we were in clover. As a matter of fact we were.

I remember Arne's coming to New York in 1931. That was in the dog days of the Trotskyist movement. On top of all of our other troubles we had a terrible factional conflict, which later exploded in the split of 1940. We came to a deadlock and couldn't get to first base. We had a small New York branch and they had a majority in it. And I knew I couldn't leave. If I left the whole damn thing would go to pieces—I was determined to stay. So we finally settled on a compromise, asking Arne to come in to act as National Secretary. Now you might think that's a simple thing—just transfer from Chicago to New York. The difference was that Arne was a skilled worker who was working, one of the few members of our organization at that time who had a job, making money. And he was supposed to give up this good paying job and come to New York and go to work for the party and then whistle for his wages. Arne came to New York.

Rose and I were evicted from a place on Third Avenue which was then already the edge of the slums, and we moved over onto First Avenue into a cold-water flat, and things got so tough and so tight that we learned to appreciate the virtues of the pushcart. There were pushcarts all along First Avenue, and right around the corner was a bakery that sold day-old bread, and I'd come home from the office with fifty cents in my pocket and get a loaf of day-old bread. Then we'd go to the pushcart and get a nickel's worth of this and a dime's worth of that and all of a sudden we had a big supper—and didn't know it was any trouble at all. Or if we knew it, we didn't admit it, and we never complained about it. Things are a little better now, but not so much relatively. Our comrades in the center, who carry the weight and burden of this organization from day to day, live on wages far less than the ordinary worker out in the branches—far less.

We have a very complicated system of "two for one" and "one for nothing." "Two for one" means if a couple both work for the party—like Farrell and Marvel, for example, or Joe and Reba—you get two for the wages of one, which is about $50 or $55 a week, plus maybe $5 extra for luxuries or something like that. Then, "one for nothing" is when the man works at a regular occupation and his wife gives full time free to the party. Or, vice versa, the woman works and the man gives full time free to the party. That's what we call the "one for nothing" deal. Then we have some comrades who have a little income and who work for nothing. And between them all together they keep the party going. They keep it rolling.

And when it runs into a crisis like the war danger that Kennedy triggered, we've got a young, vigorous organization with a competent leadership right on top of it. And I tell you that we in Los Angeles ought to take special pride in the fact that our small organization managed to put our ticket on the ballot in the state of New York. It meant they had to go and get at least fifty valid signatures in every county in that whole state. And getting on the ballot entitled them to a certain amount of free TV and radio time. And, two days after Kennedy's blockade of Cuba, Carl Feingold, using his legal right to get on the radio and television, was on television for a half-hour denouncing the Kennedy administration and all those who supported it, and defending the Cuban Revolution. We ought to be proud of that here in L.A. because Carl Feingold is our own boy. And there are others like that.

I'd like to end my speech tonight—not a speech, but off-the-cuff remarks—with an appreciation of those who have succeeded us and who are doing so well. You know, Trotsky wrote in his *Diary*—I hope most of you have read his *Diary* of the year 1935, when he was on the run from the fascists in France and unable to participate in public activities—he was already fifty-five years old and he wrote then: "I must live five more years to prepare the succession." To prepare the succession! Five more years of preparing people to carry the movement after he would be no more. And it just turned out mathematically that was the time allotted to him. Five years later, he was assassinated.

But in those five years of fruitful work he had prepared the rest of us to carry on in some fashion or other. And we have always considered this our function, we old-timers. Our real task as leaders is to prepare our successors. And we can look with equanimity on the prospect that Rose gave us here tonight—we can retire from active leadership in the movement, and we can do it with confidence because we know the successors are qualified people. And, as she said, we are only going to give advice in the future, if it's asked—but don't take that too seriously.

# Chapter 22

# Bill Brown: A proletarian fighter

Article published in the *Socialist Appeal*, July 2, 1938.

Death struck twice with cruel perversity in recent days at the liberation movement of the oppressed. One cannot get accustomed to the thought of the Northwestern sector of the movement without Bill Brown, president of Local 544, and Rodney Salisbury, onetime Farmer-Labor sheriff of Sheridan County, Montana, and president of the Montana Farm Holiday Association. They were as indigenous to the country as the tough native grass. Both were men of unique and distinctive personality. They were rich in talents, which they freely devoted to a cause bigger than themselves or any of us. They truly reflected and expressed the movement out of which they had grown, by which they had been shaped and upon which they, in turn, had placed their own personal stamp.

Now they are both dead. But I assert with confidence that their names and their deeds will live after them in the grateful and affectionate memory of their coworkers, who numbered many thousands. More than that, their memory ought by all rights to be saluted in wider circles than those in which they lived and died, and the memory of them ought to be passed on to our youth. It should be a source of inspiration to them. Such considerations alone prompt and will perhaps justify these lines, which otherwise would not be written. It is not easy to write about the dead, especially when the wound is fresh; I have always believed, with Swinburne, that "silence after grievous things is good."

From the time that William S. Brown went to work, driving a one-horse wagon, as a boy of thirteen, until his untimely and tragic death at the age of forty-one, he was continuously and uninterruptedly associated with the workers; more specifically, the drivers, and their trade unions. Flesh of their flesh and bone of their bone, he reacted sensitively to all that concerned them—their grievances, their advantages, their victories and defeats.

Lacking formal education, he compensated to a large extent for the deficiency with a first-class diploma from the college of hard knocks, and supplemented it with mother wit and native shrewdness. When he attained to leadership in the big mass movement and had to match wits with the bosses and their slick and oily lawyers, he was able to hold his own. Without any schooling in the technique of public speaking, he revealed, in the great struggles of the union, a surprising articulateness, and he became a commanding orator and master of the felicitous phrase. Nobody could lash the rapacious employers and their murderous cops with the bitter effectiveness of Bill, and none could stir the workers so deeply.

If there is such a thing as the "typical American," he was it—tough, hard-boiled, sophisticated and, at bottom, deeply sentimental and a sucker for a hard-luck story. Like all Americans, he was an empiricist, learning as he went along and inclined to improvise answers to problems as they arose from day to day. At least, that's what he had been all his life up to the great strike of 1934. After that he stood at the head of a mass movement. He was involved more and more in big and complicated actions where rule-of-thumb practice was lost and helpless. Under the influence of his new environment, Bill was thrown more and more into the consideration of things from a broader standpoint. He assimilated the basic ideas of socialism and became inspired by its great ideal. That is the true explanation of his remarkable transformation from a more or less ordinary trade-union official to a leader of militant mass actions. In this, I think, he pioneered on a road that hundreds and thousands of minor trade-union officials in America are destined to follow.

He became a party man and a fairly assiduous student of the theoretical teachings of our great masters. Few knew this; he didn't advertise it. The hard-boiled trade unionist remained to the last a bit shy about explaining this strange business of comprehensive theory and worldwide vision which was so far removed from trade unionism of the old school, its limited outlook and its humdrum routine. Nevertheless, it opened up a new window on the world for Bill, as he freely acknowledged in the close party circles, and greatly heightened his stature as a leader of the stormily developing mass movement.

This was all the more remarkable in view of his lifelong background in the stagnant pool of old-fashioned trade unionism. Bill was president of General Drivers Union, Local No. 574 (now 544), continuously from 1921. It was a small union, and he continued to work as a driver until 1932. During all those years, up until 1934, as with most unions of the same sort, nothing much ever happened. There were a few piddling contracts with small bosses. There was the routine business of keeping an office open and collecting dues and letting well enough alone, that is so characteristic of the old craft-union school.

Bill had something in him that such an environment could not draw out. During all those years of that deadening routine, there wasn't much on the surface to distinguish him from the ordinary run-of-the-mill business agent.

But, as further developments amply proved, that was only the surface appearance. Big events and new conceptions were needed for Bill to discover himself and unfold his hidden talent and capacities for greater things. They came with the development of the crisis, which shattered for all time the stability of capitalism and cleared the road for the militant mass movement of labor that will finally put an end to its domination.

The crisis bore down with unbearable weight on the workers in the trucking industry, of which Minneapolis is the great Northwestern center. The provincial Minnesota bosses, their greed multiplied by their ignorance, slashed wages and increased hours of work with reckless abandon. The truck drivers, unorganized for the most part, were goaded to desperation; only a spark was needed to touch off the explosion that would rock the country.

The entrance into this fully ripened situation of a new group of men, and the working collaboration established between them and Bill Brown, supplied the spark. The "new men" were a group of coalyard workers who are sometimes called "Trotskyites." These studious men of theory, who were also qualified mass workers—a rare enough phenomenon—came into the Teamsters Union by way of an organization campaign in the coalyards. It is to the eternal credit of Bill Brown that he opened the door of the union to this new development and received the new dynamic forces with open arms. The compact formed between them—one of the happiest and most fruitful ever recorded in the labor movement—endured to the end and flowered into political as well as trade-union solidarity, not to speak of unshakable personal friendship.

Bill's rich experience in the trade-union movement, his charming personality, oratorical ability, and widespread popularity, were absolutely indispensable factors in the subsequent developments. He and the "new men" from the coalyards, working together, welded the new insurgent mass movement and the apparatus of the old drivers' union into one solid piece. The rest is history. They formed a combination that hasn't been beaten in a single engagement to this day.

In the great strikes of 1934—especially the July–August strike—Bill Brown came out of his shell and showed his real talent as a mass leader. Somewhat weak as an executive, and a poor office man (Bill wasn't gifted on these lines), he loomed up powerfully at moments of crisis and showed the heart of a lion in times of action and danger. He fulfilled the duties of union president best on the picket line; and if a recalcitrant scab had to be clipped, he wouldn't spare his own knuckles.

As the mass orator at critical moments in the strike, and at later fateful turning points in the life of the union, Bill was supreme. He articulated the indignation and the mass courage of the workers better than any other. In this field also he was pretty much of an improviser. I don't think he ever "prepared" a speech in his life, but he delivered some mighty fine ones; some almost-perfect speeches for the occasion. Like the true orator, he sensed and "felt" his audience and let the inarticulate mass speak through him.

All those who went together through those days of

destiny took a great personal liking to Bill. "The little guy," as he was sometimes called by his friends, who had such a big and strong heart, had a way of making people like him; one tended easily to minimize or overlook his faults, of which, by the way, he had his share. Bill was no plaster saint, but human, all too human.

His virtues outweighed his failings, and that's about the best that can be said of anybody. Bill Brown was a man who took sides and always stayed on the side he had taken. He hated the bosses as a bunch of greedy and cheating parasites; he was on the side of the underdog every time, and his big heart was full of sympathy for suffering and struggling workers everywhere. He had a fierce hatred and contempt for policemen and deputies, and all hirelings of the bosses. He loved the workers, the union, the big headquarters with the big auditorium where he presided and spoke so often. His whole life revolved around it.

With all his importance and his fame as a labor leader, Bill was a carefree, laughing fellow all the time. Everything seemed to sit lightly on his shoulders, even when in moments of desperate crisis in the union's battles he seemed for the moment to bear the whole weight himself. I never knew a man who loved life better than did Bill; never one who got more fun out of it even under the most adverse circumstances. That is why his death seems such a monstrous incongruity. He was a decidedly gregarious person. Companionship was the breath of life to him. He liked action all the time. He had a good time fighting and a good time celebrating when the fight, for the moment, was ended.

I recall Bill Brown as a herald of the happy future when social relations will be organized sanely and will be lighted up by human joy and laughter. He was a good soldier in the emancipation struggle of the toilers, and put in his licks and his blows to hasten on the day of their liberation victory. Those who survive him and carry on the struggle, which alone gives life hope and meaning, will gratefully remember the man who bore the proud title of president of Local 544, the lionhearted fighter and softhearted friend, Bill Brown.

# Chapter 23

# Address at the funeral of Inger Swabeck

Delivered in Chicago, July 12, 1948.

Dear Friends:

I will first relate Inger's biography. She was born in Horsens, Denmark, May 30, 1895. Her maiden name was Inger Lindhardtsen. She came to the United States, to stay here in Chicago, in the spring of 1916. A little later Inger met Arne Swabeck, who was also an immigrant from Denmark, in the Chicago Karl Marx Club, the local Scandinavian branch of the Socialist Party. On May 12, 1920, Inger and Arne were married. She became the mother of one son, Edgar, who was born June 11, 1921. Inger died at the age of fifty-three. Her survivors are a mother, a sister and a brother in Denmark; a sister, Mrs. Thora Hansen, a resident of Chicago; her husband Arne, and her son Edgar.

Inger was loved by all. This is testified to by the telegrams that have been pouring in from all parts of the country, from comrades and friends who knew her. And all of us here testify to the same.

Some people are called upon to play their parts on great stages, where all the world can see them and hear them. Others, and they are the great majority, do their work in quiet corners, observed and noticed only by the few who come into intimate contact with them. Inger was one of those, but she was no less important for all of that.

Inger was one of the old guard of the party. She was one of those who sustained and supported the party in its hardest days, when it seemed that the whole world was conspiring to break it, to smash it. In those hard days of the early thirties, when very few people cared for us or believed in our future, Inger cared. She believed.

We had to call Arne from Chicago to New York in 1930. We could not get along without him. He had to give up his job. They had to break up their home, dispose of their furniture and come to New York, to work under conditions of unbelievable hardship and poverty to try to hold the fragile nucleus of the party together.

Inger came uncomplainingly. And even under those difficult conditions, she set about her own chosen task, to put together a few sticks of furniture and make a home where her warrior husband might rest and recuperate from his labors and his battles, and where her young son might grow up in an atmosphere of mutual affection and mutual respect and concern for humanity.

I was privileged to be a frequent guest in the home that Inger made for her husband and her son in New York. It always seemed like an oasis. All the storms of the world were raging outside, but the home that Inger made and presided over always recalled to my mind the beautiful words of the English poet, Rupert Brooke: "There was peace and holy quiet there."

I last saw Inger two years ago, after a long separation.

She and Arne had been released from their task in New York and had returned to Chicago. Arne had gone back to work at his trade, and she had built a new home in her own town, Chicago. When I last saw her she seemed to me more beautiful than ever. With grey hair framing her fair young face, she seemed to be blooming with a second youth. Her life work was crowned with victory. Her husband, who had worn himself sick under the long stress of his tasks in New York, had been restored to health under her tender care. Her son had grown to manhood and had taken his own place in the army of labor and the army of the socialist revolution.

I will never forget the pride that glowed in her face when she told me: "Edgar is on his own now. He is grown up. He is making his own living, has joined the union, and joined the party all by himself."

It was just then, when everything seemed best, that the worst troubles of dear Inger's life assailed her. Physical illness took a cruel toll of her body; and on top of that, the dark sickness of the mind, which no medicine could cure, came over her. She fought a long time against that, but it was a losing fight. All her courage, and all her husband's tender care, and her son's solicitude—not all that was sufficient to contend with that dread enemy.

And when Inger finally yielded to it, she remained true to herself and to her real nature, which was dominated above all by her concern for others, by her love for others.

I think we can most truly describe her as we all thought of her, as we remember her, if we recall the words of the great apostle, Paul: "Though I speak with the tongues of men and of angels, and have not love, I am become as sounding brass, or a tinkling cymbal."

We remember her, we, and all who know her, all those whose paths of life touched hers—we remember her as one who "had love." Hers was the precious gift of love. Her whole life was spent in the service of others. Even in her last act she gave testimony to her love. She feared that the sickness of her mind would grow worse, not better. She feared a greater evil, a greater calamity for her family; and she wanted to choose for them the lesser evil. That is the real meaning of her last act of renunciation and sacrifice.

If we remember her that way, we will remember her truly as she really was. And we will speak the truth if we say that her last action in taking her own life was no sin, but on the contrary, a final demonstration of the basic principle of her life, of her love and concern for others.

It is not for us to inquire into the wisdom of her act, or to judge, or to criticize. It is for us only to try to understand. It is for us only, as we stand here with the grief-stricken family of this blameless woman—the blameless husband and the blameless son and the grieving sister—it is for us only to say to them that we, their friends and comrades, do understand. We stand here with our arms around them in sympathy and solidarity. And we entreat them: dear friends, do not refuse to be comforted. Be rather comforted and consoled by the memory of all that Inger gave to you, to all of us. We are all better for that, and our lives are brighter.

But even here, as we say farewell to Inger, we must not forget our duty. We must not forget that we are soldiers in the war for the liberation of humanity. We must remember, too, that Inger in her own way, in her own fashion, was also a soldier of the revolution. For that, her grave, as the poet Heine said, should be marked not with a cross, but with a sword. We must all try to do a little more now to make up for her loss and to honor her memory.

The strongest warrant for living is the sense of being needed. The world needs us; the party needs us. I venture to remind the stricken husband of this dear woman; I venture to remind him that, for the old guard of the party, to which he and she both belong, duty is the first commandment. And when duty calls, even though they have been knocked to the earth and have to crawl on their hands and knees, the old guard will answer and obey.

We who have this philosophy dare to end even a funeral service on a martial note. We will say farewell now to this dear child who blessed our lives with her love. And then we will rise, all of us together, rise from the ashes of grief to go back to work, back to the battle.

Chapter 24

# Goldie Geldman

Delivered at memorial services in Los Angeles, October 15, 1952.

Comrades:

In a letter to Comrade Farrell Dobbs the day after Goldie Geldman died, I wrote: "Goldie had been with us since 1930. The history of her entire conscious life is virtually a history of our movement, that part written in simple deeds by the rank and file. In many respects she was a symbolic representative of the socialist movement. She was a living demonstration of that social revolt which is generated by oppression and discrimination. She was symbolic in another respect. She showed, herself, by her background and her evolution, how the most backward environment of ignorance and prejudice can produce representatives of the most modern, the most progressive and the most revolutionary ideas."

Goldie was born in St. Paul, October 29, 1907, the eldest of eight children. Her parents were Joe and Rose Cooper,

Goldie Geldman

who immigrated to America from the Ukraine. They came from Jewish peasant stock. They arrived in Minneapolis in 1905, along with that swarm of millions of others who have sought in this country a refuge and an opportunity. Her father worked as a foundryman in St. Paul. He often worked double shifts to make ends meet for a large and growing family.

Despairing of the difficulties, he left St. Paul with his family in 1916, tying all his worldly goods and five children to a horse and wagon, to seek his fortune in the countryside. They landed in Chaska, Minnesota, a village of 2,000 people, after three days' journey. Chaska is twenty-five miles from the Twin Cities. The natives of Chaska had never before seen such people as these nomads, suddenly arrived in their midst. They called them gypsies.

In Chaska, the Coopers started a small store in one room of the house where they lived. And there they raised eight children, a little island of Russia and Israel in a provincial inland sea. The Cooper family was isolated in that little village, ridiculed, discriminated against by the people who didn't understand that the immigrants represented an older and, in some respects, a superior culture.

The Cooper children did not have to learn about discrimination from books or from agitators. They experienced it every day of their lives. Without knowing what they were doing, the ignorant Jew-baiters of Chaska, Minnesota, were plowing up the soil of Goldie Cooper's mind and preparing it for the seed of socialism. It germinated and grew there into a luxurious plant. They fired her with a lifelong hatred of every form of discrimination and injustice, of every offense against the dignity of the human personality. She grew up to fight throughout her entire adult life against the social system which engenders such outrages.

Her first revolt against the environment of provincial prejudice and ignorance, as with so many rebels in history, took the form of flight. After graduating from Chaska High School and attending three years at the University of Minnesota, Goldie decided to explore the great world on her own account. With one of her sisters she landed in Chicago in 1929, at the age of twenty-two. It was there that she met Max Geldman and formed an association in marriage, and in common work for common ideas, which lasted for twenty-three years, until her death in Los Angeles three days ago.

Her activity in our movement extended over twenty-two years, in four different centers: New York, Minneapolis, Chicago and Philadelphia, and included a visit to Los Angeles where she made her last fight against the fatal illness that had overtaken her.

Goldie's political biography reads about as follows: She joined the Communist League of America, the predecessor of the Socialist Workers Party, in New York in 1930. She was part of the generation that joined the movement under the double necessity of understanding the general struggle for socialism and the struggle against Stalinist betrayal at the same time. She was active in New York from 1930 to 1934, attended classes, participated in general activities of the Communist League, and helped to form the Spartacus Youth Club.

From New York in 1934 she moved to Minneapolis with her husband. The major part of her political life took place in the Twin Cities. She played a key role in integrating and educating the great number of people who were attracted to our party from the mass organizations. Her house in Minneapolis, at 2518 Cortland Avenue, was always a party center. She took over the direction of the federal workers' section of Local 544, the unemployed section, during the period 1939–1940, when the leaders of that movement, including her husband, were imprisoned in Sandstone.

She took charge of the commissary at the party headquarters during the trial of the eighteen leading people of the Socialist Workers Party in 1941, and in that capacity she was invaluable in keeping conflicting elements working harmoniously together. She was loved and respected by hundreds of workers in the Twin Cities area, as telegrams here have testified, to whom her warm compassion for the oppressed and her great sense of social justice symbolized the socialist movement and the socialist future.

In 1941 and 1942 she was in Chicago, took part in the general activity of the party there, and was the first secretary of the Civil Rights Defense Committee, which was formed to defend the eighteen defendants of the SWP. When the trial took place in Minneapolis, she returned there.

In 1945, after the release of the prisoners of the SWP from Sandstone prison, including her husband, Goldie went to Philadelphia to take up with Max Geldman the task of building a political center in that area. Her greatest maturity took place there in Philadelphia. Her prior years in New York, Minneapolis and Chicago had been a preparation for her expanded role as a political worker in Philadelphia.

Besides her general party activity of recruiting and educating and integrating new people, she played an outstanding role in the party's public activities—three of them in particular. She was local secretary of the European Workers Relief Committee, which made possible the collection of tons of clothing and substantial sums of money for the relief of our hard-pressed comrades in Europe in the postwar period.

She played an outstanding role in the National Association for the Advancement of Colored People, organized the most effective campaign against police brutality in the history of Philadelphia. Her house in Philadelphia, like her home in Minneapolis, was the center for all the oppressed to call for help. She achieved outstanding recognition for attracting members to the National Association through door-to-door activity. She was known as a leading figure in the struggle against Jim Crow discrimination.

Third, she was local secretary of the Kutcher Defense Committee in Philadelphia. She took the Kutcher case to the Philadelphia labor movement and obtained dozens of endorsements and financial contributions for the support of the case.

Thus, her entire conscious life—twenty-two years—was spent in the Trotskyist movement, in our party. In that entire life, as all who knew her would testify, she exemplified warm compassion for human life, a keen sense of social justice, staunch and stubborn will to fight for socialism, optimism and integrity. That is her story. But there is even more to be added, for her life was full and complete in all respects.

She was a family person, strongly attached to her own

people, and she was the pioneer who led two of her brothers, Jake and Dave, and her sister Phyllis, into the party. She was a daughter devoted to her own parents, and likewise a devoted and attentive wife and mother of her own two children. Thus she lived a complete and full and rounded life which left her little time or thought for self.

She worked all her life for others, for her own family and for all mankind; for all members of the universal human family, whom she had adopted as her own. And Goldie would have scoffed at any suggestion that her role of leading and doing represented a sacrifice on her part. In doing for others, she simply realized herself. That was her principle, and she lived up to her principle. She believed, as the great Daniel De Leon believed and once said, that the only person who makes a real sacrifice is the one who compromises his principles. Goldie left us the heritage of this wisdom, not in words only, but in simple deeds that live and shine and light up our memory of her, even in these moments of grief and sorrow when we have to say goodbye to her.

The Greek philosophers enjoined people that the most important subject of investigation and study was themselves. And they thought that in this investigation they could find wisdom. Man, know thyself, they said. But even today, after the lapse of more than 2,000 years, the real nature of human beings, what they really are and what they may be, remains an undiscovered country, explored only by a few. In their insatiable hunger for knowledge, in their unceasing upward striving for enlightenment and progress over the centuries, people have learned much, but they do not yet know themselves.

We see people as they appear before our eyes, in a given moment of human evolution, reacting to the pressures and compulsions of contemporary society, and think that what we see about these people is fixed and final. That is the greatest error we could possibly make, for nothing is fixed and final. Everything flows, said the Greek philosopher Heraclitus. History teaches us that this is true of human society. And it is true of human nature, too. Human nature, like everything else in the universe, is subject to change and is constantly changing.

Our study of history, illuminated by the science of Marxism, gives us the unshakable conviction that people can and will conquer and control their own social organization—which up to now has controlled them—and change it for the better. And by doing this, and even in the process of doing it, they will also learn to know themselves, and to change themselves for the better.

When it is given to us to know such a selfless person as Goldie Geldman, we tend to think of her as altogether exceptional, as a deviation from the human norm, as one unaffected by the laws and compulsions which shape human nature in general. Yet it is a striking anomaly that such people—and there are more of them than we think—command almost universal admiration from others who think they are strange. Those who have the grace and the fortune to come into contact with such a personality as Goldie Geldman, and to warm their hands by her fire, always remember with love and gratitude.

But in our blindness, in our ignorance of ourselves, we think of her as different from us, as one of another race. That is not really so. She was one of us. If we but knew it, we all have many selves. Goldie was simply a representative of our better selves. We think of her as a child of heaven, as indeed she was, but she was a daughter of earth, too. She was a striver and a fighter in the dust and heat of the day, as all are and must be in the struggle called life.

But the difference consisted in this, that she did not waste her life in the vain pursuit of trifles. She concerned herself with the large affairs and great goals which are in themselves ennobling. That is the significance of her beautiful and heroic life. Her life, thus inspired by ennobling ideals, was full and satisfying because she knew that she was contributing to a movement that would survive her and carry on her work.

If we memorialize her in this sense, I think we will do her the most justice. We mourn for her, for we loved her deeply, but we celebrate her too. Her life, her associations with us, her contributions to our cause, were one of our victories, and not a small victory either. The movement which can attract the Goldie Geldmans, and call out their full devotion, already has the pledge of its future victory, for such people as she really represent the future.

We offer here, at this meeting, our sympathy and condolence to Goldie's family in their great loss, to the grieving husband and children, to her mother, and her brothers and sisters. But they, like we, must surely be sustained by all that she left behind as a heritage. By her example, she helped to give us something to believe that has value beyond computation. By her example, she not only strengthened our faith in the future, but also our faith that people in the present can be worthy of the future they are fighting for.

Is it possible, one might ask—is it possible to take part in a savage struggle against injustice and pettiness and not become tainted by injustice and pettiness ourselves? Is it possible to know what the world is, to know what people really are in a class society—which makes so many of them betray their better selves—and still remain pure in heart, still believe in people and their socialist future? Goldie Geldman could, and did. Her whole life was a testimony to that faith in people and in their socialist future. And that is her most important bequest to us.

Chapter 25

# Joseph Vanzler

Delivered in Los Angeles, June 25, 1956.

To comrades throughout the world who are familiar with his writings and translations of Trotsky's works, he was known as John G. Wright. His real name was Joseph Vanzler. His friends never called him anything but "Usick." The obituary articles by other comrades will, I am sure, give an account of the essential facts of his life and the many contributions he made to our movement over the past quarter of a century. It is an imposing record.

Here I wish only to say a few words in memory of Usick as a friend. I first remember meeting him twenty-three years ago at a party forum on the German crisis, in the days when Hitler was coming to power. He was obviously deeply disturbed by the German events and spoke excitedly at the forum. Soon afterward he joined our organization, and I gradually came to know him. It took time to know him as he really was, however, because the real

Joseph Vanzler (John G. Wright)

man didn't reveal himself very well in branch debates.

It took personal association, over a long time, to know the real Usick. Our association during the first year or so was dominated by conflict over one question of party policy and another. In 1934 we came to agreement on party policy and perspectives for the long pull and were reconciled in an unbroken union that lasted twenty-one years. We became more than comrades in the political struggle. We became friends.

Over that long stretch of time, without a break at any point, Usick gave me what everyone needs—I, perhaps most of all—and that is simple friendship. It is the hardest thing to find, but it can't be got in any other way except by finding it. In present-day business and politics, people tend to think of "friendship" as a relation based on the exchange of favors. It implies calculation and dependence of one kind or another. But friendship, as I understand it, is no good unless it is disinterested, free from any taint of self-concern.

The friendship that gives freely without counting is the only friendship worth talking about. That, I imagine, will be the normal, taken-for-granted relation of congenial people in their communion with each other in the future. But in the class society of the present, with its lack of freedom and its artificial values, such friendship is exceptional. When such a person as Usick comes along, with his simple, almost childlike trust, his appeal to the best in others and his readiness to believe the best about them, it is hard at first to believe that it is real.

Usick lived for more than fifty years in a transition period of the history of humanity. It is a mere interlude in the long evolution of the human race, but it has encompassed all our lives, and the lives of many generations. In this historical interlude, mankind, losing even the memory of its communal solidarity of earlier millenniums, has descended into the underworld of competitive class society in order to forge there the weapons for its liberation from helpless dependence on nature, and to create the material conditions for its reemergence in the communal solidarity of classless society in the future.

The present world of class society, wherein all human relationships are tainted by conflicts of interests, was a world Usick never made and he was not made for it.

He was our most learned man. Indeed, in the many broad fields which were the subject of his thought and study—the whole range of Marxism, history, philosophy and world literature—it is doubtful that the workers' movement anywhere in the world possessed a comrade so roundly learned as Usick was. He was an intellectual. If there is such a thing as a pure intellectual, one concerned with theoretical ideas as a primary interest, Usick was one. He was also a pure idealist, in that his whole life was devoted to the socialist ideal, but he knew and taught that the ideal must rest on material foundations and can be realized only in the struggle of classes.

Usick's learning and his idealism were his strength—and also his weakness. At home in the broad ocean of theoretical concepts, Usick floundered helplessly in the narrow creeks of practical affairs in the workaday world; and that included the political and party struggle, which, unfortunately, is not always free from the malignant influences of the class society it strives to change. Usick, the scholar and idealist, didn't know how to take care of himself in the rough-and-tumble business of the political fight, which others handle by reflex action, almost without thinking about it. He needed help there, lest he be taken advantage of.

It was here that a few of us, who had learned how to fight for our place under the banner without forgetting the larger aims of our struggle; how to survive in the political alley-fights and protect ourselves and others against the groin-kickers and eye-gougers—came to Usick's aid. We valued him for his learning, for his real and solid contributions to the cause, and we would not allow him to be thrust aside. I am proud of that, and it is my consolation in sorrow today.

Usick gave a lot to the party and thereby to the great cause it represents. His contributions of steady daily work—his articles, lectures and translations—added considerably to the sum total of the party's capital, and all those who have inherited this capital are his debtors.

To his friends he has left the memory of uncounted acts of generosity and kindness, of simple service simply given, which helped to take the rough edges off many a tough personal situation. The grief is too deep for tears, but we hope and believe that the memory of Usick, as he was in life, will be stronger than the grief. Usick helped the cause he believed in, and helped his friends to persevere. He helped to build our faith in men by showing us the example of a communist man. None of us can hope to do more. His life was not lived in vain.

# Chapter 26

# A wake for Usick

Letter to Doris Vanzler, June 29, 1956.

Dear Doris,
Wednesday night the Los Angeles branch meeting was turned into a memorial meeting for Usick. All of Usick's old friends who are colonized here—Vincent, Novack and Evelyn, Milt Alvin, Arne, Rose and I—spoke about different aspects of Usick's life and work and gave the branch members here, who previously knew him only by his writings, a more rounded and intimate picture of Usick as a revolutionary intellectual, comrade, man and friend. I heard many of the younger branch members say that they were inspired by the meeting and felt enriched by this more intimate knowledge of him and all that he had meant for our movement.

After the meeting, Vincent, Arne and Hildegarde, Novack and Evelyn, Rose and I, adjourned to our house and held an old-fashioned Irish wake for Usick—with sandwiches, drinks and reminiscences for several hours. We had all been too sad to talk much before that; but at the wake we felt a release of the tension and talked about Usick freely and intimately. One after another and, at times, all talking at once, we recalled incident after incident illustrating all sides of his many-sided personality. I think we enjoyed most the free exchange of reminiscences about his foibles, which were always just as dear to us as anything else about him.

We all felt better when the wake was over. We felt that we had now said farewell to Usick in the simple and sincere Irish fashion I remember so well, when friends and neighbors used to make a reverential ceremony of the departure of one who was dearly loved. The beautiful memory of Usick as a comrade and friend has finally triumphed over the grief that stunned us in the first days. I think we will keep it that way, and that we will all be better and stronger for having known him so long and so well.

Our hearts' sympathy has been with you in your deep bereavement. But we have also felt, and we spoke about it at the wake, that you have been richly privileged by your companionship with Usick, which wrought such great changes in your life and left you a treasure of memory that cannot be taken away or changed, no matter what other changes the world may see.

We thought it especially right that Usick did live to see, in his last days, the beginning of the great change in the Soviet Union and thereby in the whole world, to which he had contributed so much and which had been at the center of his life's work. With his deep insight into the historical process and his great faith in man, he was undoubtedly sure at the time of his leaving that the dawn was breaking; that the new events already signalize the beginning of an irreversible chain of developments which will bring the complete realization of the socialist ideal for which he lived and died, and that the life he contributed to that cause had not been lived in vain.

As ever,

*James P. Cannon*

## Chapter 27

# A tribute to Miles Dunne

Article published in *The Militant*, May 19, 1958.

For the past year the press has been filled with exposures of union leaders who abused their trust for personal gain. Other "labor statesmen" and exponents of business unionism, who draw down fat salaries and expense accounts and think and live like capitalists, are praised because they don't steal from the union treasury.

The death of Miles (Mick) Dunne reminds us that the union movement of our time has known labor organizers and leaders of a different breed. Indeed, the high-salaried officials, who today dictate in air-conditioned suites and ride in chauffeured Cadillacs, are living off the achievements of these pioneering militants.

Mick Dunne, of mixed Irish, French and Indian ancestry, was a true son of that generation of hard-fighting, incorruptible labor organizers to which Big Bill Haywood, Frank Little and Gene Debs belonged and which traced its lineage back to Albert Parsons and the Haymarket martyrs. The activities of such men were guided by two stars.

Three Dunne brothers (Vincent, Grant, and Miles) getting out the strike paper of the Minneapolis Teamsters.

One was the organization of the unorganized into powerful unions to buck the tightfisted corporations. The other was the ideal of a workers' world which could build a socialist society, where men could at last be free and equal.

These became Mick's aims, too, as soon as he reached the age of reason. He steered his whole life course by them. Like his well-known brothers, Vincent and Grant, he shared the ups and downs, the hard knocks and good times of a wandering worker's life from the days of the First World War to the end of the big boom of the twenties.

Destiny knocked on his door during the depths of the depression, when he was slaving as a driver in the coalyards of Minneapolis. Together with his brother Vincent, Farrell Dobbs, Carl Skoglund, Harry DeBoer and others, he formed the initial nucleus of that group of rank-and-file truckdrivers who were to inscribe an unforgettable page in the history of the Minneapolis—and American—labor movement.

With nothing but firm wills, a sound class-struggle policy, and confidence in the capacities of their fellow workers, they organized the coal drivers, wrested recognition from the companies, and then proceeded to extend unionism to other sections of the teamsters. Mick Dunne showed what stuff he was made of in those turbulent battles of 1933–1935, when the foundations of the new unionism were established.

The struggles for union recognition and conditions in those days were fought out and decided on the streets and in front of the plants, and often involved pitched battles with scabs, police, deputies. There were government arbitrators at work, too, but the men of Minneapolis knew the score and never relied upon their good will. They depended upon the force of an alert, informed, educated rank and file.

By such methods the team of leaders including Mick Dunne overturned the open shop in Minneapolis, created the most militant and democratic union in the Northwest, and expanded the power of the teamsters through the Middle West. Rising with his union, Mick became president of the Teamsters Joint Council. His advice was cherished and heeded because it had proved its worth in action. He was often called upon by workers in adjoining areas to lend a hand in their organizing drives, notably by the gasworkers in St. Louis.

Mick could be as serious as the next fellow when the occasion demanded, but he did not practice the creed of postponing enjoyment until the millennium. "He took his fun where he found it," and he found it wherever he was. Always ready with a quip or a practical joke, and willing to hoist another one with the boys at the bar, he was undoubtedly the best-liked person in Minneapolis labor circles.

Mick stood ace-high in the estimation of his brother teamsters. He could have kept his posts and climbed still higher—had he agreed to disregard his conscience and class feeling. But he wasn't born or built that way. He could rise with his class but never out of it and beyond it at the workers' expense.

The unpostponable collision with the forces of bureaucratism and corruption brought him face to face with this decision in 1940–1941. Prodded by the employers, and for his own reasons as well, President Tobin of the Teamsters International demanded that Local 544 line up for the approaching war, abandon its progressive, class-struggle policies, sacrifice its autonomy and democracy, and become part of the bureaucratic machine.

Mick and his associates answered that ultimatum with one of their own: "We'll resist—and go down, if necessary, with colors flying." Tobin hurled all the resources of a despotic administration against the stiff-necked rebels of Minneapolis: receivership, expulsions, attacks by hundreds of imported goons, court injunctions, intervention by city and state officials. All that was not enough. Then Tobin appealed to Roosevelt for aid: the FBI and Justice Department stepped in, and the Local 544 and Socialist Workers Party leaders were indicted in the first applications of the Smith Act.

Mick went on trial with the rest but his case was dismissed on a technicality. After that he returned to the life of a worker who had to pay the penalty for his beliefs and loyalty to his fellows by being hounded from job to job. He died as he lived—an unflinching soldier of labor with brilliant capacities for leadership and unshakable devotion to the cause of his class.

It is important for the young generation, who view the labor upsurge of the thirties across the span of two decades, to grasp the significance of the career of men like Mick, both in his period of prominence and in his days of obscurity.

Through the boom years of the twenties, militants such as Mick labored in the hope that the labor skates who dominated and misdirected the AFL would be unseated and swept aside by a vigorous upheaval of the ranks that would result in the cleansing of the old unions and the organization of the industrial workers. They prepared themselves for that time and those tasks.

When the crash of 1929 and its consequences set the stage for a new turn of affairs, these militants were ready to come forward, thrust aside the old-line officials, and assume direction of the seething rank-and-file movements. The tremendous advances made by unionism during that decade are the imperishable monument to their initiative and their work.

However, when the new movement ebbed back, became stabilized and bureaucratized with the advent of the Second World War and its aftermath, these builders of the unions who wouldn't go along were shoved aside or tossed out by the upstart bureaucrats. The crushing of Local 544 was one of the first and most dramatic episodes in this process.

The Becks, Brewsters, Brennans and Hoffas rose to eminence on this strangulation of democracy within the unions. These apostles of business unionism were encouraged and supported in their efforts to housebreak the unions by the very representatives of the employers who later turned upon them. The bosses could never make "sweetheart agreements" with leaders like Miles Dunne. That's why they had to mobilize the full array of their power outside and inside the unions to eliminate these spokesmen for the rank and file, and put more pliant and corruptible tools in their places. Big business got the kind of labor leaders they preferred—patriotic members of the Elks, Rotary and Knights of Columbus, Republicans and Democrats who never passed up a fast buck and operated according to the standard: "Every man has his price."

Mick Dunne never went along with that. He despised and rejected it. He went down to defeat—but not disgrace.

He left behind a spotless reputation for integrity, for honesty, for loyalty to his fellow workers and his socialist ideals.

We confidently predict that when the next great resurgence of labor militancy comes—as it surely will—the names of men like Mick Dunne will shine still brighter because they did not falter, in good times or bad, in preparing that better future.

Some of the "Old Guard": Arne Swabeck, James P. Cannon, Rose Karsner, Oscar Coover, and Carl Skoglund.

**Chapter 28**

# Carl Skoglund: One of the old guard

**THE MAN WHO HAD NO PAPERS**

Speech recorded on tape in Los Angeles and sent to New Jersey to be played at Carl Skoglund's seventieth birthday celebration, April 7, 1954.

This jubilant birthday celebration is testimony that Carl Skoglund has done pretty well for himself in this country, considering the fact that he got started off on the wrong foot and has been standing on it—so to speak—ever since. He picked Sweden for his birthplace, without realizing that Swedish birth does not confer the right to live and breathe in this country.

 Nobody told Skogie that he had made a mistake, and he didn't ask. He arrived on these shores in 1911 and, finding the gates open, just walked in. He has been traveling around the forty-eight states for forty-three years without proper identification papers. This sort of thing

Carl Skoglund

couldn't go on forever.

Thirteen years ago, the authorities picked him up and checked their files and made an alarming discovery, which has been troubling them ever since. They looked through a thick dossier marked "Skoglund, Carl"—and what did they see?

They saw that his doings and wanderings had been under observation for a long, long time; and none of the previous investigators, who had left their grimy thumbprints on the records, had had anything good to say about him. The record showed that he had always worked for a living, a very suspicious occupation for a red-blooded American. Nobody ever got rich and won the right to wave the flag by chopping down trees, fixing automobiles, driving trucks, heaving coal and working on the railroad to make the trains run on time. But that's what "Skoglund, Carl" had been up to in these United States.

The record shows further that he had been a labor agitator, strike leader, Socialist, Communist, and general troublemaker, kicking and complaining all the time about the way things are run in this country. That was bad enough, for every right-thinking American knows that things couldn't be better. But while the official headshakers were shaking their heads over the long list of bad reports about the man under investigation, they accidentally stumbled over a still more suspicious dereliction.

In ransacking the voluminous files of the Immigration Department, the Department of Justice, the FBI and the local constable, they found plenty of incriminating reports. But there was one thing they couldn't find. That was any definite proof that the subject of their inquiry had any legal existence whatever. There was no birth certificate, no entry permit, no passport, no certificate of naturalization. Nothing at all.

By the absence of any proof to the contrary, they established the fact that "Skoglund, Carl," who was standing right there before them, had no legal right to be there or anywhere else. Officially, he was not in this country and never had been. He stood before his inquisitors naked, without an identification paper to his name. Nevertheless, they had to tag him some way. So they just wrote down on the cover of the dossier, under the name of "Skoglund, Carl," in bright red ink: *"Has no papers."*

This was an absolutely intolerable situation, for how can this country stand if Skoglund's records are not in order? Something had to be done about it. The first thing that entered their minds, naturally, was to throw him into jail. Then his friends posted bond for him; and that created another problem for the department in charge of putting people in the right place and making sure they don't pop up in the wrong place.

The man who had no papers had no right to be footloose in this country; but, since bond had been posted, they had no right to keep him in jail either. It was a hell of a mess, and it hasn't been straightened out yet. The whole ponderous machinery of the United States government has been working ever since to put the man who is here but shouldn't be, in some place where he should be, but isn't. But they have never yet been able to get the time and the place and Skoglund all together.

So it turns out that, while the mills of justice grind so slowly to a final decision in his case, we have him here with us on his seventieth birthday, at a party in his honor under the auspices of the students of the Trotsky School. This is the right time and the right place and the right man all together, with more justice and more respect for the fitness of things, than the law could ever arrange.

You students of the Trotsky School do honor to yourselves and to your purpose in honoring Carl on this festive day. For he is a witness for the truth of the theory you are studying; a living exemplar of the transfusion of this theory into the green tree of life. Here is such a man as the poet Edwin Markham celebrated; a man who has "crammed his doctrine into deed."

Engels said of the theory you are studying that it is not a dogma, but a guide to action. His reference was to the action of the masses in the class struggle; a warning that the revolutionists cannot substitute themselves for the masses, but can realize their theory only with the masses and through their action. Carl Skoglund, the socialist mass worker who carried the living theory of Marxism into the labor movement, is the example par excellence of Engels's words.

But Engels's maxim can apply also to the individual's application of the theory in his own life, his own action. It is not enough to know the Marxist formulas. Not a few scholastic bystanders know the theory of Marxism, as it is written in the books; but that does not make them Marxists. The real Marxist, that is to say, the revolutionist, is one who—to quote Trotsky—assimilates the formulas into his flesh and blood; who not only knows the doctrine but lives by it and for it.

Here again, comrades of the Trotsky School, your guest of honor today is your best example. In Carl Skoglund you see a man who has lived a consistent socialist life under all circumstances, and has asked no other compensation than the satisfaction of serving the socialist cause. He has lived to see his life and his labor crowned by many achievements, which are lodged in the foundations of our great movement. And he is garlanded, on his seventieth birthday, with the affectionate regard of old comrades whom he has sustained in many a battle and of young comrades whom he has inspired for battles to come.

You cannot aim for higher rewards than that, for there are none.

## SPEECH AT MEMORIAL MEETING

Delivered at memorial meeting at Forum Hall, Los Angeles, January 7, 1961.

Comrade Chairman:

Whatever you want to call it, I can't make a conventional, sad, memorial sermon, because I don't *feel* that way about Carl. I have to talk about him the way I feel, and the way most of us feel who were associated with him for so long.

We don't deny a big sense of personal loss, his presence, his company and so on, but it is not that debilitating sadness that comes over you when someone dies before his work is finished.

Carl lived long enough and fully enough to accomplish what he was capable of, and he died in a good way, as I will inform you later in quotations from letters of comrades who were present in his last hours.

I think that this is the kind of memorial meeting that Carl Skoglund would appreciate and approve. Sadness, as I said, is not the dominant note here. It was not that of either of the other speakers or of the remarks of the chairman. And it shouldn't be. It shouldn't be an occasion for a funeral sermon and extravagant eulogy, which would be out of place when you are talking about Skogie.

The meeting, as it has been arranged by our local executive committee, is not only a tribute to a comrade who is dead; it is also, and even more so, a celebration of a life that was fully lived, up to the very last hour. The combined features of the meeting are a faithful representation of the way Carl lived, and worked, and relaxed among friends and comrades when the work was done.

Our meeting, as it has been planned by the committee, has three parts and purposes. First and properly, is that part where we pay respectful and affectionate tribute to Carl as we remember him. A second feature of the meeting is the announcement of the kick-off of a new action by the party in the local election campaign, as has already been indicated by the chairman. And then the third part, a quiet, friendly social at the end of the meeting. I don't think it is customary to have socials at the end of memorial meetings, but for Skogie's meeting, what else could you do? That's the way Skogie always did things. That's the way he did things all his life, and that's the way he died.

As you know, from what has been printed in *The Militant* and your personal knowledge and the remarks of the other speakers, Carl was one of the old guard, one of the founders of our movement, thirty-two years ago. And before that, he was one of the founders of the Communist Party in 1919. And before that, he was active in the Socialist Party in this country since the day he illegally set foot on our sacred soil. He was even a socialist before that, in Sweden, or wherever he came from—he never had any papers to prove it.

I first met Carl in 1923—that's thirty-seven years ago—in Minneapolis, while I was on a speaking tour after I had returned from the Soviet Union for the first time. We have been together ever since that first meeting, without a break of any kind, except squabbles among ourselves. But in the Communist Party we were always together in the same faction. We were together in the foundation of the Trotskyist movement in the revolt against Stalinism. We have been together in the Socialist Workers Party ever since then, and in all party work. We were together in the big strikes in Minneapolis, where I had a chance to get closer to him and to see him in action in the mass movement and get a profounder appreciation of his many qualities than I had before.

And we were together in prison, and everywhere else. Carl was not alone. I can't think of him as a single individual. He was one of that remarkable group of worker-Bolsheviks in Minneapolis, who worked and fought so long and so consistently and brought so much credit and glory to our movement in the Minneapolis struggles. And all that remains with us and can never be taken away.

The whole world, I suppose, knows about the Minneapolis strikes. When I was in Europe in the fall of 1934, after the second big strike, I was told by comrades there that every paper in France carried the story of the Minneapolis strikes on the front page, from day to day. It was worldwide news.

The world knows about the big union success in Minneapolis, which played a tremendous role in the creation of the new union movement, beginning with 1934. Carl played a big role in that. As Arne remarked, he was always one of the leading cadre of Trotskyists who were the center of the whole storm. And later he was elected president of Local 544. That was a pretty big honor in those days. And that was the time when Skoglund almost brushed the edge of acceptance and respectability in Minneapolis.

The Scandinavian Society of the Twin Cities, which consists primarily of middle-class people who like to exploit any achievements of any of their *landsmann,* as they call them, suddenly discovered that they had a member of their ethnic community who had become president of the biggest union in town. And they decided to honor, these bourgeois Scandinavians, they decided to honor Carl Skoglund. And they arranged a ceremonial dinner in his honor. That must have been a spectacle.

Carl went through with it, in the course of his official duties. Six months later he was in jail. And I really believe he was more at home there.

Now I say that the world knows about the union movement in Minneapolis and its effect on this country and the labor movement throughout the country. But I personally remember Carl best and most affectionately and most gratefully for the quiet, unobtrusive things he did to help keep *The Militant* alive in the first hard years, when his name was not known outside the borders of the labor movement in Minneapolis; when he had been blacklisted in three different ways. He had been kicked out of the Central Labor Union because he was a Communist. He had been kicked out of the Communist Party because he was a Trotskyist. And he had been blacklisted on the railroad, where he was a mechanic, a good-paying job, because he had been the chairman of the strike committee in the big strike in 1923.

And in those early days, before he became famous along with the rest of the Minneapolis group, we in New York were isolated and dead broke, didn't know where to turn to find a few dollars to pay the bills from week to week. Every week was a financial crisis. I sometimes sympathize with the United States government when they claim they're having trouble with their gold reserves. We had trouble of that kind, and I know what an agonizing thing it is to be out of money and have to pay bills—or else close up shop. We couldn't close up shop because we had taken upon ourselves the obligation to tell the world the truth about Stalinism and the Russian Opposition and so forth.

Now in those days, Carl Skoglund, as you have been told, worked in a coalyard. And he earned his meager wages by wielding a great big shovel, shoveling coal, long hours a day. And out of the wages he got for that, he donated every week a part to *The Militant;* sometimes as much as half his week's wages would be sent to New York to make it possible for us to get the paper out. That's the way it was done in those days, and that's what I remember tonight most gratefully about him, even more than his achievements which were so widely advertised and so deservedly famous.

Now Carl was that kind of a socialist! He was always preaching socialism. He talked about it to the workers he met on the job or wherever he would run into them. He talked about it all the time, wherever he was, and he converted many people. Many people in this party owe their first interest in socialism to Carl Skoglund's persistent efforts.

But preaching socialism was only one part of his work, of his promotion of the great ideal of a better-organized human society. He worked, as I have said, he made a little money and donated a part of everything he made to the party. That was the pattern of Skogie's life. Right up to the very end, right to the very end.

I thought his death and the circumstances of it were so representative and symbolic of his whole life that there is a certain cause even for rejoicing in our sorrow about the way it happened.

You know we run a school, a Trotsky school for six months of the year, and there is a special building on this campsite that houses the students, heated by steam heat. And just a few days before the death of Skoglund, the boiler, the old boiler, gave out and broke down. The weather is very severe there—it is not like California—and they had to vacate the building and huddle in the farm house until the boiler could be fixed.

Skoglund, being a mechanic who knew a little of everything about fixing things, looked it over and said, "We've got to get a new boiler, we can't fix that anymore, it's been fixed once too often."

So they scurried around and they got a new boiler, from Sears, and then the problem was to put it together and make it work. And in the last two or three days of Skoglund's life—how symbolic this is—he was there over the crew of comrades working, supervising the whole job, until all the parts were put together and the final test was made to see whether it would work or not, until it worked perfectly, and the building was heated, and the students could go back to their quarters. And then they decided to have a little celebration, after their job was done, and it's told about in a letter I'll quote, a letter from our own George and Evelyn, who are there.

She says, "Sunday demonstrated that it was a perfect installation—" Why shouldn't it be? It had a conscientious mechanic directing it, and it had to be perfect or he would never have approved. ". . . it was a perfect installation, the crowd moved back to their quarters. We had all been huddled up here during the interim, and everybody was in the best of spirits, Carl above all. He was glad we had swung the deal on the new furnace, rather than try to get some old one to replace it. We even had a financial meeting on it, right after Sunday dinner." And they decided they would try to raise the money to pay the expense of the new installation without calling on the National Office, because the National Office is in financial trouble. And there they began a collection, and she says, "Carl offered $100 toward it. Later we discovered he had just $174 to his name."

Those were Carl's last two acts. He was sitting in the social gathering, celebrating the installation of the new boiler, the new achievement, discussing all kinds of problems in which he was taking part, drinking a cocktail or two with the others and exchanging banter and ideas, and then taking up the collection to pay the bill, in which he participated. All three sides of his systematic, persistent, representative life were represented in his last hour—talk about socialism, work for socialism, and even give a little money for it, even if you've only got $174 to your name at the end of a lifetime of labor. That's Carl.

Now as for the circumstances under which he died, it's told in another letter, which I think should be read to you. It's a letter from George and Evelyn to Milt. I think you will be interested in the circumstances, and it softens the sadness somewhat because of the way it came about.

"By this time you will have received the news of Skogie's death. It occurred less than twenty-four hours ago, here in this house. It had been an exceptionally fine day, socially speaking. We were all cheerful because we had just succeeded in repairing a big catastrophe, the breakdown of the furnace in the lodge. For a week there had been no heat there and the students and us were all huddled in the main house, and so on.

"We felt the occasion called for celebration, and so we did. A fitting setting was provided by the first big snowfall of the year, which when it wound up, made us snowbound. From five to six-thirty we had cocktails. All of us in the finest humor and waiting for the dinnerbell in the main room. Carl was resting in his special chair near the stove. All of a sudden, he keeled sideways, gasped for breath and, within one minute, it was his last. It was about as swift and merciful a death as anyone could want, and as he himself could have wished it." And here is something I think should be of special interest to you, that you helped to contribute to the happiness of his last times.

"The Los Angeles comrades will be glad to know that since Carl returned from his visit,"—that's to the camp here, last fall, after his visit here in town—"he has been in better humor and apparently more vigorous than in several years. There is no question but that the comradely welcomes and hospitality he received during the five weeks was the tonic. He ended his remarkable life, working up till the last minute for the camp, for the school, for the party, for the movement, and happy to be able to do so. We of course are not yet adjusted to his death. He was sitting in the chair, and he fell over and he died, within a minute."

I like the circumstances that he died with his shoes on, after he had finished his work. That surely is a good way to die. He gave a lot to the movement for the emancipation of mankind. In fact he gave all that he had. But he did not regard it as a sacrifice. For by identifying himself with the human race as a whole, and working for its better future, he found himself and realized himself, and lived a satisfying, purposeful life to the very end. That's about the best that any of us can hope to do.

Carl Skoglund suffered a great deal of persecution and hardship in his time, but he was always ready for a little fun and relaxation when the day's work was done. We will honor his memory tonight in his own spirit if we follow the program outlined by the committee. After the memorial tributes to Carl, we will hear from the chairman about the planned city election campaign; that's an action in the spirit of Skoglund. And then we will relax at a social, and that's certainly also in the spirit of Skoglund and the pattern he set forth.

I wish, in closing, to recite a rather irreverent poem, if I may. It kept recurring in my head ever since the news of the death of Carl came. It's not the kind of a poem that you say at an ordinary funeral, but it's one that fits Carl's memorial, and I wouldn't mind having it said about me, in due time. I forget the name of the poet, but it goes something like this:

> When I die, don't just throw me away,
> Give me a nice big grave, and let me lay
> Among the literati and illuminati,
> And the cognoscenti, and intelligenti,
> And invite all the other people to the party—
> And drink hearty!

# Chapter 29

# Socialist electoral policy

Delivered at a dinner meeting sponsored by the Socialist Workers Party at Forum Hall, Los Angeles, at which Cannon and Vincent Hallinan both spoke on "United Socialist Political Action in 1958 and the Outlook for American Socialists," March 1, 1958.

The subject assigned to us tonight, as it appears in the advertisements, reads: "United Socialist Political Action in 1958—and the prospects for American socialists." This two-sided subject proposes action today and suggests, at the same time, that we look ahead and try to see where we are going.

In my opinion, the two sides of the subject are equally important and they are properly joined together. Unless we consider our outlook, it's not easy to take any kind of meaningful action. On the other hand, if we content ourselves with looking at the future as we would like to see it, and do nothing about it today, take no action in the direction of our goal, we debase our vision into a daydream of mopers and idlers.

Direction without motion is just about as useless as motion without direction. If we want to do anything meaningful and purposeful in the present day, we have to look ahead and see the general direction of our goal. And if we want to reach the desired goal without too much delay, we have to get started. We have to get going. That, I think, is the double meaning of the subject assigned to us for our discussion tonight.

Our vision and our goal, to which our lives are committed and which makes our lives worthwhile, is the socialist society of the free and equal. And as a next practical, experimental step on the road to that glorious objective, we ought to take a census of the socialist population of this country. We should try to find out how many people will make out their ballots for socialism if the issue is presented to them squarely. To that end we are proposing an electoral coalition of socialist forces for united socialist political action in 1958.

I believe that a survey of the present situation in the American socialist movement will show the feasibility and the timeliness of this proposed next step. There are important historical precedents for this procedure, as I will relate a little later on.

We have to start from where we are. In the discussion and exchange of views that have been taking place, particularly in the past two years, many writers in different publications have turned their attention to this question of just where we stand right now. The trend of opinion seems to range from sober to gloomy.

Some say we're "at rock bottom." Others say "we have no place to go but up." And then some real calamity howlers have expressed the opinion that we can't even go up or down or sideways; that all we can do is just sit there and "think," and twiddle our thumbs, and perhaps wait for a new Moses to be discovered in the bullrushes who will lead us out of this capitalist Egypt.

Well, I don't believe in unfounded optimism at all, but, as I see it, the reality is a little better than some socialists picture it. There is no doubt, no doubt whatever, that the present position of American socialism is far from good, and far from strong. That's obvious. But what about the other side of the present reality—what about the position of American capitalism? Well, she ain't what she used to be, that's for sure.

This small capitalist segment of the world, that aspired only yesterday to rule the whole world, has fallen on evil days, and everybody knows it. Even the professional boasters are singing the blues. As I read the comments, ranging all the way from the colonial world to the very centers of American power in these days, the general opinion of American capitalism is that it's in a hell of a fix. I am only telling you what I read, but I must admit that I think so, too. Nobody has any confidence except Eisenhower. And he's out on the golf course and doesn't know what's going on. They say he doesn't even read the newspapers.

Now, we socialists don't need to conceal our own troubles—we have plenty of them. We who have survived the storms of these last terrible years know very well that we have been hurt. The socialist movement in the United States has suffered heavy blows, one on top of another, for at least seventeen consecutive years.

First, there were the terrible reactionary effects on the labor movement, and on all American radicalism and even liberal thought, of the Second World War. And the cold war that followed it. And the Korean War. The effects were reactionary in all directions.

Then we had to contend with the conservatizing influence

of the long, artificially propped-up prosperity, which sapped the strength of American radicalism in all its departments.

And then we had to put up with the devastation and terror of the long witch-hunt, which decimated the ranks of American radicalism and liberalism and all sections of the socialist movement.

And then, last but not least, the socialist movement has been sapped by a moral sickness—the calculated lies and slanders, the suppression of free and independent thought, the violations of class solidarity, the disruption of fraternal relations and free discussion among socialists of different tendencies. All this dirty business has worked to demoralize the movement and to discredit the name of socialism.

We have been hit hard from all sides. But in spite of that—and this is our great capital for the future—a considerable nucleus of undaunted and incorruptible socialists have survived all this adversity. More than that, the adverse factors have been changing in recent times. For several years now, if we have looked closely enough, we have seen a turn of the tide.

Antiwar sentiment is stronger in this country today than it has been at any time in the last quarter of a century. The most striking proof of that is the fact that, for the first time since the early thirties, Hollywood dares to make antiwar movies again. And they are turning out to be the most popular movies on the screen today. There is a world of significance in this simple fact which the movie manufacturers never dreamed of when they were making something to sell.

Not only is the antiwar sentiment strong and growing, but economic troubles are beginning to engender a new radicalism. The unprecedented boom, propped up by military spending, was dragged out so long that many people began to think that capitalism finally had found a way to escape from its own laws. This artificial boom, according to what I read in the most conservative financial journals of the country, has entered into a decline. They call it a "recession," but they admit there are five million unemployed in this country; and that means that there are probably six to seven million actually unemployed.

And nowhere have I been able to read in the financial and economic columns of the various journals—nowhere except in Eisenhower's speeches—any promise that it will get better "next month." Or, more correctly, this month—this is the first of March already, and Eisenhower is already one day down on his fatuous prophecy.

Antiwar sentiment is growing, and the capitalist economy is in decline and with it the conservatizing influence of prosperity is spending its force. And also in recent years we've seen the witch-hunt slow down. It isn't stopped by any means, but the witch-hunt terror, that all sections of American radicalism had to contend with in the past ten years, has been decidedly moderated. People are raising their courage again in wider and wider numbers. All that is in our favor.

And no less important than these favorable turns in the situation, is a new atmosphere in the circles of American radicalism—in all circles. Socialists of different tendencies have begun to think of each other as comrades. Free discussion and fraternization, and sentiment for united action and regroupment of all the scattered forces, are the order of the day now everywhere. I say that's a good day for us and for our cause—the cause of American socialism.

It doesn't bother me at all that, in a meeting such as ours, we have some criticism of each other; and that some things are said by one speaker that another can't fully endorse—that's not the significant thing about this great meeting tonight. The significant thing is that socialists of different tendencies stand together here on the same platform and urge united action against the capitalist class.

All these changes I have mentioned are in our favor, and we should take advantage of them. We should see in them the opportunity for American socialism to enter a new stage of revival which will carry it to new heights, on the road to victory over American capitalism.

In spite of all that has happened to discourage, to terrorize, to weaken and demoralize the movement, there are still a lot of socialists in this country. The sentiment for socialism in the United States, even today, after all that has happened, is much bigger than all of them put together. And the potential sentiment for socialism, which the bankruptcy of American capitalism will generate in the next period, is a hundred or a thousand times greater than the conscious socialist sentiment at this present moment. That's the real situation as I see it, and the real prospect before us. We ought to take it as the starting point in a new struggle to put socialism on the map and wipe capitalism off the map.

The basic aim in rebuilding for the future—as I think all present will agree—the basic aim for which we are all striving, is to regroup the scattered socialist forces, and eventually to get all honest socialists together in one common party organization. But that can't be done in a day. The experience of the last two years shows that it will take time. We'll have to take the process of collaboration and unification in stages, one step at a time.

The starting point of the process is for all genuine socialists of all tendencies, whether presently affiliated to one organization or another, or independent at present, to recognize that we are all part of one movement, and that we ought to work together fraternally in one field of action after another, work together against the injustices and oppressions of capitalism. That sounds almost like a revolutionary assertion after the terrible experience of the disruption of solidarity. But it used to be the unvarying practice and tradition of the old socialist and radical movement in America.

In the time of Debs and Haywood and Vincent St. John, there were many differences of opinion and different organizations, and many quarrels and squabbles and debates. But it was taken for granted, as a matter of course, that when there was an issue of common interest against the class enemy—whether it was a strike or a labor leader arrested or some act of injustice committed against any section of the movement—all should work together in solidarity against the injustice.

On this point I am a reactionary—I want to turn the clock back to the good old days of solidarity and cooperation in practical action against the common enemy. Fraternal cooperation and solidarity in practical action do not exclude differences of opinion, do not exclude discussion and debate as we go along. There is no socialist life without free discussion of differences. But while we discuss our differences, we should also remember what we have in common as socialists, and act together in support of it.

Many different opinions are being expressed in the course of debate on the American road to socialism. I think all suggestions and ideas should get an attentive hearing. But however one may think socialism is going to come to the United States, one thing is sure—it's not going to be smuggled in. It's a shame to have to say that, isn't it?

The cause of socialism can be advanced only by counterposing it to capitalism—simply, honestly, openly and directly. Clever tricks designed to fool people into socialism are self-defeating, as well as dishonest and contemptible. I think we have had more than enough of that indecent horseplay already. The revival of the American socialist movement will really begin to get underway when we get back to fundamentals and come out in the open as socialists every day in the week, and twice on Sunday.

When we say that socialists should find a way to work together, especially in electoral campaigns, we mean of course real socialists, socialists who, to use the words of the *Communist Manifesto,* "disdain to conceal their aims." Socialists without false faces.

What is a socialist? Well, I can tell you very quickly what he is not. He is not a Republican. And he is not a Demo-Dixiecrat. And he is certainly not a shamefaced supporter of the war program of the U.S. State Department. He is not a member of, or supporter of, any capitalist party whatever. I'm not submitting this as an argument. I'm stating this as the summary conclusion from established facts.

Capitalism rules and exploits the working people through its control of the government. That's fact number one. And capitalism controls the government through the medium of its class political parties. That's fact number two. The unconditional break away from capitalist politics and capitalist parties is the first act of socialist consciousness, and the first test of socialist seriousness and sincerity. That's fact number three.

Where did I learn that? Marx and Engels explained it over a hundred years ago, so it's not hot off the wire. I personally heard Debs explain it fifty years ago. That's what they said—Marx and Engels and Debs.

They were very simple fellows who couldn't understand that the way to get what you want is to vote for what you don't want. They couldn't understand that the really slick and clever way to get socialism is to vote for capitalism. And to tell you the truth, we don't understand it either. And we don't intend to play that game.

About twenty years or so ago there was an aviator who flew out of the New York airport on a trip to Los Angeles and landed in Ireland. They called him "Wrong Way Corrigan," and he became a popular symbol of the man who doesn't know where he's going. That's the trouble with the Wrong Way Corrigans of politics—they don't seem to know where they're going; and it would be imprudent to follow them.

This is not a general public meeting, but a sort of invitational meeting of socialists of different tendencies. All of us present here, I take it, are socialists of one tendency or another. Now let us ask ourselves, honestly and directly: How did we become socialists? How did we acquire our certain confidence in the bright socialist future of humanity—the great vision which has transformed and inspired our lives and sustained us through the darkest days of struggle against this insane social system? Did we acquire our socialist consciousness because of our superior wisdom? I don't think so. We became socialists, each and every one of us, in the same way—because others who went before us explained it to us in earlier years. They wrote pamphlets and books, and distributed journals, and made speeches, and explained things—and from them we learned.

And the fact that we had to learn from others—does not that suggest the idea that others may learn from us? Does not that impose upon us the obligation to explain socialism to others yet to come? And if we socialists don't speak up for socialism, who will? Who will spread the inspiring word of a socialist outcome of this mad world of capitalism, if we don't? And if we have to do it, when do we begin? I believe the sooner the better.

And here comes the importance of the subject we have under discussion tonight. The best time of all—the most fruitful time to explain socialism—is during election campaigns, when public interest is highest and we stand the best chance to get a hearing. The capitalist class rules this country in a complicated way, through the machinery of bourgeois democracy. They can't shut off all avenues of public communication, even to minority parties—although they try their best.

The Socialist Workers Party, even with its limited forces, has demonstrated in these recent years how we can get through cracks in the wall and compel them to give us access to TV and radio audiences and to carry notices in the newspapers. We get a greater hearing for the ideas of socialism in the few months of the election campaign than in all the rest of the time put together. This makes every election campaign a socialist success.

The main purpose of participating in elections, as a socialist organization or as a coalition of socialist organizations, is to take full advantage of the expanded opportunity to make socialist propaganda. And in the economic and social storm that is now beginning to blow up in this country, with fear and insecurity about war and making a living or even existing on this planet—there will be more interest in social and political questions, and more people will be listening than at any time in recent decades.

What can we do to make the most of this exceedingly favorable opportunity to advance our cause? The National Committee of the Socialist Workers Party has expressed the opinion, and made the proposal in an announcement in the *National Guardian* and in *The Militant*, that all socialists get together for united political action—for socialism and against capitalism—in the state and congressional elections of 1958, and that this action in 1958 be regarded as the springboard for a united presidential campaign in 1960.

That's an outlook worth looking at, isn't it? It opens up

the prospect, if accepted by other groups and tendencies, of pushing the whole socialist movement a bit forward. It is really a first-class idea, but there is nothing new or original about it. We learned that, where we learned so many things, by looking at the books and studying the history of what others have done before us. Electoral coalitions were a common practice of socialists of different tendencies in the past.

In the year 1900, Debs was a candidate for president, not of a single party, but of a coalition—exactly what we are proposing today. A split-off section of the Socialist Labor Party, headed by Hillquit and Harriman, and the Social Democratic Party of Debs and Berger agreed upon a common election slate—with Debs, from the Social Democratic Party, for president; and Harriman, from the split-off Socialist Labor Party, for vice-president. The coalition ticket was supported by the *Appeal to Reason* and other independent socialist papers. The united presidential campaign in 1900 aroused so much enthusiasm and so much sentiment for unity that nine months later they were able to bring the forces together in a new party. That's the way the Socialist Party of America was founded in August 1901.

There are other examples. In Russia the Bolsheviks and the Mensheviks were split and at loggerheads over many issues. But when it came to the elections to the Duma, they conducted a poll among themselves to determine the proportion of candidates for each side, and ran a joint electoral slate in the general election. At the outbreak of the First World War, there were Bolshevik and Menshevik deputies in the Duma, the Russian parliament, all elected on a joint slate.

Besides the historical examples, some actions taken by individuals and by groups in recent times have led up to our proposal and made it realistic and timely. You recall that in 1956, the SWP, at the cost of tremendous effort and sacrifice and the immeasurable labor of comrades bucking the reactionary election laws to get on the ballot, ran a presidential slate of Dobbs and Weiss. In that election campaign a new note of socialist solidarity was sounded. Whereas for many years in the recent past no socialist or radical party ever cooperated with or supported or helped another party, in that election campaign in 1956, Vincent Hallinan in San Francisco and Clifford McAvoy in New York came out in support of the SWP candidates.

That was the first break in the logjam. Then again, last year, in the municipal elections in San Francisco, where Frank Barbaria and Joan Jordan ran as candidates of the SWP, Hallinan and Billings and Hitchcock and Olshausen and others, all not members of the SWP, differing with us on many points, nevertheless recognized the importance of a socialist vote and endorsed our candidates and helped the campaign. The *National Guardian* supported the SWP candidates in Detroit, New York, and San Francisco on the same grounds. The *National Guardian* played a role in this progressive development similar to that of the independent *Appeal to Reason* in the early days.

It seems to us that these new developments, taken all together, have set the stage for another step forward. The SWP National Committee has taken the initiative and made the proposal for a more formal electoral coalition, after full deliberation. We mean every word we say, and we are ready to go through with it. The matter is now under discussion throughout all sections of the movement, and we hope for a favorable outcome.

The American socialist movement has been badly battered in the storms of recent years. But the new events, which I have briefly summarized, show that the movement is still alive and kicking, and is even looking up a bit. The prospects are brighter than they have been for a long time. We should take heart and hope, as Debs used to say, and work diligently in the coming days to turn the bright prospects into new achievements and new advances.

The forces for an imposing demonstration of socialist sentiment in the 1958 elections are already present. They are waiting for the go-ahead signal. They need only to be aroused and encouraged and organized. And for this, as is almost always the case, there is no eloquence equal to the eloquence of action. United socialist political action in the 1958 elections will be the right action at the right time.

Chapter 30

# Socialism and democracy

Delivered to a meeting at the West Coast Vacation School, September 1, 1957.

Comrades, I am glad to be here with you today, and to accept your invitation to speak on socialism and democracy. It is a most timely subject, and in the discussion of socialist regroupment it takes first place. Before we can make real headway in the discussion of other important parts of the program, we have to find agreement on what we mean by socialism and what we mean by democracy, and how they are related to each other, and what we are going to say to the American workers about them.

Strange as it may seem, an agreement on these two simple, elementary points, as experience has already demonstrated, will not be arrived at easily. The confusion and demoralization created by Stalinism, and the successful exploitation of this confusion by the ruling capitalists of this country and all their agents and apologists, still hang heavily over all sections of the workers' movement. We have to recognize that. Even in the ranks of people who call themselves socialists, we encounter a wide variety of understandings and misunderstandings about the real meaning of those simple terms, socialism and democracy. And in the great ranks of the American working class, the fog of misunderstanding and confusion is even thicker. All this makes the clarification of these questions a problem of burning importance and immediacy. In fact, it is first on the agenda in all circles of the radical movement.

The widespread misunderstanding and confusion about socialism and democracy has profound causes. These causes must be frankly stated and examined before they can be removed. And we must undertake to remove them, if we are to try in earnest to get to the root of the problem.

Shakespeare's Marc Antony reminded us that evil quite often outlives its authors. That is true in the present case also. Stalin is dead; but the crippling influence of Stalinism on the minds of a whole generation of people who considered themselves socialists or communists lives after Stalin. This is testified to most eloquently by those members and fellow travelers of the Communist Party who have formally disavowed Stalinism since the Twentieth Congress, while retaining some of its most perverted conceptions and definitions.

Socialism, in the old days that I can recall, was often called the society of the free and equal, and democracy was defined as the rule of the people. These simple definitions still ring true to me, as they did when I first heard them many years ago. But in later years we have heard different definitions which are far less attractive. These same people whom I have mentioned—leaders of the Communist Party and fellow travelers who have sworn off Stalin without really changing any of the Stalinist ideas they assimilated—still blandly describe the state of affairs in the Soviet Union, with all its most exaggerated social and economic inequality, rifled over by the barbarous dictatorship of a privileged minority, as a form of "socialism." And they still manage to say, with straight faces, that the hideous police regimes in the satellite countries, propped up by Russian military force, are some kind of "People's Democracies."

When such people say it would be a fine idea for all of us to get together in the struggle for socialism and democracy, it seems to me it would be appropriate to ask them, by way of preliminary inquiry: "Just what do you mean by socialism, and what do you mean by democracy? Do you mean what Marx and Engels and Lenin said? Or do you mean what Stalin did?" They are not the same thing as can be easily proved, and it is necessary to choose between one set of definitions and the other.

This confusion of terminology has recently been illustrated by an article of Howard Fast, the well-known writer, who was once awarded the Stalin Prize. For a long time Fast supported what he called "socialism" in the Soviet Union, with his eyes shut. And then Khrushchev's speech at the Twentieth Congress, and other revelations following that, opened Fast's eyes, and he doesn't like what he sees. That is to his credit. But he still calls it "socialism." In an article in *Masses and Mainstream* he describes what he had found out about this peculiar "socialism" that had prevailed in the Soviet Union under Stalin and still prevails under Stalin's successors.

This is what Howard Fast said: "In Russia, we have socialism without democracy. We have socialism without trial by jury, habeas corpus or . . . protection against the abuse of confession by torture. We have socialism without civil liberty. . . . We have socialism without public avenues of protest. We have socialism without equality for minorities. We have socialism without any right of free artistic creation. In so many words, we have socialism without morality."

These are the words of Howard Fast. I agree with everything he says there, except the preface he gives to all his qualifications—that we have "socialism" without this and that, we have "socialism" without any of the features that a socialist society was supposed to have in the conceptions of the movement before Stalinism. It is as though Fast has discovered different varieties of socialism. Like mushrooms. You go out and pick the right kind and you can cook a tasty dish. But if you gather up the kind commonly known as toadstools and call them mushrooms, you will poison yourself. Stalinist "socialism" is about as close to the real thing as a toadstool is to an edible mushroom.

Now, of course, the Stalinists and their apologists have not created all the confusion in this country about the meaning of socialism, at least not directly. At every step for thirty years, the Stalinist work of befuddlement and demoralization, of debasing words into their opposite meanings, has been supported by reciprocal action of the same kind by the ruling capitalists and their apologists. They have never failed to take the Stalinists at their word, and to point to the Stalinist regime in the Soviet Union, with all of its horrors, and to say: "That is socialism. The American way of life is better."

It is these people who have given us, as their contribution to sowing confusion in the minds of people, the delightful definition of the capitalist sector of the globe, where the many toil in poverty for the benefit of the few, as "the free world." And they describe the United States, where the workers have a right to vote every four years, if they don't move around too much, but have no say about the control of the shop and the factory; where all the means of mass information and communication are monopolized by a few—they describe all that as the ideal democracy, for which the workers should gladly fight and die.

It is true that Stalinism has been the primary cause of the demoralization of a whole generation of American *radical* workers. There is no question of that. But the role of Stalinism in prejudicing the great American working class against socialism, and inducing them to accept the counterfeit democracy of American capitalism as the lesser evil, has been mainly indirect. The active role in this miseducation and befuddlement has been played by the American ruling minority, through all their monopolized means of communication and information.

They have cynically accepted the Stalinist definition and have obligingly advertised the Soviet Union, with its grinding poverty and glaring inequality, with its ubiquitous police terror, frame-ups, mass murders and slave-labor camps, as a "socialist" order of society. They have utilized the crimes of Stalinism to prejudice the American workers against the very name of socialism. And worst of all, comrades, we have to recognize that this campaign has been widely successful, and that we have to pay for it. We cannot build a strong socialist movement in this country until we overcome this confusion in the minds of the American workers about the real meaning of socialism.

This game of confusing and misrepresenting has been facilitated for the capitalists and aided to a considerable extent by the social democrats and the labor bureaucracy, who are themselves privileged beneficiaries of the American system, and who give a socialist and labor coloring to the defense of American "democracy." In addition to all that, we have to recognize that in this country, more than any other in the world, the tremendous pressures of imperialist prosperity and power and the witch-hunt persecution have deeply affected the thinking of many people who call themselves radicals or ex-radicals. These powerful pressures have brought many of them to a reconciliation with capitalist society and to the defense of capitalist democracy, if not as a paradise, at least as a lesser evil and the best that can be hoped for.

There is no doubt that this drumfire of bourgeois propaganda, supplemented by the universal revulsion against Stalinism, has profoundly affected the sentiments of the American working class, including the bulk of its most progressive and militant and potentially revolutionary sectors.

After all that has happened in the past quarter of a century, the American workers have become more acutely sensitive than ever before to the value and importance of democratic rights. That, in my opinion, is the progressive side of their reaction, which we should fully share. The horrors of fascism, as they were revealed in the thirties, and which were never dreamed of by the socialists in the old days, and the no less monstrous crimes of Stalinism, which became public knowledge later—all this has inspired a fear and hatred of any kind of dictatorship in the minds of the American working class. And to the extent that the Stalinist dictatorship in Russia has been identified with the name of socialism, and that this identification has been taken as a matter of course, the American workers have been prejudiced against socialism.

That's the bitter truth, and it must be looked straight in the face. This barrier to the expansion and development of the American socialist movement will not be overcome, and even a regroupment of the woefully limited forces of those who at present consider themselves socialists will yield but little fruit, unless and until we find a way to break down this misunderstanding and prejudice against socialism, and convince at least the more advanced American workers that we socialists are the most aggressive and consistent advocates of democracy in all fields and that, in fact, we are completely devoted to the idea that socialism cannot be realized otherwise than by democracy.

The socialist movement in America will not advance again significantly until it regains the initiative and takes the offensive against capitalism and all its agents in the labor movement precisely on the issue of democracy. What is needed is not a propaganda device or trick, but a formulation of the issue as it really stands; and, indeed, as it has always stood with real socialists ever since the modern movement was first proclaimed 109 years ago. For this counteroffensive against bourgeois propaganda we do not need to look for new formulations. Our task, as socialists living and fighting in this day and hour, is simply to restate what socialism and democracy meant to the founders of our movement, and to all the authentic disciples who followed them; to bring their formulations up to date and apply them to present conditions in the United States.

This restatement of basic aims and principles cannot wait; it is, in fact, the burning necessity of the hour. There is no room for misunderstanding among us as to what such a restatement of our position means and requires. It requires a clean break with all Stalinist and social democratic perversions and distortions of the real meaning of socialism and democracy and their relation to each other, and a return to the original formulations and definitions. Nothing short of this will do.

The authentic socialist movement, as it was conceived by its founders and as it has developed over the past century, has been the most democratic movement in all history. No formulation of this question can improve on the classic statement of the *Communist Manifesto,* with which modern scientific socialism was proclaimed to the world in 1848. The *Communist Manifesto* said:

"All previous historical movements were movements of minorities, in the interest of minorities. The proletarian movement is the self-conscious, independent movement of the immense majority, in the interest of the immense majority."

The authors of the *Communist Manifesto* linked socialism and democracy together as end and means. The "self-conscious, independent movement of the immense majority, in the interest of the immense majority" cannot be anything else but democratic, if we understand by "democracy" the rule of the people, the majority. The Stalinist claim—that the task of reconstructing society on a socialist basis can be farmed out to a privileged and uncontrolled bureaucracy, while the workers remain without voice or vote in the process—is just as foreign to the thoughts of Marx and Engels, and of all their true disciples, as the reformist idea that socialism can be handed down to the workers by degrees by the capitalists who exploit them.

All such fantastic conceptions were answered in advance by the reiterated statement of Marx and Engels that "the emancipation of the working class is the task of the workers themselves." That is the language of Marx and Engels—"the task of the workers themselves." That was just another way of saying—as they said explicitly many times—that the socialist reorganization of society requires a workers' revolution. Such a revolution is unthinkable without the active participation of the majority of the working class, which is itself the big majority of the population. Nothing could be more democratic than that.

Moreover, the great teachers did not limit the democratic action of the working class to the overthrow of bourgeois supremacy. They defined democracy as the form of governmental rule in the transition period between capitalism and socialism. It is explicitly stated in the *Communist Manifesto*—and I wonder how many people have forgotten this in recent years—"The first step," said the *Manifesto*, "in the revolution by the working class, is to raise the proletariat to the position of ruling class, *to establish democracy.*"

That is the way Marx and Engels formulated the first aim of the revolution—to make the workers the ruling class, to establish democracy, which, in their view, is the same thing. From this precise formulation it is clear that Marx and Engels did not consider the limited, formal democracy under capitalism, which screens the exploitation and the rule of the great majority by the few, as real democracy. In order to have real democracy, the workers must become the "ruling class." Only the revolution that replaces the class rule of the capitalists by the class rule of the workers can really "establish democracy," not in fiction, but in fact. So said Marx and Engels.

They never taught that the simple nationalization of the forces of production signified the establishment of socialism. That's not stated by Marx and Engels anywhere. Nationalization only lays the economic foundations for the transition to socialism. Still less could they have sanctioned, even if they had been able to imagine, the monstrous idea that socialism could be realized without freedom and without equality; that nationalized production and planned economy, controlled by a ruthless police dictatorship, complete with prisons, torture chambers and forced-labor camps, could be designated as a "socialist" society. That unspeakable perversion and contradiction of terms belongs to the Stalinists and their apologists.

All the great Marxists defined socialism as a classless society—with abundance, freedom and equality for all;

a society in which there would be no state, not even a democratic workers' state, to say nothing of a state in the monstrous form of a bureaucratic dictatorship of a privileged minority.

The Soviet Union today is a transitional order of society, in which the bureaucratic dictatorship of a privileged minority, far from serving as the agency to bridge the transition to socialism, stands as an obstacle to harmonious development in that direction. In the view of Marx and Engels, and of Lenin and Trotsky who came after them, the transition from capitalism to the classless society of socialism could only be carried out by an ever-expanding democracy, involving the masses of the workers more and more in all phases of social life, by direct participation and control.

And, in the course of further progressive development in all fields, as Lenin expressed it, even this democracy, this workers' democracy, as a form of class rule, will outlive itself. Lenin said: "Democracy will gradually change and become a habit, and finally wither away," since democracy itself, properly understood, is a form of state, that is, an instrument of class rule, for which there will be no need and no place in the classless socialist society.

Forecasting the socialist future, the *Communist Manifesto* said: "In place of the old bourgeois society, with its classes and class antagonisms, we shall have an association." Mark that: "an association," not a state—"an association in which the free development of each is the condition for the free development of all."

Trotsky said the same thing in other words when he spoke of socialism as "a pure and limpid social system which is accommodated to the self-government of the toilers . . . and uninterrupted growth of universal equality—all-sided flowering of human personality . . . unselfish, honest and human relations between human beings."

The bloody abomination of Stalinism cannot be passed off as a substitute for this picture of the socialist future and the democratic transition period leading up to it as it was drawn by the great Marxists.

And I say we will not put the socialist movement of this country on the right track and restore its rightful appeal to the best sentiments of the working class of this country and above all to the young, until we begin to call socialism by its right name as the great teachers did. Until we make it clear that we stand for an ever-expanding workers' democracy as the only road to socialism. Until we root out every vestige of Stalinist perversion and corruption of the meaning of socialism and democracy, and restate the thoughts and formulations of the authentic Marxist teachers.

But the Stalinist definitions of socialism and democracy are not the only perversions that have to be rejected before we can find a sound basis for the regroupment of socialist forces in the United States. The definitions of the social democrats of all hues and gradations are just as false. And in this country they are a still more formidable obstacle because they have deeper roots, and they are tolerantly nourished by the ruling class itself.

The liberals, the social democrats and the bureaucratic bosses of the American trade unions are red-hot supporters of "democracy." At least, that is what they say. And they strive to herd the workers into the imperialist war camp under the general slogan of "democracy versus dictatorship." That is their slippery and consciously deceptive substitute for the real "irrepressible conflict" of our age, the conflict between capitalism and socialism. They speak of democracy as something that stands by itself above the classes and the class struggle, and not as the form of rule of one class over another.

Lenin put his finger on this misrepresentation of reality in his polemic against Kautsky. Lenin said: "A liberal naturally speaks of 'democracy' in general; but a Marxist will never forget to ask: 'for what class?' Everyone knows, for instance (and Kautsky the 'historian' knows it too), that rebellions, or even strong ferment, among the slaves in antiquity at once revealed the fact that the state of antiquity was essentially a *dictatorship of the slaveowners.* Did this dictatorship abolish democracy *among,* and *for, the slaveowners?* Everybody knows that it did not."

Capitalism, under any kind of government—whether bourgeois democracy of fascism or a military police state—under any kind of government, capitalism is a system of minority rule, and the principal beneficiaries of capitalist democracy are the small minority of exploiting capitalists; scarcely less so than the slaveowners of ancient times were the actual rulers and the real beneficiaries of the Athenian democracy.

To be sure, the workers in the United States have a right to vote periodically for one of two sets of candidates selected for them by the two capitalist parties. And if they can dodge the witch-hunters, they can exercise the right of free speech and free press. But this formal right of free speech and free press is outweighed rather heavily by the inconvenient circumstance that the small capitalist minority happens to enjoy a complete monopoly of ownership and control of all the big presses, and of television and radio, and of all other means of communication and information.

We who oppose the capitalist regime have a right to nominate our own candidates, if we're not arrested under the Smith Act before we get to the city clerk's office, and if we can comply with the laws that deliberately restrict the rights of minority parties. That is easier said than done in this country of democratic capitalism. In one state after another, no matter how many petitions you circulate, you can't comply with the regulations and you can't get on the ballot. This is the state of affairs in California, Ohio, Illinois, and an increasing number of other states. And if you succeed in complying with all the technicalities, as we did last year in New York, they just simply rule you out anyhow if it is not convenient to have a minority party on the ballot. But outside of all these and other difficulties and restrictions, we have free elections and full democracy.

It is true that the Negro people in the United States, ninety-four years after the Emancipation Proclamation, are still fighting for the right to vote in the South, and for the right to take a vacant seat on a public bus; or to send their children to a tax-supported public school, and things of that kind—which you may call restrictions of democracy in the United States.

But even so, with all that, a little democracy is better than none. We socialists have never denied that. And after the experiences of fascism and McCarthyism, and of military and police dictatorships in many parts of the world, and of the horrors of Stalinism, we have all the more reason to value every democratic provision for the protection of human rights and human dignity; to fight for more democracy, not less.

Socialists should not argue with the American worker when he says he wants democracy and doesn't want to be ruled by a dictatorship. Rather, we should recognize that his demand for human rights and democratic guarantees, now and in the future, is in itself progressive. The socialist task is not to deny democracy, but to expand it and make it more complete. That is the true socialist tradition. The Marxists, throughout the century-long history of our movement, have always valued and defended bourgeois democratic rights, restricted as they were; and have utilized them for the education and organization of the workers in the struggle to establish full democracy by abolishing the capitalist rule altogether.

The right of union organization is a precious right, a democratic right, but it was not "given" to the workers in the United States. It took the mighty and irresistible labor upheaval of the thirties, culminating in the great sit-down strikes—a semirevolution of the American workers—to establish in reality the right of union organization in mass-production industry.

And yet today—I am still speaking under the heading of democracy—twenty years after the sit-down strikes firmly established the auto workers' union, the automobile industry is still privately owned and ruled by a dictatorship of financial sharks. The auto workers have neither voice nor vote in the management of the industry which they have created, nor in regulating the speed of the assembly line which consumes their lives. Full control of production in auto and steel and everywhere, according to the specific terms of the union contract, is still the exclusive prerogative of "management," that is, of the absentee owners, who contribute nothing to the production of automobiles or steel or anything else.

What's democratic about that? The claim that we have an almost perfect democracy in this country doesn't stand up against the fact that the workers have no democratic rights in industry at all, as far as regulating production is concerned; that these rights are exclusively reserved for the parasitic owners, who never see the inside of a factory.

In the old days, the agitators of the Socialist Party and the IWW—who were real democrats—used to give a shorthand definition of socialism as "industrial democracy." I don't know how many of you have heard that. It was a common expression: "industrial democracy," the extension of democracy to industry, the democratic control of industry by the workers themselves, with private ownership eliminated. That socialist demand for real democracy was taken for granted in the time of Debs and Haywood, when the American socialist movement was still young and uncorrupted.

You never hear a "democratic" labor leader say anything like that today. The defense of "democracy" by the social democrats and the labor bureaucrats always turns out in practice to be a defense of "democratic" capitalism, or as Beck and McDonald call it, "people's capitalism." And I admit they have a certain stake in it, and a certain justification for defending it, as far as their personal interests are concerned.

And always, in time of crisis, these labor leaders—who talk about democracy all the time, as against dictatorship in the "socialist countries," as they call them—easily excuse and defend all kinds of violations of even this limited bourgeois democracy. They are far more tolerant of lapses from the formal rules of democracy by the capitalists than by the workers. They demand that the class struggle of the workers against the exploiters be conducted by the formal rules of bourgeois democracy, at all stages of its development—up to and including the stage of social transformation and the defense of the new society against attempts at capitalist restoration. They say it has to be strictly "democratic" all the way. No emergency measures are tolerated; everything must be strictly and formally democratic according to the rules laid down by the capitalist minority. They burn incense to democracy as an immutable principle, an abstraction standing above the social antagonisms.

But when the capitalist class, in its struggle for self-preservation, cuts corners around its own professed democratic principles, the liberals, the social democrats and the labor skates have a way of winking, or looking the other way, or finding excuses for it.

For example, they do not protest when the American imperialists wage war according to the rules of war, which are not quite the same thing as the rules of "democracy." When the atomic bombs were dropped on Hiroshima and Nagasaki, the most abominable atrocity in all history—the bombing of a defenseless civilian population and the wiping out of whole cities of men, women and children—the best these liberals, labor fakers and social democratic defenders of American democracy could offer was the plaintive bleat of Norman Thomas. You know, he was supporting the war, naturally, being a social democrat. But Norman Thomas rose up after Nagasaki and Hiroshima were wiped off the face of the earth and said the bombs should not have been dropped "without warning." The others said nothing.

These professional democrats have no objection to the authoritarian rule of the military forces of the capitalist state, which deprives the rank-and-file soldiers of all democratic rights in life-and-death matters, including the right to elect their own officers. The dictatorial rule of MacArthur in Japan, who acted as a czar over a whole conquered country, was never questioned by these professional opponents of all other dictators. They are against the dictators in the Kremlin, but the dictator in Japan—that was a horse of another color. All that, you see, concerns war; and nothing, not even the sacred principles of "democracy," can be allowed to stand in the way of the victory of the American imperialists in the war and the cinching-up of the victory afterward in the occupation.

But in the class struggle of the workers against the capitalists to transform society, which is the fiercest war of all, and in the transition period after the victory of the workers, the professional democrats demand that the formal rules of bourgeois democracy, as defined by the minority of exploiters, be scrupulously observed at every step. No emergency measures are allowed.

By these different responses in different situations of a class nature, the professional democrats simply show that their class bias determines their judgment in each case, and show at the same time that their professed devotion to the rules of formal democracy, at all times and under all conditions, is a fraud.

And when it comes to the administration of workers' organizations under their control, the social democrats and the reformist labor leaders pay very little respect to their own professed democratic principles. The trade unions in the United States today, as you all know, are administered and controlled by little cliques of richly privileged bureaucrats, who use the union machinery, and the union funds, and a private army of goon squads, and—whenever necessary—the help of the employers and the government, to keep their own "party" in control of the unions, and to suppress and beat down any attempt of the rank and file to form an opposition "party" to put up an opposition slate. And yet, without freedom of association and organization, without the right to form groups and parties of different tendencies, there is and can be no real democracy anywhere.

In practice, the American labor bureaucrats, who piously demand democracy in the one-party totalitarian domain of Stalinism, come as close as they can to maintaining a total one-party rule in their own domain. Kipling said: "The colonel's lady and Judy O'Grady are sisters under the skin." The Stalinist bureaucrats in Russia and the trade-union bureaucrats in the United States are not sisters, but they are much more alike than different. They are essentially of the same breed, a privileged caste dominated above all by motives of self-benefit and self-preservation at the expense of the workers and against the workers.

The privileged bureaucratic caste everywhere is the most formidable obstacle to democracy and socialism. The struggle of the working class in both sections of the now-divided world has become, in the most profound meaning of the term, a struggle against the usurping privileged bureaucracy.

In the Soviet Union, it is a struggle to restore the genuine workers' democracy established by the revolution of 1917. Workers' democracy has become a burning necessity to assure the harmonious transition to socialism. That is the meaning of the political revolution against the bureaucracy now developing throughout the whole Soviet sphere, which every socialist worthy of the name unreservedly supports. There is no sense in talking about regroupment with people who don't agree on that, on defense and support of the Soviet workers against the Soviet bureaucrats.

In the United States, the struggle for workers' democracy is preeminently a struggle of the rank and file to gain democratic control of their own organizations. That is the necessary condition to prepare the final struggle to abolish capitalism and "establish democracy" in the country as a whole. No party in this country has a right to call itself socialist unless it stands foursquare for the rank-and-file workers of the United States against the bureaucrats.

In my opinion, effective and principled regroupment of socialist forces requires full agreement on these two points. That is the necessary starting point. Capitalism does not survive as a social system by its own strength, but by its influence within the workers' movement, reflected and expressed by the labor aristocracy and the bureaucracy. So the fight for workers' democracy is inseparable from the fight for socialism, and is the condition for its victory. Workers' democracy is the only road to socialism, here in the United States and everywhere else, all the way from Moscow to Los Angeles, and from here to Budapest.

# Chapter 31

# The trend of the twentieth century

*Delivered to a meeting at the Cornish Arms Hotel, New York City, celebrating the thirty-second anniversary of the Russian Revolution, November 4, 1949.*

The stream of history became a torrential flood in the first half of the twentieth century and rages and flows even higher toward the second half. Never have events moved so fast. Never have social convulsions been so deep and so destructive of old and apparently fixed conditions. The first half of the twentieth century is already behind us. Our concern now turns to the second half. But if we want to see what this second half of our century has in store for humanity, we must first look back into the fifty years now expiring—and even into the century which preceded them—and mark out their most important events and developments. From the examination of these events and developments we can best ascertain the course and the direction which will determine the shape of things to come in the years which lie ahead of us.

The nineteenth century was that brief space in the vast history of mankind which was especially assigned to the triumph and development of the capitalist system of production, and the social and political institutions based upon it. Under the mighty impulse of the Great French Revolution, which freed the productive forces from the constricting fetters of the outlived feudal society, capitalism flourished and expanded and developed the productive forces of society—the true foundation of all social progress—with a speed and efficiency unknown before, and even undreamed of in all the centuries since men had begun to make their history and to record it. All the past achievements in this field put together were dwarfed beside the accomplishments of capitalism in a single century. The whole of the nineteenth century stands out now in history as an unprecedented march of triumph of the capitalist class, which had overthrown feudalism by revolution and cleared a path for the development of a new and progressive system of production.

To be sure, the expansive productivity of capitalism, even in the century of its heyday, was interrupted by periodic economic crises which the capitalists themselves could neither foresee nor understand. But these economic crises, which paralyzed the forces of production at approximately ten-year intervals, turned out every time to be new starting points from which the productivity of labor was intensified and raised to new heights. In the periods of prosperity which emerged from every crisis, the capitalist machine of production expanded, and the products of labor flooded the world in unprecedented volume. This gave rise to a vast illusion, a blind confidence, in the camp of the triumphant capitalist class and their ideologists, in a continuing progressive development of the forces of production under capitalism, without limit and without foreseeable end.

But right in the middle of capitalism's "Nineteenth Century of Progress," with the publication of the *Communist Manifesto* in 1848, Marx and Engels challenged the prevailing opinion. Analyzing the economic laws by which capitalism operates, and placing the epoch of capitalism in its historic context, Marx and Engels declared: capitalism is not the fixed and final form of human society, but only a stage in its evolution. The contradictions which represent the dynamics of its development will eventually and, historically speaking, rapidly, bring it to a blind alley from which no exit and no further development will be possible for the social system based on the private ownership of the means of production and their confinement within the outlived borders of the national states.

Capitalism, said Marx and Engels, produces the modern proletariat, the wage workers, who are alienated from any stake in the ownership of the vast machinery of production which they operate, and who have nothing to lose but their chains. At the same time, the capitalist owners are completely alienated from any necessary part in production and have become a parasitic obstruction to its further development. The wage workers, the useful producers, are condemned to accumulating misery and poverty, while the parasitic capitalists accumulate wealth and riches beyond the dreams of avarice. Capitalism will be broken and destroyed by this contradiction. In the modern working class, said Marx and Engels, capitalism is producing its gravedigger. The workers will be driven inexorably, by the very conditions of their existence, to revolt against capitalism, to overthrow it, and to replace it by a socialist order, which will plan and develop economy for the benefit of all. The downfall of capitalism and the victory of the proletariat are equally inevitable.

So said the voices crying in the wilderness, the farseeing prophets, Marx and Engels in 1848.

When the two great geniuses of the working class formulated their theory and confidently uttered their prediction, capitalism had not yet reached the apex of its development. On the contrary, it was then only really beginning its most spectacular expansion and development. The fifty-odd years which followed the publication of the *Communist Manifesto* saw world capitalism attain ever greater stability, ever wider scope of increasing productivity, and ever greater confidence in its thousand-year destiny. This is the way matters stood at the beginning of the twentieth century, which opened with the great fireworks of capitalist progress in the field of production and in scientific achievements.

Capitalism ruled the world securely and confidently. Everything appeared to be fixed and final; and the ideologists of triumphant capitalism had a field day celebrating the refutation of the Marxist prophecy. The watchword of the ruling circles was progress, ever more progress, along the same line. In the prevailing psychology of the time, optimism was uppermost. The belief in gradual, uninterrupted, peaceful and harmonious improvement, within the framework of things as they were, took possession of the masters of society and all their retinue like a smug religion revealed to the chosen few. There was no room in their outlook for the social convulsions, wars and revolutions which had been the motive forces of the previous history of mankind.

The socialist and labor movements that had grown up in Europe on the revolutionary teachings of Marx and Engels, began to succumb to the prevailing atmosphere. A stratum of privileged workers, who had shared in the crumbs of capitalist prosperity at the expense of the great mass of the unskilled workers and the colonial slaves, began to adapt themselves to the prevailing state of affairs. They traded off their vision and hope of the socialist future for a few privileges and comforts of the present. A conservative bureaucracy, likewise sharing in the crumbs of prosperity and privilege, imposed on the workers' organizations the opportunist theory of a gradual, peaceful transition to socialism along the road of social reform. The conquest of the world labor and socialist movement by theories of reformist gradualism was well under way.

Against the whole tide of things as they seemed to be in the first years of the twentieth century, and against all the theories and beliefs founded on this apparent reality, a small minority in the labor movement—Lenin and the Bolsheviks, Trotsky, Luxemburg, Liebknecht, a small left wing in various countries—contended that the basic analysis and prognosis of Marx and Engels retained all their validity. They held that the period of the peaceful expansion of capitalism was approaching its culmination. They proclaimed that the accumulating contradictions of ascending capitalism were destined to explode in a mighty series of social convulsions, wars and revolutions, which could have no outcome short of the revolutionary transformation of society and the replacement of capitalism by a new social order.

In the tumultuous developments which were to unfold in the first quarter of the twentieth century, these conflicting theories confronted each other like armies in battle. They influenced the course of developments; for social theories are not merely views of history, but also active forces in shaping the course of its development. Men make their own history, as Marx and Engels said, even if they don't make it out of the whole cloth; and ideas are active forces in this making of history—for progress, if they read social reality aright, or for derailment and temporary regression, if they read it falsely.

Events did not wait long to pass their judgment on this great conflict of theories. In the first quarter of the twentieth century, the contradictions of capitalism, which had been pointed out by the Marxists and overlooked by their opponents, began to assert themselves and to take their revenge on the high priests of bourgeois optimism and socialist reformism.

The private ownership of the means of production and the exploitation of the wage laborers led to an enormous overproduction of goods and capital in all the countries of the great powers. This anomaly irresistibly drove each of them to seek new markets and fields of investment. But since there were no new continents to discover and exploit; and since the world market did not and could not expand with the expansion of the productive powers of modern industry; and since, moreover, this geographically limited world was already divided up by the dominant and competing powers—none of them could expand its markets and dispose of its surpluses, except at the expense of others. The modern capitalist states, which had been consolidated by smashing feudal provincialism to provide a broader arena for the unrestricted development of the capitalist productive process, were already becoming too small to permit any further development within their restricted borders.

Expansion is the law of life for the capitalist system of production; and the separate national states could no longer provide the field for it. The forces of production, in Trotsky's winged phrase, began to revolt against their national barriers. The tension between the great powers in the struggle for markets and fields of investment, in a world already divided up, increased and mounted from year to year. Behind an imposing facade of pacifist talk and diplomatic hypocrisy, a feverish armaments race got underway; and the accumulating contradictions finally exploded in the great World War of 1914–1918. Bourgeois optimism in regard to the prospects of uninterrupted, peaceful and harmonious development of the productive forces crashed up against the greatest orgy of destruction of human life and material culture in the war. The pernicious theory of reformist gradualism, which had taken possession of the aristocracy and bureaucracy of the labor movement, paralyzed the workers in each of the warring countries and drove them into the slaughter against each other in the interest of their exploiters. The downfall of international socialism was widely celebrated. Marxism was subjected to ridicule in the camp of the imperialists and the renegades who had joined them.

But this celebration of the death of Marxism and the refutation of its revolutionary theory was premature. The revolutionary Marxists, reduced to a small handful, carried on their work in all countries—under the most onerous conditions. Meanwhile, the drawn-out war, bringing death and destruction on every side, was doing its work of sapping the economy of the contending powers, and undermining the confidence of the people in the social system which had brought this calamity upon them. By the very fact of the war, conducted on such a scale and at such a cost, capitalism branded itself a reactionary obstacle to the aspirations of the people to live secure and prosperous lives. The revolutionary storm which the war was preparing was first heralded by sheet lightning when the Russian Czar was overthrown in February 1917. And then, eight months later, the storm itself broke in all its magnificent fury with the Bolshevik Revolution, which put the Russian working class in power.

This was the great turning point. November 7, 1917, is the moment in history from which the new age begins. Never before in the history of the human race was such a gigantic leap forward taken. Never before was there such a beneficent promise and assurance of the good future of mankind written into deed as on that day thirty-four years ago, when the Russian workers took power into their own hands and declared an end to the old things and the beginning of the new.

The Russian Revolution abolished the private ownership of the industries and the land, and demonstrated in practice that neither capitalists nor landlords are necessary to modern production, but are rather parasitic obstacles to it.

The Russian Revolution demonstrated that the working class, even in a backward country, is capable of taking power from the palsied hands of outlived exploiters; and is capable likewise of forging out of its own ranks a vanguard party capable of leading the struggle. The Russian Revolution awakened tens of millions of colonial slaves to political life and aspiration for political independence for the first time. It released the pent-up rage and hatred of the betrayed workers of Europe and inspired them with the will to follow the Russian example by Russian methods.

The revolutionary will of the masses, especially in Europe, was so strong, and bourgeois economy and self-confidence had been so weakened and shaken by the war, that successful revolutions in one country after another, sweeping the whole of Europe, were undoubtedly possible in the years immediately following the termination of the war of 1914–1918. The situation was there, the opportunity was there, but the revolutionary party capable of organizing and leading the revolutionary struggle was lacking. Reformist social democracy, still controlling the apparatus of the workers' organizations, although greatly discredited and weakened by its treachery in the war, was still strong enough to paralyze and defeat the revolutionary struggle of the masses. In those few sentences are stated the main reason—one might even say the only reason—why the Russian Revolution was not extended and consolidated over the continent of Europe in the five or six years which followed the victory of 1917.

The failure of the European workers to take the power, for the reasons already stated, enabled the European bourgeoisie to regain a certain measure of their self-confidence and to reestablish a shaky stabilization of their economy and their rule. On the other hand, the Russian Revolution consolidated its victory, prevailed in the civil war against the bourgeois counterrevolution, and defeated the numerous military interventions of the capitalist powers. A great bridgehead had been established, so to speak, and the revolutionary workers had the opportunity and the space to dig in, to entrench themselves, and to prepare for the next assault. The working class on a world scale was immeasurably stronger than it had been at the beginning of the century, and the capitalist class was weaker. The capitalist system, on a world scale, had irrevocably entered the period of its decline and decay.

This is the way matters stood at the end of the first quarter of the twentieth century. One great battle in the worldwide struggle between socialism and capitalism had been decided in favor of the workers. Other, still greater battles remained undecided.

The inconclusive stalemate in the great historic conflict between socialism and capitalism, which marked the beginning of the second quarter of the twentieth century, gave rise to a new set of illusions, misconceptions and improvised theories as ill-founded as those which had dominated mass thinking at the beginning of the century. These misconceptions and false theories penetrated deeply into the revolutionary labor movement. They disoriented and demoralized it, and thus had their effect on social developments.

The isolation of the Soviet Union, combined with the harsh poverty of the country, inherited from Czarism and aggravated by the heavy costs of the civil war and the interventions, created the conditions for the rise of a privileged bureaucracy. This bureaucracy, like all privileged strata of society, grew conservative. It sought to protect its privileges at all costs. The Soviet bureaucrats developed the mentality of all privileged bureaucrats in the labor movement in all countries, which is summed up in the fervent desire to "let well enough alone." Looking at the world with the myopia of immediate self-interest, they imagined those things which appeared momentarily under their eyes to be the only reality.

The Soviet bureaucrats saw the temporary recovery of capitalist economy, enormously exaggerated its stability, and endowed it with the quality of permanence. They saw the stagnation of the European Communist movement after the great postwar revolutionary wave had subsided and lost faith in its potentiality to expand and grow again with a new revolutionary revival. In the service of these moods and sentiments, in order to justify and try to maintain the status quo, which had brought a limited prosperity at least to the bureaucrats, the leaders of the conservative bureaucracy began to tinker with theory. The crowning monstrosity of this irresponsible theoretical tinkering was the Stalinist theory of "socialism in one country."

This theory, which the Stalinist faction passed off as an extension and development of revolutionary Marxism, was in fact blood brother to the revisionism of the social democratic reformists which had wrought such havoc in the labor movement in the first quarter of the century. The theory of socialism in one country expressed the overpowering desire of the privileged bureaucracy to preserve their privileges within the borders of the Soviet Union and let the rest of the world labor movement go hang. It signified a renunciation of the perspective of international revolution; the recognition and expectation of the permanent existence of capitalism in five-sixths of the world, and the willingness of the Soviet bureaucracy to adapt themselves to it and live with it.

Trotsky denounced the new improvisation. The theory of socialism in one country, and a backward country at that, is utopian, he said. The construction of a harmonious socialist order of society requires the highest productivity of labor, with international collaboration and a division of labor between associated countries to produce plenty and abundance for all. This theory of socialism in a single country is also reactionary, he said, and downright false in its international perspectives. The stabilization of world capitalism is only limited and temporary. Conditions are maturing for a devastating crisis and new revolutionary explosions in various parts of the world. That is the underlying reality. There will be no lack of revolutionary situations, said Trotsky; and there is no reason to change our course, which has had as its central aim the extension of the Russian Revolution to other countries, and eventually to unite the whole world in one socialist federation.

To the Stalinist theory of socialism in one country Trotsky counterposed the Marxist theory of the permanent revolution. The second quarter of the twentieth century was dominated by this conflict of theories.

Again, as in the first quarter of the twentieth century, events did not wait long to pass judgment on the contending theories. The conservative international outlook of Stalinism completely misjudged great events in the making and, at the same time, worked mightily to influence their unfavorable outcome.

The Chinese revolution of 1925–1927, which had every reasonable chance of success, was a great demonstration and warning that the days of imperialist domination of the Orient were numbered. The British General Strike of 1926, fraught with enormous revolutionary potentialities, was a startling revelation of the shakiness of bourgeois rule in the most conservative of bourgeois countries. The devastating worldwide economic crisis, touched off by the stock-market crash in New York in 1929, served notice that the supposedly permanent stabilization of the capitalist economic system had already run its brief course and could never be fully restored. The Spanish civil war; the French sit-down strikes of June 1936; the breathtaking rise and sweep of industrial unionism in the United States under the banner of the CIO—all gave powerful testimony against the illusion that the struggle of the classes could be suspended and the status quo between the Soviet Union and the capitalist countries permanently maintained.

In this great complex of world-shaking events, all crowded together within the brief space of a dozen years in the second quarter of the century, there was undoubtedly the making of a world revolutionary movement of such power that nothing could have stopped it. The uncontrollable crisis wracking the capitalist system through those fateful years cried aloud for a revolutionary solution. But the revolutionary road was blocked by the Stalinist leadership, which had demoralized and corrupted the communist movement with the theory of socialism in one country and all the unbridled practices of class collaboration which flowed from this reactionary theory.

Humanity had to pay for the crimes of Stalinism with the unspeakable horrors of fascism and another world war.

The terrible experiences of Stalinism and fascism, and the Second World War, and all that led to them and followed from them, changed many things, disappointed many expectations, and raised new problems for theoretical investigation. Once again new phenomena, unforeseen by people who notice only what is immediately before their eyes and always imagine that it will last forever, produced a crop of superficial impressions masquerading as worked-out theories.

The rise of fascism in Germany strengthened and reinforced the fascist regime of Mussolini in Italy and contributed heavily to the fascist victory in Spain. A section of the bourgeoisie, imagining that the class struggle, the real driving force of history, had been eliminated because it had been pressed down under the iron lid of police-state terror, began to indulge themselves in a new theory of fascism as "the wave of the future," wherein social tranquillity and profits would both be permanently assured. Others in the socialist and labor movement, or on its fringes, bowing before the terrifying fact of the present and taking fright from it, likewise endowed fascism with a vitality and longevity that it by no means deserved and could not live up to.

Out of the dark pool of their own fears and terrors, these panic-mongers fished up the so-called theory of "retrogressionism." They announced that the historic process is definitely moving backward toward barbarism, not forward toward socialism. But this capitulatory pessimism was just as worthless as the delighted optimism of a section of the capitalists in providing a real appraisal of the role and prospects of fascism.

The Trotskyists maintained—and events have already proved—that fascism is not a new social order, but the diseased expression of a dying one. Fascism, in fact, is latent in decadent capitalism; the specific form of its rule in times of highest social tension and crisis. If decaying capitalism is not overthrown in time and replaced by a socialist order, fascism will appear again in one part of the world after another, including the United States. But even in that case, the rule of neofascism will not last longer, nor will its fate be different, than that of the fascist regimes of Mussolini and Hitler. The very fact that capitalism in one country or another is forced to resort to the desperate expedient of fascism is the most convincing sign of its instability, of its unviability, and of its imminent downfall.

Hitler and Mussolini, in their boasts and pretensions, and also in their ultimate fate, stand out in history as representative symbols of all fascist dictators who may yet make their brief appearance in one country or another. Hitler, at the height of his madness, boasted that his Nazi regime would last for a thousand years. But he had to settle for a mere twelve years, and then throw his own head into the bargain with the ignominious collapse of his regime. Mussolini, strutting on the Roman balcony, impressed many people as an impervious superman. But his regime fell apart "like a rotten apple" after a mere twenty years. And Mussolini himself ended upside down, hanging by his heels in the public square like a slaughtered pig in a butcher shop. There was poetic justice, as well as prophecy, in the ignominious end of the two fascist supermen.

The fate of the Stalinist criminals will be no more glorious. The world-conquering historical mission ascribed to Stalinism by frightened Philistines and professional pessimists is no less chimerical than that formerly attributed to fascism. At the moment of its apparently greatest triumph of expansion, Stalinism has been overtaken by a mortal crisis. The revolt of Yugoslavia, which is already spreading like a virulent infection throughout the Stalinist domain in Eastern Europe—and tomorrow will spread to China—heralds the death sentence of history on the right of Stalinism to expand or even to survive as anything but a horrible interlude in the march of humanity.

Humanity is marching forward to socialism and freedom, not backward to barbarism and slavery. Neither fascism nor Stalinism has any historical right to stand in the way. Fascism is the degenerate product of dying capitalism, a social system which has remained too long on the scene after exhausting all its progressive potentialities and has become reactionary through and through. Stalinism is a degenerate growth of the labor movement—the product of undue retardation and delay of the proletarian revolution after all the conditions for it have become rotten-ripe. Neither fascism nor Stalinism represents "the wave of the future." Both are reactionary and transitory phenomena. Neither fascism nor Stalinism represents the main line of historic development. On the contrary, they are deviations from it, which must and will be obliterated in the next tidal wave of colonial uprisings and proletarian revolutions.

In order to form a correct appraisal of everything that has happened, it is necessary, first of all, to get a clear view of the most important and decisive factors and to subordinate those which are secondary and incidental. The most important fact revealed by the Second World War, as well as the insane preparations for a third, is the crisis and death agony of the capitalist system of production, its complete inability to operate any longer on a basis of social stability and peace. The Second World War did not culminate in a series of successful revolutions in the advanced countries, as the Marxists expected and hoped. But it is completely false to say that revolutionary situations did not arise; that the working class was definitively defeated; and that the bourgeoisie emerged with a secure and stable victory. Nothing could be a greater misrepresentation of reality than that.

The end of the war released such a tremendous revolutionary movement of the workers in Italy and France, as well as in Eastern Europe, that the capitalists were nowhere able to rule in their own name. In Italy, after more than twenty years of fascist suppression, during which all independent working-class action and propaganda had been suppressed, the workers emerged from the war with an almost unanimous cry for communism or socialism. The Italian example is the most striking and reassuring proof of the indestructibility of the proletariat and of its socialist consciousness. The overwhelming majority of the French working class at the end of the war followed the Communist Party only because of the mistaken belief that it could lead them to a French version of the great Russian Revolution.

The unparalleled upsurges of the colonial masses, which came in the wake of the war, have revealed the startling weakness of the Western imperialist powers and their inability to maintain and secure their colonial domination anymore. The doom of Western imperialism is clearly written in the flaming skies of the Orient. Outlived capitalism has no secure future anywhere.

The workers of Europe had their second chance for revolution in the immediate postwar period, and in the main they were ready for it. They failed of this objective once again only because they still lacked a sufficiently influential revolutionary party to organize and lead the struggle. The conclusion to be drawn from this is not to write off the revolution, but to build a revolutionary party to organize it and lead it. That's what we are here for.

The perspective of the coming years, as we read it in the course of events as they have transpired in the half-century behind us, is that of a continuing crisis and increasing weakness of bankrupt capitalism; of new colonial uprisings on an ever-vaster scale; of more strikes and class battles in the main countries of capitalism. In the course of these struggles the workers will learn the most necessary lessons from their own experiences. They will settle accounts with perfidious Stalinism and social democracy and drive them out of the workers' movement. They will forge revolutionary parties worthy of the century of blood and iron. And these parties will organize their struggles and lead them to their revolutionary goal.

The years of the first half of the twentieth century have been years of storm and strife. And the barometer reads: more storms to come. Those who want peace and security, without fighting or taking any risks, have simply chosen the wrong time to be born. But for those who are not afraid of storm and strife, who see social progress riding with the storm—for them matters stand differently. For those who are in tune with this century, who understand the laws of its development, who see the course and direction in which it is moving and must move—for us, this is a great century to be alive in. This is our century.

Many people have been overwhelmed by great events which they could not foresee and do not yet understand. They have seen their theories and beliefs refuted and swept away by reality and have not been able to find new ones. For such people, this is a time of great confusion and discouragement and despair of their own fate, and even of the fate of humanity. The pacifist optimism, which presided over the inauguration of the twentieth century, has given way to a profound pessimism. Those people who look only at the surface of events and refuse to see the social reality which underlies it, wake up in the morning with pessimism and go to bed at night with despair.

We Marxists have no part of this nightmare world. We see the course of development for the next fifty years already foreshadowed by the main course it has taken in the fifty years now behind us. The course has not been straight. There have been zigzags and even regressions. There have been frightful catastrophes. But the general direction toward social transformation has been clearly delineated. Hitler's gas chambers, Truman's Hiroshima and Nagasaki, and Stalin's prisons and forced-labor camps—they are all part of the terrible reality of our time. But they are not the whole of it. They are not even the most important part of it. They represent horrible aberrations from the main course of history, as revealed in the first half of the twentieth century. The Russian Revolution of 1917 is the great signpost, showing the real course of development and pointing the way to the future: to the final emancipation of humanity from the oppression of outlived capitalism, and from all fear of poverty, insecurity and war, which are its evil progeny.

We Marxists face the struggle for this future with full confidence. And we bring to this struggle faith in men and good will to work for the common good of all. Faith in man and his capacity to survive and improve his lot is not a religious superstition, as the skeptics and snivelers say. It is the recognition of reality, the most important and decisive reality there is. Faith in man and his communist future is at the core of Marxism, the central element of its unshakable optimism. The gloomy prophets of the eclipse of civilization and perhaps even the obliteration of human society ignore the history and the evolution of man, which demonstrates above all else his unconquerable will and capacity to survive and go forward.

Shall man, who came down out of the trees, and learned to stand on his feet and look the world in the face; shall man who has come so far and done so much, fall victim now to his own inventions and achievements? Shall he cease now to do and dare and aspire and achieve, and even to exist? We do not think so. The great men who taught us and inspired us never thought so. All the great revolutionaries and leaders of the people have believed in men and their better future. They never doubted, never stood aside, never yielded to pessimistic despair, no matter how dark the situation might be at the moment. We should remember that, and turn to the great men of the people for inspiration and guidance, so that we too may be imbued with their spirit; that we may see light ahead at the end of our difficult and heavy struggle, and go bravely forward to meet it.

It is true that the human race, threatened with another war of atomic bombs and bacterial poisons, is indeed confronted with a problem of survival on this planet. But the human race will survive. And in order to survive, it will do away with the social system which threatens its survival.

That is the supreme task assigned by history to the twentieth century, and it will be accomplished. The work is in progress, and the goal is in sight. The first half of the twentieth century saw the beginning of the necessary social transformation of the world. The second half of the twentieth century will see it carried through to a triumphant conclusion. Socialism will win the world and change the world, and make it safe for peace and freedom.

# Chapter 32

# The coming American revolution

Delivered to the twelfth National Convention of the Socialist Workers Party, Chicago, in a report on the "Theses on the American Revolution," November 14–18, 1946.

We have undertaken as our central task at this twelfth convention of the Socialist Workers Party to analyze the present stage in the development of United States imperialism as it emerged from the Second World War—and its further perspectives—and to draw the necessary conclusions from this analysis.

In our main thesis we deal exclusively with the perspectives of the American revolution. Secondary questions of tactics, and even of strategy, are left for consideration under another point on the agenda after we have discussed and decided the main question of perspective.

The question might be asked: Why are the theses on perspectives needed now? In order for the party to see clearly on the road ahead it is necessary to have a main orientation and a long-range view of future developments. The theses we have presented are needed at the present moment for a number of reasons.

First, the whole Trotskyist concept of our epoch as the epoch of revolutions, has been challenged by a new school of revisionists of Marxism. What answer do we give to this challenge, with specific reference to the United States of America?

What conclusions do we draw from the war and its consequences; from the new power of American imperialism; from the postwar prosperity; and from the retardation of the European revolution? What conclusions do we draw from these great events for the conduct of our own work and for our own future outlook in the United States?

Secondly, what shall we say to our cothinkers in other lands about revolutionary prospects in the United States? They are surely waiting to hear from our convention on this question, for it is of the most vital and decisive importance for them. This applies to the workers of Europe, but not only to them. It applies to the workers of Russia, of South and Central America, of China, Japan, Asia as a whole, India—in fact, to the workers of the whole world which lies today under the shadow of American imperialism.

And finally, what shall the party teach the new members who today are streaming into our ranks by hundreds and who will come to us tomorrow in thousands? What shall we tell them concretely about the prospects of the revolution in the United States? That is what they want to know above everything else.

Our document undertakes to give straight answers to all these questions.

Another question may well be asked: What is new in the "Theses on the American Revolution" presented by the National Committee?

In one sense it can be said that nothing is new; for all our work has been inspired by, and all our struggles with opportunist tendencies have been derived from, a firm confidence on our part in the coming victory of the American workers.

In another sense it can be said that everything is new; for in the theses of the National Committee on the American revolution we are now stating, explicitly and concretely, what has always been implied in our fights with opportunist organizations, groups and tendencies over the questions which were derivative from this main outlook of ours.

That has been the underlying significance of our long struggle to build a homogeneous combat party. That has been the meaning of our stubborn and irreconcilable fight for a single program uniting the party as a whole; for a democratic and centralized and disciplined party with a professional leadership; for principled politics; for the proletarianization of the party composition; for the concentration of the party on trade-union work ("trade unionization of the party"); and, if I may say so without being misunderstood, for its "Americanization." All of this derived from our concept of the realism of revolutionary prospects in America, and of the necessity to create a party with that perspective in mind.

In short, we have worked and struggled to build a party fit to lead a revolution in the United States. At the bottom of all our conceptions was the basic idea that the proletarian revolution is a realistic proposition in this country, and not merely a far-off "ultimate goal," to be referred to on ceremonial occasions.

I say that is not new. In fact, it has often been expressed by many of us, including Trotsky, in personal articles and speeches. But only now, for the first time, has it been incorporated in a programmatic document of the party. That's what is new in our "Theses on the American Revolution." We are now stating explicitly what before was implied.

For the first time, the party as a party is posing concretely the fundamental question of the perspectives of the American revolution.

You will note in your reading of the theses that secondary questions of tactics and even of strategy, with all their importance, are left out. And this is not by accident or negligence, but by design. The theses deal only with analysis and perspectives—and these only in the broadest sense—*because that is the fundamental basis from which we proceed.*

Tactical questions and even questions of great strategical importance—such as the alliance of the labor movement and the Negro people, the role of the returned war veterans, the relations between the workers and the poor farmers and the urban petty bourgeoisie, the questions of fascism and of the labor party—these questions with all their great subordinate importance are left out of the main theses for separate consideration in other documents. They will be considered at another time in the convention, because the correct answer to all of them depends in reality on a correct answer to the main question of general perspective posed in the theses of the National Committee.

Of course, a general line, a general perspective, does not guarantee that one will always find the right answer to the derivative questions, the secondary issues. But without such a general orientation, without this broad overall ruling conception, it is quite hopeless to expect to find one's way in tactical and strategical questions.

The theses have been criticized already by people who deal exclusively in "the small coin of concrete events." We have been criticized because we "do not mention concrete tasks" and "pose no concrete problems."

That is true. But what is wrong with that procedure?

We are Marxists; and therefore we do not begin with the small questions, with the tactics, or even with the strategy. We first lay down the governing line from which the answers to the secondary questions derive.

Those who preoccupy themselves primarily with tactics reproach us for our procedure, and allege that it reveals the difference between their political *method* and ours. That is quite correct. We proceed from the fundamental to the secondary; they proceed by nibbling at the secondary questions in order to undermine the fundamental concepts. There is indeed a difference in method.

Our theses specifically outline the revolutionary perspectives in America and require the party to conduct and regulate all its daily activity in light of these perspectives.

Our preoccupation at this convention with American affairs and American perspectives does not signify a departure on our part from the time-honored internationalism that has always distinguished our tendency. Rather, we are taking a step forward in the application of our internationalist concepts to American affairs. That means to bring them down from the realm of abstraction and give them flesh and blood.

We began in 1928 with a struggle for internationalism against the dogma of "socialism in one country" which had been imposed on the Comintern and all its sections by the Stalinist revisionists. That was the most fundamental of all the principled questions which have shaped and guided the development of our movement in America for the past eighteen years.

We said then, and we still believe, that the modern world is an economic unit; and that not a single important social problem—and certainly not the most important problem, the socialist reorganization of society—can be definitively solved on national grounds.

With the presentation of the theses of the National Committee on the perspectives of the American revolution, we are adding a correlative idea to the following effect: it is no longer possible to speak seriously about the world socialist revolution without specifically including America in the program. Today that would be almost as utopian as was the theory of "socialism in one country" when it was first promulgated by Stalin for Russia in 1924.

This was always true, but it is truer now than ever in the light of the Second World War and its outcome. The United States has emerged from the war as the strongest power in the world, both economically and militarily. Our theses assert that the role of the United States in further world developments will be decisive in all respects.

If the workers in another country, or even in a series of other countries, take power before the revolutionary victory in the United States, they will have to defend themselves against the American colossus, armed to the teeth and counterrevolutionary to the core.

On the other hand, a revolutionary victory in the United States, signalizing the downfall of the strongest bastion of capitalism, would seal its doom on an international scale.

Or, in a third variant, if the socialist revolution should be defeated in other countries or even on other continents, and pushed back and retarded, we can still fight and win in the United States. And that would again revive the revolution everywhere else in the world.

The world situation makes it quite clear that platonic internationalism is decidedly out of date in this country. Internationalism, as the Trotskyists have conceived it, means first of all, international collaboration. But in our view this international collaboration must signify not only the discussion of the problems and tasks of cothinkers in other countries—this is where platonic internationalism begins and ends—but also the solution of these problems, above all our own specific problems, *in action*. That is our conception of internationalism as we mean to apply it and as we have expressed it in the theses.

One-sided internationalism—preoccupation with far-off questions to the exclusion and neglect of the burning problems on one's own doorstep—is a form of escapism from the realities at home, a caricature of internationalism. This simple truth has not always been understood, and there are some people who do not understand it yet. But our party can justify its existence only if, beginning with an international program, it succeeds in applying this program to the conditions of American life and confirming it in action.

This presupposes first of all an attentive study of America and a firm confidence in its revolutionary perspectives. Those who are content with the role of commentators on foreign affairs—and it is surprising how many there are—or that of a Red Cross society to aid other revolutions in other countries, will never lead a revolution in their own country; and in the long run they will not be of much help to other countries either. What the other countries need from us, above everything else, is one small but good revolution in the United States.

Trotskyism—which is only another name for Bolshevism—is a world doctrine and concerns itself with all questions of world import. But let us not forget—or rather, let some of us begin to recognize for the first time—that America, the United States, is part of the world; in fact, its strongest and most decisive part whose further development will be most fateful for the whole.

It is from this point of view that we deem it necessary now to outline more concretely and more precisely than before our estimation of American perspectives, and to concentrate on the preparation for them. When we speak of the "Americanization" of the party in this sense we are not speaking as vulgar nationalists—far from it—but as genuine internationalists of the deed as well as of the word.

Our theses on the perspectives of the American revolution proceed in accord with the Marxist method and the Marxist tradition by analyzing and emphasizing first of all the objective factors that are making for the revolution. *These are primary. These are fundamental.* Any other approach than that which begins with the objective factors is unrealistic, mere wishful-thinking utopianism, no matter how revolutionary-minded its proponents may be.

This characterization of unrealism applies also to the new revelation of those who have exalted the subjective factor—meaning thereby the party and its strength or weakness at the given moment—to first place.

It would be incorrect, however, to add the supplementary qualification that these latter-day experts of the subjective factor, these latter-day revisionists, are "revolutionary minded." They are unrealistic, but not revolutionary-minded, for they employ their new "theory" exclusively for the explanation of past defeats and anticipation and prediction of new ones. I don't see anything revolutionary about that.

Our theses pay due acknowledgment to the great strength of United States imperialism. Let no one accuse us of failing to give the American imperialist power its due. We paid due acknowledgment to it. This is correct and proper in a document which aims at scientific objectivity; for the might and resources of the Yankee colossus are so imposing in relation to all other countries, and in relation to anything that has ever been seen in the world before in the realm of material power—and have been so well advertised in the bargain—that no one could possibly overlook them.

But our theses—and here we demarcate ourselves from

all those who are hypnotized by the superficial appearance of things—point out not only the strength of American imperialism but also its inherent weaknesses; the contradictions from which it cannot escape; and the new, even greater, power which it has created and which is destined to be its gravedigger—the American working class. That is also part of the American picture which has to be observed and noted if one wants to have a completely true and objectively formulated document.

A one-sided view of the American capitalist system—overestimation of its power and awestruck prostration before it—is the source of many illusions. And these illusions, in turn, are the chief source of American labor opportunism in general; of the capitulation and treachery of the radical intellectuals en masse; of Stalinism; and of all varieties of reformism and Menshevism.

In considering the perspectives of the American capitalist system in general and of the present postwar prosperity in particular, we observe a peculiar and rather interesting anomaly. The capitalist masters of society, and their ideologues and economic experts, enter the new period with doubts and fears which they do not conceal; while the greatest confidence in the long life and good health of the present order of society in America is either openly expressed or tacitly implied by those who set themselves up as representatives of the workers—namely, the official leadership of the labor movements and the Mensheviks of all grades.

The American bourgeoisie entered the great boom of the twenties with the exuberant confidence and enthusiasm of alchemists who had finally discovered the philosopher's stone which turns everything into gold. In that golden age of American capitalism a new school of bourgeois economists came from the colleges to proclaim the glad tidings that Marx had been refuted by Henry Ford; that American business genius had discovered the secret of full employment and permanent prosperity without interfering with the private ownership of the means of production, but on the contrary, strengthening it and aiding its concentration.

They continued to beat the drums on this theme up to the year, the month and even to the day when the stupendous myth of the twenties was exploded in the stock-market crash of 1929. The very week in which the whole structure came tumbling down, the most learned articles were published in the name of the most eminent college professors explaining that this prosperity was going to go higher and would continue endlessly.

It is true that the labor leaders and the social democrats in this country and throughout the world were captivated by the myth of permanent prosperity in the twenties and were enlisted in the great parade. But they only followed; they did not lead. The capitalists were in the lead, full of confidence and optimism in those days. The capitalists and their economists were fortified in their faith by their ignorance, and that is a wonderful fortification for some kinds of faith.

They simply observed that profits rolled in and productivity increased at a rate and on a scale never known before, and that this continued year after year. Hypnotized by the marvelous empirical phenomenon, they mistook a passing phase for a permanent condition.

This misunderstanding was widely shared. The myth of the twenties penetrated deeply into all social strata in the United States and imbued even the great mass of the workers with future hopes of prosperity and security under capitalism. Those were the conditions under which the pioneer communists had to lay the foundation for a party aiming at the revolution. The confidence and illusion in the permanence of the prosperity of capitalism penetrated down into the depths of the working class itself.

The great boom of the twenties developed under the most favorable conditions. The American sector of capitalist economy was still in its healthy prime, relying on a vast internal market of its own which extended from coast to coast and from Canada to the Gulf, and on an expanding foreign trade. All other conditions were most favorable then.

But in spite of that, it is now a matter of historical record that this great boom ended with the stock-market crash of 1929. It is a matter of record that the crisis lasted, with some fluctuations, for ten years.

The salient facts and figures about the crisis of the thirties are recited in our theses. They show the depth and intensity of the crisis, its horrible effects in terms of human misery, and the irreparable blows it dealt to the American capitalist system. National income was cut in half, and with it the living standards of the workers were cut in half. Unemployment reached the figure of twenty million out of a working-class population of no more than forty million at the time.

The partial recovery, brought about in large measure by huge government expenditures, only led to a second sharp drop in 1937, a crisis within the crisis. The crisis as a whole lasted for ten solid years. And even then, a way out to the revival and increase of production and the absorption of the unemployed was found only in the war and the colossal expenditures connected with it.

And this artificially induced recovery, which greatly expanded the productive plant of the country and the numerical force of the working class, has only deepened the contradictions and has prepared all the conditions for the explosion of another crisis, far worse than the thirties and fraught with far more serious social implications.

So, in surveying the future prospects of American capitalism, we simply heed the counsel of realism by putting the question: If American capitalism was shaken to its foundations by the crisis of the thirties, at a time when the world system of capitalism—and America along with it, and America especially—was younger, richer and healthier than it is now; if this crisis lasted for ten years, and even then could not be overcome by the normal operation of economic laws; if all the basic causes and contradictions which brought about the crisis of the thirties have been carried over and lodged in the new artificial war and postwar prosperity, with new ones added and old ones multiplied many times; if all this is true—and nobody but a fool can deny it, for the facts are clearly to be seen—then what chance has the capitalist boom of the forties, that we are living under now, to have a different ending from the boom of the twenties?

Marxist realism tells us that it can be different only insofar as the crisis must go far deeper, must be far more devastating in its consequences, and must come sooner than it came in the boom of the twenties.

The specious theory expounded by the foolishly optimistic bourgeois economists in the heyday of the capitalist boom of the twenties, to the effect that Marx had been outwitted by American business genius, was refuted by the ten-year crisis of the thirties—and that crushing refutation remains in the memory of all.

How inexcusable, then, how absurd, how downright reactionary is the cultivation of this myth under the new conditions today!

In justice to the bourgeoisie and their ideologists it must be admitted that they, instructed by the experiences of the past, now take a far more sober and cautious position in their prognostications of the future. The burnt child fears the fire—that is, if he is a bourgeois economist, a businessman, and not a theoretical trifler.

The bourgeois economists and businessmen talk today far more of "boom and bust" than of boom without end. Any businessmen's economic review you may pick up at random expresses dark forebodings for the economic future. They speak quite casually—as though it is a matter of course, to be taken for granted—of an impending "shake-out" which will slow down the wheels of production and bankrupt the smaller firms which have flourished on the fringes of the boom.

At first, they referred to this process as a "shakedown," but that expressed their thoughts too truthfully. And since bourgeois economists cannot live without lying and dissimulating, they stopped talking about the "shakedown" and finally hit on the euphemistic substitute of a "shake-out."

That sounds better but it will not be one cent cheaper.

The sole chorus of optimism, where the economic prospects of American capitalism are concerned, is that raised by the American variety of Mensheviks. And that is a thin, piping chorus of trebles and tremolos, without a bass voice in it, or a baritone, or even a first-class tenor. It is a eunuch's chorus.

Our fundamental theses on the American revolution do not tie themselves to the economic prospects of the next month or the next year. They deal exclusively with the long-range inevitable outcome of the present artificial prosperity. From the point of view of our theses it makes no difference whether the deepgoing crisis begins in the early spring of 1947, as many bourgeois economists are predicting; or six months later, as many others think; or even a year or two later, as is quite possible in my opinion. Our theses do not consider immediate time schedules, but the *general perspective*. That is what we have to get in mind first.

We take the position that the crisis is *inherent* in the situation; that it may not be escaped or avoided; and that this crisis, when it strikes in full force, will be far deeper and far more devastating than was the crisis of the thirties. As a consequence it will open up the most grandiose revolutionary possibilities in the United States. That conception must be at the base of the policy and perspectives of our party from now on.

I proceed from the discussion of the objective factors in the broadest sense, as our theses do, to go over to another of the most fundamental factors making for the coming American revolution and its victory.

The American working class which confronts the next crisis will not be the disorganized and helpless mass which met the crisis of the thirties in bewilderment and fear, and even with an element of despair. Great changes have taken place in the meantime, and all these changes redound to the advantage of the revolution.

The proletariat greatly increased in numbers with the expansion of industry during the war. Millions of Negroes, of women, and of the new generation of youth have been snatched up out of their former existence and assimilated into the processes of modern industry. Thereby, they have been transformed from a multitude of dispersed individuals into a coherent body imbued with a new sense of usefulness and power.

Most remarkable of all, the most pregnant with consequences for the future, is the truly gigantic leap which the American workers made from disorganized individual helplessness to militant trade-union consciousness and organization in one brief decade. The trade-union movement in the early thirties embraced barely more than three million members. Today the figure stands at *fifteen million members of organized labor in the United States.*

One can point to this fact and say that this represents a remarkable growth. But these bare figures, eloquent as they are, do not in themselves tell the whole story, the true story. For of the three million-odd members of the trade unions in the early thirties, the great majority were composed of the thin stratum of the most skilled and privileged workers, who are the most conservative in their social thinking. The great bulk of workers in the mass-production industries—the most decisive section of the proletariat—were entirely without benefit of organization and had never even known the experience of it.

In spite of that—or more correctly, because of that—when these mass-production workers took the road of trade-union organization, with the partial revival of industry in the middle thirties, they were not impeded by the old baggage and deadening routine of the conservative craft unions. They started from scratch with the modern form of organization—the industrial union form—and with the most militant methods of mass struggle, which reached their apex in the great wave of sit-down strikes in 1937.

The benefits these mass-production workers derived from trade unionism were wrested from the employers in open struggle, and therefore were all the more firmly secured. The stability and cohesiveness of the trade-union organizations created in these struggles were put to the test in the strike wave of the past year. Here we saw a clear demonstration of the great difference in the relationship of forces between the workers and the capitalists at the end of World War II from that which prevailed at the end of World War I, a difference entirely in the favor of the workers.

After the successful termination of the First World War "to make the world safe for democracy," the ruling class of America embarked on a furious reactionary campaign to break the unions, to establish the open shop and to suppress all forms of labor radicalism. In the "Palmer Red Raids" of 1919, hundreds of political meetings were broken up and thousands of radical workers were arrested; hundreds were sent to prison; whole shiploads of foreign-born workers were deported. The newly founded Communist Party was savagely persecuted, its leaders were arrested and indicted, and the party was driven underground.

Simultaneously, the steel strike was broken, in part by ruthless violence and in part by the wholesale importation of strikebreakers; unions newly formed during the war were broken up and scattered right and left; the railway shopmen's strike was defeated in 1922. American capitalism, smashing all opposition before it, marched confidently into the strikeless, open-shop paradise of the great boom of the twenties.

The same thing was attempted, or at least contemplated, for the period immediately following World War II, but the result was a miserable fiasco. This time it was the organized workers who were victorious on every front.

The great industrial unions of the steel, auto, oil, packinghouse, electrical and maritime workers demonstrated their capacity to bring production to a complete stop until the employers came to terms. So great was the newfound solidarity and militancy of the workers that neither violence nor the importation of strikebreakers—the decisive factors in the defeat of the strikes following World War I—could even be attempted by the bosses.

Millions and tens of millions of workers in other industries, profiting by the example of the auto, steel, packinghouse, electrical and other strikes, and riding on the wave created by them, gained wage increases by "collective bargaining," while keeping their unions intact and even strengthening them.

Where did this marvelous labor movement come from? Who created it?

Here we must pay due acknowledgment to American

capitalism. By the blind operation of its internal laws and method of operation, it has created the greatest power in the world—the American working class. Here is where Marx takes revenge on Henry Ford. Capitalism produces many things at a rapid rate and in great quantities. But its richest contribution to the further and higher development of human civilization is the production of its own gravedigger—the organized working class.

American capitalism, as we know, could not work the miracle of boom-without-crisis. But in the period of the twenties and thirties, working blindly and unbeknownst to itself, it wrought some other wonders which border on the miraculous.

American capitalism took millions of bare-footed country boys from the bankrupted farms of the country; put shoes on them and marched them into the regimented ranks of socially-operated modern industry; wet them in the rain of the man-killing, speed-up exploitation of the twenties; dried them in the sun of the frightful crisis of the thirties; overworked them on the assembly line, starved them on the breadline, mistreated and abused them; and finally succeeded in pounding them into a coherent body which emerged as a section of the most powerful and militant trade-union movement the world has ever known.

American capitalism took hundreds of thousands of Negroes from the South and, exploiting their ignorance, and their poverty, and their fears, and their individual helplessness, herded them into the steel mills as strikebreakers in the steel strike of 1919. And in the brief span of one generation, by its mistreatment, abuse and exploitation of these innocent and ignorant Negro strikebreakers, this same capitalism succeeded in transforming them and their sons into one of the most militant and reliable detachments of the great victorious steel strike of 1946.

This same capitalism took tens of thousands and hundreds of thousands of prejudiced hillbillies from the South, many of them members and sympathizers of the Ku Klux Klan, and, thinking to use them, with their ignorance and their prejudices, as a barrier against unionism, sucked them into the auto and rubber factories of Detroit, Akron and other industrial centers. There it sweated them, humiliated them and drove and exploited them until it finally changed them and made new men out of them. In that harsh school the imported southerners learned to exchange the insignia of the KKK for the union button of the CIO, and to turn the Klansman's fiery cross into a bonfire to warm pickets at the factory gate.

You won't find Ku Kluxers or Black Legionnaires in the auto and rubber factories today—or at any rate, not many of them. But there is a mighty sight of first-class shop stewards and picket captains who originally came down out of the hills and up from the bayous of the backward South at the summons of American capitalism.

The American working class covered the great distance from atomization, from nonexistence as an organized force, to trade-union consciousness and organization, in one gigantic leap, in one brief decade.

What grandiose perspectives this achievement opens up for the future! What are the limits to the future possibilities and powers of this remarkable class? There are no limits. All things are possible; and all things that are necessary will be achieved.

If someone had predicted in 1932, at the depths of the crisis, that in ten years' time ten million new workers who had never known unionism would organize themselves into industrial unions of the most modern type and demonstrate their ability to force the absentee owners of the steel and auto and rubber and other mass-production industries to come to terms and not even to dare to attempt to break the strikes—the skeptics would have said: "This is fantasy. This is ultraleft radicalism."

But it happened just the same.

The American workers do not always move when impatient revolutionists call them, as many of us have learned to our sorrow. But they do move when they are ready, and then they move massively.

Industrial unionism is not a new idea. It was projected long before it found its realization on a mass scale in America, and the pioneers of industrial unionism in America suffered many disappointments. In 1930, the IWW dolefully observed its twenty-fifth anniversary. At the end of a quarter of a century, the organization which had proclaimed the program of industrial unionism twenty-five years earlier was completely defeated, a hollow shell comprising far fewer members than it had started with in the bright year of promise, 1905, under a great galaxy of leaders. Industrial unionism seemed to be a defeated program in 1930. But only ten years later the majority of the most important basic industries were completely organized in industrial unions under a new name.

The workers did not move when the IWW called them in 1905. They didn't move when many of us called them later than that. But they moved when they were ready and when conditions were mature for it, and then they moved on a scale and at a speed scarcely dreamed of by the pioneers of industrial unionism.

The scale of the difference is remarkable. Bill Haywood, the great captain of the IWW—I love to mention his name—used to dream and speak in his intimate circle of the goal of a "million members" in the IWW. As a matter of fact, the organization never had more than 100,000 at any one time in all its history, and most of the time only a fraction of that number. The great strikes of the IWW which took place in its heyday, those great pioneer battles which heralded and blazed the way for the CIO—Lawrence, Akron, Paterson, McKees Rocks, the lumber strikes in the Northwest—never involved more than ten to twenty thousand workers at any one time.

But in 1946 nearly two million workers of the CIO, with only a few years of trade-union experience behind them, were on strike at one time!

These comparative figures show not growth, not simply progress, but a veritable transformation of the class. And what has been seen up to now are only the preliminary movements, the promise and the assurance of far greater movements to come. Next in order—and not far away—comes the political awakening of the American workers. That will be at the same pace and on the same scale, if not greater. The American workers will learn politics as they learned trade unionism— "from an abridged dictionary." They will take the road of independent political action with hurricane speed and power.

That will be a great day for the future of humanity, for the American workers will not stop halfway. The American workers will not stop at reformism, except perhaps to tip their hats to it. Once fairly started, they will go the whole way.

He who doubts the socialist revolution in America does not believe in the survival of human civilization, for there is no other way to save it. And there is no other power that can save it but this almighty working class of the United States.

The younger generation entering the revolutionary movement today, with the goal of socialism shining bright in their far-reaching vision, come at a good time. A lot of pioneer work has been done. Many obstacles have been cleared out of the road. Many conditions for success have matured.

The young generation coming to us today comes to a party that foresees the future and prepares for it. They come to a great party with a glorious record and a stainless banner, a party that has already been prepared for them and awaits their enlistment. They come to a strong party, firmly built on the granite rock of Marxism. This party will serve them well, and is worthy of their undivided allegiance.

This twelfth convention coincides with the eighteenth anniversary of the party. The experience and tradition of the party are the capital of the new generation. The work of many people for two decades has not been done in vain. And, besides that, the new recruits can find in a realistic examination of the objective facts many assurances that the course of development is working mightily in favor of the realization of their ideal.

Our economic analysis has shown that the present boom of American capitalism is heading directly at a rapid pace toward a crisis; and this will be a profound social crisis which can lead, in its further development, to an objectively revolutionary situation.

Our analysis of the labor movement has shown that the workers have already demonstrated the capacity to move massively and rapidly forward in the field of trade unionism; and we have every right to confidence that they will move even more massively and with even greater speed on the political field in the days to come.

The objective prerequisites for the social revolution in America will not be lacking. Capitalism itself will provide them. The manpower of the revolution will not be lacking either. The many-millioned masses of the organized workers of America will provide this manpower. It is already partly assembled and partly ready.

The rest is our part. Our part is to build up this party which believes in the unlimited power and resources of the American workers, and believes no less in its own capacity to organize and lead them to storm and victory.

Cannon in 1938

# Chapter 33

# What socialist America will look like

*Delivered as the last in a series of six lectures on "America's Road to Socialism" at the Friday Night Forum in Los Angeles on January 23, 1953.*

We Marxists conceive of socialism not as an arbitrary scheme of society to be constructed from a preconceived plan, but as the next stage of social evolution. The preceding five lectures dealt with the struggle for socialism, which develops in succeeding stages foreseen, understood and consciously organized by the revolutionary party on the basis of a program. The subject of this lecture—what socialist America will look like—carries us beyond our formal program.

Our discussion tonight deals with the socialist society itself, which will grow out of the new conditions when the class struggle will have been carried to its conclusion—that is, to the abolition of classes and consequently of all class struggles. Our preview of the socialist society, therefore, is not a program for struggle, but a forecast of the lines of future development already indicated in the present.

The architects and builders of the socialist society of the future will be the socialist generations themselves. The great Marxists were quite sure of this and refrained from offering these future generations any instructions or blueprints. Their writings, however, do contain some marvelous flashes of insight which light up the whole magnificent perspective. The insights of these men of transcendent genius will be the guiding line of my exposition tonight.

Auguste Blanqui, the great French revolutionist, said, "Tomorrow does not belong to us." We ought to admit that and recognize at the same time that it is better so. The people in the future society will be wiser than we are. We must assume that they will be superior to us in every way, and that they will know what to do far better than we can tell them. We can only anticipate and point out the general direction of development, and we should not try to do more. But that much we are duty-bound to do; for the prospect of socialism—what the future socialist society will look like—is a question of fascinating interest and has a great importance in modern propaganda.

The new generation of youth who will come to our movement and dedicate their lives to it will not be willing to squander their young courage and idealism on little things and little aims. They will be governed by nothing less than the inspiration of a great ideal, the vision of a new world. We are quite justified, therefore, in tracing some of the broad outlines of probable future development; all the more so since the general direction, if not the details, can already be foreseen.

In attempting an approximate estimate of what life will be like under socialism, we run up against the inadequacy of present-day society as a measuring rod or basis for comparison with the future. We must project ourselves into a different world, where the main incentives and compulsions of present-day society will no longer be operative, where in time they will be completely forgotten and have merely a puzzling interest to students of an outlived age.

Socialism will undoubtedly bring about a revolutionary transformation of human activity and association in all fields previously conditioned by the division of society into classes—in work, in education, in sports and amusements, in manners and morals, and in incentives and rewards.

But all these changes, which can be anticipated and predicted, will begin with and proceed from the revolutionary transformation of the system of production and the consequent augmentation and multiplication of the productivity of labor. This is the necessary material premise for a society of shared abundance. The revolutionary reorganization of the labor process—of the manner of working and of regulating, measuring and compensating the labor time of the individual—will take place first and should be considered first, because it will clear the way for all the other changes.

Here at the start we lack an adequate standard of comparison. The necessary amount of productive labor time which will be required of each individual in the new society cannot be calculated on the basis of the present stage of industrial development. The advances in science and technology which can be anticipated, plus the elimination of waste caused by competition, parasitism, etc., will render any such calculation obsolete. Our thought about the future must be fitted into the frame of the future.

Even at the present stage of economic development, if everybody worked and there were no waste, a universal four-hour day would undoubtedly be enough to provide abundance for all in the advanced countries. And once the whole thought and energy of society is concentrated on the problem of increasing productivity, it is easily conceivable that a new scientific-technological-industrial revolution would soon render a compulsory productive working day of four hours, throughout the normal lifetime of an individual, so absurdly unnecessary that it would be recognized as an impossibility.

All concepts of the amount of necessary labor required from each individual, based on present conditions and practices, must be abandoned in any serious attempt to approach a realistic estimate of future prospects and possibilities in this basic field. The labor necessary to produce food, clothing, shelter and all the conveniences and refinements of material life in the new society will be cooperative, social labor—with an ever-increasing emphasis on labor-saving and automatic, labor-eliminating machinery, inventions and scientific discoveries, designed to increase the rate of productivity.

This labor will be highly organized and therefore disciplined in the interests of efficiency in production. There can be no anarchy in the cooperative labor process, but only freedom from labor to an ever-increasing extent as science and technology advance productivity and automatically reduce the amount of labor time required from the individual.

This progressive reduction of the labor time required of each individual will, in my opinion, soon render it impractical to compute this labor time on a daily, weekly or even yearly basis. It is reasonable to assume—this is my opinion, but only my opinion, and not a program—that the amount of labor required of the individual by society during his whole life expectancy will be approximately computed, and that he will be allowed to elect when to make this contribution. I incline strongly to the idea that the great majority will elect to get their required labor time over with in their early youth, working a full day for a year or two.

Thereafter, they would be free for the rest of their lives to devote themselves, with freedom in their labor, to any scientific pursuit, to any creative work or play or study which might interest them. The necessary productive labor they have contributed in a few years of their youth will pay for their entire lifetime maintenance, on the same principle that the workers today pay for their own paltry "social security" in advance.

On the road to that, or some similar arrangement, beginning already in the transition period which we discussed last week, there will be an evolutionary change of labor regulations, calculations and payments. Emerging from capitalism, the transitional society will carry over some of the capitalist methods of accounting, incentives and rewards. People will first work for wages. They will be paid in money, backed by the gold in Fort Knox, for the amount of work performed. But after a certain period, when there is abundance and even superabundance, the absurdity of strict wage regulation will become apparent. Then the gold will be taken out of Fort Knox and put to some more useful purpose, if such can be found.

When people have no further use for money, they will wonder what to do with all this gold, which has cost so much human labor and agony. Lenin had a theory that under socialism gold could be used, maybe, to make doorknobs for public lavatories, and things like that. But no Marxist authority would admit that in the socialist future men will dig in the earth for such a useless metal.

The accounting arrangements automatically registered by money wages based on gold, will at a certain stage be replaced by labor certificates or coupons, like tickets to the theater. But even that, eventually, will pass away. Even that kind of accounting, which would take up useless labor and be absolutely purposeless, will be eliminated. There will be no money, and there will not even be any bookkeeping transactions or coupons to regulate how much one works and how much he gets. When labor has ceased to be a mere means of life and becomes life's prime necessity, people will work without any compulsion and take what they need. So said Marx.

Does that sound "visionary"? Here again, we must make an effort to lift ourselves out of the framework of the present society, and not consider this conception absurd or "impractical." The contrary would be absurd. For in the socialist society, when there is plenty and abundance for all, what will be the point in keeping account of each one's share, any more than in the distribution of food at a well-supplied family table? You don't keep books as to who eats how many pancakes for breakfast or how many pieces of bread for dinner. Nobody grabs when the table is laden. If you have a guest, you don't seize the first piece of meat for yourself; you pass the plate and ask him to help himself first.

When you visualize society as a "groaning board" on which there is plenty for all, what purpose would be served in keeping accounts of what each one gets to eat and wear? There would be no need for compulsion or forcible allotment of material means. "Wages" will become a term of obsolete significance, which only students of ancient history will know about. "Speaking frankly," said Trotsky, "I think it would be pretty dull-witted to consider such a really modest perspective 'utopian.'"

The ethic of capitalism and its normal procedure, of course, are quite different. But don't ever, dear comrades, make the mistake of thinking that anything contrary to its rules and its ethics is utopian, or visionary, or absurd. No, what's absurd is to think that this madhouse is permanent and for all time. The ethic of capitalism is "from each whatever you can get out of him—to each whatever he can grab." The socialist society of universal abundance will be regulated by a different standard. It will "inscribe on its banners," said Marx, "from each according to his ability—to each according to his needs." I speak now of the higher phase of socialist society, which some Marxist authorities prefer to call communism.

In the present society people are haunted by insecurity. Their mental health is undermined by fear for their future and the future of their children. They are never free from fear that if something happens, if they have a sickness or an accident for which they are not responsible, the punishment will be visited upon their children, that their children will be deprived of an education and proper food and clothing.

Under such conditions this "human nature," which we hear so much about, is like a plant trying to flower in a dark cellar; it really doesn't get much chance to show its true nature, its boundless potentialities. In the socialist society of shared abundance, this nightmare will be lifted from the minds of the people. They will be secure and free from fear; and this will work a revolution in their attitude toward life and their enjoyment of it. Human nature will get a chance to show what it is really made of.

The present division of society into classes, under which the few have all the privileges and the many are condemned to poverty and insecurity, carries with it a number of artificial and unnatural divisions which deform the individual and prevent the all-around development of his personality and his harmonious association with his kind.

There is the division between men's work and women's

work, to say nothing of men's rights and women's rights. There is the division of race prejudice between the Negroes and the whites, which is cruelly unjust to the former and degrading to the latter. There is the division between manual and intellectual labor, which produces half-men on each side. There is the division between the city and the country, which is harmful to the inhabitants of both.

These divisions are not ordained for all time, as some people may think. They are the artificial product of class society and will fall with it. And a great fall it will be.

The emancipation of women will begin in the very first days of the workers' government, and very probably will be fully completed before the socialist society emerges from the transition period. The first condition for the real emancipation of women is their economic emancipation. That must presuppose the scientific organization of housework, like all other work, so that women too can have time and leisure for cultural activity and the free choice of occupation. That will imperatively require the establishment of communal kitchens, housekeeping services, nurseries and kindergartens.

The average poor housewife in this country is made to think that she was born into this glorious world for the chief purpose of fighting dust and wrestling pots and pans. That's not true. Women are capable of participating in all avenues of activity, in all trades, in all sciences, in all arts. Enough have already broken through to demonstrate that.

One thing I'm absolutely sure is going to happen early in the period of the workers' government, maybe during the first five-year plan. Under the slogan of more efficiency in production, reinforced by moral arguments which are powerful in the case—the rights of women to leisure and freedom for cultural and spiritual growth—there will be a tremendous popular movement of women to bust up this medieval institution of forty million separate kitchens and forty million different housewives cooking, cleaning, scrubbing and fighting dust.

Thirty or forty million women every day of the year trudging to the market, each one loading her separate basket and lugging it home to cook thirty or forty million different meals for thirty or forty million different families. What a terrible waste of energy, waste of productivity; to say nothing of the cultural waste; to say nothing of the imposition upon the women victims. The enlightened socialist women will knock the hell out of this inefficient, unjust and antiquated system. The mass emergence of the socialist women from the confining walls of their individual kitchens will be the greatest jailbreak in history—and the most beneficent. Women, liberated from the prison of the kitchen, will become the free companions of free men.

The drudgery of housework will be organized like any other division of labor, on an efficient communal basis, so that women can begin to have some leisure too. Cooking and house-cleaning, like any other work, can be done much better, much quicker, in an organized, scientific manner. Proper air-conditioning and dust-catching "precipitrons"—which will be standard equipment for every home—will take care of most of the house-cleaning automatically.

I cannot see why the average housewife, who isn't specially trained for it or specially adapted to it, should want to bother with it. I cannot see why cooking, housecleaning and janitor work shouldn't be one of the national divisions of labor, for which various people take their turns in the process for a certain number of hours a day, a certain number of weeks in a year, however it may be allocated. Or, if some people prefer to live communally, as many have found it advantageous, they'll do that, and simplify things still more.

By this forecast I do not mean to draw a picture of regimentation. Just the opposite, for any kind of regimentation such as that imposed by the present social order will be utterly repugnant to the free and independent citizens of the socialist future. They will live the way they want to live, and each individual—within the limits of his general obligation to society—will decide for himself. Better, in this case, say "herself"—for old-fashioned reactionaries who ignorantly think they know what "woman's place" is, will run up against the hard fact—for the first time since class society began—that women will have something to say about that, and what they will say will be plenty.

What kind of homes will the people have under socialism, what kind of home life? I don't know, and neither does anyone else. But they will have the material means and the freedom of choice to work out their own patterns. These two conditions, which are unknown to the great majority today, will open up limitless vistas for converting the "home" from a problem and a burden into a self-chosen way of life for the joy of living.

Homes will not be designed by real-estate promoters building for profit—which is what the great bulk of "home-building" amounts to today. The people will have what they want. They can afford to have it any way they want it. If some of them want a house of their own in the country, and if they want to have their cooking and their house-cleaning done on the present basis, nobody will stop them. But I imagine they will evoke public curiosity and quizzical glances. People will say: "They've got a perfect right to do that, but they don't have to."

Every man can have his little house as he has it now, and his little wife spending her whole time cooking and cleaning for him—provided he can find that kind of a wife. But he will not be able to buy such service, and he'll be rather stupid to ask for it. Most likely his enlightened sweetheart will tell him: "Wake up, Bud; we're living under socialism. You've been reading that ancient history again and you've a nostalgia for the past. You've got to break yourself of that habit. I'm studying medicine, and I have no time to be sweeping up dust. Call up the Community House-Cleaning Service."

I must also break the news to the Southern crackers and their Northern cousins, and other members of the Jim Crow fraternity, that under socialism America will no longer be "a white man's country." It will belong to the colored people too. They will own as much of it as anyone else and share to the full, without let or hindrance, all its bountiful prosperity and abundance, all its freedoms, rights and privileges—without any exceptions whatever.

The socialist society based on human solidarity will have no use for such unscientific and degrading and inhuman notions as the idea that one man is superior to another because, many thousands of years ago, the ancestors of the first lived in an environment that produced in the course of time a lighter skin color than was produced by the environment of the ancestors of the second.

The Jim Crow gangsters who strut around in self-satisfied ignorance as representatives of the "superior" race may have to learn their mistake the hard way, but they will learn—or "be learned"—just the same. The Negroes will play a great and decisive role in the revolution, in alliance with the trade unions and the revolutionary party; and in that grand alliance they will demonstrate and conquer their right to full equality.

The Negroes will very probably be among the best revolutionists. And why shouldn't they be? They have nothing to lose but their poverty and discrimination, and a whole world of prosperity, freedom and equality to gain. You can bet your boots the Negroes will join the revolution to fight for that—once it becomes clear to them that it cannot be gained except by revolution. The black battalions of the revolution will be a mighty power—and great will be their reward in the victory.

As in the emancipation of women, the emancipation of the Negroes will begin with the absolute and unconditional abolition of every form of economic discrimination and disadvantage, and proceed from that to full equality in all domains.

Race prejudice will vanish with the ending of the social system that produced and nourished it. Then the human family will live together in peace and harmony, each of its sons and daughters free at last to make the full contribution of his or her talents to the benefit of all.

The present big and crowded, ugly, unhealthy cities—I was asked at a previous lecture—what will happen to them? They will be no more. Once the transition period has been passed through, once all the problems of abundance and plenty have been solved, the people will want also to live right in the larger sense—to provide for their cultural and esthetic aspirations. They will have a great hunger and thirst for beauty and harmony in all the surroundings of their lives. These monster cities we live in today are blights of modern society. They will certainly give way to planned cities interlinked to the countryside. Everybody will live with the natural advantages of the country and the cultural associations of the town. All the Marxist authorities were emphatic on this point. The crowded slums and the isolated, godforsaken farmhouses will be demolished at about the same time.

A new science and new art will flower—the science

and art of city planning. There is such a profession today, but the private ownership of industry and real estate deprives it of any real scope. Under socialism, some of the best and most eager students in the universities will take up the study of city planning, not for the profitable juxtaposition of slums and factory smokestacks, but for the construction of cities fit to live in. Art in the new society will undoubtedly be more cooperative, more social. The city planners will organize landscapers, architects, sculptors and mural painters to work as a team in the construction of new cities which will be a delight to live in and a joy to behold.

Communal centers of all kinds will arise to serve the people's interests and needs. Centers of art and centers of science. Jack London, in *The Iron Heel*, speaking in the name of an inhabitant of the future socialist society, referred as a matter of course to the numerous "wonder cities" which had been given poetic names—"Ardis," "Asgard" and so on—wonder cities designed for beauty, for ease of living, for attractiveness to the eye and to the whole being.

Farming, of course, will be reorganized like industry, on a large scale. The factory farm is already in existence to a large extent in the West. Tens of thousands of acres in single units are operated with modern machine methods and scientific utilization of the soil, for the private profit of absentee owners. These factory farms will not be broken up. They will be taken over and developed on a vaster scale. Eventually the whole of agricultural production will be conducted on the basis of factory farms. The agricultural workers will not live in cultural backwardness, in lonely, isolated farmhouses. They will live in the town and work in the country, just as the factory worker will live in the country and work in the town.

The separation between manual and intellectual labor

will be broken down. The division between specialized knowledge of single subjects and ignorance of the rest, which is a characteristic feature of capitalism, will be eliminated. The half-men produced by these artificial divisions, who know only one thing and can do only one thing, will give way to the whole men who can do many things and know something about everything.

There will be a revolution in art. The class society, which splits the population into separate and antagonistic groups of the privileged and the deprived, splits the personality of the artist, too. A few selected people have the opportunity to study and practice art, remote from the life of the people. At the same time, not thousands but millions of children have the spark of talent, or even of genius, snuffed out before it has a chance to become a flame. Children of the poor, who like to draw already in school, soon have to put all those ideas out of their minds. They can't afford to be drawing pictures. They have to learn some trade where they can make a living, and forget about their artistic aspirations.

In the new society, everybody will be an artist of some sort or other, and every artist will be a worker. Education will be for intellectual pursuits and manual occupations simultaneously, from childhood to old age. Marx was of the emphatic opinion that children should engage in productive labor from the age of nine, not at the expense of their "education" but as an essential part of it. From an early age, children will learn to use tools and to make something useful to the people. The child will have the satisfaction of learning by doing and the satisfaction of being useful and productive even when he's a child.

Then older people will begin to treat him more respectfully. They will regard him, also, from an early age, as a human being, as a citizen, as a producer who shouldn't be treated as a baby any longer. He will be reasoned with and talked to and treated as an equal, not beaten or scolded or shouted at, or pushed into a corner. Marx said "Children must educate their parents." And in some respects they will do that, too, when they get a fair chance.

There will be such a revolution in the relations of children and parents as we can hardly conceive of in this monstrous class society of the present. Parents often think they have been endowed by some mysterious supernatural power with the right to abuse and mistreat children. Primitive man never had such rights, never dreamed of such things. It is only due to the degeneration which followed the introduction of private property, that the mistreatment of children and the double mistreatment of women became the rule. Primitive man in his natural state never knew such things. And the future society will know them still less.

Every child who has a talent for music or drawing or sculpture or molding or writing—and there is no such thing as a child without some talent—can become an artist of one sort or another. One who has an instinct and feeling for words can become a writer. There will be poets who will glorify the great theme of human solidarity, and they will not be starved and ridiculed as they are in this ignorant society. The poets will be honored, perhaps above all, because they have more insight than any others.

All-sided cultural development under socialism will not be some special gift or opportunity for favored individuals, but the heritage of all. The socialist man will have the most priceless of all possessions. He will have time. He will have leisure. He will have time and the means to live, to play, to grow, to travel, to realize to the full the expression of his human personality. And that will not be the exception, but the rule. There will be a whole race of people enjoying and expressing all those things.

I have a theory—again a personal opinion and not a program—that there will be two kinds of labor under socialism. All, without exception, will participate in the organized productive process, the source of the people's maintenance and abundance. But that will take up only a small amount of time, as already indicated. Then, I visualize another form of purely voluntary labor, unorganized, anarchistic, practiced as a means of artistic self-expression, and freely given for the general good or as a service of friendship.

Handicrafts, once the basic form of production, were virtually wiped out by the development of capitalism because of their comparative inefficiency, and many of the old skills of the artisans have been lost. The cooperative machine process, which produced more things faster and more easily, eliminated handicraft as a serious factor in the productive process, and this progressive historical development can never be reversed.

But under socialism, where machine industry will be developed to the highest degree, producing even more abundantly many times over what it can at the present stage of its development, I can foresee a revival, a new flowering of handicrafts on a new basis. If this is theoretically inadmissible as a form of labor in the socialist society, perhaps my speculative suggestion can be considered under the heading of art.

I spoke before of the artificial division between intellectual and manual labor, and the half-man this division produces. The whole man of the socialist future will not be content merely to know what he reads in books, or to write books, or to confine himself exclusively to any other purely intellectual occupation. He will be trained from childhood to use his hands productively and creatively, and he will have plenty of time to exercise his skills in any way he sees fit; to do what he wants to do, what he likes to do.

I should imagine that under such conditions man, the tool-using animal, will assert himself once again. There will be a resurgence of freelance cabinetmakers, shoemakers, hand tailors, bookbinders, etc. These artisans of the future won't compete with machine industry—that would be anachronistically absurd—but will ply their crafts as a special form of recreation and artistic self-expression, and to make gifts for friends. If they want to do it that way, who is going to stop them?

In the present society, very few get a chance to do the work they really want to do, and thereby they are deprived of life's most solid satisfaction. "Blessed is he who has found his work," said Carlyle. But how many are so blessed? Most people do what seems best to make a living. Those who are able to choose their work, and to persist in it at all costs, are very rare.

Taking the present society as it is, I personally have had the work I wanted, that I thought the time required, the occupation I was made for—that of a professional revolutionist. But in a socialist society, where there will be no need and no room for social struggles or revolution, the likes of me would have to find another trade. I have thought that under such circumstances I would be a cabinetmaker, as my grandfather was, a man who took pride in his fine work with wood and tools. Another would be a bookbinder, another a shoemaker, another a tailor—there are a lot of fine old crafts which will challenge the ingenious and the tool-minded.

Under socialism, people will not fear to love their neighbor lest they be taken advantage of, nor be ashamed of disinterested friendship, free from all self-interest and calculation. There will be powerful impulses to give things to each other, and the only possible way of giving will be by doing, by making. There will be no chance to "buy" a present for anybody—because nothing will be for sale; and besides, everybody will be free to take anything he needs from the superabundant general store of material things rolling from the assembly line. Presents, to mean anything, will have to be *made,* outside the general process. I think they will be, and such gifts will be really treasured and displayed on special occasions.

I imagine that when a man goes to his wedding, he'll wear a coat of many colors, like Joseph in the Bible, hand-made for him by a friend who is an expert tailor, who has made it for him as a service of love. On holidays, he'll wear hand-made shoes, molded to his own feet by a friend who is a craftsman, who takes pride in his perfect work. And when he, in turn, wants to present a gift to a friend, he will make it for him.

Your house, the house of the well-regulated family, will have as the things it is proudest of certain things specially made for you by people who like you. This easy chair made to your own measure by your friend so-and-so. This hand-mortised hardwood bookcase made for you by a cabinetmaker, as a gift. And those pictures and decorations on the walls—they were not machine-stamped at the factory, but hand-painted especially for you by an artist friend. And your important and most treasured books, which came well-bound from the print shops of the socialist society, have been rebound in fancy leather, by an old-fashioned bookbinder, a real craftsman. He does this outside his general contribution to the cooperative labor process, as a form of creative self-expression and as an act of friendship. I think it will be a great joy and satisfaction to be an expert craftsman in the coming time.

Morality, which in class society is either a hypocritical cover for material self-interest, or an escapist withdrawal from the harsh realities of the class struggle, will be changed inside out. The advancement of individual special interests at the expense of others—the highest standard of capitalist society—is summed up in the slogan "getting ahead," which means: getting ahead of others. It is the root cause of the lying, demagogy and deception which are the central features of every election campaign, of advertising, and of all media of information and communication. The people are bombarded with lies every day of their lives. Capitalist morality itself is a lie.

There can be no doubt whatever that the new society will have a different morality. It will be a social morality based on human solidarity, having no need of lies, deception, demagogy and hypocrisy. Those who cannot conceive of any human relationship without the "getting ahead" philosophy of capitalism say socialism would not "work" because people would have no incentives. They really have a low opinion of the human race. Incentives will not be lacking. But they will be different.

For one thing, public opinion, uncontaminated by phony propaganda, will be a powerful force, as it was in the unspoiled primitive societies before people knew anything about private property and special class interests. The desire to be approved by one's associates will be a powerful incentive. In the new society the most useful people will be acclaimed, not the most "successful" in the business of getting ahead of others, not the rich exploiters, the slick fakers, the lying politicians, and the generals famed for slaughter.

The youth will venerate heroes of a new type—the scientist; the artist; the poet; the inventor who discovers a means of shortening the labor time necessary in this or that occupation; the agricultural expert who discovers a new way of breeding seed and making bigger crops. The applause and approval of the people will be the highest incentive and the highest reward of the socialist man.

Scope for ambition will not be lacking either. The socialist people will be completely alive and animated by driving ambitions. But their ambitions will have a different motivation and a different direction. Struggle is the law of life, and so it will be under socialism. But under socialism the struggle of men against each other for personal gain will give way to the struggle for ideas, to competition and rivalry in serving and advancing the general good of all, and to their cooperative struggle to complete the conquest of nature.

The people will struggle cooperatively—and through the competition of alternate plans—to move mountains, to change the course of rivers, to control climate and to get the full benefit of all its changes. They will organize huge migrations with the seasons. Why should only the birds have the right to move south when it gets cold in the North? The rich have already claimed this right. The people who own New York, for example, don't live there much of the time. They spend their summers in Bar Harbor, Maine, where it's cool and breezy, and their winters in Florida, on the sunny beach. Some of them travel to other countries with the changing seasons. They stop over in New York only in the spring and fall when the New York weather is better than that of Maine or Florida. That, it seems to me, is a very sensible way to live—if you can afford it.

Under socialism everybody will be able to afford to live comfortably and to travel freely, without passports. Can you imagine people living in Chicago in the wintertime, when they might be in California on a six-month vacation? Nobody ever saw the sun in Chicago from Labor

Day to the Fourth of July; but here—I am told—it shines every day in the year—even when it's raining.

Some people who have lived in a frost-bound place all their lives may continue for some years, even under the new society, just from tradition, habit and ignorance. But once you get them to come to the Land of the Sundown Sea on a trial journey and see what California is like on the twenty-third day of January, they will never be the same again. And the daring souls, the pioneers who will find this out, will write letters back and the word will pass, and the idea will grow up amongst the people in the frozen North: "Why shouldn't we, with all our abundance—we can afford it, we have plenty—why shouldn't we travel around and enjoy climate with the seasons—just like the birds?"

The people will have ambition, under socialism, to explore the great universe and to unlock its secrets, and to extract from their knowledge new resources for the betterment of all the people. They will organize an all-out war against sickness and disease and there will be a flowering of the great science of medicine. They will look back with indignation when they read in their history books that at one time people had to live in a society where there was a shortage of doctors, artificially maintained.

I believe it can be said with certainty that among the heroes of the new society, whom the youth will venerate, will be the doctors of all kinds who will really be at the service of man in the struggle for the conquest of those diseases which lay him low. Man's health will be a major concern, and sickness and disease a disgrace, not to the victim, but to the society which permits it.

Having conquered nature, having solved the problems of material existence, having taken care of the problem of health, the socialist man will begin finally—as Trotsky forecast in his brilliant work *Literature and Revolution*—to study, to know and to conquer himself. The study and mastery of the body and the mind will bring the socialist man to physical and mental harmony and perfection, to the realization in life of the old aspiring motto, "a sound mind in a sound body"—producing a new race, the first worthy of the name of man.

Under socialism there will be no more private property, except for personal use. Consequently there can be no more crimes against private property—which are 90 percent or more of all the crimes committed today—and no need of all this huge apparatus for the prevention, detection, prosecution and punishment of crimes against property. No need for jails and prisons, policemen, judges, probation officers, lawyers, bondsmen, social workers, bureaucrats; no need for guards, bailiffs, wardens, prosecutors, stool pigeons, informers and professional perjurers. No need for this whole mass of parasitical human rubbish which represents the present-day state and which devours so much of the substance of the people.

With the end of classes and their conflicting interests, there will be no more "politics," because politics is essentially an expression of the class struggle; and no more parties, as they are now known, for parties are the political representatives of classes. That is not to say there won't be differences and heated debates. Groupings, we must assume, will arise in the course of these disputes. But they will not be based on separate class interests.

They will be "parties" based on differences of opinion as to what kind of an economic plan we should have; what great scheme of highways should be developed; what system of education; what type of architecture for the wonder cities. Differences on these, and numerous other questions of public interest and general concern, will give the competitive instincts of the people all kinds of room for free expression. Groupings will be formed and contend with each other for popular support without "politics" or parties in the old sense of class struggle and the conflict of material interests.

In the classless society of the future, there will be no state. The Marxist formula that the state will wither away and die out has a profound ultimate meaning, for the state is the most concentrated expression of violence. Where there is violence, there is no freedom. The society of the free and equal will have no need and no room for violence and will not tolerate it in any form. This was the profound conception of the great Marxists.

I recall that when I was very young, I read Jack London's *Iron Heel* and got from there for the first time, in one single reference, a glimpse of the socialist future wherein violence will be unknown. In a footnote to the manuscript in this great book about the ruthless class war in capitalist society, ostensibly written by an editor in the socialist society, the author calls attention to an enigmatic expression in the story. One of the characters is described as having the build of a prizefighter, and the editor thought it necessary to explain to the citizens of the socialist society what prizefighting meant. This footnote reads, "In that day it was the custom of men to compete for purses of money. They fought with their hands. When one was beaten into insensibility, or killed, the survivor took the money." That had to be explained in the socialist society, because they wouldn't know it otherwise.

Trotsky, in his last testament, written in anticipation of death, said, "Life is beautiful. Let the future generations cleanse it of all evil, oppression and violence and enjoy it to the full." Just ponder those words—Trotsky was a writer who weighed every word. His last injunction to the people who would follow him was: "Cleanse life of all violence."

In a talk with Gorky, Lenin said the same thing in almost the same words: "Our ideal is not to use force against anyone."

It is difficult for us to comprehend such a possibility, living in a society where even the smallest children are taught that they have to fight and scramble to protect themselves in a hostile world. We can hardly visualize a world without violence. But that's what socialism means. That was the ultimate meaning of our far-seeing teachers when they said that the state will wither away and eventually die out. They meant that eventually all violence of people against each other will wither away and cease to be.

The people will turn their attention then to that most important problem of all—the problem of the free development of the human personality. Then human nature will begin to change, or rather, to assert its real self. People will recover some of the virtues of primitive society, which was based on solidarity and cooperation, and improve them and develop them to a higher degree.

Leisure is the condition for all cultural development. "The glory that was Greece," justly celebrated in song and story, was the first great confirmation of this law. Ancient Greece, borrowing from other civilizations, produced the first truly cultured class. In some important respects it touched the highest peaks our race has yet known, and in the Golden Age of Pericles it came to its fullest flower. Its attainments in literature, the drama, sculpture, architecture, philosophy, in the beginnings of science and in the graces and amenities of civilized intercourse are the original pattern from which Western civilization stems.

But that glorious Greece had a fatal flaw. Its leisure—and therefore its culture—was limited to a very narrow stratum of privileged aristocrats. It lacked the technological basis for *universal* leisure and culture. The society of ancient Greece rested on a base of dehumanized slave labor. It was surrounded by a world of barbarism. It was constantly embroiled in wars and eventually went down in ruins, and nothing was left of it but what is scratched on stone and preserved on parchment. A few ruins of the marvelous sculpture and architecture still stand to give an intimation of what was known and done twenty-five hundred years ago.

Socialist society will stand immeasurably higher than that of ancient Greece, even in its Golden Age. Machines and science will be the slaves, and they will be far more productive, a thousand, ten thousand times more productive, than the human slaves of ancient Greece. Under socialism, all will share in the benefits of abundance, not merely a favored few at the top. All the people will have time and be secure for an ever higher development.

All will be artists. All will be workers and students, builders and creators. All will be free and equal. Human solidarity will encircle the globe and conquer it, and subordinate it to the uses of man.

That, my friends, is not an idle speculation. That is the realistic perspective of our great movement. We ourselves are not privileged to live in the socialist society of the future, which Jack London, in his far-reaching aspiration, called the Golden Future. It is our destiny, here and now, to live in the time of the decay and death agony of capitalism. It is our task to wade through the blood and filth of this outmoded, dying system. Our mission is to clear it away. That is our struggle, our law of life.

We cannot be citizens of the socialist future, except by anticipation. But it is precisely this anticipation, this vision of the future, that fits us for our role as soldiers of the revolution, soldiers of the liberation war of humanity. And that, I think, is the highest privilege today, the occupation most worthy of a civilized man. No matter whether we personally see the dawn of socialism or not, no matter what our personal fate may be, the cause for which we fight has social evolution on its side and is therefore invincible. It will conquer and bring all mankind a new day.

It is enough for us, I think, if we do our part to hasten on the day. That's what we're here for. That's all the incentive we need. And the confidence that we are right and that our cause will prevail, is all the reward we need. That's what the socialist poet, William Morris, had in mind, when he called us to

> Join in the only battle
> Wherein no man can fail,
> For whoso fadeth and dieth,
> Yet his deeds shall still prevail.

# Notes

### Chapter 1
### Speech at the first Workers Party convention

This speech was first printed in *The Toiler,* published in Cleveland, January 7, 1922.

The **Third International,** also called the Communist International and the Comintern for short, was founded in March 1919 at a congress in Moscow. It was dissolved by Stalin in June 1943 as an assurance to his capitalist allies in World War II of his nonrevolutionary intentions.

The **Second International** was founded in 1889. Prior to World War I it embraced all the socialist or social democratic (as some were called) parties. The support of its leading sections for their own imperialist powers in waging World War I marked its demise as a revolutionary socialist organization and its moral bankruptcy. It continues to exist to this day as a reformist and opportunist organization.

The **Two-and-a-half International** was a short-lived organization formed in 1921 by Karl Kautsky, Otto Bauer, and their followers. Its chief component was the centrist USPD (Independent Social Democratic Party), which had been a belated antiwar splitoff from the German Social Democracy, but most of which had voted to join the Third International. The remnant USPD led the Two-and-a-half International until 1923, when it fused with the Second International.

The **American Civil Liberties Union** was formed in January 1920 as the successor to the National Civil Liberties Bureau, which had defended and sought amnesty for political prisoners, conscientious objectors, and other victims of the wartime persecution and postwar witch-hunt.

The **SP Amnesty Committee** was the Political Amnesty Committee set up by the Socialist Party to petition and agitate for the freeing of Eugene V. Debs and other political prisoners.

The **Red Trade Union International** or Red International

of Labor Unions (also known as the *Profintern,* from a contraction of its Russian title) had its first congress in Moscow in July 1921. A number of syndicalist-led unions, including the IWW, sent delegates.

**George Hardy** was an IWW political prisoner who later joined the Communist Party.

**J.W. Johnstone** was prominent in the Chicago Federation of Labor. Later, within the Communist Party, he became a secondary leader in the Foster faction.

**Socialist Party**: After the mass expulsions conducted by the right-wing leadership and the splits of 1919, the SP had less than one-third of its former membership.

**Farmer-Labor Party**: Following World War I, there were a number of local labor-party developments based on the trade unions. The most important of these was led by the Chicago Federation of Labor, which had spearheaded the great organizing drives in the meatpacking and steel industries. The leaders of the local labor parties came together in Chicago at the end of 1919 and formed a national Labor Party, which later changed its name to Farmer-Labor Party in order to attract agrarian support. In the 1920 election, its presidential ticket received about 250,000 votes, mainly in Washington, South Dakota, and Illinois.

Under the direction of the Pepper-Ruthenberg faction, the Communist Party in 1923 took control over the movement, alienating most of the trade-union elements in the process, so that they withdrew. The Pepper-Ruthenberg faction then became involved, through its renamed Federated Farmer-Labor Party, in an opportunist maneuver with the supporters of the insurgent Progressive Republican LaFollette. The CP hastily extricated itself from this situation shortly before the 1924 presidential election by putting its own ticket in the field and having the executive committee of the Federated Farmer-Labor Party withdraw its candidates in favor of the CP ticket.

**Gompers bureaucracy**: Samuel Gompers (1850–1924) was president of the American Federation of Labor from its founding in 1886 until his death, with the exception of the year 1895. The outlook of the AFL bureaucracy, which was fashioned in his image, was narrow and class-collaborationist. It abhorred militancy and socialist ideas, and its philosophy was that of craft exclusivism and business unionism.

## Chapter 2
## Our appeal against expulsion

This speech was first printed in *The Militant,* January 1, 1929.

**Twenty-one comrades expelled**: Cannon, Max Shachtman, and Martin Abern were tried on charges of Trotskyism by the Political Committee of the Workers (Communist) Party and expelled (with the right of appeal to the December plenum of the National Committee) on October 27, 1928. The party leadership thereupon ordered all party units to hold meetings to vote approval of the expulsions. Individuals or at-large members were sent letters giving them one week to express their attitude. Those who demurred at endorsing the expulsions for any reason—desiring more information or wanting to hear the defendants' arguments—were themselves immediately expelled. Thus in Minnesota twenty-one members, who knew nothing about Trotskyism but did know the expelled leaders and wanted to hear what they had to say, were expelled.

**John Pepper** was the pseudonym in the U.S. of Josef Pogany, a Hungarian who played an undistinguished role in the short-lived revolutionary government in Hungary in 1919. He came to the U.S. in 1922 in the company of a Comintern delegation and remained. He was put on the American party's top committees. He formed a faction with Ruthenberg, was Lovestone's mentor, and was mastermind of the Communist takeover of the Farmer-Labor Party and the flirtation with LaFollette's third party in 1924. He was recalled to Moscow in 1924, where he continued to serve the Lovestone faction's ends in Comintern politics. He was an early and notorious anti-Trotskyist. He returned to the U.S. in 1928 and went immediately into the top leadership of the Communist Party, but was recalled to Moscow in 1929.

**Lovestone faction**: Following the death of Charles E. Ruthenberg in the spring of 1927, Jay Lovestone became the leader of what had been the Ruthenberg-Pepper faction. It represented a right-wing tendency and was allied in Comintern politics with

Bukharin, who was then in a bloc with Stalin.

When Stalin turned on his rightist allies in 1929, Lovestone was deposed as head of the U.S. party and then expelled. The Lovestone group maintained an independent organizational existence until the outbreak of World War II, when it disbanded. Lovestone himself entered the service of the U.S. labor bureaucracy as an anticommunist expert. He is currently chief advisor on foreign policy to AFL-CIO President George Meany.

**Foster faction**: In 1923 Foster and Cannon formed a caucus to oppose the policies of the Pepper-Ruthenberg leadership, which were damaging party work in the trade unions. This faction continued until 1925, when it split into the Foster faction and the Cannon faction. In 1927, the two factions formed a bloc against the Lovestone leadership. This continued until the fall of 1928, when the Foster faction realized that Cannon had been won over to the ideas of Trotsky. Thereupon the Fosterites broke the bloc and, to forestall any charges against themselves, brought charges of Trotskyism against the leaders of the Cannon faction before the party's Political Committee.

**William Z. Foster** (1881–1961) was the most important trade-union figure to join the U.S. Communist Party. In the pre–World War I years he had embraced the ideas of the French syndicalists, which on the American scene translated into working within the AFL and opposing all attempts to build rival or dual unions. He gained the support of the leaders of the Chicago Federation of Labor, who backed him in the famous organizing drive and strike in the stockyards in 1917 and in the massive but unsuccessful steel strike of 1919. He joined the Workers Party in the fall of 1921. His early stance within the party was for realistic work within the AFL unions and opposition to attempts to create dual unions; but after the American party was completely Stalinized, he went along with the party's dual-union adventures of the "third period" and all the subsequent twists and turns of the party line. He was kept from the party's top post until the end of World War II, when Stalin deposed Earl Browder as a scapegoat and elevated the long-suffering Foster in his place.

**William W. Weinstone** was a leader in the Ruthenberg-Pepper faction. He became New York district secretary after his faction had been given the party leadership as a result of Comintern intervention, but distinguished himself by a conciliatory attitude toward factional opponents. In 1926–1927 he developed a position favoring the end of chronic factionalism in the party and creation of a collective leadership. He formed a bloc with the Cannon faction and the Foster faction to oppose Lovestone's complete takeover of the party apparatus. After Lovestone, with Moscow backing, triumphed at the September 1927 party convention, Weinstone abandoned his oppositional role and returned to the Lovestone faction; in return he was allowed to retain his post as New York district secretary.

**Moissaye J. Olgin** was editor of the Jewish newspaper *Freiheit* and a leader in the Jewish Federation, the Yiddish-speaking units of the party. He had been a close associate and follower of Ludwig Lore, whom Pepper had driven out of the party in 1925 with accusations of Trotskyism. In the 1930s, Olgin became the CP specialist on Trotskyism, writing such works as *Trotskyism, Counterrevolution in Disguise*.

**Alexander Trachtenberg,** like Olgin and Kruse, remained in the Socialist Party in 1919 when the left wing was expelled, only to leave it in 1921 with a belated left splitoff.

**William F. Kruse** was sent by the U.S. party to the Lenin school in Moscow, where he served as Ruthenberg's unofficial ambassador and source of inside information. He was district organizer in Chicago at the time of Lovestone's expulsion in 1929 and was himself expelled for refusing to denounce Lovestone; he did not, however, become active in Lovestone's independent organization.

## Chapter 3
### The fifth year of the Russian Revolution

This speech was first printed as a pamphlet by the Workers Party in 1923; it was published in the magazine *Fourth International,* November 1942, and it was issued as a pamphlet by Pioneer Publishers in March 1944.

**Genoa Conference**: In April and May of 1922, representatives of thirty-four nations met in Genoa, Italy, in an attempt to alleviate the dislocation of Europe's economy and commerce.

This was the first postwar diplomatic conference at which representatives from the Soviet Union and Germany were permitted by the victorious allies of World War I. Policy divergences between Britain and France prevented the conference from taking any important measures. However, in the course of the gathering, the Soviet and German delegates met in the nearby town of Rapallo and signed an important pact there regarding Soviet-German relations. The Genoa Conference was important for the USSR as a step towards regularizing its diplomatic position and towards later recognition by the capitalist nations.

**David Lloyd George** (1863–1945) was a British politician noted for his flamboyance and demagogy. A member of the Liberal Party from Wales, he was successively chancellor of the exchequer, munitions minister, and war minister. In 1916 he became prime minister and later headed the British delegation to the peace conference at Versailles. In 1922, when his political popularity was waning, he engineered the invitation of the Soviet Union and Germany to the Genoa Conference in the hope that a diplomatic success there would restore his political fortunes in Britain. His government fell later in 1922.

**Trial of the SRs**: Founded at the beginning of the century, the Social Revolutionary Party openly embraced terrorism as a principal tactic in the fight against Czarism. The party split in 1917, the left wing entering a coalition with the Bolsheviks to form the Soviet government in October. But they opposed signing the Brest-Litovsk peace treaty with Germany and quit the government in protest. They then tried to provoke a resumption of hostilities with Germany by encouraging military clashes in the Ukraine and by assassinating the German ambassador in Moscow. They also tried to overthrow the Bolsheviks through a campaign of assassination and insurrection. The Bolshevik leaders Mikhail Uritsky and V. Volodarsky were assassinated, and Lenin was shot, but survived. Two attempts were made to blow up Trotsky's military train. The SR military uprisings in Moscow and the provincial centers were quickly put down, except for that in Yaroslavl, which lasted several weeks. The SRs split into numerous factions; some renounced the use of terror against the Soviet regime, and their deputies were reinstated in the soviets; others set up governments in areas held by the

White Guards and engaged in terrorist conspiracies in areas held by the Soviets.

In June 1922, thirty-four members of the SR Party were tried on charges of terrorism and conspiracy against the Soviet government. The 1922 trial stands in dramatic contrast to the frame-up trials of the Stalin era. In prison, the defendants were accorded the rights and privileges of political prisoners, and they were allowed to defend their views freely in the courtroom. The Second International sent eminent foreign counsel to assist in their legal defense. Emile Vandervelde, long the president of the Second International and himself a lawyer and former minister of justice in the Belgian government, accompanied by Artur Wauters, a Belgian social democratic colleague, and the German social democrat Kurt Rosenfeld, went to Moscow to aid the defense. They held private interviews and conferences with their clients.

After a two-month trial, fully covered by the international press, all but a few of the defendants were found guilty. Fourteen were given suspended death sentences; the others, varying terms of imprisonment.

**The King of Egypt**: In 1922, archaeologists discovered the tomb and mummy of Tut-ankh-amen, dead for 3,271 years. The newspapers sensationalized the find, and the public was fascinated by the story of "King Tut."

**NEP** stood for **New Economic Policy.** This was a forced retreat on the economic front adopted by the Soviet government at the end of the civil war because of the USSR's economic paralysis. In place of the stringent controls of the period of "war communism," private trading in the domestic economy and consumer goods production were allowed; provision was also made for some foreign investment on a concession basis.

**Nepmen** was a popular term for traders, merchants, and others who took advantage of the opportunities for profitmaking under the NEP.

**Seval Zimmand** (1891–1967) was born in Rumania and came to the U.S. in 1913. He was a factory worker, a teacher, and finally a prominent liberal journalist. He was a correspondent for *The New York Times* and *Survey Graphic* magazine in the Far East. In 1922–1923 he was a special correspondent for the *New York Evening Post* in Europe and the Soviet Union. He wrote *Modern Social Movements* (1921), *The Open Shop Drive* (1922), and *State Capitalism in Russia* (1926). In his later years he was active in the public health field and wrote principally about issues related to that.

**Gregory Y. Zinoviev** (1883–1936) was Lenin's closest collaborator in the decade preceding 1917, and was chairman of the Comintern from its founding in 1919 until 1926. Following Lenin's death, Zinoviev, Kamenev, and Stalin formed the ruling bloc (the "troika"). Breaking with Stalin in 1926, Zinoviev and Kamenev united with Trotsky's Left Opposition to form the United Opposition. In 1928, when the Oppositionists were expelled from the party, Zinoviev recanted and was readmitted to the party. He was again expelled in 1932 and again capitulated; in 1934 he was again expelled and imprisoned. In 1936 he "confessed" at the first big Moscow frame-up trial and was executed.

**Alexei I. Rykov** (1881–1938) was an Old Bolshevik leader who succeeded Lenin as premier (chairman of the Council of People's Commissars). With Bukharin he led the right-wing tendency in the party in the NEP period. When Stalin broke with the right wing in 1929, Bukharin was dismissed from the Politburo and Rykov was warned; both then recanted. Rykov was removed from the post of premier at the end of 1930. He was a defendant in the third great Moscow frame-up trial in March 1938; he "confessed" and was executed.

**West Virginia**: A nationwide strike of coal miners was called by the United Mine Workers in April 1922. Though not unionized, the West Virginia miners struck in solidarity and in hopes of winning union recognition. However, when the UMW settled the strike in August, no provision was made for the West Virginia miners. The strike continued, despite hunger, evictions from company housing, and brutal repression by the coal and iron police, company-hired thugs, and the National Guard. But the miners were ultimately defeated.

**General Semyon N. Budenny** (1883–1973) won fame in the civil war as a cavalry commander and was one of the few leading military figures to escape execution or imprisonment in Stalinist purges.

**The Internationale** is the anthem of the working-class movement. Written in France by the Communard Eugene Pottier, it was translated and adopted by all sections of the socialist movement. It was similarly adopted by the communist movement upon the formation of the Third International and was the official anthem of the USSR until 1944, when Stalin replaced it with the conventionally nationalistic *Hymn of the Soviet Union.*

The **November Revolution** is the October Revolution of 1917. At that time, Russia still used the older, Julian calendar, which had been abandoned in Western Europe between the sixteenth and eighteenth centuries in favor of the Gregorian calendar. The Soviet government adopted the Gregorian calendar, making anniversaries of prerevolutionary dates fall thirteen days later.

**Recognition of the USSR**: Although the other world powers gradually accorded diplomatic recognition to the Soviet Union, the United States refused to do so until 1933.

## Chapter 4
### The twenty-fifth anniversary of the Russian Revolution

This speech was printed in *The Militant,* November 21, 1942, and as a Pioneer Publishers pamphlet in March 1944.

The **Black Hundreds** was the popular name for the Association of the Russian People and the Association to Combat Revolution. These were gangs of reactionaries and "patriotic" hoodlums, organized with the Czarist government's clandestine backing, which specialized in such actions as anti-Semitic pogroms.

The **White Guards** was the name that, by extension, came to cover all the reactionary or counterrevolutionary forces in the civil war in the Soviet Union. It derived from the White Guard organized in Finland in 1918 to destroy the revolutionary forces there. White was the color associated with monarchy since the French Revolution; it was the color of the Bourbon flag.

**Axis Powers** was the name applied before and during World War II to the alliance of Germany, Italy, and Japan. It originated in the 1936 declaration of a Rome-Berlin "axis" against communism; it was later extended to include Japan when that country signed the Anti-Comintern Pact.

**Central Powers** was the name given to the Quadruple Alliance of Germany, Austria-Hungary, Bulgaria, and Turkey during World War I. The name refers to Germany and Austria's central geographic position within Europe.

## Chapter 5
## The AFL and the start of the CIO

This speech was first printed in *The New Militant,* December 14, 1935.

**Craft unions**: The AFL was overwhelmingly an organization of craft unions, i.e., workers organized by their particular skills into unions of painters, or machinists, or carpenters, etc. This outmoded form of organization presented an insurmountable barrier to organizing modern industry, for the craft-union leaders demanded that the workers in a factory or enterprise be split up into their appropriate and separate craft unions. Industrial unionism, by contrast, meant organizing all the workers of a single factory or enterprise in a single union, regardless of their distinct jobs or skills.

The **National Recovery Administration (NRA),** set up by the National Industrial Recovery Act of 1933, was the New Deal's principal measure against the depression. It suspended antitrust laws in favor of codes, adopted by the various branches of industry and given government sanction, which fixed standards and eliminated "unfair" competition. It gave labor merely a vaguely worded clause—the famous 7(A)—stating employees' right to bargain collectively through representatives of their own choosing. Militant workers, however, seized upon this clause and in attempting to apply it engaged in a nationwide rash of strikes, most of which were defeated by the employers and the government after having been debilitated and sold out by the AFL craft-union leaders.

**Daniel J. Tobin** (1875–1955) was president of the International Brotherhood of Teamsters prior to World War II. He tried to break the strikes of Teamsters Local 574 in Minneapolis in 1934 because they were led by communists (i.e., Trotskyists) and because they violated craft principles by taking the "inside" men (warehousemen) into the union. After the strikes were won, Tobin expelled Local 574 "for ninety-nine years," and set up a rival local in an attempt to destroy it. This also failed, and 574 was finally readmitted into the Teamsters union, with the number 544.

**July strike**: There were two great strikes in the battle to organize the truck drivers in Minneapolis in 1934, the first in May, the second in July. The blast against Local 574 took the form of an editorial by Tobin in the *Teamsters' Journal,* the union's national publication; it was printed by the employers as a paid advertisement in the Minneapolis newspapers on July 7, 1934.

**William Green** (1873–1952) was president of the American Federation of Labor from the death of Gompers in 1924 until his own death in 1952.

The **Citizens Alliance** was the employers' antiunion and strikebreaking organization, which had kept Minneapolis an open-shop city until 1934. In the May Teamsters' strike of that year, it organized a "citizens' army" of hundreds of deputized supporters to reinforce the police in a battle with the strikers at the city's main market. The deputies and cops were decisively beaten and driven off the streets. After the success of the 1934 strikes, the Citizens Alliance was never able to regain the dominant position it had formerly occupied.

**John L. Lewis** (1880–1969) was president of the United Mine Workers from 1920 until his death. He headed the minority in the AFL executive council in the early 1930s which favored the industrial form of unionism, and he was the principal founder and leader of the Committee for Industrial Organization (later the Congress of Industrial Organizations) from its beginning in 1935 until 1940, when he resigned.

**Sidney Hillman** (1887–1946) was president of the Amalgamated Clothing Workers and the second figure in the leadership of the CIO.

**William L. Hutcheson** (1874–1953) was president of the AFL Brotherhood of Carpenters and Joiners. An arch-conservative, he personified craft hatred of industrial unionism, and it seemed quite natural that at the 1935 AFL convention he and Lewis came to blows during the debate on industrial unionism.

**Meyer Lewis** was the special emissary of AFL President

Green who was sent to Minneapolis in 1935 to raise a red scare against Local 574. Teamsters President Tobin had expelled 574 and set up an officially approved Local 500 in Minneapolis. Then, with great fanfare, Green announced that the AFL was beginning a national campaign to purge the labor movement of communism and that it would begin in Minneapolis, where he was sending Meyer Lewis. Despite the red scare and weeks of physical violence by imported goon squads against the leaders and members of "Red 574," the attempt to break the union failed.

**David Dubinsky** (1892–) was president of the International Ladies Garment Workers Union from 1932; he was an important figure in the forming of the CIO.

**Resignation of Lewis**: Shortly after the 1935 AFL convention in Atlantic City, which voted down proposals for a campaign of organizing industrial unions, John L. Lewis and seven other presidents of AFL unions met and formed the Committee for Industrial Organization. AFL President Green and a majority of the AFL executive council demanded the immediate dissolution of the CIO. Lewis refused and, in a dramatic move, resigned from the AFL council.

The **National Civic Federation** was dedicated to the preaching and practice of class collaboration. It was founded in 1901 after a series of conferences on arbitration and conciliation of labor disputes. It was composed of leading industrialists and financiers, top AFL labor bureaucrats, and representatives of the "general public," such as ex-President Grover Cleveland and steel magnate and philanthropist Andrew Carnegie. Long denounced by socialists and militants as a softening-up chamber for labor leaders and the citadel of sellouts, it was so openly antilabor by 1935 that Matthew Woll, president of the AFL Photo-Engravers Union, was forced by the AFL convention to resign as acting president of the National Civic Federation, though the point was made that Gompers had been its vice-president and many other top labor leaders had been proud members.

**The Communists left the AFL**: In 1928, the Stalinists decreed the so-called third period, in which capitalism was supposedly on the point of collapse. The Communist parties of the world went into a frenzy of ultraleft activity that was to last until the policy was abandoned for the People's Front line in 1935. In the trade-union field, the Comintern "third period" line was one of building "revolutionary" or dual unions. In the U.S., this meant setting up CP-controlled unions of miners, textile workers, garment workers, maritime workers, etc. Though these dual unions almost invariably remained small and ineffective, their creation involved the withdrawal and isolation of Communists and their sympathizers from the existing AFL unions; in addition, it meant that the mass of the unionized workers were abandoned to the control and misleadership of the AFL bureaucrats.

## Chapter 6
## Sixty years of American radicalism

This speech was first printed in the magazine *International Socialist Review*, Winter 1960; it was reprinted in the same publication, February 1971.

**Socialist Party split of 1919**: The right wing split the party by means of wholesale expulsions of those adhering to the left; in a period of six months, two-thirds of the membership was expelled or suspended. Even so, when the right wing convened the SP convention in Chicago, August 30, 1919, it had to call in police to help eject delegates adhering to the left. For the next several days, there were walkouts by delegates disgusted with the convention's undemocratic procedures. The expelled left-wingers held their own convention and constituted themselves the Communist Labor Party.

**Referendum of 1919**: Before the split in the Socialist Party, a referendum on a proposal by the left wing to quit the Second International and affiliate with the Third or Communist International had been carried by a vote of more than ten to one. In other SP referendums in the spring of 1919, the left wing won on its proposal for a new national executive committee and won twelve of the fifteen seats on that committee.

The **Palmer Raids** were so called after Democratic Attorney General A. Mitchell Palmer. The post-World War I repression culminated in a series of nationwide raids and mass arrests of radicals of all tendencies early in January 1920. Thousands were jailed and hundreds of foreign-born radicals were deported. Civil liberties and due process of law were completely disregarded by federal and local authorities. The newly formed Communist movement was driven into *de facto* illegality and had to begin underground organizations. The repression and the officially induced hysteria against "reds" continued until the Republican administration of Warren G. Harding took office in 1921, when it slowed down and gradually tapered off.

The **stock-market crash** of October-November 1929 heralded the beginning of the great depression of the 1930s.

**John Gates** joined the Young Communist League in 1931. He became a party activist and functionary and received a five-year prison sentence in the 1949 Smith Act trial. He was editor of the *Daily Worker,* the Communist Party newspaper, at the time of Khrushchev's revelations of Stalin's crimes in 1956. He then formed a neo-Browderite faction, calling for party reform and making some criticisms of the Soviet Union. The faction melted away as members quit the party, and he was expelled in 1957. In 1958 he wrote *The Story of an American Communist* (foreword by Earl Browder).

**Alfred M. Landon** (1887–) was the Kansas governor who was the Republican candidate for president in 1936. He was overwhelmingly defeated by Franklin D. Roosevelt's second-term bid.

**Julius A. Wayland** (1854–1913) was a publisher and (until 1904) editor of the *Appeal to Reason,* the most popular American socialist paper in the pre–World War I era. Wayland became a socialist in 1890; he founded the *Appeal to Reason* in 1895 in Kansas City and moved it the next year to Girard, Kansas, where it was published thereafter.

The **"right-to-work" laws** were antilabor laws banning any form of union shop or closed shop. Under pressure from employers' lobbies, state legislatures began passing them in 1944; by 1958 they were on the statute books of nineteen states. As the employers' propaganda machine went into high gear in its campaign for such laws in the late 1950s, the laws were falsely and demagogically dubbed "right-to-work" legislation. In the 1958 elections this legislation was on the ballot in referendum form in six states. It was defeated in five, including the key industrial state of Ohio, where an intensive campaign involving unionists at a local-union level had been waged against the laws.

The **Landrum-Griffin Act** was a federal antilabor law passed in 1959, extending and amplifying the government regulation and interference in trade unions instituted by the Taft-Hartley Act. It is sometimes referred to as the Kennedy-Landrum-Griffin Act, because John F. Kennedy, then a senator, played the major role in securing its passage.

**Citations from Trotsky**: Both quotations are from *Germany, the Key to the International Situation* (November 26, 1931), first published in the U.S. in 1932. It has been reprinted in *The Struggle Against Fascism in Germany* (Pathfinder Press, 1971).

## Chapter 7
## The end of the Comintern

This speech was first printed in *The Militant,* June 12, 1943; it was published as a pamphlet by Pioneer Publishers in September 1943.

The **Voorhis Act,** passed by Congress in 1940, placed penalties on political parties affiliated to international organizations.

**Zimmerwald** and **Kienthal,** both villages in Switzerland, were the scene of two antiwar conferences during World War I. The Zimmerwald Conference, on September 15, 1915, brought together thirty-eight delegates from left-wing social democratic parties or groups, including Lenin and Trotsky. It issued the famous Zimmerwald Manifesto, drawn up by Trotsky, opposing the imperialist war. A still more strongly antiwar conference, which condemned the betrayal of the Second International, was held at Kienthal on April 16, 1916. The Zimmerwald movement led to the formation of the Third International. Lenin, Trotsky, and a handful of delegates from Zimmerwald were able to make the final break with the Second International and see the necessity for the Third.

The **Criticism of the Draft Program of the Comintern** appears under the title "The Draft Program of the Communist International: A Criticism of Fundamentals," in Leon Trotsky, *The Third International After Lenin,* Pathfinder Press, 1970.

The **London Bureau** was a loose international association of centrist parties in the 1930s which were not affiliated to either the Second or the Third International, but were opposed to the formation of a Fourth International. Among its components were the Independent Labour Party of Great Britain, the POUM of Spain, the SAP of Germany, and the PSOP of France.

**GPU murder machine**: Although the Soviet secret police underwent several changes of name (GPU, OGPU, NKVD, and, after Stalin's death, MVD), the name which persisted in general usage was the original GPU. In addition to its activities within the USSR, it carried out missions such as assassinations and kidnappings of anti-Stalinists in other countries.

## Chapter 8
## The downfall of Browder

Excerpts from this speech were printed in *The Militant,* September 8, 1945.

**Browder . . . J.P. Morgan**: Earl Browder (1891–) was elevated to the post of general secretary of the U.S. Communist Party by Stalin's directive in 1930; he was similarly deposed in 1945 and was expelled from the party in 1946. Except for his first few years in office (the end of the ultraleft "third period") and the brief interlude of the Stalin-Hitler pact, his regime coincided with those years in which the Communist Party abandoned the class struggle and engaged in blatant class collaboration of the People's Front variety. During the World War II alliance of the U.S. and the Soviet Union, Browder ardently supported U.S. imperialism and publicly urged that the wartime class collaboration continue after the war ended. One of his gestures to prove the Communists' devotion to class peace was his public offer to shake hands with J.P. Morgan, the multibillionaire financier and world-famous personification of U.S. capitalism.

**From Moscow via Paris**: When Stalin decided to dump Browder, the device he utilized was to have Jacques Duclos, a leader of the French Communist Party, write an article in the French CP press denouncing the leader of the American Communists for excessive class collaboration. The Duclos article, entitled "On the Dissolution of the Communist Party of the U.S.," was translated and printed in the *Daily Worker,* the American Communist paper, on May 24, 1945, whereupon Browder went immediately into eclipse.

**Communist Political Association** was the name adopted by the American Communist Party when it dissolved itself as a party on May 20, 1944. The move was designed to achieve on a national scale what Stalin's dissolution of the Comintern the previous year had aimed at internationally, that is, to give assurance to the "democratic" capitalist allies that Stalinism represented no revolutionary danger.

**Robert Minor** (1884–1952) was a cartoonist and an anarchist who joined the Communist Party in its early days. Though a prominent figurehead, he was never politically important in the top party circles. After the party's degeneration, he slavishly supported whomever Stalin designated to head the American party.

**Eugene Dennis,** who later became Communist Party general secretary, was one of the eleven leaders jailed following the 1949 Smith Act trial.

**John Williamson** was one of the eleven Communist Party leaders jailed after the 1949 Smith Act trial.

**Benjamin J. Davis** (d. 1964) was a prominent black leader in the Communist Party. He was elected to the New York city council on the Communist Party ticket in 1943. Before the expiration of his first term in 1945, a deal was made with Tammany Hall (the name of the New York County Democratic Party machine) by which Davis was to receive the Democratic Party nomination. Davis registered as a Democrat and Tammany officials announced his nomination at a public rally; later in the campaign, however, growing opposition from red-baiting elements inside the Democratic machine persuaded Tammany to withdraw the nomination. Nevertheless, Davis was reelected and served a second term. Then a reactionary campaign to end proportional representation in city elections was successful, and Davis was defeated in the 1949 election. He was then on trial under the Smith Act. Convicted with ten other party leaders, he was given a five-year sentence. In prison he wrote an autobiography, *Communist Councilman From Harlem,* in which he bitterly criticized himself and his close friend and comrade Peter V. Cacchione, the Communist councilman from Brooklyn, for having voted with the Democrats in the council to institute a city sales tax and to extend the term of office from two to four years, and for having abandoned the fight to force an end to the Jim Crow exclusion of blacks from Stuyvesant Town, the huge housing project built with state and city assistance by the Metropolitan Life Insurance Company. He ascribed his and Cacchione's errors to the line imposed by Browder.

## Chapter 9
## The trial of the Stalinist leaders

This speech was first printed in *The Militant*, February 14, 1949.

**Farrell Dobbs,** now National Secretary of the Socialist Workers Party, was reporting the Smith Act trial of the eleven Communist Party leaders from the courtroom for *The Militant*. He had spoken before Cannon at this meeting. Dobbs, like Cannon, was one of the eighteen SWP leaders and truck drivers' union officials convicted in the first Smith Act trial in Minneapolis in 1941.

**Moyer and Haywood trial**: On December 30, 1905, Frank Steunenberg, an ex-governor of Idaho, was killed by a bomb explosion. In March 1906, officials in Denver, Colorado, secretly arrested William D. Haywood, leader of the IWW and the Western Federation of Miners, Charles H. Moyer, president of the WFM, and George Pettibone, WFM activist. They were shoved onto a special train and taken to Idaho, thus preventing any appeal against extradition. This "legal" kidnapping and the murder charges placed against the trio led to one of the greatest mass defense campaigns in U.S. labor history. Debs embarked on a national speaking tour for the defense and wrote his famous "Arouse Ye Slaves" in the *Appeal to Reason,* in which he recalled the frame-up and hanging of the Haymarket martyrs twenty years earlier and declared: "If they attempt to murder Moyer, Haywood and their brothers, a million revolutionists, at least, will meet them with guns." The defendants were tried separately, with Haywood first. Clarence Darrow, the defense attorney, exposed the case as a frame-up by the Mineowners Association and the Pinkerton Detective Agency. In August 1907, the jury found Haywood not guilty; the trials and acquittals of the other two defendants were mere formalities.

**Ettor and Giovannitti**: Joseph Ettor, an IWW organizer, and

Arturo Giovannitti, poet and editor of an Italian socialist paper in New York, became the outstanding leaders of the 1912 strike of textile workers in Lawrence, Massachusetts. Annie LoPizzo, a striker, was shot dead when police and National Guardsmen broke up a picketing demonstration. Frame-up charges of murder were then brought against Ettor, Giovannitti, and Joseph Caruso, a rank-and-file striker. The three were held in prison without trial until seven months after the strike was won. The IWW launched a national defense campaign that was marked by numerous protests and solidarity strikes. On November 23, 1912, all three were found not guilty.

**Mooney and Billings**: Thomas J. Mooney was the outstanding left-wing labor leader in San Francisco in the pre–World War I period. Warren K. Billings was a young left-winger in the same union movement. Both opposed the impending U.S. entry into the war. On July 22, 1916, "Preparedness Day," a day of military parades and propaganda to whip up public sentiment for entering the war, a bomb exploded in downtown San Francisco, killing six people. Frame-up charges based on faked evidence and wholesale perjury were brought against Mooney and Billings. Mooney was sentenced to death, Billings to life imprisonment. International protests, especially by the Bolsheviks in Russia, led to a commutation of the death sentence. Though the perjured evidence was refuted in detail as the years passed, and though the labor movement demanded the prisoners' release, it was not until 1939 that Mooney was pardoned; Billings was released some months later.

The **IWW war trial** was a mass trial of 101 leaders and members of the IWW in Chicago in 1920. This was the biggest of the many trials of IWW members.

**Eugene V. Debs** (1855–1926) was a railroad worker, a militant union leader and founder of the American Railway Union jailed for his leadership of the Pullman strike. He became a socialist in prison and was a founder of the Socialist Party. He was the most popular socialist leader in U.S. history; he got nearly a million votes when he campaigned for president in 1912. He was jailed under the Espionage Act during World War I for his antiwar speeches. When the war was over, a growing movement demanded amnesty for him and other political prisoners. Debs ran for president in 1920 from his cell in the federal prison in Atlanta. President Harding acceded to the amnesty demands and released Debs on December 25, 1921.

**Sacco and Vanzetti** were the victims of the post–World War I anti-red campaign, and are among American radicalism's most famous martyrs. Niccolo Sacco (1891–1927), a minor leader in a shoe workers' strike in 1918, had been active in the defense campaign for Ettor and Giovannitti. Bartolomeo Vanzetti (1888–1927) had organized and led a long strike in a rope mill, but had been blacklisted in the industry and, at the time of his arrest, earned his living peddling fish. The two were friends and members of an anarchist group. In May 1920, while organizing a meeting to protest the killing in the Department of Justice prison in New York of Andrea Salsedo, an Italian printer "suspected of radicalism," they were arrested by police in Brockton, Massachusetts, and framed up on charges of payroll robbery and murder. At the trial, the judge did not conceal his hatred of them as immigrants, "slackers," and anarchists. Their death sentences aroused worldwide protests, which managed to stave off their execution for a number of years. They were finally electrocuted on August 22, 1927.

**McNamara and Schmidt** were labor prisoners serving life sentences in the *Los Angeles Times* bombing case of 1910. John J. McNamara, secretary-treasurer of the AFL Bridge and Structural Iron Workers Union, and his brother, James B. McNamara, had been convicted in the celebrated trial, with the former receiving a life sentence. Three years later, Matthew Schmidt and David Kaplan, who had been indicted with the McNamaras but had evaded arrest, were caught. Schmidt received a life sentence, Kaplan a lesser sentence.

**Centralia prisoners**: Wartime strikes of the IWW-led lumberjacks in the Northwest were smashed with unprecedented ferocity. In 1918 the IWW was still able to maintain an open headquarters and meeting hall only in the bigger towns in the lumbering area, like Centralia, Washington. But in the spring of 1918, a patriotic parade in Centralia turned into an organized raid on the IWW hall. The hall was wrecked, and the Wobblies found there were beaten unconscious. A year later the IWW felt strong enough to open another hall in Centralia. On Armistice Day (November 11) in 1919, the American Legion and Chamber of Commerce organized another patriotic parade and routed it to pass the new IWW hall. When the "patriots" attacked the hall, they were met by gunfire and four of the assailants were killed and several wounded. All Wobblies suspected of defending the hall were arrested. The next night one of them, Wesley Everest, was turned over to a mob of Legionnaires and businessmen who castrated him and then hanged him from a railroad bridge. Seven others were convicted of second-degree murder and sent to Walla Walla prison with sentences ranging from twenty-five to forty years.

**James Kutcher,** a member of the Newark, New Jersey, branch of the Socialist Workers Party who was drafted into the infantry during World War II, lost both legs in Italy. He learned to walk on artificial legs and after the war obtained a clerical job in the Veterans Administration office in Newark. During the cold war the Attorney General issued a "subversive list" which included the SWP, and Kutcher was fired for his open and avowed membership in that party. He fought the firing on constitutional grounds through all the boards set up for administering the "loyalty purge" and into the federal courts. In the eight years that the case lasted, from its beginning in 1948, Kutcher and the defense committee created to aid him received broad support from labor, liberal, and civil rights organizations, as well as from numerous individuals—despite opposition in the first five years of the case from the Communist Party, which maintained that it was not a legitimate civil liberties issue because no Trotskyist was deserving of any sympathy or support from progressive-minded people. The case was finally won in 1956, and Kutcher was reinstated in his job with back pay. In the course of this fight, Kutcher was involved in two other cases. First, the government tried to evict his elderly parents, with whom he lived, from a federally financed housing project on the grounds that no member of a family in such housing could be a "subversive." This case was also won in the courts, and subsequently Congress allowed the law to lapse. Then, just prior to Christmas in 1955, the Veterans Administration announced that it was cancelling

Kutcher's disability pension because of his SWP membership. This evoked a tremendous public protest, and after a widely publicized administrative hearing, the VA backed down and restored his pension. In 1953 Kutcher wrote a book entitled *The Case of the Legless Veteran.*

## Chapter 10
## The end of the Stalin cult

This speech was printed in *The Militant,* March 26, 1956.

**John Foster Dulles** (1888–1959) was secretary of state in the Eisenhower administration.

**East German workers**: In June 1953, three months after Stalin's death, a spontaneous walkout of construction workers in East Berlin, whose workloads had been arbitrarily increased, snowballed into a general strike and demonstrations throughout East Germany. Street battles with the police showed that East German officials were unable to defeat the uprising, and Soviet troops and tanks were called in. Though these were able to turn the tide, strikes continued in various parts of the country late into July.

**Vorkuta,** located in a coal-rich area of Siberia, is the center of a complex of forced-labor camps run by the Soviet secret police. In July 1953 a great wave of strikes began in the camps and mines there and spread as far as the camps of Central Asia and Pacific Siberia.

## Chapter 11
## Khrushchev's report to the Twentieth Congress

This speech was printed in *The Militant,* July 2, 1956, and in the pamphlet, *The Twentieth Congress and World Trotskyism,* New Park Publishers, Ltd., London, February 1957.

**I.F. Stone** was formerly a Washington reporter and columnist for *The Nation* and the newspaper *PM* and its short-lived successors, the *New York Star* and the *Daily Compass.* In 1953 he launched *I.F. Stone's Weekly* which, although issued in small newsletter format, soon wielded considerable influence in left and liberal circles and commanded respect from those in the field of journalism.

## Chapter 12
## Leon Trotsky: To the memory of the Old Man

This speech was printed in *Socialist Appeal,* September 7, 1940, and as a pamphlet by Pioneer Publishers the same year. It was reprinted in Joseph Hansen (ed.), *Leon Trotsky: The Man and His Work,* Merit Publishers (now Pathfinder Press), 1969.

The **Russian Bulletin** was the Russian-language *Bulletin Oppozitsii (Bulletin of the Opposition)* published under the editorship of Leon Sedov, Trotsky's son, from 1929 until his mysterious death in 1938. The *Bulletin* was started in Paris and then moved to Berlin. After Hitler suppressed it, it was moved back to Paris. At the end of 1939 it was moved to New York. Publication was suspended one year after Trotsky's death, in August 1941.

**Assault of May 24**: Around four a.m. on May 24, 1940, Trotsky's house in Coyoacan, a suburb of Mexico City, was attacked by a group of some twenty men dressed in police and army uniforms. Overpowering or tricking the young American guard on duty at the gate, they gained entry and immobilized the remainder of the guard by spraying their sleeping quarters with machine-gun fire. Then a squad entered the house and machine-gunned the room where Trotsky and Natalia slept. The couple had been awakened by the initial noise and were lying hidden in a corner of the dark room. They miraculously escaped injury, but Trotsky's young grandson, Seva, received a slight wound. The assailants left, throwing incendiary and explosive bombs to deter pursuit, taking the guard, Robert Sheldon Harte, with them. His body was found a month later on a farm which had been rented by known Stalinists. It was also learned that the well-known painter and Mexican Communist Party henchman David Alfaro Siqueiros had led the attack. Siqueiros, released on bail, left the country for several years; when he returned he was not prosecuted for the attack or murder.

**Dead body of Leon Trotsky**: After Trotsky's assassination in Coyoacan on August 21, 1940, the Socialist Workers Party sought to bring his body to New York for a funeral. U.S. government authorities, who during Trotsky's last exile had repeatedly rejected his requests to enter or visit the U.S., also refused to permit his body to be brought across the border.

## Chapter 13
## How we began and where we are going

This speech was first printed in *The Militant,* November 9, 1953.

**David Weiss, Cathy Gratta, and Joyce Cowley** were the Socialist Workers Party candidates respectively for mayor, president of the city council, and comptroller in the New York City elections of November 3, 1953.

**Haymarket martyrs**: The campaign initiated by the Federation of Organized Trades and Labor Unions (which later became the AFL) for the reduction of the working day to eight hours was to culminate in strikes and demonstrations on May 1, 1886. The action was particularly successful in Chicago, where 40,000 downed tools and marched on May Day. On the following day the number doubled. The employers hastened to take countermeasures. On May 3, police killed six pickets at the McCormick reaper plant, where 1,400 workers had been locked out for many months. Anarchists who were prominent in the union and eight-hour movements called a protest meeting in Haymarket Square the following night. The meeting was peaceful and the crowd was departing when suddenly a large troop of police attacked. Then a bomb was thrown (whether by a hater of the police or a hired provocateur is unknown). Police fired on the crowd, which attempted to defend itself. Seven police and four workers were killed. Immediately there were dragnet arrests of radicals and labor leaders. A trial was held. The court made no pretense of fairness, nor were the defendants linked to the bombing; it sufficed to show that their words or writings could indirectly have encouraged the unknown bomber. August Spies, Albert Parsons, Adolph Fischer, and George Engel were hanged on November 11, 1887. Louis Lingg cheated the gallows by committing suicide the day before; Oscar Neebe, Samuel Fielden, and Michael Schwab were imprisoned until 1893, when Illinois Governor John P. Altgeld pardoned them. Altgeld's pardon message declared that a thorough investigation showed that none of those tried were guilty.

**Haywood, St. John and Frank Little**: Though William D. ("Big Bill") Haywood was the leading public spokesman of the Industrial Workers of the World, secretary-treasurer Vincent St. John was the main organizational leader. Frank Little, lynched in Butte, Montana, on August 1, 1917, was a member of the IWW general executive board.

## Chapter 14
## How to put an end to imperialist war

This speech was first printed in *The Militant,* November 7, 1942.

**Wall Street . . . Russian Revolution**: In August 1918, U.S. troops were sent to northern Russia, where, along with British forces, they occupied Murmansk and Archangel. At the same time U.S. troops stationed in the Philippine Islands were sent to Siberia, where, along with Japanese forces, they occupied Vladivostok and took over the Trans-Siberian railway. U.S. troops were withdrawn early in 1920. Not only had the intervention by fourteen capitalist nations failed to overthrow the Bolsheviks, but their own troops had been infected with the revolutionary "virus," and there were a number of instances of mutiny and mutinous behavior, including the case in northern Russia of a U.S. army company refusing to return to the line.

**Bonus Army**: In the depression year 1932, World War I veterans marched on Washington demanding immediate payment of their promised bonus, that is, their adjusted compensation insurance benefits. They set up camps and built shanties on vacant land and demonstrated and lobbied congressmen. Finally, President Herbert Hoover ordered them removed. Army troops, commanded by General Douglas MacArthur, drove them out and burned down their shantytowns.

## Chapter 15
## Youth and foreign policy

This speech was first printed in the magazine *Fourth International,* May–June 1951.

**Differences of Truman and MacArthur**: On April 4, 1951, in the midst of the Korean War, President Truman fired General MacArthur on the grounds of insubordination and pursuit of policies which would lead to the outbreak of World War III. This sudden dismissal of the commanding general of the U.S. forces in Korea had been preceded by the so-called great debate over foreign policy in Congress and in the press. Launched by the Republican Party leaders, the "great debate" expressed their tactical differences with the Truman administration on diplomatic-military policy. It concerned such matters as military priorities in Asia versus commitments in Europe, limiting the use of ground forces on the Asian mainland, and greater dependence on air and naval power.

Ex-President **Herbert Hoover** (1874–1964), the Republican Party's principal elder statesman, had spoken out on December 20, 1950, a week before the "great debate" officially began in the new Congress. He questioned the feasibility of full U.S. troop commitments to Europe when such a great effort was required in Asia; urged that the European capitalist nations be made to shoulder more of the military burden there; stressed greater use of air and naval power in Asia as opposed to a ground-force invasion of mainland China. His position soon came to be considered too "defensist" or not aggressive enough by the Eastern wing of the Republican Party, whose spokesman on foreign policy more and more became John Foster Dulles.

**Sidney Hook** was an ex-radical who became one of the most vocal of the liberal and social democratic supporters of the cold war and witch-hunt. He had written an article for the March 11, 1951, issue of *The New York Times Magazine* urging the U.S. government to engage in a propaganda offensive against procommunist and pro-Soviet forces throughout the world. Hook was a professor of philosophy at New York University, and the student organization sponsoring Cannon's talk had invited Hook to debate him. Hook refused, whereupon the college newspaper chided him and urged him to reconsider. The sponsors of the meeting announced that equal time was being reserved for Hook in case he appeared; however, he did not appear.

**Lewis Corey** was a writer on political and economic subjects and a professor. Under his original name, Louis C. Fraina, he had been an important figure in the Socialist left wing and the founding of the Communist Party. He dropped out of the party and political activity after he had been repeatedly tried on charges that were apparently false. Wild rumors about his alleged misdeeds circulated in left-wing circles for years. Reemerging into political activity in the 1930s as Lewis Corey, he became a supporter of the Lovestoneite organization and in 1940 repudiated Marxism. He died in 1953.

**James T. Farrell** (1904–), the novelist, had been a sympathizer of the Socialist Workers Party for some years, but during and after World War II he had gradually moved to a social democratic position.

Novelist **Upton Sinclair** (1878–1968) had been a member of the Socialist Party until 1917, when he quit in protest against the party's antiwar stand.

**Norman Thomas** (1884–1968) was the leader of the Socialist Party and six times its candidate for president after Debs.

**Thomas E. Dewey** (1902–1971) was then governor of New York; he had been the Republican candidate for president in the 1948 election. He had made a speech calling for preparation for all-out war, the building of a 100-division army, and the adoption of a "Spartan course" domestically in order to win the coming "struggle for survival," that is, World War III.

**Aneurin Bevan** (1897–1960), leader of the left wing in the British Labour Party and minister of labour in the government of Clement Attlee, resigned along with two other ministers in protest against the policy being followed by the Labour government. In an April 24, 1951, speech in the House of Commons, Bevan denounced Britain's heavy military spending, which made impossible the expansion of social-welfare services, saying it was being forced on Attlee by Washington.

**Labor Mobilization Board**: Dissatisfaction with the attempt of the Wage Stabilization Board, set up by the Truman administration during the Korean War, to institute a wage freeze—while prices climbed steadily—led the board's labor members finally to walk out. The unions then convened a National Conference of Labor in Washington on March 21, 1951, to discuss the crisis. Despite brave speeches made there, the labor bureaucrats soon accepted posts on a National Advisory Board on Mobilization Policy newly set up by the administration. There the same dispute broke out again, as the big business figures who dominated the board refused to yield any concessions to the labor leaders.

## Chapter 16
## What it means to be a young revolutionist today

This speech has not been printed before.

**Rose Karsner** (1890–1968) was a leading member of the SWP. She was Cannon's wife and companion from 1924, and was present at this speech. Born Rose Greenberg in Rumania, she came to the U.S. when a child. In 1908 she joined the Socialist Party in New York City and was in the party's left wing. During World War I she was secretary of the magazine *The Masses*. She rallied to the Russian Revolution and was a founding member of the Communist Party. An early marriage to David Karsner, socialist journalist and biographer of Debs, ended in divorce. During the days of the famine in Russia, she worked in the national office of the Friends of Soviet Russia, which later became the Workers International Relief. She helped organize the International Labor Defense and was its assistant secretary. In 1928 she was expelled from the Communist Party for Trotskyism and became a founder of the first U.S. Trotskyist organization. The remainder of her life was linked with that movement, and she held many different posts in it. She was business manager of *The Militant* and manager of Pioneer Publishers; in the post–World War II period, she organized and was secretary of the American Committee for European Workers Relief. In 1952, at the age of sixty-two, she moved with Cannon from New York to Los Angeles, where she continued activity in the SWP to the extent that her health permitted. One of her last talks, on women's liberation, was given at the West Coast Vacation School in September 1966.

The **Center for the Study of Democratic Institutions** was the successor to the Fund for The Republic, an independent foundation which had been set up by the Ford Foundation. The Center afforded opportunity for study and scholarly discussion of social and political problems.

The **Triple Revolution document** (full title: "The Triple Revolution: An Appraisal of the Major U.S. Crises and Proposals for Action") saw mankind at a historic conjuncture as the result of a "cybernation revolution" in production, a "weaponry revolution" in the military field, and a "human rights revolution" in the consciousness of oppressed people throughout the world. This interacting combination made radical new solutions necessary and possible. The document was issued by an Ad Hoc Committee of some two dozen leftist and liberal figures, among them W.H. Ferry, head of the Center for the Study of Democratic Institutions. The Triple Revolution document was printed in full in the *International Socialist Review,* Summer 1964.

**The Dynamics of World Revolution Today** was the major political resolution adopted by the Reunification Congress of the Fourth International, June 1963. The resolution was printed in the *International Socialist Review,* Fall 1963.

## Chapter 17
### Before the Minneapolis trial

This speech has not been printed before.

**Those fainthearts . . . renegades**: From its beginning, a basic principle of the Trotskyist movement had been the defense of the Soviet Union in the coming war. After the signing of the Stalin-Hitler pact and the outbreak of World War II in 1939, a minority in the SWP, led by James Burnham, Max Shachtman, and Martin Abern, demanded the abandonment of this position. An intensive factional struggle ensued, and when the minority position was voted down in 1940, the minority split from the SWP and formed the now defunct Workers Party.

**If the Soviet Union really comes to catastrophe**: The German invasion of the USSR had begun on June 22, 1941, less than four months before the delivery of this speech. Yet in that brief period the military picture had indeed become ominous. All three army groups which Hitler had unleashed on the Soviet Union were making incredible advances. Army Group North had swept up through the former Baltic states and had already begun the siege of Leningrad, which would not be broken until January 1943. Army Group Center had taken Smolensk and driven on to the outskirts of Moscow. Five days after this speech, the Stalinist bureaucrats would begin their panicky evacuation of the capital to Kuibyshev. Army Group South, routing Budenny's armies and taking a half-million prisoners on the Dnieper, had occupied nearly the entire Ukraine and the coast of the Azov Sea.

**Scissorbill,** a slang term coined by members of the IWW, which entered into wider usage, is a derogatory term for a politically and culturally backward or stupid worker, such as one who is against unions. Usually a noun, it is also used sometimes as an adjective.

**Francis Biddle** was Roosevelt's Attorney General, under whose orders the indictments and prosecutions in the Minneapolis Labor Case were carried out.

**Albert Goldman** was one of the eighteen convicted in the Minneapolis Labor Case, the first use of the Smith Act. Goldman was a lawyer and acted as chief defense counsel. After the prison sentences had been served, Goldman and Felix Morrow organized a faction within the SWP which failed to gain a majority for its position. Goldman then left the SWP and some years later renounced the socialist program.

**Felix Morrow** was one of the eighteen prisoners in the Minneapolis Labor Case; at the time of the trial he was editor of *The Militant*.

**Vincent Raymond Dunne** (1890–1970) was one of the eighteen prisoners in the Minneapolis Labor Case. A founding member of the Trotskyist movement in the U.S., Dunne was a leader in the Minneapolis truck drivers' strikes. He remained active in the SWP in Minnesota until his death.

**Farrell Dobbs** was one of the eighteen prisoners in the Minneapolis Labor Case. A leader in the Minneapolis truck drivers' strikes, he later became an official of the AFL Teamsters union and directed the organization of over-the-road drivers and warehousemen in an eleven-state area of the Midwest. He then resigned his post and became labor secretary of the SWP; today he is the SWP National Secretary.

The **letter from Comrade Natalia Trotsky** to James P. Cannon was dated October 7, 1941.

## Chapter 18
### Speech on the way to prison

This speech was first printed in *The Militant*, January 8, 1944. It was also included in the pamphlet *Why We Are in Prison*, issued by Pioneer Publishers in 1944.

The **Supreme Court** stubbornly refused to hear the appeal of the eighteen Trotskyists, although they were the first people convicted under the Smith Act.

**Ben Hanford** (1859–1910) was a socialist leader and pamphleteer. Long an activist in the International Typographical Union, he was the Socialist Labor Party candidate for governor in New York in 1898. He ran for the same office in 1900 on the ticket of the Social Democratic Party (which the next year became the Socialist Party) and was Debs's running mate in the presidential campaigns of 1904 and 1908. Hanford created the legendary character Jimmie Higgins, the unsung but devoted rank-and-file activist who constituted the movement's strength.

### Chapter 19
### Sixtieth birthday speech

This speech was first printed in James P. Cannon, *Notebook of an Agitator,* New Park Publications, Ltd., London, 1958.

**Farleys or Baruchs**: James A. Farley (1888–) was the personification of the big-time capitalist political boss—the ward heeler magnified to a national scale. He had been Roosevelt's 1932 campaign manager and thereafter chairman of the Democratic National Committee. Bernard M. Baruch (1870–1965) was an American financier who was head of the War Industries Board during World War I and was famous thereafter as "advisor" to every U.S. president during his lifetime.

### Chapter 20
### Revolutionary journalism

This speech was first printed, in abridged form, in *The Militant,* December 15, 1958.

**Comrade Novack**: George Novack, a leading member of the SWP, author of many books and a frequent contributor to *The Militant,* was the chairman of the meeting.

**Labor Action**: The paper to which Cannon is *not* referring was the organ of the Workers Party. When the Burnham-Shachtman minority split from the SWP in 1940 and set up the Workers Party, it adopted the name *Labor Action* for its paper.

**Iskra (The Spark)** was the newspaper of the Russian social democrats, published abroad and smuggled into Russia. It was founded by Lenin, Martov, Plekhanov, Potresov, and Axelrod. Its first issue appeared on December 21, 1900, printed in Germany; in 1902 it was moved to England and in 1903 to Switzerland. It became the principal voice and organizing center of the Russian social democratic party. Although the 1903 party Congress gave the Bolshevik position a majority, thus vindicating Lenin's leadership of *Iskra,* a switch of position later in the year by Plekhanov put Lenin in a minority on the editorial board, and he resigned from the paper.

**For Harriman or for Rockefeller**: In 1958, New York voters were presented by the major parties with a choice between two members of America's Sixty Families as candidates for governor: the incumbent, Averell Harriman, and the challenger, Nelson A. Rockefeller.

**Independent Socialist Party** was the ballot name of the slate of candidates put forward by the United Independent Socialist Campaign Committee in New York's 1958 elections. The committee had been created by a conference held June 13–15, 1958, of various socialist groupings, unaffiliated socialists, and independents. Members of the SWP, readers of the *National Guardian,* and prominent figures of the defunct American Labor Party who had resisted the Communist Party's decision to liquidate the ALP all played an active role. The conference adopted a minimal socialist program on international and domestic issues and empowered the committee to select candidates. The candidates were Corliss Lamont for U.S. senator, John T. McManus for governor, Annette T. Rubinstein for lieutenant governor, Captain Hugh N. Mulzac for comptroller, and Scott K. Gray, Jr., for attorney general. The vote totals were: Lamont, 49,087; McManus and Rubinstein, 31,658; Mulzac, 34,038; and Gray, 31,746. Some supporters expressed discouragement with the outcome, since a vote of 50,000 on the gubernatorial line was required to obtain automatic ballot status for a party in the next election, thus rendering unnecessary the laborious and expensive task of getting on the ballot by petition.

**Diary in Exile, 1935** had just been published; its full title is *Trotsky's Diary in Exile, 1935,* Harvard University Press, 1958.

## Chapter 21
## The lives of two revolutionaries

These speeches have not been printed before.

**Oscar G. Coover** had just been the SWP write-in candidate for governor of California.

**Arne Swabeck** was prominent in the labor movement and in the Communist Party in Chicago, and was a founding member of the Trotskyist movement. When he retired from his trade, he moved to Los Angeles. He was at the banquet and was one of the speakers.

**Fred Halstead,** a writer on *The Militant* staff, came from Los Angeles.

**Theodore Draper** is the author of two books, *The Roots of American Communism* (Viking, 1957) and *American Communism and Soviet Russia* (Viking, 1960).

**Edith Bartell** was a former member of the Los Angeles SWP branch.

**Farrell Dobbs** and **Marvel Scholl** both worked in the SWP national office in New York, as did *Joe* and *Reba Hansen*.

The **war danger** referred to was the Cuban missile crisis of October–November 1962. On October 22, President Kennedy announced a U.S. naval blockade of Cuba and the intention to search or turn back Soviet ships approaching the island.

**Carl Feingold,** SWP candidate for U.S. senator from New York, utilized his scheduled television and radio time on the day after Kennedy's brink-of-atomic-war speech to refute the president's arguments and to call for an end to the war moves. Before moving to New York, Carl Feingold had been a member of the Los Angeles SWP branch.

## Chapter 22
## Bill Brown: A proletarian fighter

This speech was first printed in the *Socialist Appeal,* July 2, 1938.

The **Farm Holiday Association** was the Farmers' Holiday Association, a movement of agrarian revolt that became powerful in the Northwest during the depression years of the 1930s. It organized strikes by dairymen and other farmers for a guaranteed return of their cost of production. It halted or frustrated mortgage foreclosure sales of farms by preventing bidding or so arranging it that the only bid entered was $1 on behalf of the dispossessed family. Another tactic was to pack the courthouse entrances with crowds so dense that the sheriff couldn't get through to hold a sale. It finally forced passage of moratorium laws on foreclosure sales in the legislatures of a number of farm states. The organization was founded by radical farmers on the initiative of John Bosch, who was its principal leader. During the 1934 truck drivers' strikes in Minneapolis, the Farmers' Holiday Association was a strong supporter of the union.

**Rodney Salisbury** was sheriff of Plentywood, Montana. His jail was famous among the many itinerant workers of the Northwest because of its open door and free sleeping quarters for the night for anyone who wished to avail himself of the hospitality. It was also the only jail in the U.S. which had a big "Free Tom Mooney" poster on the wall.

## Chapter 23
### Address at the funeral of Inger Swabeck

This speech was first printed in *The Militant,* July 19, 1948.

## Chapter 24
### Goldie Geldman

This speech was first printed in *The Militant,* October 27, 1952.

## Chapter 25
### Joseph Vanzler

This speech was first printed in *The Militant,* July 9, 1956. It was also included in James P. Cannon, *Notebook of an Agitator,* New Park Publications, Ltd., London, 1958.

**Usick's old friends**: Those listed only by first name are Vincent R. Dunne, Evelyn Reed, Arne Swabeck, Rose Karsner, and Hildegarde MacLeod.

## Chapter 26
### A wake for Usick

This letter has not been printed before.

## Chapter 27
## A tribute to Miles Dunne

This article was first printed in *The Militant,* May 19, 1958.

**Harry DeBoer** was one of the eighteen prisoners in the Minneapolis Labor Case.

**Dave Beck** was head of the Teamsters in Seattle, became the principal Teamsters official on the West Coast, and finally became president of the International Brotherhood of Teamsters. He was sent to prison on charges of income-tax evasion after a federal prosecution.

**Frank Brewster** was a West Coast official of the IBT, one of Beck's men.

**Sidney Brennan** was formerly a job steward in Minneapolis Teamsters Local 544; he went over to the side of IBT President Tobin when the latter opened the fight to destroy the local in conjunction with the Roosevelt administration's arrest of Local 544 leaders on Smith Act charges. Brennan was rewarded by the IBT leadership, which made him the principal Teamsters official in Minneapolis.

**James R. Hoffa** was a Detroit-based Teamsters official; he succeeded Dave Beck as IBT president and was later sent to prison on charges of corrupt use of union funds and jury tampering, after a federal prosecution.

## Chapter 28
## Carl Skoglund: One of the old guard

"The Man Who Had No Papers" was first printed in *The Militant* of December 26, 1960, the second issue following Carl Skoglund's death.

The speech at the memorial meeting has not been printed previously.

## Chapter 29
## Socialist electoral policy

This speech was first printed in *The Militant,* March 17, 1958; it was also published as a pamphlet entitled *Socialist Election Policy in 1958* by Pioneer Publishers, 1958.

**Vincent Hallinan** is a noted attorney, prominent in labor and left circles; he was presidential candidate of the Progressive Party in 1952.

**Clifford T. McAvoy** (1904–1957) was the central leader of those in the American Labor Party who opposed the Communist Party's decision to liquidate the ALP and get its supporters to work within the Democratic Party. McAvoy had been the ALP candidate for mayor of New York City in 1953.

**Frank Barbaria and Joan Jordan** were the SWP candidates for city supervisors in the San Francisco municipal elections of 1957.

**Warren K. Billings** was the Billings of the famous Mooney-Billings case.

**George Hitchcock** was a playwright and chairman of the Independent Socialist Forum in San Francisco.

**George Olshausen** was a prominent civil liberties attorney in San Francisco.

## Chapter 30
### Socialism and democracy

This speech was first printed in the *International Socialist Review,* Fall 1957; it was also issued as a pamphlet entitled *Socialism and Democracy* by Pioneer Publishers, 1959.

**Beck and McDonald***:* Dave Beck was the Teamsters president; David J. McDonald was president of the United Steelworkers of America.

## Chapter 31
### The trend of the twentieth century

This speech was first published in the magazine *Fourth International,* July–August 1951.

## Chapter 32
### The coming American revolution

This speech was first published as a pamphlet entitled *The Coming American Revolution,* Pioneer Publishers, 1947.

## Chapter 33
## What socialist America will look like

This speech was first printed in *The Militant,* July 27, 1953; it was later published in the pamphlet *America's Road to Socialism,* issued by Pioneer Publishers in 1953.

**Preceding five lectures***:* The six lectures were given on December 5, 12, and 19, 1952, and January 9, 16, and 23, 1953. Their titles were: *America Under Eisenhower, The International Prospects of Capitalism and Socialism, Prospects of Capitalism and Socialism in America, The Coming Struggle for Power, America Under Workers' Rule,* and *What Socialist America Will Look Like.*

**Louis Auguste Blanqui** (1805–1881) was a French revolutionary socialist famous for his devotion to the cause despite repeated imprisonments and for his tactic of the revolutionary seizure of power by a well-trained body of armed men. He joined an unsuccessful Paris insurrection in 1827 and was thereafter connected with every revolutionary attempt until his death. He played an active role in the July Revolution of 1830; he was sentenced to prison for articles in the paper he edited; he was sentenced again in 1836, but pardoned in 1837. He was condemned to death for leading an unsuccessful insurrection in 1839, but his sentence was commuted to life imprisonment; he was freed by the February Revolution of 1848, but given a ten-year sentence in 1849 as reaction gained the upper hand. Amnestied in 1859, he was reimprisoned in 1861 but escaped in 1865 and continued his propaganda against the Second Empire government from exile. Returning to France under the general amnesty of 1869, he led two armed demonstrations against the government of Louis Napoleon in Paris in 1870 and temporarily seized power on October 31, 1870. He was condemned to death on March 17, 1871. The Paris Commune broke out a few days later. Blanqui was elected a member of the revolutionary government, but he was unable to take his seat since he was in the prison of the counterrevolutionary Versailles regime, which had a well-grounded fear that, with his energy and military ability, he might lead the Commune to military victory. He was kept in prison until 1879, when he was elected to the Chamber of Deputies by the workers of Bordeaux. Although the government declared his election invalid, it released him from prison, broken in health. He immediately resumed his agitation. At the end of 1880, he had a stroke after giving a speech at a meeting in Paris, and he died New Year's Day, 1881.

**The Iron Heel** is the most remarkable of Jack London's socialist novels. Written in 1906 and published early in 1908, it is uncannily prophetic in its descriptions of workers' uprisings and of fascism. The form of the novel is the discovery and publication, with footnotes, in the fourth century of the socialist era of an unfinished document, written in 1932, describing the smashing of the labor movement and civil liberties in the period 1912–1932 by what today would be called a fascist regime. In 1932, when the manuscript suddenly ends, the fascist regime, known as the Iron Heel, has crushed the first uprising of the workers, but a second revolt is being secretly planned.

**Thomas Carlyle** (1795–1881) was a Scottish essayist and historian.

**Land of the Sundown Sea**: In 1952, at the age of sixty-two, Cannon moved from New York City to Los Angeles. He immediately became an ardent, if somewhat ironic, booster of Southern California.

**Trotsky's testament** was written on February 27, 1940, with a brief addition dated March 3, 1940. It was printed in *Trotsky's Diary in Exile, 1935* (Harvard University Press, 1958) and in *The Age of Permanent Revolution* (a Trotsky anthology edited by Isaac Deutscher with the assistance of George Novack, Dell Publishing Co., 1964).

**Maxim Gorky** (1868–1936) was a Russian writer who rallied to the Bolshevik movement in 1905 and became a friend of Lenin. He was an off-and-on sympathizer thereafter, but opposed the October Revolution and was highly critical of the Soviet regime despite the attempts of Lenin and other Soviet leaders to win him over. He left Russia in 1924, returning for a visit in 1928–1929. Then he returned permanently in 1931, and gave up all criticism of the regime, becoming an apologist for Stalinism. He was made the elder statesman of Soviet literature. He was apparently out of favor when the great purges of the mid-1930s began, and was refused a passport to leave the Soviet Union for a visit to France; though his death, it now appears, was from natural causes, it was charged at the Moscow trials that he had been murdered by Trotskyists.

**William Morris** (1834–1896) was a British poet, artist, and socialist. He came to socialism as a result of his efforts to overcome the degradation of art by commercialism and the alienation of the individual in capitalist society. He attempted to introduce standards of craftsmanship and beauty in objects of everyday use by designing—and then starting workshops to produce—furniture, wallpaper, printing type, books, etc. In 1885 he was instrumental in founding the Socialist League. He was active in mass demonstrations of the unemployed and upheld the Marxist position in the long struggle with the anarchists, who were prominent in the radical movement in that period. He remained an active socialist as well as one of Britain's leading poets until his death. Among his socialist writings are *Art and Socialism, Signs of Change, Useful Work versus Useless Toil*, and the fictional *A Dream of John Ball* and *News From Nowhere*.

# ALSO BY JAMES P. CANNON

### The History of American Trotskyism, 1928–38
Report of a Participant

"Trotskyism is not a new movement, a new doctrine," Cannon says, "but the restoration, the revival of genuine Marxism as it was expounded and practiced in the Russian Revolution and in the early days of the Communist International." Talks by a founding leader of American communism on building a proletarian party in the United States. $17. Also in Spanish and French.

### The Struggle for a Proletarian Party

"The workers of America have power enough to topple the structure of capitalism at home and to lift the whole world with them when they rise," Cannon asserts. On the eve of World War II, a founder of the communist movement in the US and leader of the Communist International in Lenin's time defends the program and party-building norms of Bolshevism. $20. Also in Spanish and Farsi.

### The Left Opposition in the U.S.
Writings and Speeches, 1928–31

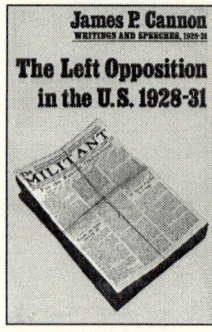

How veteran leaders of the American communist movement, expelled in 1928 by a growing Stalinist faction, joined with Bolshevik leader Leon Trotsky to continue building a party to carry out the program for world revolution developed by the Communist International under Lenin's guidance. $23

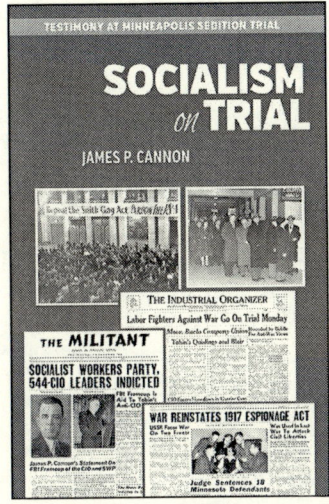

### Socialism on Trial
Testimony at Minneapolis Sedition Trial

The revolutionary program of the working class, presented in response to frame-up charges of "seditious conspiracy" in 1941, on the eve of US entry into World War II. The defendants were leaders of the Minneapolis labor movement and the Socialist Workers Party. $15. Also in Spanish, French, and Farsi.

### Notebook of an Agitator
From the Wobblies to the Fight against the Korean War and McCarthyism

Spans four decades of working-class battles—defending IWW frame-up victims and Sacco and Vanzetti; battles on the San Francisco waterfront; labor's fight against the McCarthyite witch-hunt. Includes the 1934 strike call and seven articles from *The Organizer*, daily bulletin of the Minneapolis Teamster strike. $20

### Letters from Prison
A Revolutionary Party Prepares for Post–WWII Labor Battles

The prison letters of a communist leader, jailed for his party's opposition to the US imperialist war effort in World War II. Cannon discusses organizing a revolutionary party in wartime and preparing its postwar political course. $20

### The Socialist Workers Party in World War II, 1940–43
Preparing the communist workers movement in the United States to campaign against wartime censorship, repression, and anti-union assaults. $23

**WWW.PATHFINDERPRESS.COM**

# BUILDING A PROLETARIAN PARTY

## Capitalism's World Disorder
Working-Class Politics at the Millennium
JACK BARNES

The social devastation and financial crises, the coarsening of politics, the cop brutality and acts of imperialist aggression accelerating around us—all are products not of something gone wrong with capitalism but of its lawful workings. Yet the future can be changed by the united struggle and selfless action of working people conscious of their power to transform the world. $20. Also in Spanish and French.

## The First Five Years of the Communist International
LEON TROTSKY

During its first five years, the Communist International, guided by V.I. Lenin, Leon Trotsky, and other central Bolshevik leaders, sought to build a world movement of Communist Parties capable of leading the toilers to overthrow capitalist exploitation and colonial oppression. This two-volume collection contains Trotsky's speeches and writings from the first four Comintern congresses. Volume 1, $22; volume 2, $22.

## The Revolutionary Party
Its Role in the Struggle for Socialism
JAMES P. CANNON

The necessity of creating a leadership capable of carrying through to the end the struggle of working people to conquer power. $5

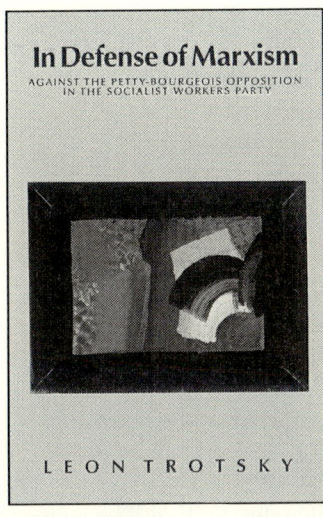

## In Defense of Marxism
Against the Petty-Bourgeois Opposition in the Socialist Workers Party

LEON TROTSKY

A reply to those in the revolutionary workers movement in the late 1930s bending to bourgeois patriotism during Washington's buildup to enter World War II. Trotsky explains why only a party fighting to bring workers into its ranks and leadership can steer a communist course. In the process, he defends the materialist and dialectical foundations of Marxism. $17. Also in Spanish.

## Revolutionary Continuity
Marxist Leadership in the U.S.
*The Early Years, 1848–1917*
*Birth of the Communist Movement, 1918–1922*

FARRELL DOBBS

"Successive generations of proletarian revolutionists have participated in the movements of the working class and its allies.... Marxists today owe them not only homage for their deeds. We also have a duty to learn what they did wrong as well as right so their errors are not repeated." —*Farrell Dobbs*. Two volumes, $17 each.

## What Is to Be Done?
V.I. LENIN

The stakes in creating a disciplined organization of working-class revolutionaries capable of acting as a "tribune of the people, able to react to every manifestation of tyranny and oppression, no matter where it appears, to clarify for all and everyone the world-historic significance of the struggle for the emancipation of the proletariat." Written in 1902. $20

**WWW.PATHFINDERPRESS.COM**

# FROM PATHFINDER

## The Low Point of Labor Resistance Is Behind Us
The Socialist Workers Party Looks Forward

JACK BARNES, MARY-ALICE WATERS STEVE CLARK

The global order imposed by victors of the inter-imperialist slaughter of World War II is shattering, with explosive ramifications for workers and farmers worldwide. A long retreat by the working class and unions has come to an end. More and more workers—of all ages, skin colors, and both sexes—are saying, "Enough is enough!" This book highlights opportunities ahead for class-conscious workers to forge a labor party built on fighting unions. And a mass proletarian vanguard able to lead the struggle to end capitalist rule, opening a future for humanity. $10. Also in Spanish and French.

## In Defense of the US Working Class
MARY-ALICE WATERS

Drawing on the fighting traditions of the oppressed and exploited of all colors and national origins, in 2018 tens of thousands of teachers and other working people in West Virginia, Oklahoma, and other states waged victorious strikes. They fought for dignity and respect for themselves, their families, and for all working people. $7. Also in Spanish, French, Farsi, and Greek.

## Teamster Rebellion
Farrell Dobbs

The 1934 strikes that won union recognition for truckers and warehouse workers in Minneapolis and helped pave the way for the working-class social movement that built the industrial unions. The first of four volumes by a central leader of these battles. $16. Also in Spanish, French, Farsi, and Greek.

# 'THE HISTORY OF EXISTING SOCIETY IS THE HISTORY OF CLASS STRUGGLES'

## Labor, Nature, and the Evolution of Humanity
The Long View of History

FREDERICK ENGELS, KARL MARX
GEORGE NOVACK
MARY-ALICE WATERS

Without understanding that social labor, transforming nature, has driven humanity's evolution for millions of years, working people are unable to see beyond the capitalist epoch of class exploitation that warps all human relations, ideas, and values. Only the revolutionary conquest of state power by the working class can open the door to a world free of capitalist exploitation, degradation of nature, subjugation of women, racism, and war. A world built on human solidarity. A socialist world. $12. Also in Spanish and French. Ebook for the blind or low vision: visit Bookshare.org.

## The Communist Manifesto
KARL MARX AND FREDERICK ENGELS

Communism, say the founding leaders of the revolutionary workers movement, is not a set of ideas or preconceived "principles" but workers' line of march to power, springing from a "movement going on under our very eyes." $5. Also in Spanish, French, Farsi, and Arabic. Ebook for the blind or low vision: visit Bookshare.org.

## Understanding History
Marxist Essays
GEORGE NOVACK

How did capitalism arise? Why and when did this exploitative system exhaust its once revolutionary role? Why is revolutionary change fundamental to human progress? $15

**WWW.PATHFINDERPRESS.COM**

# CAPITALIST CRISIS AND THE FIGHT FOR WORKERS POWER

### Are They Rich Because They're Smart?
Class, Privilege, and Learning under Capitalism
JACK BARNES

Exposes growing class inequalities in the US and the self-serving rationalizations of well-paid professionals who think their "brilliance" equips them to "regulate" working people, who don't know what's in our own best interest. $10. Also in Spanish, French, Farsi, and Arabic. Ebook for the blind or low vision: visit Bookshare.org.

### The Clintons' Anti-Working-Class Record
Why Washington Fears Working People
JACK BARNES

What working people need to know about the profit-driven course of Democrats and Republicans alike over the last three decades. And the political awakening of workers seeking to understand and resist the capitalist rulers' assaults. $10. Also in Spanish, French, Farsi, and Greek.

### The Transitional Program for Socialist Revolution
LEON TROTSKY

The Socialist Workers Party program, drafted by Trotsky in 1938, still guides the SWP and communists the world over. The party "uncompromisingly gives battle to all political groupings tied to the apron strings of the bourgeoisie. Its task—the abolition of capitalism's domination. Its aim—socialism. Its method—the proletarian revolution." $17. Also in Farsi.

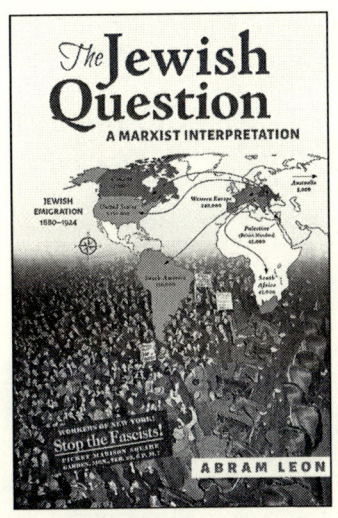

### The Jewish Question
A Marxist Interpretation
ABRAM LEON

Why is Jew-hatred still raising its ugly head? What are its class roots—from antiquity through feudalism, to capitalism's rise and current crises? Why is there no solution under capitalism? The author, Abram Leon, was killed in the Nazi gas chambers. Revised translation, new introduction, and 40 pages of illustrations and maps. $17. Also in Spanish and French.

### Is Socialist Revolution in the US Possible?
A Necessary Debate among Working People
MARY-ALICE WATERS

Fighting for a society only working people can create, it is our own capacities we will discover. And along that course we will answer the question posed here with a resounding "Yes." Possible but not inevitable. That depends on us. $7. Also in Spanish, French, and Farsi.

### "It's the Poor Who Face the Savagery of the US 'Justice' System"
The Cuban Five Talk about Their Lives within the US Working Class

How US cops, courts, and prisons work as "an enormous machine for grinding people up." Five Cuban revolutionaries framed up and held in US jails for 16 years explain the human devastation of capitalist "justice"—and how socialist Cuba is different. $10. Also in Spanish, Farsi, and Greek.

**WWW.PATHFINDERPRESS.COM**

# THE RUSSIAN REVOLUTION'S WORLD EXAMPLE

### Lenin's Final Fight
Speeches and Writings, 1922–23
V.I. LENIN

In 1922 and 1923, V.I. Lenin, central leader of the world's first socialist revolution, waged what was to be his last political battle—one that was lost following his death. At stake was whether that revolution, and the international communist movement it led, would remain on the revolutionary proletarian course that brought workers and peasants to power in October 1917. $17. Also in Spanish, Farsi, and Greek.

### The History of the Russian Revolution
LEON TROTSKY

How, under Lenin's leadership, the Bolshevik Party led millions of workers and farmers to overthrow the state power of the landlords and capitalists in 1917 and bring to power a government that advanced their class interests at home and worldwide. Unabridged, 3 vols. in one. Written by one of the central leaders of that socialist revolution. $30. Also in French and Russian.

### The Revolution Betrayed
What Is the Soviet Union and Where Is It Going?
LEON TROTSKY

In 1917 workers and peasants of Russia were the motor force for one of the deepest revolutions in history. Yet within ten years a political counterrevolution by a privileged social layer, whose chief spokesperson was Joseph Stalin, was being consolidated. The classic study of the Soviet workers state and its degeneration. $17. Also in Spanish, Farsi, and Greek.

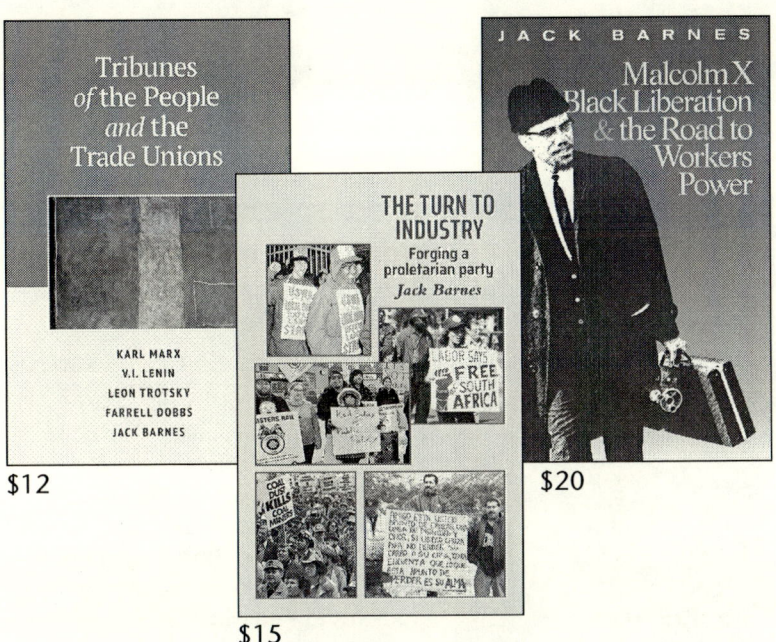

$12

$20

$15

## Three books to be read as one...

**about building a party that's working class in program, composition, and action. One that recognizes, in word and deed, the most revolutionary fact of our time...**

... that working people have the power to create a different world as we act together to defend our own class interests—not those of the privileged classes who exploit our labor, not of those who fear us as "deplorables," or just plain "trash."

As we advance along a revolutionary course toward workers power, we will transform ourselves and awaken to our own worth. Also in Spanish and French.

**Special Offer!**
All three $30

*The Turn to Industry* and *Tribunes of the People and the Trade Unions*   $20

Either book plus *Malcolm X, Black Liberation, and the Road to Workers Power*   $25

**WWW.PATHFINDERPRESS.COM**

# CUBA'S SOCIALIST REVOLUTION

## Women in Cuba: The Making of a Revolution within the Revolution
VILMA ESPÍN, ASELA DE LOS SANTOS YOLANDA FERRER

The integration of women in the ranks and leadership of the Cuban Revolution was intertwined with the proletarian course of the leadership of the revolution from the start. This is the story of that revolution and how it transformed the women and men who made it. $17. Also in Spanish, Farsi, and Greek.

## Cuba and the Coming American Revolution
JACK BARNES

This is a book about the struggles of working people in the imperialist heartland, the youth attracted to them, and the example set by the Cuban people that revolution is not only necessary—it can be made. It is about the class struggle in the US, where the revolutionary capacities of workers and farmers are today as utterly discounted by the ruling powers as were those of the Cuban toilers. And just as wrongly. $10. Also in Spanish, French, and Farsi. Ebook for the blind or low vision: visit Bookshare.org.

## Colombia: Fidel Castro on the Debate around Revolutionary Strategy and Lessons of the Cuban Revolution
FROM THE PAGES OF THE *MILITANT*

Excerpts from Fidel Castro's *Peace in Colombia* and articles from the *Militant*. In describing the Cuban leadership's efforts to end decades of war between the FARC guerrilla movement and Colombia's brutal regime, Castro in his prologue, afterword, and other statements explains why Cuban revolutionaries, unlike FARC leaders, rejected taking hostages and organized working people to win state power, not pursue a "prolonged people's war." $5. Also in Spanish.

# New International
## A MAGAZINE OF MARXIST POLITICS AND THEORY

### Capitalism's Long Hot Winter Has Begun
JACK BARNES

Today's global capitalist crisis is but the opening stage of decades of economic, financial, and social convulsions and class battles. Class-conscious workers confront this historic turning point for imperialism with confidence, Jack Barnes writes, drawing satisfaction from being "in their face" as we chart a revolutionary course to take power. In *New International* no. 12. $14. Also in Spanish, French, Farsi, Arabic, and Greek.

### Imperialism's March toward Fascism and War
JACK BARNES

"There will be new Hitlers, new Mussolinis. That is inevitable. What is not inevitable is that they will triumph. The working-class vanguard will organize our class to fight back against the devastating toll we are made to pay for the capitalist crisis. The future of humanity will be decided in the contest between these contending class forces." In *New International* no. 10. $14. Also in Spanish, French, Farsi, and Greek.

### U.S. Imperialism Has Lost the Cold War
JACK BARNES

The collapse of regimes across Eastern Europe and the USSR claiming to be communist did not mean workers and farmers there had been crushed. In today's sharpening capitalist conflicts and wars, these toilers are joining working people the world over in the class struggle against exploitation. In *New International* no. 11. $14. Also in Spanish, French, Farsi, and Greek.

**WWW.PATHFINDERPRESS.COM**

# PATHFINDER AROUND THE WORLD

**UNITED STATES**
(and Caribbean, Latin America, and East Asia)
> Pathfinder Books, 306 W. 37th St., 13th Floor
> New York, NY 10018

**CANADA**
> Pathfinder Books, 7107 St. Denis, Suite 204
> Montreal, QC H2S 2S5

**UNITED KINGDOM**
(and Europe, Africa, Middle East, and South Asia)
> Pathfinder Books, 5 Norman Rd.
> Seven Sisters, London N15 4ND

**AUSTRALIA**
(and New Zealand, Southeast Asia, and the Pacific)
> Pathfinder Books, Suite 2, First floor, 275 George St.
> Liverpool, Sydney, NSW 2170
> Postal address: P.O. Box 73, Campsie, NSW 2194

## JOIN THE PATHFINDER READERS CLUB
## BUILD YOUR LIBRARY!

**$10 / YEAR**
**25% DISCOUNT ON ALL PATHFINDER TITLES**
**30% OFF BOOKS OF THE MONTH**
Valid at pathfinderpress.com and local Pathfinder book centers

Go to: www.pathfinderpress.com/
products/pathfinder-readers-club

# New International
### A MAGAZINE OF MARXIST POLITICS AND THEORY

## Capitalism's Long Hot Winter Has Begun
JACK BARNES

Today's global capitalist crisis is but the opening stage of decades of economic, financial, and social convulsions and class battles. Class-conscious workers confront this historic turning point for imperialism with confidence, Jack Barnes writes, drawing satisfaction from being "in their face" as we chart a revolutionary course to take power. In *New International* no. 12. $14. Also in Spanish, French, Farsi, Arabic, and Greek.

## Imperialism's March toward Fascism and War
JACK BARNES

"There will be new Hitlers, new Mussolinis. That is inevitable. What is not inevitable is that they will triumph. The working-class vanguard will organize our class to fight back against the devastating toll we are made to pay for the capitalist crisis. The future of humanity will be decided in the contest between these contending class forces." In *New International* no. 10. $14. Also in Spanish, French, Farsi, and Greek.

## U.S. Imperialism Has Lost the Cold War
JACK BARNES

The collapse of regimes across Eastern Europe and the USSR claiming to be communist did not mean workers and farmers there had been crushed. In today's sharpening capitalist conflicts and wars, these toilers are joining working people the world over in the class struggle against exploitation. In *New International* no. 11. $14. Also in Spanish, French, Farsi, and Greek.

**WWW.PATHFINDERPRESS.COM**

# PATHFINDER AROUND THE WORLD

**UNITED STATES**
(and Caribbean, Latin America, and East Asia)
> Pathfinder Books, 306 W. 37th St., 13th Floor
> New York, NY 10018

**CANADA**
> Pathfinder Books, 7107 St. Denis, Suite 204
> Montreal, QC H2S 2S5

**UNITED KINGDOM**
(and Europe, Africa, Middle East, and South Asia)
> Pathfinder Books, 5 Norman Rd.
> Seven Sisters, London N15 4ND

**AUSTRALIA**
(and New Zealand, Southeast Asia, and the Pacific)
> Pathfinder Books, Suite 2, First floor, 275 George St.
> Liverpool, Sydney, NSW 2170
> Postal address: P.O. Box 73, Campsie, NSW 2194

## JOIN THE PATHFINDER READERS CLUB
### BUILD YOUR LIBRARY!

**$10 / YEAR**
**25% DISCOUNT ON ALL PATHFINDER TITLES**
**30% OFF BOOKS OF THE MONTH**
Valid at pathfinderpress.com and local Pathfinder book centers

Go to: www.pathfinderpress.com/products/pathfinder-readers-club